D1208481

Managing the Multinationals

NEW HORIZONS IN INTERNATIONAL BUSINESS

General Editor: Peter J. Buckley
Centre for International Business,
University of Leeds (CIBUL), UK

This series is aimed at the frontiers of international business research. The study of international business is important not least because it gives researchers the opportunity to innovate in theory, technique, empirical investigation and interpretation. The area is fruitful for interdisciplinary and comparative research. This series is established as a central forum for the presentation of new ideas in international business.

Titles in the series include:

Managing the Multinationals

An International Study of Control Mechanisms

Anne-Wil Käthe Harzing

*Lecturer in International Management, Management Centre,
University of Bradford, UK*

NEW HORIZONS IN INTERNATIONAL BUSINESS

Edward Elgar
Cheltenham, UK • Northampton, MA, USA

Published by
Edward Elgar Publishing Limited
Glensanda House
Montpellier Parade
Cheltenham
Glos GL50 1UA
UK

Edward Elgar Publishing, Inc.
6 Market Street
Northampton
Massachusetts 01060
USA

A catalogue record for this book
is available from the British Library

Library of Congress Cataloguing in Publication Data

Harzing, Anne-Wil Käthe.
    Managing the multinationals: an international study of control
mechanisms / Anne-Wil Käthe Harzing.
        (New horizons in international business)
    Includes bibliographical references and index.
    1. International business enterprises—Management. 2. Comparative
management. I. Title. II. Series.
HD62.4.H375 1999
658'.049—dc21   98–31842
                                                   CIP

ISBN 1 84064 052 9

Printed and bound in Great Britain by Bookcraft (Bath) Ltd.

Contents

List of figures

List of tables

Preface

This book is based on my doctoral dissertation. Writing a dissertation is an individual and sometimes very lonely task. However, this task was supported, either directly or indirectly, by a whole number of people. I would like to take this opportunity to thank some of them.

First of all the two people who kindly offered to be my thesis advisors: Arndt Sorge and Jaap Paauwe. Arndt Sorge has been comfortably present during much of my academic career and provided comments that were few in number, but always exactly to the mark. What helped me even more than his comments, however, were his humorous emails that cheered me up in difficult times. Jaap Paauwe showed that a reversal of roles (I criticised his manuscripts for a textbook for the Open University) can lead to a very fruitful interaction of ideas. We have spent quite a lot of hours in a restaurant near Utrecht Central Station discussing the draft version of the manuscript. When I decided to finish my dissertation in Bradford, both Arndt and Jaap were very supportive. In Bradford, Hafiz Mirza proved that the roles of supervisor and colleague need not conflict and offered guidance through the idiosyncratic British system. My external examiners, Neil Hood and Peter Lawrence showed me that a Viva can be trying and satisfying at the same time.

I would also like to thank all members of my international committee of recommendation, who were so kind as to lend their name to the project. A sincere word of thanks to John Dunning, Paul Evans, Anthony Ferner, Carlos Garcia Pont, Gunnar Hedlund, Martin Hilb, Geert Hofstede, Jorma Larimo, Christian Maroy, Aahad Osman-Gani, Victor Prochnik, Gordon Redding, Marino Regini, Oscar Risso Patrón, Bill Roche, Danny Van Den Bulcke, Yoko Sano, Steen Scheuer, Udo Wagner and Denice Welch. Thanks are also due to Philip Dewe who kindly offered to cast his critical eye over the study's statistics.

A word of thanks also goes to participants of EIBA-conferences in 1994, 1995 and 1996, and other international colleagues I came in touch with during the last five years. They made me discover the comforting reality, that, although I did not have direct colleagues working on the same research themes, there was a large international research community I could fall back on.

Four jobs in seven years means there are a lot of colleagues to thank. I would like to thank my colleagues at the Open University for giving me the opportunity to gather writing experience and publications before starting with my dissertation, my colleagues at Tilburg University for helping me to realise that where International HRM is concerned, it is the International and not the HRM part that interests me most, my colleagues at Maastricht University for their understanding of my frequent "home-working" and my current colleagues at Bradford University for making me realise that there is life after the dissertation.

I thank my parents for bringing me up in a stimulating environment. Although my choice of career might be unfamiliar to you, I am sure there is a link between arts and scholarly work: both require lots of inspiration and perspiration. Most of all, however, I would like to thank Ron, who has supported me with his love and insight before I even thought of going to university. I do not have to make the usual apologies about time not spent with him during the dissertation process. Normally, he was far too busy to notice. Nevertheless, he helped me in more ways than even he will realise, not in the least by asking awkward questions and by patiently listening to my stories.

Bradford, October 1998

Introduction

1. BACKGROUND

This book investigates control mechanisms in multinational companies (MNCs). The project was first induced by an article of Edström and Galbraith (1977b), in which they analyse the international transfer of managers in four MNCs. One of these MNCs transferred a far greater number of managers than its direct competitor, despite their being of the same size, operating in the same industry and having nearly identical organisation charts. Edström and Galbraith hypothesised that in this company international transfer of managers was being used to develop a process of control based on socialisation and informal communication.[1]

Since then, and especially since the last decade, the number of studies on both international transfers and control mechanisms within multinational companies has increased considerably. Concurrent with developments in general management theory (the learning organisation, the network organisation, the "end of bureaucracy", the firm as a brain), the general idea is that more and more MNCs are or should be moving towards a kind of loosely coupled network organisation (Bartlett and Ghoshal, 1989; Galbraith and Kazanjian, 1986; Hedlund, 1986, Porter, 1986a/b, Prahalad and Doz, 1987, White and Poynter, 1990). In this kind of organisation the management of human resources is of paramount importance (Evans, 1986) and coordination emphasis is said to shift from formal mechanisms to more informal and subtle mechanisms (Martinez and Jarillo, 1989).

Within this informal or subtle type of coordination, the international transfer of managers is often claimed to play a key role (Bartlett and Ghoshal, 1987b; Child, 1984; Daniels and Radebaugh, 1989; Edström and Lorange, 1984; Evans, 1991; Kobrin, 1988; Kuin, 1972; Mascarenhas, 1984; Ondrack, 1985a/b; Robock and Simmonds, 1983; Roth and Nigh, 1992). The role of

---

[1] Later in the research project, it appeared that there had been earlier authors signalling this relationship, though in a less explicit way. Wiechmann (1974) for instance mentions that people transfer (including long-term assignments) enhances corporate acculturation, which is seen as an alternative to centralisation in order to integrate multinational marketing activities. Since the article by Edström and Galbraith is the only one that is consistently cited in publications on control/coordination in MNCs, we decided to keep this article as the basis for further research.

1

international transfers in this type of coordination is hardly ever "proved" empirically, however. Most of the authors simply refer to Edström and Galbraith (1977b) to substantiate their argument. Apart from a limited number of case studies (Ferner, Edwards and Sisson, 1995; Welch, Fenwick, and De-Cieri, 1994), no one seems to have conducted any empirical research in this field.[2] It therefore appeared to be a worthy subject for our empirical investigations. However, international transfers should not be considered in isolation, since - in spite of their acclaimed importance - they are only *one* of the many ways to control MNCs. This book therefore aims to provide a much broader picture by considering a variety of control mechanisms, exploring their application in various circumstances and relating them to other MNC characteristics in a configuration type of analysis. The study's specific research questions will be discussed in the next section.

2. RESEARCH QUESTIONS

When contemplating interesting research opportunities related to control mechanisms in MNCs, several questions came to mind. *First,* we wondered whether the informal and subtle type of control described above was indeed the "control mechanism of the future", since it might be a rather expensive and indirect way to coordinate a company. Wouldn't there be companies or parts of companies (subsidiaries) that would better be managed with more direct and possibly less expensive control mechanisms? More specifically, could we distinguish characteristics of both headquarters and subsidiaries of MNCs that might explain differences in the application of control mechanisms between and within MNCs? This then led to our first research question:

> **Research question 1**: Which characteristics of both headquarters and subsidiaries of multinational companies can explain differences in the composition of the portfolio of control mechanisms that is used by headquarters in respect of its subsidiaries?

In international management literature, the topic of control has been a source of considerable discussion and has resulted in a large number of publications usually classified under the heading headquarters-subsidiary relationships. Most of these studies were limited in the sense that they considered only one or two control mechanisms and/or considered a limited number of predictor

---

[2] Later in the project it appeared that quite a number of German publications are available about the functions of expatriation, which seem to be totally neglected in the mainstream English literature on this subject. These studies will be reviewed in Section 3 of Chapter 1, where we discuss the organisational functions of international transfers.

variables (headquarters and subsidiary characteristics). Further, many of the previous studies focused on MNCs from one country of origin (usually the USA) and investigated subsidiary operations in one or two countries only. Our study explicitly addresses these limitations by identifying and including a full range of control mechanisms and predictor variables. In addition, MNCs headquartered in nine different countries and subsidiaries located in 22 different countries are included in the empirical part of this study. Finally, the sample was constructed in such a way that the industry in which the MNC operates, a variable usually neglected in previous research, could also be used as a predictor variable.

As indicated above, our attention was originally drawn to the role of international transfers as an informal and indirect type of control mechanism. Our *second* research question is therefore related to this specific way to control MNC subsidiaries. The contrast between the general acceptance of the role of expatriation as an informal control mechanism and the lack of solid empirical confirmation for this relationship spurred us to try to measure this hypothesised relationship in a more quantitative way than had been done so far. However, expatriates could very well play a role in *directly* controlling foreign subsidiaries, and there might be alternatives to international transfers in achieving a high level of informal control in MNC subsidiaries. Therefore, our second research question is formulated in general terms:

Research question 2: What role do international transfers play in controlling MNC subsidiaries? Are there alternative ways to achieve a high level of informal control in MNC subsidiaries?

As identified above, not many studies have investigated this strategic role of international transfers. Of those that did, many questioned headquarters managers about their perceptions of the different functions of expatriation. The advantage of our study is that it measures the relationship between actual expatriate presence in a specific subsidiary and the importance of informal control in this subsidiary. Although we had to rely on single respondents, this method is expected to give a more objective representation of the possible role of international transfers in achieving an informal type of control. Further, our study would be the first to identify and measure in a quantitative way the alternatives to international transfers in this respect.

Because of the breadth of this study and the number of variables included, we decided to use configuration analysis to reduce the study's complexity. Configurations are defined as multidimensional constellations of conceptually distinct characteristics that commonly occur together (Meyer et al, 1993). Some recent well-known configurations are Mintzberg's typology of organisations (Mintzberg, 1979) and Miles and Snow's typology of strategies (Miles and Snow, 1978). The advantage of configurations is not only that they reduce the complexity of organisational reality into a manageable number of related characteristics, but also that these organisational typologies or archetypes can be used in a predictive way. If certain characteristics are shown to cluster in distinct typologies, the presence of one or more of these characteristics in other samples can lead to a prediction of the remaining elements, thus facilitating comparison across and integration of different studies. Therefore, our *third* research question is formulated as follows:

> **Research question 3a**: Can we distinguish (both theoretically and empirically) MNC configurations that integrate the various MNC characteristics included in our study?

In our study we will therefore not only construct typologies of MNCs, but also test these typologies empirically, thus accommodating the problems associated with using either a typological (theoretically derived configurations) or a taxonomical (empirically derived configurations) approach. Up until now, few studies in international management literature have tried to derive and test configurations of MNCs. The available studies (e.g. Ghoshal and Nohria, 1993; Roth, Schweiger and Morrison, 1991) focus on a limited number of variables. Bartlett and Ghoshal (1989) performed the most extensive configuration-type of analysis. Their study, however, was based on case studies in nine MNCs only, so that our study could be a valuable extension.

An important assumption of configuration analysis is that companies that show a higher level of internal consistency, that is, conform to the ideal-type configurations more closely, should outperform companies with a lower level of consistency. In addition, performance implications (however measured) are the "bottom line" of most if not all research in the field of management studies (see e.g. Summer et al., 1990). Since a company's performance is influenced by a multitude of different factors, we have formulated our last research question in a rather general way:

> **Research question 3b**: Which of the MNC characteristics included in this study can be used to explain differences in performance between MNCs?

The advantage of our study is that many of the characteristics that have been identified in previous literature as being important factors in influencing performance had already been included in our research design in order to enable us to answer the other research questions. This then allows us to assess the relative importance of variables such as: country of origin, industry, size, diversification, internationalisation, strength of the corporate culture and configurational fit in explaining performance differences between companies.

3. BUILDING BLOCKS AND CROSS-CULTURAL RESEARCH

Many of the studies on control mechanisms in MNCs and the role of international transfers as a control mechanism are very difficult to compare since researchers use very different definitions, concepts, classifications and operationalisations. In order to benefit from previous research and to be able to build upon and extend previous studies, we decided to discuss first the three main building blocks of this thesis. This meant that we performed an extensive literature review into the different kind of organisational control mechanisms, into the environment, strategy and structure of MNCs and finally into the subject of international transfers within MNCs.

These three building blocks have largely developed as separate fields of research, usually broadly referred to as: organisation studies, international management and expatriate management. Various authors have urged international management scholars to pay more attention to available organisation theory (and vice versa) and research in the field of expatriate management is often claimed to lack an integrative and strategic perspective[3] (see e.g. Boyacigiller and Adler, 1993; Ghoshal and Westney, 1993; Martinez and Jarillo, 1989; Melin, 1992; Negandhi, 1975). This book therefore also plays an integrative role in combining these different fields of research.

As discussed above, the empirical part of this study investigates the application of control mechanisms in subsidiaries located in 22 different countries, while their headquarters are located in nine different countries. Our study can therefore be truly called international and cross-cultural. Since this type of research is associated with many problems that are less prominent in purely domestic research, we will also pay quite a lot of attention to the research process itself.

4. STRUCTURE OF THE BOOK

In view of the length of this book and the number of subjects to be discussed, we have made every effort to make the book's basic structure as straightforward as possible. Figure 1 visualises this structure. Chapter 1 presents the literature review of the three building blocks of this study: control mechanisms, multinational companies and international transfers. Subsequently, Chapter 2 combines these three building blocks into the three research ques-

---

[3] See Section 3 of Chapter 1 for a discussion of the limitations of most research in the field of international transfers.

tions identified above. Chapter 3 is then completely devoted to the research design and methodology. It discusses the problems associated with cross-cultural research and describes the selection of the research method and the operationalisation of variables. This chapter also gives a detailed description of the mail survey process and the final sample. Chapters 4 and 5 are then the empirical mirrors of the theoretical Chapters 1 and 2. These chapters discuss the empirical results concerning the three building blocks (Chapter 4) and the three research questions (Chapter 5). A sixth and final chapter then summarises and discusses the study's main findings, signals its limitations and offers some suggestions for future research. This final chapter also briefly indicates the study's managerial implications.

Figure 1: Structure of the book

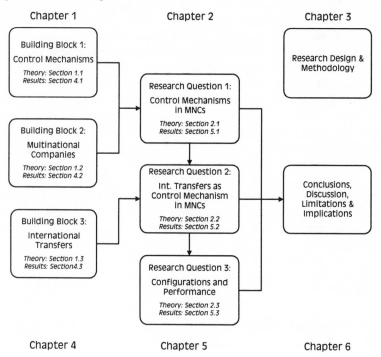

1.   Theoretical building blocks

As indicated in the introduction, this book focuses on control mechanisms in MNCs and puts a special emphasis on the role of international transfers in this respect. This first chapter will therefore review the current state of knowledge about control mechanisms (Section 1), multinational organisations (Section 2) and international transfers (Section 3) respectively. The products of this chapter in terms of definitions and classifications will then be used in the next chapter, where these three theoretical building blocks will be integrated.

1. CONTROL MECHANISMS IN ORGANISATIONS

Introduction

In the discussion of the first building block of our theoretical framework, we will ask ourselves three fundamental questions: first, what is control, second, what is an organisation and third, what forms of control can we distinguish within organisations? To answer these questions, we will first examine the differences between control and coordination. Subsequently, we will show that coordination is one of the major foundations of economic (organisation) theory. In doing so, we will discuss transaction cost theory, which claims that coordination can occur through either markets or organisations. Organisational theorists, however, point out that *within* an organisation different coordination or control mechanisms can be used. Unfortunately, virtually every writer has his or her own classification of control mechanisms. Therefore, we will discuss and synthesise these different approaches into a coherent classification of control mechanisms. The pattern of control mechanisms used by MNCs in respect of their subsidiaries is likely to be influenced by their country of origin. Consequently, we will propose some hypotheses on this "country-of-origin" effect.[4]

---

[4] As the relationships identified in this chapter are a by-product of the main research questions of this book , the hypotheses formulated in this chapter are mainly based on previous research. No effort has been made to construct an original research model. However, a test of the hypotheses included in this chapter is an important means to validate the empirical data that will be used in the remainder of this book.

Control and coordination defined

In this section, we will try to come to a definition of control and coordination and if possible make a distinction between these two concepts. In order to do this, we have included citations of a number of authors that have tried to define control or coordination and their relation to one another.

Control

All formal organisations are concerned with how to channel human efforts towards the attainment of organisational objectives. The organisation employs a set of instruments and processes designed to influence the behaviour and performance of organisational members, groups, subunits and/or the organisation as a whole towards goal congruence and goal achievement. The sets of instruments and processes are designated herein as either control systems or control instruments. (Leksell, 1981:76)

Control within organisations is a process whereby management and other groups are able to initiate and regulate the conduct of activities so that their results accord with the goals and expectations held by those groups. (Child, 1984:136)

Control is seen as having one basic function: to help ensure the proper behaviours of people in the organisation. These behaviours should be consistent with the organisation's strategy, if one exists, which, in turn, should have been selected as the best path toward achievement of the organisation's objectives. (Merchant, 1985:4)

The term control refers to the mechanisms used to assure the execution of organisational goals and plans. (Youssef, 1975:136)

According to Child (1973:117) control is essentially concerned with regulating the activities within an organisation so that they are in accord with the expectations established in policies, plans and targets. This is consistent with Tannenbaum's definition (1968) which states that the importance of control is to ensure achievement of the ultimate purposes of the organisation. (Baliga and Jaeger, 1984:25).

Two important elements stand out in these definitions of control. First, management can use it a means to direct behaviour of individuals in an organisation towards the goals of this organisation. Second, there is an element of power in this relationship.

Coordination

Coordination means integrating or linking together different parts of an organisation to accomplish a collective set of tasks. (Van de Ven, Delbecq and Koenig, 1976: 322)

Coordination of sub-units may be defined as the function of insuring that sub-units behaviours are properly interwoven, sequenced and timed so as to accomplish some joint activity or task completion. (Tuggle and Saunders, 1979, cited in Mascarenhas, 1984:94)

A mechanism of coordination is any administrative tool for achieving integration among different units within an organisation. Therefore, the terms mechanisms of coordination or mechanisms of integration will be used as synonyms. (Martinez and Jarillo, 1989:490)

The fundamental theme in the definition of coordination appears to be the integration, harmonisation or linking of different parts of an organisation towards a common goal. In contrast to control, the power element is much more implicit. The final aim, however, appears to be the same as in the definitions of control, namely the direction towards common organisational goals. What *is* the difference between coordination and control?

Control and coordination

Organisational control systems represent mechanisms that convey information to initiate and regulate individual activities. They are needed to integrate individual goals and organisational diversity to create order and coordination out of potentially diffuse individual behaviours and diverse interest (Tannenbaum, 1968, cited in Pucik and Katz, 1986:122).

Management control is the process by which an organisation ensures that its subunits act in a coordinated and co-operative fashion, so that resources will be obtained and optimally allocated in order to achieve the organisation's goals. (Lebas and Weigenstein, 1986:259)

On the relationship between coordination and control. [...] Coordination ... [involves] various means. These can be referred to as coordinating mechanisms, although it should be noted that they are as much concerned with control and communication. In footnote 1 Mintzberg [1979] quotes Litterer (1965, p. 233): "recent developments in the area of control, or cybernetics, have shown [control and coordination] to be the same in principle". In our view, these concepts should be distinguished at the theoretical level, even though in practice they are highly intertwined. Theoretically, however, we would argue that coordination refers to the tuning of different tasks or activities. Control refers to the ways and means by which coordination is monitored and preserved. In this view control is instrumental in achieving coordination in organisations. (Schreuder et al, 1988:8)

These three citations point in the same direction: control is a means to achieve an end called coordination, which in turn leads towards the achievement of common organisational goals. Most of the definitions of control as reproduced above skip the coordination step and assume control to lead directly to the achievement of common organisational goals. In the remainder of this book, we will use the term control mechanisms. These control mechanisms are then used to achieve coordination. This does not mean that we are past confusion. Numerous authors use the terms of control and coordination as interchangeable (see among others Hennart, 1991; Martinez and Jarillo, 1989), consistently speak of "coordination and control mechanisms" (see for instance Edström and Galbraith, 1977b and Bartlett and Ghoshal, 1989) or use yet other terms to denote the same idea: governance mechanisms or integrative mechanisms (Ghoshal and Nohria, 1993). We will therefore discuss a selection of all classifications that bear any relationship to the assurance that common organisational goals or objectives are met.

First, we will take a short dive into history. Why do we need coordination? In the next section, we will see that the need for coordination is a relatively recent phenomenon, which comes forth out of specialisation and the division of labour, maybe the most fundamental cornerstones of our modern economy.

Organisation as opposed to market

Adam Smith and the division of labour
Prehistoric people were almost completely self-sufficient. They caught or gathered their own food, made their own clothes, and built their own houses. The only division of labour they knew was within the family, between men (hunting, building) and women (preparing food and making clothes). This gradually changed and specific professions arose. Goods and services were traded on the market against other goods and services or against money (or some equivalent). The massive increase in the division of labour, however, did not occur until the industrial revolution. At this time Adam Smith, usually credited as the father of modern economics, wrote his now famous book *The Wealth of Nations* (1776) in which he attaches great importance to the division of labour. He begins the first chapter of his book with the following sentence:

> The greatest improvement in the productive powers of labour, and the greater part of the skill, dexterity, and judgement with which it is anywhere directed, or applied, seem to have been the effects of the division of labour.

The example of the pin factory, in which Adam Smith shows that even a simple task, such as the making of pins, can be subject to large increases of productivity by a division of labour, has become famous. Adam Smith indicates three reasons for the division of labour to lead towards an increase in the amount of work that can be done in the same time by the same number of people. *First*, if the work is split into different tasks we can all choose a task we like and which specifically suits our capabilities. When we subsequently specialise in that task, our ability to perform this task increases. Because we can devote all our attention to this specific task, we will probably improve our efficiency. First, we learn by doing and second, we can use this experience to think of ways and instruments to improve our execution of the task at hand. Therefore, specialisation breeds more efficient task performance. *Second*, when we only have to perform one specific task, we do not lose any time in changing from one task to another. This is very important when different tasks are separated physically (for instance performed in different buildings) and/or require quite different tools. However, even if the two kinds of work are done behind the same desk with the same tools (for instance pen and paper or a personal computer), it still takes time to switch from one task to another. Most academics, for instance, have trouble when switching from preparation of courses to writing an academic article, although both tasks use the same tools and are performed behind the same desk.[5] *Finally*, we can use our experience in performing a job to think of ways *and instruments* to improve the execution of the task at hand. Workers who are looking for easier and faster ways to perform their jobs often initiate the construction of labour saving machinery.

In short,[6] division of labour allows people to specialise themselves in a particular task and increases efficiency. There are, however, limits to this kind of specialisation (Douma and Schreuder, 1991). For the individual worker specialisation leads to higher performance, but it also restricts his freedom to perform different tasks. From the individual point of view specialisation can only be carried through to the extent that the dissatisfaction resulting from a narrowly defined task (boredom and the frustration of not being able to use one's capabilities) is compensated by the satisfaction received from higher performance (and most importantly higher rewards). Henry Ford, for instance, offered relatively high wages to induce individuals to take up the narrowly defined tasks in assembling cars. Individual factors are only one limit to increasing the amount of specialisation, however. The other limit is the focus of our attention in this thesis: the need for coordination.

Coase and the need for coordination: markets and organisations

Basically, we can distinguish two different (ideal) types of coordination: market and organisation.[7] In the market system, buyers and sellers do not have to meet each other personally. Accumulated supply and accumulated demand lead to a market price. This market price contains all the information an individual needs to decide whether or not to perform a transaction. The price

---

[5] In fact, switching between these two particular tasks might even be easier if they were physically *separated* and used *different* tools.

[6] This paragraph and parts of the following section are loosely based on chapter 1 of Douma and Schreuder (1991).

[7] As we will discuss later, this basic distinction is somewhat too simplistic since organisations can have many different control mechanisms, including internal markets.

mechanism is the control mechanism in the market system; it takes care of an efficient allocation process. Why then are not all transactions performed on the market? In our society of today organisations are present everywhere. We are of course not the first to ask this question. Coase (1937) put it this way:

> [...] in economic theory we find that the allocation of factors of production be-
> tween different uses is determined by the price mechanism. The price of factor A
> becomes higher in X than in Y. As a result, A moves from Y to X until the differ-
> ence between the prices in X and Y, except in so far as it compensates for other
> differential advantages, disappears. Yet in the real world, we find that there are
> many areas where this does not apply. If a workman moves from department Y to
> department X, he does not go because of a change in relative prices, but because
> he is ordered to do so. [...] The example given above is typical of a large sphere in
> our modern economic system. [...] But in view of the fact that it is usually argued
> that coordination will be done by the price mechanism, why is such organisation
> necessary? (Coase, 1937: 387/388)

Therefore, outside the firm price movements direct production, but within a firm it is the entrepreneur/coordinator who directs production. The main rea-son, according to Coase, is that there are costs involved in using the price mechanism. In some cases, conducting transactions in the market systems is more costly than forming an organisation to perform that same transaction. The costs of internal coordination within the organisation are lower than the costs involved in market transactions in this case. But how do we know in which cases this would apply: when would an organisation come into exis-tence? In the next section, we will discuss Oliver Williamson's transaction cost theory that tries to give an answer to this question.

Williamson and the transaction cost theory
Williamson's (1975, 1981; Williamson and Ouchi, 1981) transaction cost theory starts with the axiom that humans are boundedly rational and some-times behave opportunistically. Bounded rationality refers to human behav-iour that is "*intendedly* rational, but only *limitedly* so" (Simon, 1965:xxiv). Human beings try to make rational decisions, but they are bounded by their limited capacity to formulate and solve problems. The limited capacity to formulate problems is due to language limits. Sometimes, language fails us to describe the problem at hand. Our limited capacity to solve problems is due to the fact that human beings are physically limited in their power to "receive, store, retrieve and process information without error" (Williamson, 1975:21). Fortunately, this *bounded rationality* is only important if "the limits of ration-ality are reached - which is to say, under conditions of *uncertainty and/or complexity*" (ibid.:22). Internal organisation has several advantages under conditions of uncertainty and/or complexity. Internal organisation can deal with uncertainty/complexity in an adaptive, sequential way without fearing

opportunism (see below). Instead of specifying everything in advance (as would be necessary with market contracting), "events are permitted to unfold and attention is restricted to only the actual rather than all possible outcomes" (ibid.: 25). Furthermore, in organisations a kind of idiosyncratic language can be developed to handle the complex situation and "economise on bounded rationality" (ibid.: 25). Finally, internal organisation often leads to converging expectations so that uncertainties resulting from the fact that independent parties can make independent decisions when situations are changing are becoming less important.

The second characteristic is opportunism. Behaving opportunistically means using a situation to your own advantage. Williamson does not claim that all human beings behave opportunistically. He only indicates that some human beings do so some of the time and that it is difficult or even impossible to tell the bad guys from the good guys. Even if you could, you would not know beforehand if the bad guy were going to behave opportunistically this time. Fortunately, this *opportunism* is only a problem if there is only a small number of trading partners, called *small numbers bargaining*. Internal organisation has several advantages compared to markets when opportunism is combined with small numbers bargaining. First, as compared with autonomous trading parties, parties within an organisation are less likely to behaviour opportunistically. While this may result in subgroup gains, the organisation as a whole will suffer. General management can tie rewards to organisational performance as a whole, thereby promoting a more cooperative behaviour. Secondly, related to the first argument, an internal organisation can more easily be audited than a market-contracting party, thereby reducing the possibility of opportunism. Finally, might disputes occur, they are more easily settled within a firm than between market-contracting parties. The latter are more likely to involve costly litigation.

Transaction cost theory tries to answer the following question: given the above-mentioned conditions of bounded rationality and opportunism, can we distinguish situations in which either markets or hierarchies (organisations) are clearly most efficient to use? To answer this, Williamson distinguishes three critical dimensions of transactions: asset specificity, complexity/uncertainty and frequency. *Asset specificity* refers to transaction-specific investments that have been made to execute the transaction. An asset is transaction-specific if it cannot be sold to other buyers without a significant decrease in value (for instance a custom-made software package). We also call transactions involving transaction-specific investments idiosyncratic. So the seller of the asset is in fact "locked into the agreement" and is subject to opportunistic behaviour by the buyer (who can for instance demand a price reduction). However, once the agreement has been made, the buyer will usually also make asset-specific investments (for instance training of employees to work with the package) and be locked into the agreement as well, with possible opportunistic behaviour of the seller (who can for instance demand a higher price) as a result. Seller and buyer are locked into a bilateral monopoly, in fact a special case of small numbers exchange. To prevent both sides from behaving opportunistically, incorporating the software bureau into the buyer's company would be a solution; the market is replaced by the organisation. The second dimension is *complexity/uncertainty*. We already saw above that when transactions are characterised by complexity and/or uncertainty, bounded rationality is a problem, and the transactions are least costly performed within an organisation. If asset specificity and complexity/uncertainty were high we would expect transactions to be carried out within organisations rather than across markets. However, there are certain fixed costs involved in setting up an organisation. Therefore, we would hardly consider doing this for one specific transaction. However, if the transaction occurs frequently, the fixed costs are more easily recovered. Therefore, *frequency* is a third important dimension of transactions.

In sum, transactions will take place where the costs are lowest. These costs are dependent on certain transaction dimensions discussed above. Transactions characterised by a high asset specificity, a high complexity/uncertainty and a high frequency will probably lead to the emergence of an organisation in which coordination is achieved by the direction of the entrepreneur or, as Williamson calls it, hierarchy. However, is the application of the price mechanism really restricted to market transactions and is the application of hierarchy strictly restricted to internal organisation? And is hierarchy the only control mechanism that can be used to achieve coordination within an organisation? The answers to these questions will be discussed in the next section.

Price and hierarchy: the only possible control mechanisms?
In the previous sections, we have shown that coordination of transactions, the necessary consequence of the division of labour, can occur through the price system on the market and by hierarchy within an organisation. The choice of one or the other is dependent on the characteristics of a transaction as distinguished by Williamson. Hennart (1991) however, while recognising price and hierarchy as two control mechanisms, explicitly distinguishes them from the market and the firm, which he calls economic institutions. These economic institutions will "generally use a mix of both price and hierarchy, although the mix in firms is heavily biased towards hierarchy, while markets predominantly use the price system" (Hennart, 1991:74). The same is put forward by Imai and Itami (1984): "The basic hypothesis of this paper is that resource allocation in the market as the arena is done not *only* by the market principle but also, to a great extent by the organisation principle. On the other hand, the market principle is used to a great extent in the resource allocation within the

firm as the arena alongside the organisation principle" (Imai and Itami, 1984:286). This process is called interpenetration. They subsequently distinguish, apart from pure organisations and pure markets, organisation-like markets, market-like organisations and intermediate organisations. The latter are characterised by a more or less evenly balanced mixture of the market principle and the organisation principle and are said to be characteristic of the way Japanese organisations are structured.

These authors, however, still make the basic distinction between coordination through price or hierarchy. Schreuder (1990) argues that this is a far too simplistic view of organisations. He shows that Williamson was already somewhat uncomfortable himself with this strict distinction. In the original description of the transactions cost approach (then called Markets and Hierarchies approach, Williamson, 1975) Williamson discusses "peer groups" and "atmosphere". Peer groups are described in the following quote:

> In order to avoid imputing the benefits to hierarchy that can be had, in some degree, by simple non-hierarchical associations of workers, it will be useful to begin with an examination of worker peer groups. These groups involve collective and usually co-operative activity, provide for some type of other-than-marginal productivity and income-sharing arrangement, but do not entail subordination. (Williamson, 1975:41-42)

According to Williamson, peer groups, which he calls the simplest non-market alternative, have a number of advantages over market relationships. They will not replace the market system, but will attract that part of the population "who find market transactions less satisfying than a non-market relationship" (Williamson, 1975:45). According to Williamson, however, peer group limitations in dealing with bounded rationality and opportunism will soon cause it to be replaced by hierarchy. Therefore, although the alternative is not long-lived, Williamson suggests another alternative.

The concept of atmosphere is hardly elaborated upon in the Markets and Hierarchies approach. According to Williamson: "Concern for atmosphere leads to seeing the issue of 'supplying a *satisfying exchange relation*' as part of the economic system [...]." (Williamson, 1975:38). Reference is also made to "*a sense of well-being*" which may be joined with efficiency. Furthermore, markets and organisations differ in respect to atmosphere:

> Market exchange tends predominantly to encourage calculative relations of a transaction-specific sort between the parties. Such transactions are carefully metered; unsettled obligations do not carry over from one contract, or related set of transactions to another. Internal organisation, by contrast, is often better able to make allowance for quasi-moral involvement among the parties (Williamson, 1975:38)

Apart from a brief reference in the context of employment relations the concept of atmosphere is left for what it is until the conclusions where Williamson states (when enumerating the advantages of hierarchy over markets): "As
compared with market modes of exchange, hierarchy provides, for some purposes at least, a less calculative exchange atmosphere". Then he adds a footnote: "note however, that the peer group may be preferred to hierarchy in this
respect - at least in small organisations". As Schreuder aptly remarks, if peer
groups are superior in this respect, one cannot argue that hierarchies will replace markets because of the atmosphere characteristic. He further concludes:
"we do not normally associate *'satisfying exchange relations'* or a *'sense of
well-being'* with the hierarchical nature of organisations" (Schreuder,
1990:7).

Schreuder acknowledges the existence of hierarchy within complex organisations. He does refute, however, that hierarchy or entrepreneurial authority is
the only control mechanism within organisations and shows that Williamson
himself was not very comfortable with the dichotomy between markets and
hierarchies. Schreuder cites Mintzberg's (1989) six coordinating mechanisms
to show the possible variety of control mechanisms *within* an organisation. In
the next section, we will discuss these and a number of other classifications of
organisational control mechanisms in order to come to a synthesised classification that can be used in later chapters.

Control mechanisms in organisations

In this section, we will review the different control mechanisms that are distinguished by a variety of authors. As discussed above, we will deal with both
classifications that use the term "control" and classifications that use the term
"coordination", as long as the mechanisms have a bearing on the assurance
that common organisational goals or objectives are met. Our final aim is to
provide a synthesis of these various classifications that integrates as many of
the classifications discussed as possible. This final classification will then be
used in subsequent chapters.

A variety of control mechanisms
Table 1-1 summarises the control/coordination mechanisms distinguished by
various authors in both organisational theory and international management
literature.[8] The different classifications have been fitted into four distinct

---

[8] In addition, there is a large number of studies in the field of accounting (e.g. Birnberg and
Snodgrass, 1988; Chow, Shields and Chan, 1991; Chow, Kato and Shields, 1994; Daley et al,
1985; Flamholtz, Das and Tsui, 1985; Govindarajan and Gupta, 1985; Merchant, Chow and Wu,
1995; O'Connor, 1995) that discuss various classifications of control mechanisms or management control systems as they are usually called in this field. Their perspective on control mecha-

categories that have been constructed heuristically in the process of comparing the various classifications. A full explanation of the various categories will be given below. Of course fitting all these classifications into just four categories meant some stretching of definitions and it does not always do full justice to the contributions of different authors. However, in order to come to a workable classification, we had to make some generalisations. The authors have been classified in historical order. Sometimes, authors use equivalent terms to characterise the same mechanism or give further specification in rather general terms. In the former case the terms are separated by a '/'. In the latter case, the specification is given between brackets. When authors distinguish several different control mechanisms that we have put into the same category, the terms have been separated by a ';'. If a given term is only marginally applicable in one of our four categories, it is included between square brackets. We have made an effort to preserve the original labels whenever possible. Unfortunately, we have been able to include only one non-English contribution (Kenter, 1985). It would seem, however, that the classification made by Kenter enjoys a large popularity in the German academic community (see e.g. Festing, 1996a; Macharzina, 1993; Welge, 1987a/b, 1989; Wolf, 1994).

---

nisms is, however, fundamentally different from that used by the various authors in organisation and international management theory. More specifically, compared to the studies discussed in this section, authors in the field of accounting have a rather broad perspective of what are components of a control system. In addition to control mechanisms also referred to by authors in the field of organisation studies and international management, such as centralisation, formal rules and planning, they also include issues such as: environmental uncertainty, horizontal interdependency, slack in budgets, autonomy in purchases, the probability that an employee can attain his or her performance plan, motivation and various types of reward systems. Some of these elements can be considered as a further specification or operationalisation of the control mechanisms defined by authors in the field of organisation theory or international management. Others, however, coincide with the independent variables in our study. Since comparison of these studies with the studies in the field of organisation studies and international management would involve a lot of arbitrary decisions and in some cases would be extremely problematic, we decided to leave these studies out of the literature review altogether.

Table 1-1 Control mechanisms distinguished by various authors

Author	Personal centralised control	Formal bureaucratic control	Output control	Control by socialisation and networks
March/Simon (1958)	coordination by feedback	programmes (activity coordination)	programmes (output coordination)	(coordination by feedback)
Blau/Scott (1963)	control through personal supervision	rules and regulations	performance records (results achieved)	recruitment and training
Thompson (1967)	(coordination by mutual adjustment)	standardisation (routines or rules);	coordination by plan (schedules)	coordination by mutual adjustment
Lawrence/Lorsch (1967)	managerial hierarchy	paper system		direct managerial contact; individual/team or departmental integrative devices
Child (1973)	centralisation	bureaucratic (formalisation, standardisation)		
Galbraith (1973)	hierarchy	rules and programmes	planned targets/goal setting	creating lateral relationships (a.o. direct contact, task forces)
Edström/Galbraith (1977b, 1978)	centralising control strategy (personal/direct)	bureaucratic strategy (impersonal/indirect)		control by socialisation
Ouchi (1977, 1979, 1980)	behaviour control (direct personal surveillance)	behaviour control (rules and procedures)	output control	clan control (indoctrination, socialisation)
Mintzberg (1979, 1983)	direct supervision	standardisation of work processes	standardisation of output	mutual adjustment; socialisation; standardisation of skills

Source				
Child (1984)	personal centralised control	bureaucratic control (a.o. formalisation, routinisation)	output control	cultural control (a.o. socialisation, emphasis on selection, training and development)
Baliga/Jaeger (1984)	cultural (personal)	bureaucratic (behaviour)	bureaucratic (output)	cultural (socialisation)
Merchant (1985/1996))	action (a.o. centralisation)	action (a.o bureaucratic)	result	personnel (a.o. selection, training, cultural control)
Kenter (1985) *(our translation)*	personal control mechanisms (personal instructions)	technocratic control mechanisms (formalisation)	technocratic control mechanisms (planning)	personal control mechanisms (socialisation)
Pucik/Katz (1986)	bureaucratic (behaviour)	bureaucratic (behaviour)	bureaucratic (output)	cultural (socialisation)
Bartlett/Ghoshal (1989)	centralisation (direct intervention)	formalisation (formal systems, policies and standards)		socialisation (recruitment, development, acculturation)
Martinez/Jarillo (1989)	structural and formal (behaviour control/direct supervision; centralisation)	structural and formal (formalisation/standardisation)	structural and formal (output; planning)	informal and subtle (lateral relations; informal communication; socialisation)
Hennart (1991)	hierarchy (personal)	hierarchy (impersonal through rules and regulations)	price	selection/socialisation

A synthesis of control mechanisms

Before we give a further description of the various categories as distinguished in Table 1-1, we would like to make a few remarks regarding the labelling of different control mechanisms. *First*, it would not seem very useful, as some authors do, to characterise a particular control mechanism as behaviour control. In fact all control mechanisms are aimed at changing behaviour, even the ones that are output-based. Output is the result of a certain kind of behaviour. Generalising, we could say that control mechanisms in our first and second category aim at controlling behaviour directly and explicitly, while the mechanisms in the third and fourth category do so indirectly and implicitly. This would plead for not using the term behaviour control at all.

Second, there could be a valid argument to call control mechanisms in both the second and the third category formal, bureaucratic or technocratic (both are impersonal and formalised), as Baliga and Jaeger (1984), Kenter (1985), Pucik and Katz (1986) and Martinez and Jarillo (1989) do. As indicated above, though, these two control mechanisms are fundamentally different in their object of control (direct/explicit or indirect/implicit control of behaviour), which would be neglected by giving them the same name. Different names would therefore be preferred for categories 2 and 3.

Third, using the same term for control mechanisms in the first and last category, as Baliga and Jaeger (1984) and Kenter (1985) do, would seem equally problematic.[9] There are certainly similarities between our first and fourth categories. As Peterson (1984) aptly remarks, selection/socialisation can be regarded as internalised supervision: monitoring, evaluation and feedback take place internally by the subordinate. As also indicated above, however, there is a fundamental difference between the two categories, in that the first involves a very direct/explicit form of control, while the latter is indirect/implicit.

Finally, using the same term for control mechanisms in the first and second category, as Ouchi (1977), Merchant (1985) and Hennart (1991) do, obscures the fact that - as other authors indicate - one of them is a personal type of control, while the other is impersonal.

Combining the two dimensions referred to above, though, gives a convenient classification scheme to characterise our four different categories. Table

---

[9] Even stranger is the classification by Martinez and Jarillo, who classify direct personal types of control under the heading structural and formal control mechanisms, which further includes only impersonal types of control. It is therefore not surprising that in their empirical test of these different control mechanisms (Martinez and Jarillo, 1991), one factor was entirely composed of this personal control category. It must be said, however, that when this factor was excluded the direct personal control loaded on the same factor as the structural and formal control mechanisms.

1-2 summarises this classification and includes our suggested labels for these categories. A further explanation of these labels can be found below.

Table 1-2 Classification of control mechanisms on two dimensions

	Personal/Cultural (founded on social interaction)	Impersonal/Bureaucratic/Technocratic (founded on instrumental artefacts)
Direct/Explicit	Category 1: Personal centralised control	Category 2: Bureaucratic formalised control
Indirect/Implicit	Category 4: Control by socialisation and networks	Category 3: Output control

Personal centralised control The control mechanisms that we have arranged in the first category all denote the idea of some kind of hierarchy, of decisions being taken at the top level of the organisation and personal surveillance of their execution. Of the seventeen authors reviewed Table 1-1, five mention a control mechanism called centralisation, three mention hierarchy and eight refer to a direct personal kind of control (several authors use more than one term and three authors use other terms). We would suggest that the term used by Child (1984), *personal centralised control*, captures most of the variety in this category.

Bureaucratic formalised control The control mechanisms we have arranged in the second category have in common that they are impersonal (also called bureaucratic) and indirect. They aim at pre-specifying, mostly in a written form, the behaviour that is expected from employees. In this way, control can be impersonal because employees can and should refer to the "manual" instead of being told directly what to do. Of the seventeen authors, twelve refer in one way or another to this "written manual". The terms used are: formalisation, rules, regulations, paper system and programmes. A number of authors also use the term standardisation in this respect. In fact, standardisation can be seen as a prerequisite for formalisation. It is nearly impossible to formalise work processes that are not standardised. Six of the seventeen authors (Child, 1973/1984 mentions both terms) mainly refer to the impersonal aspect of this kind of control and use the term bureaucratic. We therefore suggest the term *bureaucratic formalised control* to describe this category.

Output control A remarkable feature of the third category is that four authors do not distinguish any mechanism in this category. As we have said before, this category bears the largest resemblance to the market way of coordination. Perhaps organisational theorists are more likely to neglect this category than the other ones. Of the thirteen authors that do define a control mechanism in this category, seven use the term output. This should not come as a surprise, because we have noticed before that the main characteristic of this category is that it focuses on the outputs realised instead of on behaviour (as the other three control mechanisms do). These outputs are usually generated by the use of reporting or monitoring systems and can take any form from rather general aggregated financial data to detailed figures regarding sales, production levels, productivity, investments, etc. Merchant and Hennart use the terms result and price, which can be regarded as equivalents of output, although in the case of price there are subtle differences (see Hennart, 1991). Four authors refer to plans (Martinez and Jarillo distinguish both planning and output). As all of these are defined by the authors as setting goals that the employee can achieve with a considerable amount of freedom of action, these were also put in the third category. The key element that distinguishes this control mechanism from the two previous ones is thus that instead of particular courses of action certain goals/results/outputs are specified and monitored by reporting systems.[10] Because of the relatively high consistency in terms used we propose the term *output control* for this category.

Control by socialisation and networks Our fourth category unfortunately has come to resemble a garbage can. It combines a lot of relatively diverse mechanisms. It is mainly defined by what it is not: it is not hierarchical, it is not bureaucratic, there are no fixed targets, it is usually not very formal, etc. Compared to the other categories this control mechanism is rather informal, subtle and sophisticated (Martinez and Jarillo, 1989:492). In spite of this diversity, we can distinguish three main sub-categories in this broad category:

- *Socialisation* - which can be defined as ensuring that employees share organisational values and goals, that is are socialised into a common organisation culture - is identified by ten authors (eleven if you include the personnel controls by Merchant). Several of them point to the importance of selection in this respect.
- *Informal, lateral or horizontal exchange of information.* Six authors point to the importance of non-hierarchical communication as a control mechanism, using terms such as: mutual adjustment, direct (managerial) contract, informal communication and coordination by feedback.
- *Formalised lateral or cross-departmental relations.* This category has the same objectives as the second one, increasing the amount of (non-hierarchical) information processing, with the difference that in this case

---

[10] Until of course the reporting system reveals failure to achieve goals/budgets. In that case, companies are likely to resort to either personal centralised control or bureaucratic formalised control for correction.

the relationships are (temporarily) formalised within the organisational structure. Examples are task forces, cross-functional teams, integrative departments (Galbraith, 1973; Lawrence and Lorsch, 1967; Martinez and Jarillo, 1989).

As a common denominator for this category, we propose the term *control by socialisation and networks*. Networks comprise both the second and third sub-category, as the aim of both mechanisms is to create a network of communication channels that supplements the formal hierarchy. The term network is chosen because in organisation theory it is frequently used to denote non-hierarchical relations.

Interaction between various control mechanisms As a final remark, we would like to stress that the different control mechanisms we have distinguished should be regarded as complements rather than substitutes. One company can use different control mechanisms for different employees, different sections of the organisation, different subsidiaries, etc. It can even use more than one control mechanism in the same situation. Some authors (Edström and Galbraith, 1977a/b, 1978; Galbraith, 1973; Lawrence and Lorsch, 1967; Martinez and Jarillo, 1989) even see the different control mechanism as cumulative, with our fourth category as the last to be added to deal with complex environmental conditions.

Concerning complementarity, some combinations are more likely to occur than others. Personal centralised control and bureaucratic formalised control are likely to be used together - with an emphasis on the first in smaller and the second in larger organisations - in situations with a low environmental variability, a simple technology and a good knowledge of the transformation process (Child, 1984:168). As indicated in Table 1-2, both control mechanisms aim at directly controlling employee behaviour. Some authors (Hennart, 1991; Merchant, 1985 and Ouchi, 1977) do not have different names for these control mechanisms. Output control and control by socialisation and networks are likely to be used together - with an emphasis on the first if outputs are measurable and on the second if they are not - in situations with high environmental variability, complex technology and limited knowledge of the transformation process (Child, 1984:168). Both control mechanisms direct behaviour in an implicit way and leave the employee considerable freedom.

Although, as discussed above, some combinations of control mechanisms are more likely than others, in principle *any* combination is possible and control mechanisms are regarded as additive instead of substitutive. This means that some firms might have a high level of application of *all* types of control mechanisms and thus have a relatively high overall level of control, while other firms rely on a heavy application of just one or two control mechanisms, thus displaying a lower overall level of control.

In Chapter 2, we will discuss the applicability of different control mechanisms in different circumstances in much more detail. One issue that we would like to discuss now, is the influence of an MNC's "country of origin" on the dominant types of control mechanisms used in this MNC. [11]

Country of origin and control mechanisms

The belief in the universality of management or organisational science has often been discarded as a myth (Adler, 1983b/c; Hofstede, 1980a/b; Laurent, 1983; Osigweh, 1989; Ronen, 1986). Further, as Clark and Mueller (1996) indicate: "The earlier tendency in management studies towards an intra-firm, universal, context-free and time-free analysis has been increasingly challenged over the last ten years or so" (1996:136). The cultural or societal[12] effect might therefore be an important factor in explaining differences among companies, even if they are multinational.

Therefore, we may find that the use of specific control mechanisms or even the relationship between various contingency factors and control mechanisms is influenced by the home base of the MNC. Of course, this influence is not likely to be completely deterministic,[13] but it certainly is a factor to take into account. In the empirical chapters, we will systematically analyse whether specific contingency relationships hold in different cultures. In this section, we will formulate a number of hypotheses on the influence of the country of origin on the control mechanisms used by MNCs.

To explore the possible differences in control mechanisms between MNCs with a different home base, we performed a literature review for studies that investigated these differences. Unfortunately, very little research focuses on

---

[11] We will not discuss the possible differences in the application of the various control mechanisms in various industries. Previous research in this field is inconsistent and usually focused on one or two industries only. Further, we will not discuss the use of different control mechanisms for different subsidiary countries. Although we would expect MNCs to differ in their use of expatriates (see Section 3) according to different subsidiary countries, we do not expect them to vary other elements of their control portfolio dependent on the subsidiary country. If differences occur between various countries, they are most likely to be due to other factors at the subsidiary level, as will be discussed in the next chapter. The same argument is put forward by Garnier (1982). According to him the degree of autonomy granted will rather be dictated by factors internal to the MNC. We assume this would also be the case for the other control mechanisms. Although Hamilton III et al. (1996) offer a three-dimensional model (based on political risk, financial/monetary policies and relative cultural distance) to choose appropriate control systems for various subsidiaries, no empirical support is offered for this model.

[12] See Sorge (1995) for a discussion of the relation between the two concepts.

[13] See Harzing and Hofstede (1996) for a discussion of the relationship between culture, choice and contingencies.

cross-cultural or international issues. Adler (1983a) found that only 4.2% of the organisational behaviour articles published in American management journals focused on cross-cultural or international issues. Of these publications, nearly half focused on one single country. Two studies that replicated Adler's findings could not find a significant increase in the number of cross-cultural articles (Godkin, Braye and Caunch, 1989; Peng, Peterson and Shyi, 1991). Therefore, the fact that we did not find too many articles on the cultural or societal influence on control mechanisms should not come as a surprise. In addition, the number of studies that included more than one or two countries was particularly small. Further, a large majority of the studies that did include more than one country compared only the United States and Japan. Still, some broad patterns can be distinguished concerning the various control mechanisms discussed above.

Personal centralised control
A relatively large number of studies have investigated the differences in decentralisation of decision-making within Japanese and American companies. Sometimes a number of other countries were included as well. Unfortunately, these studies do not show a consistent picture. We will first discuss a number of studies that claim - with or without empirical support - that centralisation is rather high in Japanese companies and rather low in American companies. Subsequently, we will review the studies that come to the opposite conclusion and try to resolve these conflicting views.

First, Agarwal (1993) hypothesises a positive relationship between power distance and centralisation and a negative relationship between individualism and centralisation. He does not test these relationships in his study, however. Harrison et al. (1994) do test the same hypotheses and find a significantly higher level of centralisation in companies located in Singapore or Hong Kong, when compared to American and Australian companies. A positive relationship between country-of-origin power distance and centralisation is also found by Wong and Birnbaum-More (1994) in a study of subsidiaries of foreign banks located in Hong Kong. Jain and Tucker (1995) assert that power is more centralised in Japanese companies than in American companies. This claim is confirmed indirectly, since Japanese MNCs had a larger observed need to delegate decision-making authority when extending operations abroad. Kustin and Jones (1996) find that the influence of Japanese headquarters on their American subsidiaries is larger than the influence of American headquarters on American subsidiaries. It may be argued, however, that this is not a valid comparison, as subsidiaries located in the same country as headquarters might be treated differently anyhow. Although the difference was not statistically significant, Zaheer (1995) found that Japanese banks showed higher levels of centralisation than American banks.

In contrast to the studies discussed above, an equal number of studies come to the opposite conclusion. Chow et al. (1994) relate centralisation to a country's score on Hofstede's power distance dimension and predict a higher preference for centralisation among Japanese respondents. Although the difference was not significant, preference for centralisation turned out to be higher among American respondents. Kriger and Solomon (1992) explicitly investigated decision-making autonomy in subsidiaries of Japanese and American MNCs. Questionnaires were distributed at both headquarters and subsidiaries. Their results consistently indicated a greater tendency for American MNCs to centralise decision-making in the parent organisation. Negandhi (1987) found the decentralisation of decision-making of subsidiaries of American MNCs to be lower than that of both German and Japanese MNCs. In a final chapter of his edited book on the management of headquarters-subsidiary relationships, Otterbeck (1981) refers to a collective database of information on autonomy of foreign subsidiaries, parts of which have been used by Hedlund, Negandhi and Baliga, Welge, Leksell and himself in the same book. In this database, autonomy was highest for subsidiaries of British MNCs. Japan and Sweden were a close second and third, while subsidiaries of German MNCs had a much lower autonomy. The lowest amount of autonomy was found in subsidiaries of American MNCs, though. Based on an extensive literature review, Wolf (1994) hypothesises centralisation to be higher in American MNCs than in German MNCs, while the latter will have higher levels of centralisation than other European MNCs. The differences found in his empirical study were in the predicted direction, but not significant. Yuen (1993) finds that American headquarters exercise a higher influence on the HRM policies of their Singaporese subsidiaries than their Japanese counterparts do. Finally, Garnier (1984) investigated autonomy in subsidiaries of MNCs headquartered in a number of different countries. In a multivariate analysis, however, only the country variable for Japan entered the regression analysis. Japanese subsidiaries had a much higher level of autonomy than subsidiaries from all other countries in the survey, including the USA.

The results of Lincoln, Hanada and McBride (1986) might shed some light on these contradictory findings. They find that centralisation of *formal* authority (centralisation in theory) is higher in Japanese organisations when compared to their US counterparts. In contrast to this, centralisation of *de facto* decision-making (centralisation in daily practice) is lower in Japanese companies than in American companies. The difference between formal and *de facto* centralisation is very small in American companies, but considerable in Japanese companies. Although the above studies do not provide enough information to verify whether formal or *de facto* authority was measured, this difference might very well explain some of the inconsistent results. As our study will focus on *de facto* centralisation and as most of the studies that focused specifically on MNCs found autonomy to be larger for Japanese subsidiaries, we come to the following hypothesis:

Hypothesis 1-1: Subsidiaries of Japanese multinationals will have a higher amount of autonomy than subsidiaries of American multinationals.

In addition to the studies discussed above, some additional information is available for different European countries. Two of the studies referred to above (Otterbeck, 1981 and Wolf, 1994) already indicated a rather low level of autonomy for German subsidiaries when compared to subsidiaries from Japanese and other European MNCs. This is confirmed by Garnier's (1982) study, in which Germany had the second highest level of centralisation of the ten countries included. A very early study by Daniels and Arpan (1972) found autonomy to be very limited in subsidiaries of both German and British MNCs when compared to both Italian and Scandinavian (mostly Swedish) firms. We will therefore add the following hypothesis:

Hypothesis 1-2: Subsidiaries from German multinationals will have a lower amount of autonomy than subsidiaries from both other European and Japanese multinationals.

For the other European countries, less empirical work is available. Finland has not been included in any study, while Switzerland, the Netherlands and France were included in one study only (Garnier, 1982). We will therefore not offer any hypotheses on these countries. The United Kingdom was included in three studies. Unfortunately one reported a very high level of autonomy (Otterbeck, 1981), one a very low level (Daniels and Arpan, 1972) and one an average level (Garnier, 1982). Sweden was also included in these studies. As all these studies report a higher level of autonomy for Swedish subsidiaries than for subsidiaries from most of the other countries except Japan, we will offer the following hypothesis:

Hypothesis 1-3: Subsidiaries from Swedish multinationals will have a higher amount of autonomy than subsidiaries from both other European and American multinationals.

A related issue that might qualify the discussion on decision-making autonomy in Japanese subsidiaries is the relatively high presence of expatriates in Japanese subsidiaries (see e.g. Kopp, 1994; Negandhi and Welge, 1984; Tung, 1982). Ferner (1997) refers to this practice as: "expatriate-intensive modes of control to allow the imposition of central authority through direct contract". In this way, a larger amount of autonomy can be granted since committed Japanese expatriates represent "mini-headquarters" within the foreign subsidiary. Bartlett and Ghoshal (1989) also refer to this phenomenon when they claim centralisation to be the dominant type of control mechanism in Japanese MNCs. This issue will be further explored in Chapter 2, when we discuss the use of expatriates as a control mechanism.

Bureaucratic formalised control

Results in the area of formalisation are less abundant, but also somewhat less contradictory. Chow et al. (1994) found the preference for formal rules to be higher among Japanese MBA students than among their American counterparts (motivated by Japan's higher score on Hofstede's uncertainty avoidance dimension). Harrison et al. (1994) found a insignificant higher level of formalisation in firms located in Hong Kong or Singapore, when compared to Australian and American firms. In Zaheer's (1995) study, Japanese banks showed significantly higher levels of formalisation than American banks.

On the other hand, Bartlett and Ghoshal (1989) - in their clinical study of nine MNCs - report formalisation to be the dominant control mechanism in American MNCs. Birnberg and Snodgrass (1988) find that American firms have more explicit control systems, while Japanese MNCs have more implicit systems. An implicit control system is defined as one in which the bureaucratic rules and standards are not clearly set out and readily knowable by both parties. In this context explicit control systems may therefore be considered to be synonymous with formalisation. Ferner (1997) contrasts control rooted in formal systems, which is said to be typical of US companies, with the more socially oriented control mechanisms supported by a heavy use of expatriates, as typical of Japanese MNCs. According to Hulbert and Brandt (1980) some American MNCs follow the American mode of control to the extreme and run the risk of drowning themselves in the morass of procedures and reports. Jaeger and Baliga (1985) use a similar distinction, when they claim that US companies will tend to use more bureaucratic control and Japanese companies more cultural control, which is seen as the internalisation of and moral commitment to the norms, values, objectives and ways of doing things of the organisation. Negandhi (1987) reports that 88% of the subsidiaries of American MNCs responded that they depended a great deal on written policies from headquarters, while this was the case for only 32% of the subsidiaries of German and 12% of the subsidiaries of Japanese firms. Wolf (1994) finds standardisation in the American MNCs to be higher than in European MNCs. Standardisation in German MNCs is also higher than in the other European MNCs. In their study of foreign banks in Hong Kong, Wong and Birnbaum-More (1994) find - contrary to their hypotheses - a significant negative relationship between uncertainty avoidance and formalisation. Countries in their sample with high uncertainty avoidance include Japan, France, Germany and Switzerland, while the group of countries with a low uncertainty avoidance hosts all the Anglo-Saxon countries. Although Germany is now in the low formalisation group, the scores of Japan and the USA are consistent with the previous studies. Considering the relative weight of the evidence with regard to American and Japanese MNCs, we put forward the following hypothesis:

Hypothesis 1-4: Subsidiaries of American multinationals will experience higher levels of bureaucratic formalised control than subsidiaries of Japanese multinationals.

Calori et al. (1994) compared the control mechanisms applied by French and American MNCs in respect of their British acquisitions. American MNCs were hypothesised to exercise greater control through procedures. Although the difference was not significant, it was in the expected direction. As in two studies French MNCs were found to have low levels of control through procedures, when compared to American or Anglo-Saxon MNCs, we put forward the following hypothesis:

Hypothesis 1-5: Subsidiaries of both American and British multinationals will experience higher levels of bureaucratic formalised control than subsidiaries of French multinationals.

Output control

Concerning output control, the picture is rather homogeneous. In an early study, Scholhammer (1971) found that American MNCs relied more heavily on reports than European firms. Conforming to this picture, Hulbert and Brandt (1980) found that American MNCs required higher levels of reports than either European or Japanese MNCs. Negandhi (1987) finds the frequency of reporting to be higher in American than in German and Japanese MNCs. In Egelhoff's (1984, 1988b) study American MNCs also tended to exercise relatively high levels of output control over their foreign subsidiaries, when compared to European firms. British MNCs were included as a separate group and showed output control levels between American and European MNCs. For financial matters, though, British MNCs had exactly as much output control as American MNCs. The differences between American and European firms did not disappear when controlling for age, size, subsidiary country, the number of subsidiaries and the international experience of the company. Finally, many of the studies mentioned above under bureaucratic formalised control do not make a distinction between this type of control and output control, and claim both of them to be higher in American companies than in Japanese companies. In view of the observations above, we put forward the following hypothesis:

Hypothesis 1-6: Subsidiaries of American and British multinationals will experience higher levels of output control than subsidiaries of both European and Japanese multinationals.

Control by socialisation and networks

Although the use of cultural or clan control in Japanese companies is well documented (see e.g. Ouchi, 1980; Ouchi and Jaeger, 1978; Zaheer, 1995), it is not clear whether the same type of control is present in Japanese MNCs. We can distinguish two different approaches in this respect. First, Japanese expatriates could indeed socialise foreign subsidiaries' employees into the Japanese way of doing things. On the other hand, control could also rely on a socialised Japanese managing director who has either internalised headquarters decisions or directly supervises decisions taken at headquarters. Snodgrass and Grant's (1986) study seems to follow the latter idea. In the Japanese firms in their study, the strength of the hierarchy as a control mechanism was emphasised. Managers in American firms were significantly more homogeneous in their values, i.e. had a higher level of shared values, than managers in Japanese companies. Further, we should note that not every subsidiary of a Japanese MNC would have an expatriate as a managing director. With respect to subsidiaries of Japanese MNCs that have a low expatriate presence, shared values with headquarters is likely to be lower than for subsidiaries of American MNCs, simply because the difference with the idiosyncratic Japanese culture will be larger. We will therefore offer the following tentative hypothesis:

Hypothesis 1-7: Subsidiaries of American multinationals will report a higher level of shared values with headquarters than subsidiaries of Japanese multinationals.

When comparing the control mechanisms applied by French and American MNCs in respect of their British acquisitions, Calori et al. (1994) found that, conforming their hypothesis, American MNCs exercised higher levels of informal control - in particular informal communication to achieve socialisation - than French MNCs. As this result relates back to Laurent's (1983) finding that Anglo-Saxons view the organisation primarily as a network of individual relationships, who influence each other through negotiation and communication, we will offer the following hypothesis:

Hypothesis 1-8: Subsidiaries of American multinationals will experience higher levels of informal control (informal communication and shared values) than subsidiaries of French multinationals.

Summary and conclusion

As the reader will undoubtedly have noticed, many of the hypotheses report on supposed differences between American and Japanese MNCs. The problem is that very few of the studies done on this subject so far include individual European countries in the picture. We therefore heartily agree with Ferner's (1997) suggestion that "the choice of countries of origin for such research should reflect the need to overcome the concentration of much existing research on USA and Japanese MNCs".[14] Therefore, as will be described in Chapter 3, we have made every effort not only to increase the chances of a high response rate, but also to achieve a distribution of responses across countries that allows us to analyse differences between a larger number of countries than the USA and Japan alone.

Conclusion

This section has discussed the first building block of our theoretical framework: control mechanisms. The different control mechanisms distinguished above will be used in the remainder of this thesis. In subsequent chapters, we will show how these control mechanisms are affected by an international context. We will also outline the role that international transfers can play in this respect. First, however, we will discuss the two other building blocks of this thesis: MNCs and international transfers in Sections 2 and 3 respectively.

2. MULTINATIONAL COMPANIES

Introduction

In this section, the relevant issues concerning MNCs - the second building block of this book - will be discussed. We will pay attention to the changing international environment, the industry, and an MNC's strategy and structure. This description will serve to substantiate our reasoning in a subsequent chapter that changing environments are not only accompanied by changing strategies and structures, but also by different processes, i.e. control mechanisms. Table 1-3 (adapted from Martinez and Jarillo, 1989) summarises these ideas. It is based on the environment-strategy-structure paradigm, which suggests that superior performance comes from a good fit between strategy and environmental demands, and between organisational structure (and processes) and strategy.

In contrast to earlier work on MNC strategy and structure (Daniels, Pitts and Tretter, 1984, 1985; Egelhoff, 1988b; Galbraith and Kazanjian, 1986;

---

[14] This problem is not only apparent in research on control mechanisms. In Section 3, we will see that the same limitations apply to research on staffing policies. A recent example in another field, subsidiary ownership patterns (Eramilli, 1996), shows clearly that research on country-of-origin effects leaves much to be desired. Conclusions on the influence of nationality on ownership patters for Swiss, Italian, French and British firms are based on data from 1, 1, 5 and 3 MNCs respectively, while the same sample included 19 American MNCs.

Franko, 1976; Stopford and Wells, 1972[15]), we do not presuppose a one-way deterministic relationship between any of these five variables. Especially the link between strategy and structure has been discussed extensively since Chandler's (1962) seminal work and various authors (see for instance Hall and Saias, 1980) have argued that strategy might be just as dependent on structure as structure on strategy. Further, changes also do not necessarily result from the environment alone (Hedlund and Rolander, 1990).

Most of the authors discussed in this section belong to the process school of international management (Doz and Prahalad, 1991) that had its origins in the dissertations of Prahalad (1975) and Doz (1976) and adhere to a more flexible and less deterministic relationship between environment, strategy, structure and process. The overall balance, fit or match is what counts. We will come back to this distinction in Section 2 of Chapter 2, where we will discuss the configuration approach and contrast it to traditional contingency theory.

Table 1-3 Environment, strategy, structure, systems and processes in MNCs

Environment: Historical	Environment: Industry	Strategy	Structural con- figuration	Systems and processes
Changes in international environment	Pattern of in- ternational competition	Company's strategic re- sponse	Company's organisational structure	Company's control mechanisms

This section on multinational companies will be structured as follows. First, we will first discuss the host of classifications that is available in this field and try to bring some clarification into the jungle of terms in use. We will then discuss the first four elements of Table 1-3 in more detail, based on research by Bartlett and Ghoshal (1987a/b, 1988, 1989, 1992a) and Prahalad and Doz (1987). Subsequently, we will discuss a number of "traditional" organisation theory approaches to the first four elements of Table 1-3. The main aim of that section is to discover whether there are some notable similarities or dif-ferences between international management literature and "traditional" man-agement literature.

Before discussing any of these subjects, we would like to stress that one very important intervening variable in the development sketched in Table 1-3 is the manager himself. Changes in the environment will not influence strat-egy unless they are enacted (Weick, 1979) and managers do have some choice

---

[15] All these authors discuss the relationship between two strategy variables, foreign product diversity and the percentage of foreign sales - Egelhoff (1988b) added a third percentage of foreign manufacturing - and the type of organisational structure an MNC chooses (international division, area division, product division or global matrix).

of action (Child, 1972). An important influential factor in this process is the societal/cultural effect (see among others Sorge, 1995 and Hofstede, 1980a/b). Society/culture can form a constraint on certain choices (e.g. democratic leadership will not work in countries where people favour hierarchical decision processes) and influences the values of managers so that certain environmental changes are not enacted and certain options are not considered (see Harzing, 1991). We will therefore discuss whether a country-of-origin effect is present in the application of the various organisational strategies and structures.

The last section discusses the links between the environment and an MNC's strategy and structure. It includes some hypotheses on the types of strategy and structure expected to be most dominant in the industries included in the empirical part of this thesis. The link between strategy and structure (summarised as organisational model) on the one hand and control mechanisms on the other, will be discussed in Chapter 2, where we will integrate the three theoretical building blocks.

Confusion of terms

Although international management as a field of research is still rather young, many authors have described typologies of multinational firms. Table 1-4 summarises the typologies found in academic and professional literature.[16] The different classifications have been fitted into four distinct categories that have been constructed heuristically in the process of comparing the various classifications. The authors are classified in historical order. '[ ]' is used to denote that the term is not fully applicable in this category. It is important to note that these typologies are either purely conceptual or based on limited case study research. Later, we will discuss a number of studies that have tried to verify these typologies empirically.

Although there are substantial differences in the details and the variables that are used to distinguish the different categories, there is a reasonable convergence in the basic characteristics of the categories distinguished by the various authors. Some of the authors refer to others themselves, pointing out comparable notions. Further, most authors implicitly or explicitly refer to an integration/coordination/globalisation versus differentiation/responsiveness/-localisation continuum.

---

[16] Not surprisingly, German authors are very popular in the German academic community. German authors also refer to Anglo-Saxon literature, although books sometimes only become popular after their translation into German (see e.g. Meffert, 1991). As could be expected, German contributions are totally ignored in the Anglo-Saxon literature.

Table 1-4 Typologies of multinational companies

Authors	Attribute	Multidomestic	International	Global	Transnational
Perlmutter (1969)	management attitudes	polycentric		ethnocentric	geocentric
Stopford and Wells (1972)	strategy, structure	area division		world-wide product division	[global matrix]
Doz (1980)	strategy (economic and political imperatives)	national responsiveness		world-wide integration	administrative coordination
Porter (1986a)	strategy (configuration and coordination), industry	country-centred strategy, multidomestic industry		purest global strategy, global industry	strategy: high foreign investment with extensive coordination among subsidiaries
Porter (1986b)	id.	id.		simple global strategy, global industry	complex global strategy, global industry
Bartlett (1986)	strategy (forces for global coordination/integration and national responsiveness/differentiation)	multinational		global	
Prahalad and Doz (1987)	strategy (need for integration and responsiveness)	locally responsive strategy		integrated product strategy	multifocal strategy
Meffert (1989) [our translation]	strategy (globally based or locally based advantages)	multinational	international	global	mixed
Bartlett and Ghoshal (1989)	environment, industry, strategy, structure	multinational	international	global	transnational

Gerpott (1990) *[our translation]*	strategy (globally based or locally based advantages)	multilocal		global	hybrid
White and Poynter (1990)	structure (globally based or locally based advantages)	geographic area structure		global product structure	horizontal
Adler and Chadar (1990)	Environment, strategy, structure, processes	international	(international)	multinational	global
Adler and Bartholomew (1992b)	id.	international	(international)	multinational	transnational
UN, *World investment report* (1993)	strategy	stand-alone strategy		simple integration strategy	complex integration strategy
Welge (1996) *[our translation]*	strategy (integration and differentiation)	multinational	international	global	dual
Macharzina and Wolf (1996) *[our translation]*	strategy (globalisation and localisation requirements)	independent market strategy	selection strategy	integration strategy	interaction strategy

Confusing, however, is that some authors use the same terms for different typologies. Adler and Ghadar use three of the terms that Bartlett and Ghoshal use, but all for different typologies. Fortunately, Adler and Bartholomew at least substituted the term global for transnational in a later publication. Even more confusion results from the use of the terms in other disciplines. In international marketing for instance the term global is used by some authors (e.g. Hout, Porter and Rudden in Buzzell and Quelch, 1988) to describe a kind of company that we would call transnational. International economists *do* use the term transnational, but they simply mean a company operating in different countries, as in the case where we would use the general term multinational.

Based on this review of previous literature, we propose five terms to characterise MNCs. First, *multinational* as a general term for a company that operates internationally. Second, *multidomestic, international, global,* and *transnational* to describe different configurations of MNCs. In the next section, we will describe these configurations in more detail, using the work by Bartlett and Ghoshal and Prahalad and Doz for this purpose. A more recent contribution (Böttcher and Welge, 1996) questions the usefulness of these generic terms in describing international strategies. The authors indicate that the strategy *content* remains largely unspecified beyond the discussion of broad categories of competitive advantage. As Böttcher and Welge also discuss, however, by limiting the analysis to a few dimensions, the typologies are very well suited to categorise and structure international strategies. As international strategy will be only one of the many variables in this book, the broad classification in generic strategies is deemed more appropriate than a more detailed analysis of strategic behaviour.

MNCs: environment, strategy and structure

We will discuss the first four elements of Table 1-3. This discussion is relatively extensive, since these elements play a crucial part in the remainder of the thesis. We will mainly be using the work by Bartlett and Ghoshal. Although, as we have seen above, quite a number of authors have written about the environment, strategy and structure of MNCs, Bartlett and Ghoshal seem to be the most influential ones. In the Social Science Citation Index, we found more references to their articles and books than to those of Prahalad and Doz and Porter, which can be regarded as their main "competitors" in this field.

A second, and perhaps more important reason to start from Bartlett and Ghoshal's work is that their focus is mainly on the first (environment/history) and last two (structural configuration, and systems and processes) elements of Table 1-3, which are most important for our purpose, while both Prahalad and Doz and Porter pay more attention to the industry and strategy elements. While Bartlett and Ghoshal work from a resource-based perspective, Prahalad and Doz and Porter take an industrial organisation viewpoint. Although of course both perspectives can offer a valid contribution (Collis, 1991), the more internally oriented work of Bartlett and Ghoshal is more suitable for this book, whose focus is also on the internal side of the organisation.

This section will therefore discuss Bartlett and Ghoshal's historical analysis of the international environment and their distinction of various types of industries and MNC strategies and structures. These four factors will then be integrated with the help of Prahalad and Doz's (1987) integration/responsiveness framework.[17] A final subsection discusses the empirical support for the typology in general and the transnational model in particular.

Historical analysis of the international environment

When analysing the environment on a global (world-wide) scale, one of the most important trends for MNCs is the increasing internationalisation of the world economy. In this section, we will briefly sketch four phases in this internationalisation process. The description is based on Bartlett (1986) and Bartlett and Ghoshal (1989).

The *Multidomestic*[18] Era (1920-1950): The period between the two world wars was characterised by a rise in nationalistic feelings. Countries became more and more protectionistic and erected high tariff barriers. There were large national differences in consumer preferences, and communication and logistical barriers remained high. These circumstances favoured national companies. For *multinational* companies, the strategy of centralised production in order to capture economies of scale, combined with exports to various countries, was made impossible by high tariff and logistical barriers. In order to be able to compete with national companies, multinational firms had to set up a larger number of foreign manufacturing subsidiaries. These subsidiaries were usually relatively small plants that produced for the national market only. Differences in consumer preferences and high communication barriers led to a decentralisation of decision-making, so that the foreign subsidiaries were relatively independent of their headquarters. European companies dominated foreign investment in this era.

The *International* Era (1950-1960): The post-war years were characterised by a world-wide boom in demand. Consumers were making up for the years of scarcity and sobriety. The United States was in a predominant economic position during this period and led the way. Most European companies were preoccupied with the reconstruction of their domestic operations, while

---

[17] This section is largely based on a similar description in Harzing (1995a) and Paauwe and Dewe (1995).

[18] Because we prefer to use the term multinational as a general term describing companies operating in more than one country, we have consistently substituted Bartlett and Ghoshal's term multinational by the comparable term multidomestic.

American companies were almost untouched by the war. US companies developed new technologies and products. They were almost forced into the international market by spontaneous export orders and opportunities for licensing. Later they started making their products in manufacturing facilities in Western Europe and in developing countries. These companies followed the classic product life-cycle pattern (Vernon, 1966). By 1960 the United States share in foreign investment had risen to 59% (Bartlett and Ghoshal, 1989:47).

The *Global* Era (1960-1980): In the sixties and seventies, the successive reductions in tariff barriers began to have their full impact. They were accompanied by declining international transport costs and communication barriers. Furthermore, new electronic technologies increased the minimum efficient scale in many industries. Finally, consumer preferences became more homogeneous because of increased international travel and communication. All these developments made centralised and relatively standardised production with exports to various countries profitable again. Japanese companies which internationalised in this period, were very successful with their large scale-intensive production facilities, which were able to produce low-cost, high-quality products under tight central control.

The *Transnational* Era (1980-?): By the late 1970s there was a rising concern on the part of host countries about the impact of MNCs on their balance of trade, national employment levels, and on the international competitiveness of their economies. Consequently, they gradually started to exercise their sovereign powers. Trade barriers were erected again to limit exports and foreign direct investments were regulated by industrial policies. In addition, other forces counteracted the previous globalisation process. Flexible manufacturing reduced the minimum efficient scale by employing robotics and CAD/CAM technologies. The use of software became important in a growing number of industries (from telecommunications to computers and consumer electronics). This development facilitated conformity to consumers who were once again asking for products tailored to their local needs. The problem is that we do not see a complete return to the multidomestic era again. The world-wide innovation of the international era and the global efficiency of the global era remain important competitive factors. Today, in more and more industries, companies struggle with three different and sometimes opposing demands: national responsiveness, global efficiency and world-wide innovation.

Industry, strategy and structure

In the analysis of the industry, strategy and structure, we re-encounter the four familiar terms: multidomestic, international, global and transnational. The description is again based on Bartlett and Ghoshal (1987a/b, 1989 and 1992a).

Multidomestic In a multidomestic industry, international strategy consists of a series of domestic strategies. Competition in each country is essentially independent of competition in other countries. Typical industry characteristics are determined by cultural, social and political differences between countries. A classic example of a multidomestic industry is the branded packaged products industry (e.g. food and laundry detergents).

Companies in these industries preferably follow a multidomestic strategy, which gives primary importance to national responsiveness. Products or services are differentiated to meet differing local demands. Policies are differentiated to conform to differing governmental and market demands. The competitive advantage of multidomestic companies often lies in downstream value chain (see Porter, 1986b for a discussion of the value chain concept) activities such as sales and marketing or service. These activities are closely related to the buyer and are usually tied to the buyer's location.

A multidomestic organisational structure completes the picture. Responsiveness to the differences in national markets led multidomestic companies to decentralise organisational assets and decision-making. This resulted in a configuration that can be described as a decentralised federation. The decentralised federation is organised by area, that is by geographical region.

International The adjective "international" refers to the international product life cycle, which describes the internationalisation process in this type of industry. The critical success factor in these industries is the ability to transfer knowledge (particularly technology) to units abroad. It involves sequential diffusion of innovations that were originally developed in the home market. A classic example of an international industry is telecommunications switching.

The preferred strategy in this industry, the international strategy, gives primary importance to the development and diffusion of world-wide innovations internationally. The competitive advantage of international companies often lies in research and development. New technologies are developed in the home country and transferred and adapted to foreign countries, following the product life cycle as discussed by Vernon (1966). They do not strive for the efficiency of global companies or the complete national responsiveness of multidomestic companies, but do pay *some* attention to both of these goals. This is the strategy traditionally followed by American multinationals.

In the international organisational structure, transfer of knowledge and expertise to countries that were less advanced in technology or market development is the essential task. Local subsidiaries do still have some freedom to adopt new products or strategies, but coordination and control by headquarters is more important than in the multidomestic type. Subsidiaries are relatively dependent on the parent company for new products, processes, or ideas.

A coordinated federation, often structured by function, is the name for the structural configuration of this organisational model.

Global In a global industry, standardised consumer needs and scale efficiencies make centralisation and integration profitable. In this kind of industry, a firm's competitive position in one country is significantly influenced by its position in other countries. The global industry is not merely a collection of domestic industries but a series of linked domestic industries in which the rivals compete against each other on a truly world-wide basis. A classic example of a global industry is consumer electronics.

The preferred strategy in these industries is the global strategy that gives primary importance to efficiency. Global companies integrate and rationalise their production to produce standardised products in a very cost-efficient manner.[19] The competitive advantage of global companies often lies in upstream chain activities such as procurement, inbound logistics (warehousing, inventory control, material handling, etc.) and operations (machining, assembly, testing, etc.). These activities are optimised on a world-wide scale. This is the strategy traditionally followed by Japanese multinationals.

In a global organisational configuration, assets, resources and responsibilities are centralised. The role of subsidiaries is usually limited to sales and/or service. Compared with subsidiaries in multidomestic or international organisations, they have much less freedom of action. The structural configuration can be described as a centralised hub and is usually based on a product structure. Within each product division, activities are centralised, but there is little, if any, linkage between the world product groups.

Transnational Transnational industries are characterised by a complex set of environmental demands. Companies in these industries must respond simultaneously to the diverse and often conflicting strategic needs of global efficiency (as a characteristic of global industries), national responsiveness (as a characteristic of multidomestic industries) and transfer of knowledge (as a characteristic of international industries).

Companies following the transnational strategy that fits the industry recognise that they should pay attention to global efficiency, national responsiveness and world-wide learning at the same time. In order to do this their strategy must be very flexible. The strategy (literally) is to have no set strategy, but to let each strategic decision depend on specific developments. Strategy becomes unclear and it may become dissolved into a set of incremental decisions with a pattern that may only make sense after the fact. Issues are shaped, defined, attended to, and resolved one at a time in a "muddling through" pro-

---

[19] See Levitt (1983) for a fervent argumentation for the benefits of product standardisation.

cess. A transnational strategy would be a deliberately planned strategy to have an "adaptive" (Mintzberg, 1988a), "incremental" (Quinn, 1988), "muddling through" (Lindblom, 1987) or "emergent" (Mintzberg, 1988b) strategy.

The type of organisation structure that fits a transnational industry and strategy is very flexible. Bartlett and Ghoshal refer to an integrated network structure that links major sub-units of the company together. Assets, resources and capabilities are neither centralised nor completely decentralised. Expertise is spread throughout the organisation and subsidiaries can serve as a strategic centre for a particular product-market combination. To use a popular term, companies are creating "centres of excellence" for each activity. It is important to realise that this concept upsets the traditional notion of having one headquarters and many dependent subsidiaries. The company becomes a kind of network with different centres for different activities. Each centre can have a strategic role for a particular area.[20]

Integration
The four configurations - combinations of industry, strategy and structure - described above can be visually summarised in the integration/responsiveness framework (see Prahalad and Doz, 1987, for an extensive description), which is reproduced in Figure 1-1.

Figure 1-1 The integration-responsiveness framework

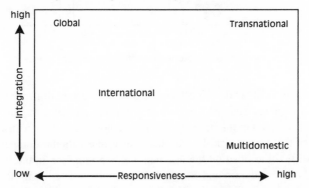

The vertical axis represents the level of global integration, and hence of central coordination by headquarters; the horizontal axis represents the extent of national responsiveness or differentiation, and consequently of the desired influence of subsidiaries in strategic and operational decisions. Although this

---

[20] A more extensive description of the transnational organisational model can be found in Ghoshal and Bartlett (1990), Hedlund (1986) and Hedlund and Rolander (1990). A longitudinal study of a company moving from a multidomestic to a transnational type of structure can be found in Malnight (1996).

framework is very convenient to summarise the different configurations, there are some additional points that should be stressed. *First*, a firm can choose to follow a strategy and choose a structure that would not provide an optimal fit with the industry, but that is more in accordance with its internal resources. *Second*, the place of the transnational in the upper right corner does not mean that it is always high on both integration and responsiveness. The transnational approach is to decide whether to stress integration or responsiveness for each particular situation. The accent can be different for each business, function, task or country. Figure 1-2 shows the varying needs for global integration and national responsiveness in Unilever's business strategies, functional strategies and tasks.

Figure 1-2 Integration and differentiation needs at Unilever (source: Bartlett and Ghoshal, 1987b)

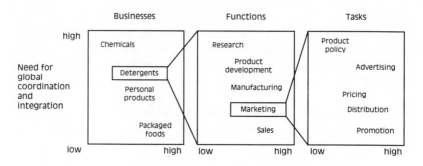

Need for national differentiation and responsiveness

Third, the aspect of world-wide learning and innovation, dominant for international companies and also important for transnational companies, is not adequately captured in this framework. This is not surprising because the constructors of this framework did not distinguish international companies. This makes it difficult to position the international configuration in the framework. Some authors (Sundaram and Black, 1992) simply equate it with the transnational configuration other authors (Ghoshal and Nohria, 1993; Welge, 1996[21]) place it in the lower left corner. As said above, an international strategy assumes *some* concern with both integration and responsiveness. We therefore argue that the actual position would lie in between, leaning somewhat more to the lower left corner.

---

[21] It should be noted, though, that these authors do not refer to the learning aspect of the international strategy. They simply consider it as a strategy that scores low on both integration and responsiveness. Our classification preserves some of the learning aspect.

Empirical support

Although Bartlett and Ghoshal's typology has received a lot of attention, by both academics and professionals, it is based on in-depth case studies of nine MNCs only. This section will therefore take stock of the empirical support for this typology. First, we will discuss a number of replications of the typology as such and second, we will investigate the occurrence of the transnational organisational model in practice.

Empirical tests of the typology found a reasonable amount of support for the organisational models described by Bartlett and Ghoshal. Leong and Tan (1993) had senior executives of MNCs all around the world classify their organisations as being multinational, global, international or transnational in nature. They further asked them to evaluate their organisation's configuration of assets and capabilities, roles of overseas operations and development and diffusion of knowledge. The global and multinational organisation types scored as hypothesised, but the international and transnational types did not differ significantly from each other or from the other types.

Moenaert et al. (1994) describe the organisational structural properties of 87 MNCs from the USA, East Asia and Western Europe. The scales they used to measure multinational, global and transnational structures had reasonably high alpha values (0.61-0.80). Transnational structural properties correlated positively with the level of multinational orientation and negatively (though with a lower magnitude) with the global orientation of a company. A strong (-0.49) negative correlation was found between the global and multinational structural properties. The signs and magnitude of these correlations support the models described by Bartlett and Ghoshal.

In a survey of business units competing in global industries, Roth and Morrison (1990) found three clearly distinguishable clusters of firms following global integration, locally responsive and multifocal strategies respectively. Johnson Jr (1995) performed a similar study in one industry - the US construction equipment industry - and found the same generic strategies. Although these results conflict with Bartlett and Ghoshal's typology in the sense that not all companies are following the strategies best suited to the particular industry,[22] they do provide support for the classification as such.

Considering the various empirical tests of the Bartlett and Ghoshal typology, we see that the global and multidomestic strategies emerge clearly and that all studies find a kind of "in-between" strategy that combines elements of global and multidomestic strategies. This strategy is usually called transnational or multifocal. No clear international strategy was found. In combination with the lack of an international strategy in many of the conceptual classifica-

---

[22] In Bartlett and Ghoshal's (1989) own study, only one in three firms had the ideal configuration.

tions as discussed above, this observation leads us to limit our analysis in subsequent chapters to just three international configurations: global, multi-domestic and transnational.

Although Bartlett and Ghoshal would be the last to claim that the transnational model is the best solution for each MNC, it is increasingly seen as an ideal type. Although we will probably not encounter many firms that completely conform to this ideal type, we can find a whole number of firms that strive for or have realised a number of transnational characteristics. Starting with the business press, the *Financial Times* describes Electrolux, IBM and Nestlé as actual or potential transnationals (Lorenz, 1989, 1990, 1991). Many company executives also describe their companies in transnational terms. Asea Brown Boveri clearly recognises the three-fold demands that are placed on companies in the transnational era. According to Percy Barnevik, ABB's former president and CEO, its competitive strategy is based on local market presence and responsiveness, on leveraging core technologies/being a technology leader and on achieving global economies of scale (Taylor, 1991). Agathe (1990), president and CEO of ABB Inc., describes ABB's structure in terms of managing the mixed marriage. Although he uses a somewhat infelicitous term (the multidomestic global corporation), his description comes close to the ideal-type transnational. Becton Dickinson is one of the firms that is trying to implement transnational management, after consulting Christopher Bartlett (Biggadike, 1990). Jeelof (1989) and van Houten (1989), at the time both members of the corporate board of management, saw the transnational company as the concept of the way they wanted Philips to function. Maljers (1992) describes Unilever as an evolving transnational.

Moving to the academic or professional literature, Forsgren (1990) reports on a study of 22 of the most internationalised Swedish firms and finds many of them to have loosely coupled multi-centre structures, in which subsidiaries can occupy important strategic roles. Turner and Henry (1994) investigated ten companies to see whether they have transnational characteristics. They describe the companies' dispersal of assets and resources, specialisation of tasks (strategic tasks for subsidiaries), interdependence of units and the way control and planning is conducted. Although firms such as Ford, Nestlé, Unilever and ABB had some transnational characteristics, none of the companies included in the survey could truly be regarded as a transnational. Sullivan and Bauersmidt (1991) analysed the views of managers of 63 Fortune 500 firms, working in international, multidomestic and global industries (Bartlett and Ghoshal's terms) and found that the concept of strategic simultaneity was supported by their respondents. An international business strategy should be "organised around the variables of multinational integration, internationalisation through innovation, and national responsiveness" (Sullivan and Bauersmidt, 1991:120).

Management consultants also discovered the transnational model. In three consecutive issues of the *McKinsey Quarterly*, Dichter (1991), Blackwell et al. (1991), and Theuerkauf (1991) describe the need for new organisational models to respond to the competitive challenges of the 1990s. Recurring elements are less hierarchical, but integrated structures, a balance between international coordination and local control and a differentiated response to the specific needs of the different business units. All these elements can be traced back to the transnational model. A similar description is given by Rall (1989), a McKinsey director in Germany. In addition, there is some evidence that one of the basic premises of the transnational, its interdependent network organisation, is becoming more important. Recent management books increasingly focus on network structures.

According to Ghoshal and Westney (1993) the evolving transnational model:

> is implicitly acknowledged in the changing definition of the MNC as accepted by the UN. In 1973 it defined the MNC as an enterprise which controls assets [such as] factories, mines, sales offices and the like in two ore more countries. The present definition is far more complex, reflecting the complexity of the new model: an enterprise (a) comprising entities in two or more countries, regardless of legal form and fields of activity of those entities, (b) which operates under a system of decision-making permitting coherent policies and a common strategy through one or more decision-making centres, (c) in which the entities are so linked, by ownership or otherwise, that one or more of them may be able to exercise a significant influence over the activities of the others, and, in particular, to share knowledge, resources and responsibilities with others. (Ghoshal and Westney, 1993:6).

Ghoshal and Westney (1993) also point our that research on MNCs in the economics paradigm increasingly incorporates four fundamental features of transnational organisations, namely dispersion of innovation, interdependence, increasingly tight coupling of sub-units and cross-unit learning. The UN's 1993 *World Investment Report* - devoted to integrated international production - signals a movement towards complex integration strategies, in which any affiliate operating anywhere may perform functions for the firm as a whole, a description clearly reflecting the strategic role of affiliates typical of Bartlett and Ghoshal's transnational company. The report includes numerous company examples of complex integration in the area of R&D, procurement, manufacturing, accounting, finance, training, corporate planning and legal activities.

In sum, we can say that at present probably very few firms can be considered transnationals in every sense of the word. The transnational model as an ideal type, however, has taken a strong foothold in the world of academics, consultants and MNCs' top executives alike. In Chapter 2, we will discuss the implications of this movement for control mechanisms in MNCs. In the next section, however, we will first try to draw some parallels between international management and "traditional" management literature.

International management and "traditional" management literature: a comparison

In this section, we will make a brief comparison between the studies discussed above and the work of authors in the field of general management and organisation studies. As above, we will discuss some studies on the environment, industry, strategy and structure. We do not claim to give a complete review. The main aim is to discover whether there are some similarities or differences between international management literature and "traditional" management literature, which does not explicitly focus on multinational firms.

Bolwijn and Kumpe and the transnational era[23]

Above, we described different eras with a focus on either national responsiveness, transfer of knowledge or global efficiency. The transnational era was characterised by the necessity to pay attention to all three market demands. In this section, we discuss a study by Bolwijn and Kumpe (1990) that also distinguishes different phases in the business environment. Although the authors briefly refer to multinationals in both the introduction and the conclusion, their article focuses on large companies in general. The research refers primarily to general management literature (e.g. Peters, Drucker, Mintzberg, Toffler, and Senge). Bolwijn and Kumpe (1990) distinguish four phases, each phase having different market demands and performance criteria and requiring a different ideal type of firm (see Table 1-5).

The sixties were characterised by growing internationalisation, partly because of trade liberalisation. A side effect of this growth of international trade was a fierce price competition, because products could be produced in low-wage countries. Price was the ruling market requirement and efficiency the overruling performance criterion. The seventies brought a new competitive weapon: quality. Customers became more critical and demanded high-quality but affordable products. Therefore, companies had to comply with the market requirements of both price and quality. Japanese companies were and are especially good at doing this. In the eighties, freaks of fashion abounded and demand became more and more whimsical. Apart from price and quality, a large choice and short delivery times were important market requirements that forced a company to be flexible. According to Bolwijn and Kumpe the new

---

[23] This section and the next are largely based on a similar description in Harzing (1995a).

market requirement of the nineties will be uniqueness. Companies will have to offer a product that is unique in one way or another. In order to be able to do this companies have to be innovative. Flexibility is a prerequisite for this; innovation requires change and change requires flexibility. However, an innovative firm also has to conform to the market requirements of price and quality. The actual practice in companies lags behind, however. According to Bolwijn and Kumpe the industrial world as a whole is only in the phase of transition to flexibility, while some companies are still struggling with quality.

Table 1-5 Market requirements, performance criteria and ideal types of firms in the period 1960-2000 (Source: Bolwijn and Kumpe, 1990)

	Market requirements	Performance criteria	Firm (ideal type)
1960	Price	Efficiency	The efficient firm
1970	Price, quality	Efficiency + quality	The quality firm
1980	Price, quality, product line	Efficiency + quality + flexibility	The flexible firm
1990	Price, quality, product line, uniqueness	Efficiency + quality + flexibility + innovative ability	The innovative firm

The market requirements and periods described above differ from those used by Bartlett and Ghoshal. There are notable similarities, however. Bartlett and Ghoshal's global firm, making its appearance in the sixties with the exploitation of economies of scale and a strict focus on efficiency, is comparable with the efficient firm of Bolwijn and Kumpe. Japanese firms combine Bolwijn and Kumpe's efficiency and quality in the global era. Flexibility, the emerging market requirement in the eighties, fits well into the transnational era, in which standard solutions no longer suffice. The combination of efficiency/quality/flexibility and innovative ability in the nineties, as described by Bolwijn and Kumpe, blends very well into Bartlett and Ghoshal's analysis of the transnational era, for which they stress a simultaneous compliance to diverging requirements. The conclusion of both studies is the same: we are living in an age in which companies have to conform to different strategic requirements at the same time.

Porter and others: competitive strategies compared
In this section, we would like to take a look at the responses to strategic requirements: a company's competitive strategy. In the "traditional" literature on competitive strategy, there are a few constantly occurring choices: a cost-efficiency or cost-leadership strategy, a differentiation strategy, a quality strategy (which can be considered as a form of differentiation) and an innovation strategy (see e.g. Porter, 1980 and Schuler and Jackson, 1987). How do these strategies relate to the strategies discussed above?

Superficially, a one-to-one linkage can be postulated. A global strategy is based on efficiency, so this would be a cost-efficiency or cost-leadership strategy. An international strategy boils down to the world-wide diffusion of innovations from the home country, so this could easily be related to an innovation strategy. Companies following a national responsiveness strategy can be said to differentiate their products according to local needs, so the differentiation strategy would be applicable. However, what about the transnational strategy? We have seen that this is a very flexible strategy, so perhaps the transnational strategy can be equated with the strategy aimed at compliance with the market requirement of flexibility (see the previous section).

On closer examination, however, this one-to-one relationship doesn't hold. Porter (Porter, 1986a), for instance, describes how a firm following a global strategy can choose between global cost leadership and global differentiation. Global differentiators such as IBM can use their scale and learning advantages to lower the cost of differentiating (e.g. offering many models and frequent changes). A national responsiveness strategy can focus on either differentiation or low cost in serving the particular needs of a national market.

This one-to-one relationship also does not conform with our picture of the transnational strategy, which should pay attention to global efficiency, national responsiveness and world-wide learning *at the same time*. Furthermore, in the previous section we already saw that Japanese companies, which are assumed to follow global strategies, were masters in complying with the demands of both efficiency and quality and later flexibility. Schuler and Jackson (1987) acknowledge that companies might be pursuing different strategies at the same time and that even different parts of the company can follow different strategies. An R&D department will often be following an innovative strategy and a production department a cost-efficient strategy.

There are some studies that confirm Porter's suggestion that a firm should choose of either cost leadership, differentiation or focus as a strategy (Dess and Davis, 1984; Hall, 1980; Hambrick, 1983). Three of the firms in Hall's sample of sixteen firms, however, combined both approaches and were very successful. Furthermore, Miller and Friesen (1986, 1987), conclude from an empirical study of the relationship between Porter's generic strategies and performance, that business units that had specific competences in the areas of differentiation, cost leadership and focus dramatically outperformed others. However, good performers did not make a choice of just one of these strategies. Instead of being stuck in the middle (Porter, 1985) they outperformed other firms, so Miller and Friesen conclude that the more strategic competences the better. In a later study Miller (1987) distinguished four strategies (among which cost, differentiation and innovation) and found that they are not mutually exclusive. Perhaps a choice of one single strategy is no longer feasible in the late eighties and nineties.

There are two conclusions that we can draw from this discussion. First, the competitive strategies described above have a high level of generality. Within these strategies, there is room for a choice among cost-efficient, quality, differentiation, innovation or other strategies. Second, a choice *between* these strategies might not be necessary or even feasible. Here we come back again to the earlier observation that perhaps today's competitive environment requires a *simultaneous* attention to all choices. This would apply to both the "general" and the "specific" competitive choices.

Organismic, adhocratic and flexible network organisations

A number of authors have argued that complex, diverse or heterogeneous, and dynamic, uncertain, unpredictable, unstable, turbulent or changing environments require flexible, multidimensional and heterogeneous organisation structures. A representative selection of these studies will be discussed below.

More than thirty years ago *Burns and Stalker* (1961) identified the organismic type of organisation with characteristics such as flexibility, continual adjustment, lateral communication and a network structure. These characteristics can be found in the description of the transnational organisation. This organismic type of organisation would be appropriate for an environment with changing conditions. Their other type of organisation, the mechanistic organisation, would be appropriate to a stable environment.

Mintzberg (1983) sees the adhocracy (one of his organisational configurations, the others being the simple structure, the divisionalised form, the machine bureaucracy and the professional bureaucracy) as the organisation of the future (Mintzberg, 1983:275). The adhocracy is a highly organic type of organisation, flexible and decentralised to cope with dynamic and complex environments, with mutual adjustment as a rather informal coordination mechanism. Mintzberg argues that diversified markets formerly led multinationals to use the divisionalised form, grouping their major divisions either by area or by product line. However, "those multinational firms with interdependencies among their different product lines, and facing increasing complexity as well as dynamism in their environment will feel drawn toward the divisionalised adhocracy hybrid" (Mintzberg, 1983:269). Of course, the last sentence describes the transnational organisation perfectly.

Miles and Snow (1984 and 1992) follow the environment-strategy-structure paradigm. Changing environments necessitate changing strategies and structures. As the organisation for the future conditions of high complexity and rapid change, they put forward the dynamic network organisation. "Properly constructed, the dynamic network organisation will display the technical expertise of the functional form, the market focus of the divisional form, and the efficient use of resources of the matrix. And, especially important, it will be able to quickly reshape itself whenever necessary" (Miles and

Snow, 1984: 27). Miles and Snow's dynamic network organisation closely resembles the transnational organisation with its flexible integrated network type of structure. Both types of organisation also encompass characteristics of the three other types of organisations distinguished. As discussed above, the technical expertise of the functional form is dominant in the international type of organisation, while a divisional orientation towards different markets is typical of the multidomestic organisation. Efficient use of means of course fits the global organisation, although this type of organisation does not usually have a matrix structure.

Finally, *Morgan*'s (1993) hybrid spider plant would be an excellent description of a transnational organisation in that it illustrates the necessity of finding different solutions within one and the same MNC. The problems come in describing the integration between the various offshoots, which is also characteristic of a transnational's integrated network structure. Morgan recommends not using formal lines of communication and coordination, because this runs the danger of tying the whole system in knots. The recommended solution relates very closely to the international transfer part of this thesis: introduce organisational bumble-bees.[24] Organisational bumble-bees fly "from plant to plant" and create cross-pollination between the various offshoots.

All of the organisational structures discussed above bear some resemblance to the transnational type of organisation. In addition, the environmental demands that were discussed fit into the transnational era very well. The transnational environment is complex, dynamic and heterogeneous. Heterogeneous because each business unit faces a somewhat different environment, complex because each business unit has to deal with opposing demands, and dynamic because these demands are likely to change continuously. Therefore, we see that the transnational concept indeed has some roots in "traditional" management literature. We will now turn to country-of-origin and industry effects on the application of the various organisational models.

Country-of-origin effect on strategy and structure

Virtually no studies have explored the country-of-origin effect concerning different types of international strategies and structures. Bartlett and Ghoshal indicated that the international organisational model was the dominant model for American MNCs, the global model for Japanese MNCs and the multidomestic model for European MNCs. The adoption of these models would be mainly based on the era in which most of the American, Japanese and Euro-

---

[24] This solution also led me to name my research design (Harzing, 1994) 'Organisational Bumblebees: International Transfers as a control mechanism in multinational companies.'

pean firms internationalised. Their study, however, was based on nine MNCs in three industries only. Further, although for instance most European firms might have started with multidomestic models, they may have adjusted - in spite of their administrative heritage - strategies and structures in the course of time. As Ghauri (1995) comments, this classification is an oversimplification of a complex issue. According to him, we can find firms from Europe following the international and global model and many Japanese firms following the international or multinational model.

To our best knowledge, only one study has empirically investigated the application of different organisational models as defined by Bartlett and Ghoshal. Kriger and Solomon (1992) suggest that "awareness of local differences and a marketing focus oriented towards diversity in customer needs and profiles is [...] at the core of quality and process management methods which are widespread in Japanese companies" (Kriger and Solomon, 1992:330). They therefore hypothesise that Japanese MNCs will pursue locally oriented strategies and simultaneous local (differentiation) and global (integration) strategies to a larger extent than American MNCs. No difference was hypothesised concerning global strategies. Strategies were measured at both HQ and subsidiary level and all three hypotheses were confirmed at both levels.

Doyle, Saunders and Wong (1992) investigated American and Japanese strategies in the British market and found among others that Japanese firms were more locally responsive in terms of adapting their promotion, pricing, distribution and overall strategies to the British market. It could therefore be concluded that Japanese firms would be more likely to follow multidomestic strategies than American firms.[25] Given the conclusions of the two larger-scale empirical studies, we put forward the following hypothesis:

Hypothesis 1-9: Japanese multinationals will be more likely to follow multidomestic strategies and have multidomestic structures than American multinationals.

In general, though, we would not expect to find too many differences between countries in the application of the various international strategies and structures. The industry effect, discussed in the next section, is likely to have a stronger effect on the strategy that is followed and the structure that is chosen than the country of origin.

---

[25] Although neither of the two articles indicates this possibility, a valid explanation for the multidomestic orientation of Japanese firms could of course also be that they *have* to adapt their policies when entering the Western market, simply because they are so different from what is usual practice in Japan. It would then only be logical that, for instance, American MNCs do not adapt their policies too much when entering the British market. Whatever the reason, though, the effect would be that Japanese MNCs would be more likely to follow the nationally responsive multidomestic strategy.

Industry effect on strategy and structure

As indicated above, the industry in which a company operates is likely to have a considerable influence on the preferred organisational model. Some industries are more likely to experience forces for global integration (global industries) or for local responsiveness (multidomestic industries), while in other industries firms have to respond to both these demands at the same time (transnational industries). Various authors have tried to classify industries in terms of these forces. In this section, we will review what these authors have said about the various industries included in the empirical part of this thesis: electronics, computer and office equipment, automobile, petroleum, food, pharmaceutical, paper and chemical.

The electronics, computer and office equipment and automobile industry are usually seen as global industries, while the food industry is often considered to be the prototype of a multidomestic industry (Bartlett, 1986; Bartlett and Ghoshal, 1989; Doz, 1986; Doyle et al, 1992; Kobrin, 1994; Porter, 1986a/b; Rall, 1989). Ghoshal and Nohria (1993) classify both the computer and the automobile industry as transnational, however. These industries are joined by the drugs and pharmaceutical industry. The food industry is again seen as multidomestic, while the paper industry is classified as operating in the relatively placid international industry. Ghoshal *and* Nohria (1993) indicate, however, that the forces of global integration appear to be getting stronger in the food industry. This would mean that the food industry is moving towards the transnational type. The chemical industry is seen as a global type of industry. Brinkgreve (1993) follows Ghoshal and Nohria's classification, but adds the petroleum industry in the global category. His empirical results show that from the ten industries included in his survey, the food industry had the highest percentage of firms following a transnational strategy and the chemical and computer industry the lowest. Transnationals also occurred more than average in the electronics and pharmaceutical industry. According to Kobrin (1991), companies in the pharmaceutical and food industry have a higher than average trade among subsidiaries, a feature that can be seen as characteristic for a transnational model (integrated network with inter-subsidiary flows).

In view of the observations above, the chemical, computer, automobile, electronics and petroleum industry are considered global industries. The food and pharmaceutical industry are considered transnational industries. Ghoshal and Nohria are the only authors who classify the paper industry. The international category in which the paper industry is classified, however, is not distinguished as a separate category in this thesis. As the paper industry is one of the industries with the lowest levels of integration (Kobrin, 1991), we will categorise it as multidomestic instead, as was also done by Kobrin (1994).

We would of course expect most companies to have strategies and structures that fit their type of industry. However, since the transnational organisational model is rather new, only a small number of firms will actually follow this strategy. Consequently, we would not expect the absolute majority of firms in the food and pharmaceutical industry to have transnational strategies and structures. Many firms in the food industry will still be likely to follow multidomestic strategies, while many firms in the pharmaceutical industry will still follow global strategies. In the hypotheses stated below, we will therefore take a relative perspective and compare industries to each other. The empirical analysis will also give an overview of the relative application of the various strategies in each industry.

Hypothesis 1-10: Firms in the electronics, computer, automobile, petroleum, chemical, and pharmaceutical industry will have a higher application of global strategies and structures than firms in other industries.

And:

Hypothesis 1-11: Firms in the paper and food industry will have a higher application of multidomestic strategies and structures than firms in the other industries.

And:

Hypothesis 1-12: Firms in both the food and pharmaceutical industry will have a higher application of transnational strategies and structures than firms in other industries.

Conclusion

In this section, we have provided an introduction to the environment, strategy and structure of MNCs, all crucial elements of the second building block of our thesis. A discussion of the various classifications used in the international management literature and a detailed description of one of these classifications led to the identification of three distinct organisational models for multinational firms: global, multidomestic and transnational. The transnational model is claimed to be the answer to changes in the international environment. Many of the elements discussed in the classification of multinational firms can be traced back to "traditional" management and organisation theory.

Two further sections offered a number of hypotheses on the influence of both the country of origin and the industry on the type of international strategy and structure that is followed. In Chapter 2, we will combine the theory on control mechanisms discussed in the previous section with the theory on multinationals and their development as discussed in this section. First, however, the third and final section of this chapter will provide a discussion of our third building block: international transfers.

3. INTERNATIONAL TRANSFERS

Introduction

In the two previous sections, we discussed different forms of organisational control and multinationals. In this section we will discuss the relevant issues related to the third major element in our thesis: international transfers. First, we will discuss various staffing policies as they were identified by Perlmutter (1969) in his seminal article "The tortuous evolution of the multinational company". These different staffing policies imply a preference for parent-country nationals, host-country nationals or third-country nationals. We will discuss the reasons multinationals have to prefer one of these groups. We will also offer some hypotheses on the choice of expatriates over host-country nationals in various circumstances. Subsequently, we will discuss the organisational functions of expatriation and offer some hypotheses on the importance of these functions in different circumstances. Finally, the major research issues in the field of international transfers are summarised and some limitations in this field of research that this study hopes to overcome are discussed.

International staffing policies

Perlmutter (1969) distinguishes three states of mind or attitudes of international executives:

- *ethnocentric* (or home-country-oriented);
- *polycentric* (or host-country-oriented);
- *geocentric* (or world-oriented).

These attitudes should be regarded as ideal types. Every firm will probably have *some* degree of ethnocentrism, polycentrism and geocentrism, but usually we can distinguish a dominant state of mind. The *ethnocentric* attitude implies that management style, knowledge, evaluation criteria, and managers from the home country are thought to be superior to those of the host country. A logical consequence is that only parent-country nationals are considered suitable for top management positions, both at headquarters and at subsidiaries. The communication and information flow consists of orders and commands from headquarters to subsidiaries, authority and decision-making is high in headquarters and the organisation is complex at headquarters, but simple in subsidiaries. The *polycentric* attitude takes a completely different point of view. It explicitly recognises differences between countries and believes that local nationals are in the best position to understand and deal with these country-specific factors. A local manager, however, will never be offered a position at headquarters, because parent-country nationals are considered more suitable for these positions. In a firm characterised by a polycentric attitude, there is little communication to and from headquarters and between subsidiaries, because subsidiaries are rather independent. Consequently, authority and decision-making at headquarters are relatively low. The *geocentric* attitude, finally, is world-oriented. A company characterised by a geocentric attitude draws from a world-wide pool of managers. Managers can be appointed at headquarters or subsidiaries regardless of their nationality. Transfers take place in all directions, from headquarters to subsidiaries, from subsidiaries to headquarters and between subsidiaries. The communication and information flow goes both ways, there is a collaborative approach to decision-making and the organisation as a whole becomes increasingly complex and interdependent. In a later publication with Heenan (1979) Perlmutter distinguishes a fourth attitude: *regiocentric*. This attitude resembles the geocentric attitude, but is regio-oriented (e.g. the European Union) instead of world-oriented.

In subsequent literature in the field of international management, Perlmutter's headquarters orientations became equated with strategies of international human resource management in general, and with different types of staffing strategies in particular (see among others Buckley and Brooke, 1992; Dowling and Schuler, 1990; Hendry, 1994; Hossain and Davis, 1989). This distinction into four different types of staffing should not be taken to imply that in reality every firm has a systematic staffing policy. Borg and Harzing (1995) describe four different staffing policies, three of which are broadly comparable to the ethnocentric, polycentric and geocentric strategies discussed above. They do distinguish a fourth strategy, an *ad hoc* strategy. Companies following an *ad hoc* "strategy" do not really have a set strategy and make decisions on an *ad hoc* basis. This usually results in the placement of parent-country nationals in important positions, a course of events also recognised by Robinson (1978). Furthermore, we must realise that, in general, staffing issues in an international setting involve filling critical higher management positions. Usually, most employees at the middle management and operative levels are recruited locally. Therefore, a polycentric staffing strategy will usually be followed for the majority of subsidiary personnel.

Choosing between PCNs, HCNs and TCNs

The policies we discussed above imply a preference for parent-country nationals (PCN), host-country nationals (HCN), third-country nationals (TCN)
or a combination of these different groups. These different groups can be defined as follows:

- A PCN is a national of the country of the MNC's headquarters (and usually worked at headquarters before being expatriated);
- An HCN is a national of the country of the subsidiary (and usually
  worked in the subsidiary before being appointed to the position of managing director);
- A TCN is a national of a country other than the MNC's home country
  and the country of the subsidiary (and usually worked at headquarters before being expatriated).

A discussion of the advantages and disadvantages of employing these different groups of employees will clarify the applicability of the different staffing
policies discussed above. The advantages and disadvantages that are frequently mentioned in the relevant literature (Banai, 1992; Briscoe, 1995;
Dowling and Schuler, 1990; Fatehi, 1996; Hamill, 1989; Hodgetts and Luthans, 1994; Negandhi, 1987; Phatak, 1989; Root, 1986; Schaffer and Rhee,
1996;[26] Scullion, 1991; Tung, 1988; Zeira and Harari, 1977) are summarised
in Table 1-6.

As is shown in Table 1-6, most of the advantages of using PCNs can be
cited as disadvantages of using HCNs and vice versa. Some of the advantages
ascribed to parent-country nationals have a rather arrogant flavour. Host-
country nationals are assumed to have fewer technical and managerial skills.
Although this is still true in some developing countries, one could hardly
maintain that for instance a local German manager has fewer technical skills
than the English expatriate manager of the parent country. In this case, the
reverse would probably be true. This attitude is even less compatible with the
concept of the transnational company as discussed in the previous chapter. In
a transnational company, subsidiaries are not simple appendages to a complex
and sophisticated (in terms of human resources as well) headquarters, but are
elements of a network, which can take a strategic role in selected areas.

---

[26] This paper is rather special in that it tries to build a well-grounded theory on the choice between PCNs and HCNs based on both economic (internationalisation theory) and organisational
(strategic context) theory concepts, while the other contributions mainly limit themselves to a
simple list of advantages and disadvantages.

Table 1-6 Advantages and disadvantages of using PCNs, HCNs and TCNs

	Advantages	Disadvantages
PCN	technical and managerial expertise and competence	difficulties in adapting to the foreign language and the socio-economic, political, cultural and legal environment/high failure rate
	familiarity with the home office's goals, objectives, policies and practices	
	effective liaison and communication with home-office personnel/PCNs act as linking pins	excessive cost of selecting, training and maintaining expatriate managers and their families abroad; feelings of injustice on part of HCNs because of generous fringe benefits for PCNs
	easier exercise of control over the subsidiary's operation	
	opportunity for management development/establishment of a pool of internationally experienced managers	the host countries' insistence on localising operations and on promoting local nationals in top positions at foreign subsidiaries
	PCNs can be advantageous if personnel in the subsidiary comprises of two or more rivalling ethnic or religious groups	family adjustment problems, especially concerning the unemployed partners of managers
HCN	familiarity with the socio-economic, political and legal environment and with the language and business practices in the host country	Difficulties in exercising effective control over the subsidiary's operations
	lower cost incurred in hiring them as compared to PCN and TCN	communication difficulties in dealing with home-office personnel
	provides opportunities for advancement and promotion to local nationals and, consequently, increases their commitment and motivation	lack of opportunities for the home country's nationals to gain international and cross-cultural experience
	responds effectively to the host country's demands for localisation of the subsidiary's operation/achieves good public relations	
	greater continuity of management	
TCN	perhaps the best compromise between securing needed technical and managerial expertise and adapting to a foreign socio-economic and cultural environment	host country's sensitivity with respect to nationals of specific countries
	TCN are usually career, international business managers	local nationals are impeded in their efforts to upgrade their own ranks and assume responsible positions in the multinational subsidiaries
	TCN are less expensive to maintain than PCN	
	TCN may be better informed about the host environment than PCN	

In the remainder of this section, we will discuss a number of factors that might influence the choice of HCNs, PCNs or TCNs. As the number of TCNs is still very small in most companies (see e.g. Tung, 1988; Kopp, 1994), we will focus our attention on the choice between HCNs and PCNs. Further, as lower-level positions are usually filled by HCNs, we will concentrate on the percentage of PCNs in top management positions.

MNC staffing policies: country factors

Although - as can be seen above - many publications focus on the advantages and disadvantages of using expatriates as opposed to local managers, surprisingly few empirical studies examine MNC staffing policies. All of the above publications refer to Tung (1981, 1982, 1987) in this respect. Although Tung's study was a primer in the field, it is now more than 15 years old. Recently, Kopp (1994) compared international human resource policies in Japanese, European and United States multinationals. One of the issues she studied was the nationality of top managers in overseas operations. Kopp's study confirmed Tung's finding that Japanese companies employ the largest number of PCNs in their subsidiaries, US companies the smallest number, while the number of PCNs in subsidiaries in European companies lies between these two extremes. Tung's study gave five explanations for the larger number of expatriates in Japanese MNCs:

- Most Japanese MNCs do not have a long history and have only recently set up overseas operations. It is very usual to rely on PCNs to set up a business abroad;
- The Japanese management is rather culturally specific and requires constant interaction and consultation between the employees of headquarters and subsidiaries. Foreigners might not fit very well into this system;
- There is a major language barrier, because most Japanese do not speak English and most foreigners do not speak Japanese. Therefore communication with headquarters is only possible with PCNs;
- Japanese companies had trouble in recruiting host-country nationals, although this might have changed recently;
- As most Japanese companies effectuate a system of life-time employment, they might be reluctant to hire foreigners.

In addition to these two studies, a number of other authors have investigated the use of expatriates by MNCs from different countries, usually as part of a larger research project on control mechanisms.[27] Dealing with these publications in chronological order, Hulbert and Brandt (1980) found that European and Japanese MNCs were more likely to use expatriates in the CEO position of Brazilian subsidiaries than American MNCs. In Dobry's (1983) study of American and German MNCs, the German MNCs were more likely to em-

---

[27] There is a handful of other studies that discuss the choice between expatriate and local managers (Franko, 1973; Youssef, 1973; Hamill, 1989; Scullion, 1991). Unfortunately, these studies focus on very limited samples (e.g. two subsidiaries of one American MNC or only British MNCs) and provide very fragmented empirical information. In general, however, these studies do confirm the above observations.

ploy PCNs in their American subsidiaries than American MNCs in their German subsidiaries. Negandhi and Welge (1984) found that both Japanese and German MNCs had only 2% HCNs in top positions in their foreign subsidiaries, while American firms had 28% HCNs. Egelhoff (1988a) indicates that, in general, European MNCs make heavier use of expatriates than both American and British MNCs. In Wolf's (1994) study, German MNCs had the largest number of PCNs in the managing director position, while there was no major difference between American and the remaining European MNCs in this respect. In a study on FDI in Taiwan, Tzeng (1995) finds American and European MNCs to more localised than Japanese MNCs. Finally, Oddou et al. (1995) report that Japanese MNCs have a stronger tendency than US and European MNCs to expatriate their personnel. No differences were found between European and American firms. In view of the observations above, we formulate the following hypothesis regarding the effect of the country of origin on the preferred staffing policy:

> Hypothesis 1-13: Japanese and German multinationals will employ the largest percentage of PCNs in top positions in their foreign subsidiaries. American and British multinationals will employ the smallest percentage of expatriates. Other European countries will fall in between these two extremes.

While the country of origin is the aspect of MNC staffing policies that has occupied the most prominent place in previous research, there are a number of other factors that have received some attention. With regard to the country of destination, Tung found that subsidiaries in Asian countries employed the largest percentage of PCNs, closely followed by subsidiaries in Latin/South American countries, while subsidiaries in both Europe and the USA employed a relatively larger amount of HCNs in top positions.[28] In a study of the staffing policies of an American bank, Boyacigiller (1990) found that the percentage of PCNs was positively related to cultural distance. This would confirm Tung's findings, as the cultural distance between headquarters from the USA and Europe and subsidiaries in Asia and Latin/South America would be rather large. The same goes for Japanese headquarters and Latin/South American subsidiaries. Wolf's (1994) study also found a higher level of PCNs when the cultural distance - whether measured objectively or subjectively - was higher. We will therefore put forward the following two hypotheses:

> Hypothesis 1-14: Subsidiaries in Asian and Latin American countries will employ a larger percentage of PCNs in top-level positions than subsidiaries in the USA and Western European countries.

---

[28] Tung also included Canada, Middle/Near East, Eastern Europe and Africa. As these countries are not included in our survey, they will not be discussed here.

And:

> Hypothesis 1-15: The percentage of PCNs in top-level positions in a subsidiary will be positively related to the cultural distance between headquarters and the subsidiary in question.

Of course, the percentage of PCNs employed in a certain country might also be dependent on the availability of qualified local personnel. This aspect will be discussed in the next section, where we discuss the organisational functions of expatriation.

MNC staffing policies: industry[29]

No previous studies have investigated the influence of the industry on the use of PCNs on a large enough scale to draw any reliable conclusions from them. The studies that have been done (e.g. Hamill, 1989; Ondrack, 1985a/b) typically looked at only one or two companies in a particular industry. We would expect, though, that industries that are characterised by a global orientation have a larger percentage of expatriates in upper levels of their subsidiary workforce than industries that are characterised by a multidomestic orientation. For the latter industries local responsiveness is more important, while for the former integration is the main challenge. Local responsiveness would be easier to achieve with HCNs, while integration is facilitated by PCNs. Wolf (1994) also found a higher percentage of PCNs in the position of managing director in firms following a global strategy than in firms following a multidomestic strategy. In view of the observations above, we will therefore put forward the following hypothesis:

> Hypothesis 1-16: The percentage of PCNs in top-level positions in a subsidiary will be higher in the electronics, computer, automobile, petroleum, pharmaceutical and chemical industry than in the paper and food industry.

MNC staffing policies: subsidiary factors

In addition to country and industry influences, a number of authors have discussed the effect of structural characteristics of the subsidiary on the presence of expatriates. With regard the factor size, various authors (Boyacigiller, 1990; Hamill, 1989; Welge, 1981; Wolf, 1994) argue that larger subsidiaries will have a higher expatriate presence, because they constitute a larger investment risk for headquarters. The empirical support for this statement is rather mixed, though. None of the studies found significant differences, and in

---

[29] Our study only includes manufacturing companies. There is some evidence that the percentage of expatriates in service companies is usually very high (Boyacigiller, 1990; Groenewald and Sapozhnikov, 1990; Harzing, 1998a).

Wolf's study a different result for absolute and relative size was found. However, in view of the strength of the argument of the importance[30] of larger (both absolute and relative) subsidiaries for headquarters, we put forward the following hypothesis:

Hypothesis 1-17: The percentage of PCNs in top-level positions in a subsidiary is positively related to its (relative) size.

In comparison to the other factors, the age of the subsidiary has received quite a lot of attention in empirical studies. Most of these studies indicate that younger subsidiaries have a higher percentage of PCNs. This is usually explained by the observation that many MNCs tend to use expatriates in the start-up phase, but gradually move to local managers (Franko, 1973; Hamill, 1989; Tung, 1982; Youssef, 1975; Wolf, 1994; Wong and Birnbaum-More, 1994). Only Boyacigiller's (1990) and Egelhoff (1998a) did not find a clear relationship between age and staffing policy. In view of the balance of evidence, we formulate the following hypothesis.

Hypothesis 1-18: The percentage of PCNs in top-level positions in a subsidiary is negatively related to its age.

Egelhoff (1988a) is the only author that empirically investigated the influence of the entry mode on the presence of expatriates. He measures the extent of foreign acquisitions at parent company level and finds a weak negative correlation for CEO staffing at subsidiaries. Hamill (1989) argues that acquired subsidiaries will be less likely to have a PCN as managing director. Unfortunately, he does not give any motivation for this. We would expect greenfield subsidiaries to employ a larger number of PCNs, especially in the position of managing director, as they have to be started up from scratch, thus needing a lot of direct steering from headquarters.

Hypothesis 1-19: Greenfield subsidiaries will employ a higher percentage of PCNs in top-level positions than acquired subsidiaries.

Although this has not been investigated before, we would expect the percentage of PCNs to be also dependent on the subsidiary's function. Sales and service subsidiaries are more oriented towards the local market and will therefore be less likely to employ a large number of PCNs than subsidiaries that

---

[30] Martinez and Ricks (1989) found that the importance of a subsidiary to headquarters was positively correlated to the percentage of expatriates in the subsidiary.

have an assembly, a production, an R&D or a country headquarters function.[31] The latter types of subsidiaries will have to be more integrated into the company as a whole. Therefore, the following hypothesis is put forward:

> Hypothesis 1-20: Sales and service subsidiaries will employ a lower percentage of PCNs in top-level positions than the other types of subsidiaries.

Another issue that has received very little attention yet is the influence of a subsidiary's performance. To our best knowledge, Wolf (1994) is the only one to have investigated this relationship. He found a very weak negative relationship between sales growth and expatriate presence. Expatriate presence was higher in subsidiaries with a lower sales growth. Anticipating our discussion on the direct control effect of expatriates, we would expect low-performing subsidiaries to attract a higher percentage of PCNs. What would be a more logical way to "correct" an under-performing subsidiary than to send a trusted PCN to put things in order? Hence, we put forward the following hypothesis.

> Hypothesis 1-21: The percentage of PCNs in top-level positions in a subsidiary is negatively related to its performance.

MNC staffing policies: parent-company factors

There are virtually no studies that have investigated the influence of the size of the parent company on the use of PCNs. Wolf (1994) refers to a study by Ondrack (1985a/b), who qualitatively investigated this relationship. No clear relationship was found. In Wolf's own study, the data gathered at subsidiary level indicated that larger MNCs more often employed PCNs as managing directors for their subsidiary, while the data gathered at headquarters showed the reverse relationship. However, neither of these relationships achieved statistical significance. Further, as we can set a plausible argument for either a positive and a negative relationship, we will not formulate a hypothesis.

With regard to the extent of internationalisation of the parent, again very few empirical studies are available. Egelhoff (1988a), however, found that the extent of foreign manufacturing - an operationalisation of the internationalisation of the company - was negatively related to the extent of expatriate staffing especially for the manufacturing and marketing functions. In Wolf's (1994) study, the extent of internationalisation (measured as foreign manufacturing, foreign sales and foreign employees) was also negatively related to expatriate staffing, though the results were only significant for foreign employees. Further, as with size of the parent company, the data gathered at

---

[31] In a conceptual paper, Torbiörn (1994) refers to the higher control needs of production and R&D subsidiaries when compared to sales units.

headquarters showed the opposite relationship. As we would expect more internationalised firms to be less ethnocentric in their staffing policies, we would also expect them to employ a larger number of HCNs in their subsidiaries. We will therefore state the following hypothesis:

> Hypothesis 1-22: The percentage of PCNs in top-level positions in a subsidiary is negatively related to the extent of internationalisation of the parent company.

Organisational functions of international transfers

Having discussed the advantages and disadvantages of different nationality policies and the specific circumstances in which PCNs will be preferred over HCNs in the previous section, we will now try to take a rather more abstract point of view. In this section, we will discuss three fundamental organisational functions of international transfers. Although these functions resemble the advantages of the use of PCNs, they are by no means in essence limited in applicability. They are reasons for the existence of international transfers *per se*, regardless of whether the transfer is made by a PCN, an HCN or a TCN.

Edström and Galbraith

There are few theoretical elaborations and concepts regarding the organisational functions fulfilled by international transfers of managers. At first sight, the study of Edström and Galbraith (1977b), seems to be the only one which theoretically explains why international transfers of managers occur. Edström and Galbraith found three company motives for making this type of transfer.

The first was to *"fill positions"*. Edström and Galbraith contend that this chiefly concerns the transfer of technical knowledge to developing countries,[32] where qualified local nationals are not available. Employees who are sent abroad to fill positions only accept one or two assignments before returning to the parent organisation.

The second major motive is *management development*. The transfer gives the manager international experience and develops him or her for future important tasks in subsidiaries abroad or with the parent company. This kind of transfer would be carried out even if qualified host-country nationals were available. Since it is difficult to select successful international managers beforehand, i.e. before the assignment abroad, a relatively large number of managers could be sent out so that those who are successful may be selected for further assignments, whereas the rest are repatriated or resign.

---

[32] Since the opening up of Eastern Europe, this reason for international transfers has acquired a new meaning. Transfer of technical but also management (e.g. marketing skills) knowledge is a very important reason for expatriation to these countries (see e.g. Hillman and Rudolph, 1996).

In the third reason for international transfer the final goal is not individual development but *organisation development*, that is, transfers are used to change or maintain the structure and decision processes of the organisation. These managerial transfers for organisational development consist of a so-cialising process and a process of creating a verbal information network. The socialisation process has two major objectives. First, to "achieve open and positive attitudes toward other nationalities and cultures" (Edström and Gal-braith, 1977b:255). Second, to create commitment to the organisation as a whole. In Chapter 2, we will come back to this function of international trans-fers when discussing international transfers as a control mechanism.

As the reader might have gathered from the discussion above, it will sometimes be very difficult to distinguish one motive from the other. An ex-tensive quotation from Edström and Galbraith will illustrate this difficulty:

> One of the sources of confusion about the motives for transfer within companies as well as between companies is the fact that motives are not mutually exclusive. Va-cancies will provide needs and opportunities to transfer managers. An organisation may then choose to select the person for expatriate service based on his training needs. In such a way, one can combine the need to fill a position with the need to provide managers with international experience. Similarly, if one is conscious of the possibility of using transfers in order to maintain or develop a particular or-ganisational structure one can let the selection of expatriates be guided by this par-ticular criteria. It makes it difficult for an outsider to distinguish motives since they are confounded. The motives also tend to be cumulative in the sense that a policy maker who agrees with the organisational development motive tends to be in agreement with the first two as well. For these reasons an analysis of motives is seldom trivial. (Edström and Galbraith, 1977a:15)

The classification by Edström and Galbraith is well accepted in the litera-ture on international transfers. Virtually every (Anglo-Saxon) publication that deals with international transfers refers to Edström and Galbraith's now clas-sic 1977 ASQ article. The empirical support for this classification is limited, however. In his thesis on international transfers, Borg (1988) used the EandG classification to summarise eight different roles that could be fulfilled by ex-patriates on their assignment. In our view, the roles he subsumed under posi-tion filling and manager development come very close to the idea of the original classification. One of the roles mentioned under organisational de-velopment (Ensuring that the company policies were pursued in accordance with the ambitions of the parent company) implies a rather more direct way of control than the control by socialisation as envisaged by Edström and Gal-braith. In general, the position-filling and organisational development roles were mentioned more often than the management development role. The three-fold role of international transfers: position filling, management development/international experience and control can also be distinguished in the description from case study research by Evans et al. (1989: 122-123).

"German" studies

As indicated above, Edström and Galbraith's study at first sight seems to have the monopoly on the theoretical foundation of the functions of international transfers. Borg perfectly describes this in his thesis: "The study of Edström and Galbraith (1977b), which is very often quoted in both articles and text-books, seems to be the only one which theoretically explains why international transfers of managers occur" (Borg, 1988:41). Ondrack (1985a/b) voices the general opinion when he cites the study by Edström and Galbraith as a rare exception that does consider strategic issues in the field of international transfers. A further investigation, however, revealed a whole number of German studies, both conceptual and empirical, on this subject. The fact that they appeared in the German language only, seems to have blocked their way to the Anglo-Saxon academic community. A summary of these studies and a comparison of their classifications to the one by Edström and Galbraith can be found in Table 1-7. The figures in brackets indicate the relative importance of the functions if this was measured in the study.[33]

As can be deduced from Table 1-7, there is a considerable consensus on the principal functions of international transfers that is well represented by the classification of Edström and Galbraith as discussed above. It would seem, though, that, as in Borg's study, in many of the German studies the focus is more on a rather direct type of expatriate control than on the rather informal type of control or coordination that Edström and Galbraith distinguish. It would therefore seem wise to include direct expatriate control into the last category. A further distinction between indirect and direct expatriate control will be made in the next chapter.

The studies do not seem to converge on the importance of the various reasons for expatriation, although (one of) the position-filling reason(s) often occupies a first place. It would seem that the importance of the various reasons is heavily dependent on specific circumstances such as the type of international strategy, the industry, the country of origin and destination, the size and age of the subsidiary, etc. In the context of this study, it would be going too far to analyse systematically all the possible influences in this respect, especially since there has not been a single previous study on which to base at least part of the hypotheses. What we can do, however, is try to further explain some of the hypothesised relationships in the previous section, by relating them to the reasons for international transfers.

---

[33] The differences between the various functions were not tested for significance in most studies, and were sometimes very small.

Table 1-7 Organisational functions of international transfers according to various authors

Edström and Galbraith (1977)	Position Filling	Management Development	Organisation Development
Pausenberger and Noelle (1977) *[our translation]*	To ensure transfer of know-how (1); To compensate for a lack of local managers (3); Training and development of local managers (5).	To develop the expatriate's management capabilities (2); To develop managers' global awareness (8).	To ensure homogeneous practices in the company (4); To ensure a common reporting system in the company (5); Presence of different viewpoints in decision-making bodies (6).
Welge (1980) *[our translation]*)	Position filling (3); Transfer of know-how (6).	International experience (2); Use management potential (5).	Coordination (1); Change management (4).
Kenter (1985) *[our translation]*	Lack of qualified local managers available (1); Transfer of know-how (2); Training of local managers (5).	Development of parent-country nationals (4).	Control and coordination (3); Increase loyalty and trustworthiness of expatriates (6).
Kumar and Steinmann (1986)*[our translation]*	Transfer of know-how-(1); The necessity to train German managers (4).	Headquarters want Japanese managers to gain international experience (5).	To ensure coordination with headquarters corporate policies and philosophies. (2); To facilitate communication (3); Desired loyalty with headquarters goals (6).
Roessel (1988) *[our translation]*	Transfer of Management know-how; Lack of qualified local personnel (1/3).[34]	Managerial development of expatriates and local managers (2).	Coordination, control and steering; Reciprocal information flows; Internationalisation of the company as a whole (1/3).
Groenewald and Sapozhnikov (1990) *[our translation]*	Transfer of technological, administrative or sales know-how (1/2); Lack of qualified local personnel (3).	Management development (4); Better career opportunities for employees (5).	Steering and coordination (1/2).
Kumar and Karlshaus (1992)[35] *[our translation]*	Transfer of know-how (1); Limited availability of local managers (3); The necessity to train foreign managers (5).	Headquarters want German managers to gain international experience (6).	To ensure coordination and communication with headquarters (2); Desired loyalty with headquarters goals (4).
Macharzina (1992) *[our translation]*	Filling vacant positions (1).	Management development (2).	Coordination (3)
Wolf (1994) *[our translation]*	Filling vacant positions (2).	Personal or managerial development (1).[36]	Coordination (3)

---

[34] For manufacturing companies, this was the most important reason; for service companies the least.

[35] A seventh function referred to the representational aspect of expatriates as in the Kumar and Steinmann study.

The expected higher expatriate presence in subsidiaries of Japanese and German MNCs is assumed to be mainly due to the high relative importance of the organisation development function of expatriation in these MNCs. There is no reason to suspect that Japanese or German MNCs would have a higher level of transfer for position filling than MNCs from other countries, as this reason would seem to depend mainly on the industry and the subsidiary country. Although the importance attached to management development might very well vary between countries, we do not have any indications to assume that Japanese or German MNCs would be leaders in this respect. Therefore:

> Hypothesis 1-23: Japanese and German multinationals will attach a higher than average importance to the organisation development function of expatriation.

Looking at the level of the subsidiary country, we would expect that part of the higher presence of expatriates in Latin American subsidiaries could be explained by the lack of locally qualified personnel. Therefore:

> Hypothesis 1-24: Subsidiaries in Latin American countries will report a higher than average importance for the position-filling function of expatriation.

Cultural distance was hypothesised to be an important reason for a high expatriate presence. This effect, however, will probably differ for the different functions of expatriation. It is expected to be strongest for the organisation development function. The perceived need for control (either direct or indirect through socialisation) and the improvement of communication channels will be stronger if the cultural difference between headquarters and the subsidiary is larger. To a lesser extent, we would also expect a positive relationship with the position-filling function. The mere fact that subsidiary employees are culturally different would probably lead headquarters managers to think that they are less suited for top-level positions and that transfer of know-how would be necessary. The management development function would probably be relatively less important for culturally distant subsidiaries as headquarters would rather choose "less difficult" locales for management development as international transfers offer enough challenges without the added cultural difference. Therefore:

> Hypothesis 1-25: There will be a positive relationship between cultural distance and both the organisation development and the position-filling function of expa-

---

[36] Wolf's study is the only one that finds management development to be most important and control very unimportant (1.56 on a scale from 1 to 5, where 1 means: this function of expatriation plays no role at all). It must be noted, however, that his study focuses on the coordination of personnel management only, while the other studies take either a general management or a differentiated perspective.

triation, although the latter relationship will be weaker. There will be a negative relationship between cultural distance and the MD function of expatriation.

No specific differences are expected concerning industry and we can think of no clear rationales why larger subsidiaries would place higher importance on one of the functions of expatriation. For younger subsidiaries, though, we would expect the organisation development function to be rather important. Making sure that the new subsidiary functions according to headquarters plans and establishing communication channels is likely to be very important in the early phases of operation. Therefore:

Hypothesis 1-26: In younger subsidiaries, the organisation development function of expatriation will be more important than in older subsidiaries.

As acquired subsidiaries have usually functioned with local personnel for quite some time, we would expect the position-filling reason of expatriation to be less important in acquisitions than in greenfields. Therefore:

Hypothesis 1-27: In acquired subsidiaries expatriation for position filling will be less important than in greenfield subsidiaries.

No clear rationales could be found for a higher importance of one of the functions of expatriation for subsidiaries with different functions. Although we did not offer a hypothesis on the influence of the size of headquarters on expatriate presence, one of the reasons to expect a positive influence would be the fact that larger MNCs will be more likely to have explicit management developments programmes in use.[37] Therefore:

Hypothesis 1-28: Large multinationals will attach a higher importance to expatriation for management development than small multinationals.

Finally, concerning the extent of internationalisation, we would expect more internationalised MNCs to place more emphasis on management development and less emphasis on position filling than less internationalised MNCs.

Hypothesis 1-29: The more internationalised a multinational is, the more important will be transfer for management development and the less important transfer for position filling.

---

[37] An unpublished master's thesis (Levolger, 1995) found transfer for management development to be the most important reason for expatriation in the larger MNCs.

Research issues in international human resource management (HRM)

In this section we will briefly discuss the major research issues in the field of international human resource management in general and international transfers in particular. Although there are some differences between domestic and international HRM (see for instance Acuff, 1984), most authors (see for instance Arvey et al, 1991; Dowling and Welch, 1988; Dowling and Schuler, 1990; Hilb, 1992; Hossain and Davis, 1989; Pucik, 1984) argue that the most important tasks in international HRM involve staffing/selection, assessment and compensation, training and development, and industrial relations and employee participation. These issues are also often considered to be the main activities in domestic HRM (Beer et al, 1984; Fombrun et al, 1984). The way in which these activities are to be performed gives rise to differences.

In the next sections, we will therefore briefly discuss the research done so far on the selection, training and appraisal and compensation of international managers. In this review we will concentrate on the company perspective and ignore the abundant literature, mostly psychological in nature, that focuses on the expatriate him/herself, discussing for instance adjustment and acculturation in an international setting or repatriation problems (see e.g. Black, 1988; Black, Gregersen and Mendenhall, 1992; Black, Mendenhall and Oddou, 1991; Brewster, 1991; DeCieri, Dowling and Taylor, 1991; Feldman and Thompson, 1993; Forster, 1992, 1994; Gaugler, 1989; Gregersen and Black, 1990; Harvey, 1982, 1985 and 1989; Harris and Moran, 1979; Mendenhall and Oddou, 1985; Napier and Peterson, 1991; Naumann, 1992; Stening and Hammer, 1992; Torbiörn, 1982). What should be noted about repatriation from a company perspective is, however, that it is considered to be one of the most urgent problems to be dealt with nowadays, especially by European and American MNCs (Forster, 1994; Forster and Johnsen, 1996; Peterson et al, 1996; Solomon, 1995). We will also not discuss industrial relations and employee participation as this is considered less relevant to the subject of international transfer of *managers*. At the end of the review, we will identify a number of limitations in this field of research that this study hopes to overcome.

Selection
One important sub-topic in the area of selection - executive nationality policies (to choose for PCNs, HCNs or TCNs) - has already been discussed extensively above. In this section, we will focus our discussion on two main subjects. First, the selection criteria for expatriate managers and the related issue of expatriate failure. Second, the role of women in international management and in particular the reasons why they are not selected for international assignments.

Expatriate selection criteria and expatriate failure Research on expatriate selection mainly focused on the competencies international managers should have and on the reasons for expatriate failure. Baumgarten (1992a) has reviewed the numerous studies aimed at determining the competencies needed for international success, which resulted in a list of more than 80 competencies, ranging from listening skills to a sense of humour, from mental alertness to leadership skills. She developed a hypothetical profile for international managers and subsequently validated this by means of a survey carried out among a stratified sample of 117 (ex) international managers of a Dutch multinational company, 94 (80%) of whom returned the completed questionnaire (Baumgarten, 1992b). The survey asked the respondents to indicate the relative importance of various competencies for success on foreign assignments. The six competencies of the hypothetical profile that were perceived as being most important for the success of international managers were (in descending order of importance) leadership skills, initiative, emotional stability, motivation, ability to handle responsibility and cultural sensitivity. A study that relates directly to our discussion above is the analysis of Bartlett and Ghoshal (1991). According to them, the global manager should be seen as a network of specialists rather than a single individual. They distinguish three different types of managers with specialised yet interdependent roles: the business manager, the country manager and the functional manager. Together they fulfil the roles necessary to implement a transnational strategy. Besides leading in the broadest sense, the main roles of the fourth type - the corporate manager - are talent scout and developer. International transfers play an important role in the further development of high potentials. Martinez and Quelch (1996) distinguish four different roles for country managers that would be applicable to the different strategies as discussed above. Unfortunately, neither of the studies tested their classifications empirically, although the different managerial roles as distinguished by Bartlett and Ghoshal were derived from their case study research.

In spite of the fact that most research suggests that personal skills are very important for success in international assignments, if we look at the actual selection criteria that are used in most MNCs, we see that technical competence is usually still considered to be most important (Baker and Ivancevich, 1971; Brewster, 1991; Cardel Gertsen, 1990; Edström and Galbraith, 1977a; Forster and Johnsen, 1996; Mendenhall and Oddou, 1985; Miller, 1972; Roessel, 1988; Stone, 1991; Tung, 1981, 1982). According to Miller (1972) there are two major reasons for this practice: firstly, the difficulty of identifying and measuring the relevant interpersonal and cross-cultural skills, and secondly, the self-interest of the selectors, who will try to minimise the personal risk involved in selecting a candidate who might fail on the job. Technical competence will usually prevent *immediate* failure on the job.

With regard to expatriate failure, there seems a consensus in the academic world that the estimated failure rate has fluctuated between 25 and 40% since 1965 (see e.g. Adler and Ghadar, 1990; Black, Gregersen and Mendenhall, 1992; Buckley and Brooke, 1992; Dowling, 1986; Dowling and Welch, 1988; Dowling and Schuler (1990); Hamill, 1989; Harvey, 1983, 1985; Hendry, 1994; Henry, 1965; Lanier, 1979; Mendenhall and Oddou, 1985, 1988; Murray and Murray, 1986; Scullion, 1991; Zeira and Banai, 1985). As with the reasons for organisational transfers, Borg (1988:31) neatly summarises this general acceptance: "The general opinion among American writers is that the failure rate, i.e. premature return of expatriates, fluctuates between 25 and 40%." In a recent article (Harzing, 1995b) we showed, however, that these figures might actually be a myth, created by massive indirect quotations without any solid empirical evidence. The ultimate source of this myth is most likely a four-page article on "Return on investment of overseas personnel" in the *Financial Executive* (Misa and Fabricatore, 1979). The authors start the article as follows: "A recent review of the overseas operations of 245 multinational corporations concludes that 'the adjustment problems of Americans abroad are severe'" (Misa and Fabricatore, 1979:42). Unfortunately the authors do not provide any clues as to which review they are citing as no references are included in the article (it could even be Tung's study, the first results of which were presented in 1978). However, a second quotation from this article is even more important: "Even when things were going right for expatriate managers overseas in the glorious days prior to the devaluation of the dollar and closing of some of the beneficial tax advantages, the premature return rate on foreign assignments ranged from 25 to 40 percent." The glorious days Misa and Fabricatore are referring to are most likely the days before the collapse of the Bretton Woods system in 1971. This collapse led to a period in which the dollar fell continuously and did not stabilise until 1978/1979 (Samuelson and Nordhaus, 1985:885). The period Misa and Fabricatore are referring to is therefore most likely the sixties. Concluding, the final source of all of the references on expatriate failure rates, both for US companies and in general, right through to 1994 is therefore two management consultants claiming, out of the blue, that in the glorious past (the 1960s) American expatriate failure rates were 25-40% (see Harzing, 1995b for a further discussion and motivation[38]).

These critical remarks do not imply that we consider expatriate failure unimportant. The criterion for failure used in the studies cited above is the return of the expatriate to his home country before the assignment has been successfully completed. The percentages cited therefore do not include expa-

---

[38] A recent NFTC/Windham International (1995) report on expatriate practices in 138 American MNCs that we received after writing the article referred to mentions a failure rate of 9%.

triates who fail to perform satisfactorily, but are not sent home early. It can be argued that these expatriates bring more damage to the firm in the long run, causing for instance missed opportunities, disturbed relations with the host-country government, loss of market share, or even in extreme cases expropriation of the subsidiary in question.

Disregarding the actual figures for a moment, what would be the most important reasons for the failure of expatriates on foreign assignments? Again, there seems to be a large amount of agreement in this area. Most authors point to the inability of either the manager's partner or the manager himself to adapt to a different physical or cultural environment as the most important reason for failure (Edström and Galbraith, 1977b; Gonzalez and Negandhi, 1967; Hays, 1974; Stone, 1991; Torbiörn, 1982; Tung, 1981; Zeira and Banai, 1984). The manager's lack of technical competence scores rather low on the list of main causes for failure of foreign assignments (Tung, 1981), which seems logical because, as we have seen, the expatriate-to-be is mainly selected for his technical competence.

Female international managers A subject that has received some special attention is the role of women in international management. In a study of American and Canadian multinationals only 3% of the 13,388 were women (Adler, 1984b).[39] This is all the more surprising, since in the USA the percentage of female managers in a domestic setting is generally higher than in European countries, with the exception of Sweden (Adler, 1992). This same study showed that there were no sex differences in relation to an interest in international careers and to the reasons for rejecting an international assignment. Generally, three reasons are suggested to explain the scarcity of women in international management. First, women's disinterest in international assignments, an assumption that was clearly rejected in Adler's (1984b) study. A second reason would be corporate resistance to send women on international assignments. A large number of male managers said that *they* wouldn't have a problem in sending female managers abroad, but that superiors, subordinates, colleagues or clients would. A variant of this behaviour can be found in a third reason for a lack of women's international presence, that is, the prejudice of foreigners with regard to women. Although there might indeed be countries were it would be difficult for women to work (e.g. African and Islamic countries), research by Adler (1987) amongst US women expatriates working in Southeast Asia challenges the validity of this assumption by finding a very high rate of success amongst women international managers,

---

[39] This percentage seems to be growing, however. A recent NFTC/Windham International (1995) survey found 13% of the expatriates to be female, 1% more than in 1994 and 3% more than in 1993.

largely due to the fact that women were seen as foreigners who happened to be women, not as women who happened to be foreigners: a subtle, but highly significant distinction. Female expatriate managers were therefore not subject to the same limitations imposed on local females. This was generally confirmed by Westwood and Leung's (1994) study in Hong Kong. Stone (1991) claims, however, that Adler is somewhat too optimistic. He finds less acceptability of women as international managers in Korea and Japan. But even if this arguments holds, why do we not see more female managers on assignment in Europe or the United States? It seems as if the reasons for not sending female managers abroad are largely based on assumptions of how other people (women themselves, superiors, colleagues, foreigners) *might* react. In some cases there is distinct evidence that these assumptions are false, so just asking these "others" might solve this problem, provided that these assumptions are not just an excuse to camouflage the manager's own reluctance to send female managers on foreign assignments, an attitude for which Stone (1991) did find some credence. In Westwood and Leung's study of female expatriate managers in Hong Kong, many of the interviewed women claimed that Western expatriate men exhibited more sexism and male chauvinism than local managers. Though sexism/sex discrimination in the society at large was generally thought to be higher than in Western countries, it was suggested that there was not much sexism/discrimination in work settings.

There is one very real problematic issue, however, in sending female managers abroad, namely the existence of dual-career couples (Punnett et al, 1992). If a female manager has a partner, the chances are more than nine out of ten that this partner has a career of his own, and is not very willing to give up this career by following his partner abroad.[40] Although male managers should increasingly face the same problem with a growing number of women pursuing careers, companies still tend to see dual-career problems as a reason for not selecting potential female expatriates (Harris, 1995). It's therefore not surprising that more than half (in the Adler, 1987 sample even nearly two-thirds) of the women on foreign assignments are single (Westwood and Leung, 1994; Reynolds and Bennett, 1991), while this goes for only 15% of the men. Almost 79% of them are married and accompanied by their wife on assignment, while this is the case for less than a quarter of the women expatriates (Reynolds and Bennett, 1991).

---

[40] A recent empirical study (Brett and Stroh, 1995) came to the surprising finding that the type of work and career ambition did not have a significant impact on a spouse's willingness to relocate internationally. One explanation the authors give is that the type of work is correlated with having children at home (spouses with managerial and professional jobs were less likely to have children at home), which has a negative impact on the willingness to relocate. Further, a recent NFTC/Windham International (1995) report on expatriate practices in 138 American MNCs found spouse career concerns to be the most important reason for refusing an assignment.

Training

Most studies regarding pre-departure training for expatriates (PCNs) conclude that a majority of companies do not provide training (Baker and Ivancevich, 1971; Harvey, 1985; Mendenhall, Dunbar and Oddou, 1987; Tung, 1981, 1984, 1988). There is some evidence, however, that this is much more prominent in American companies (Tung, 1988; Hamill, 1989) than in European and Japanese companies. It is questionable whether these results still hold true. A recent NFTC/Windham International (1995) report on expatriate practices in 138 American MNCs reports that "only" 38% provide no cross-cultural preparation. The problem is, according to the report, that many expatriates do not use the programmes. In 43% of the companies under 50% of the eligible employees participate in them. Further, a study of Japanese expatriates in Germany (Kumar and Steinmann, 1986) showed that only 43% received satisfactory pre-departure training. If training is provided at all it is usually of a one-shot nature, consisting mainly of a language course and some lectures or books on the habits and culture of the country of the assignment (Baker and Ivancevich, 1971; Mendenhall, Dunbar and Oddou, 1987; Tung, 1981, 1984, 1988). As the inability of the spouse to adapt is probably one of the most important reasons for expatriate failure, her or his inclusion in the training programme is of fundamental importance (Harvey, 1985; Tung, 1981). Not surprisingly, even fewer companies provide pre-departure training for family members (Black and Mendenhall, 1989; Harvey, 1982; Tung 1988).

Baumgarten (1995) correctly argues that most of the competencies that are needed for success on foreign assignment lie in the area of attitudes, abilities and even personality traits. Wills and Barham (1994) and Barham (1995)* make the same point when describing the deeper, core competencies that successful international managers seem to have. Even if we are prepared to accept that these competencies can be acquired through training, we should realise that most of them cannot be acquired overnight. They simply need time to develop and become strong. A short training course just before departure can therefore not be effective in changing and/or developing competencies related to attitudes, abilities or personality traits. Baumgarten (1995) therefore pleads for continuous training, using a phased, cumulative approach. The *first phase* of training and development should begin soon after initial selection has taken place and the candidate has been accepted into the company for a position with international prospects. Development in this phase should focus on strengthening those abilities needed for an international career and on reinforcing the manager's motivation to work abroad. The *second phase* of training and development should take place after the manager has been selected for an international career. In this phase, the focus should be on strengthening all required competencies for the fulfilment of an international assignment.

After the manager has been selected for a specific assignment, the *third phase* of training should be implemented. In this phase the manager is trained in specific skills needed for his assignment and is imparted the necessary knowledge of specific cultural issues in the host country, logistical information and business practices and procedures.

There are numerous cross-cultural training methods (see Baumgarten, 1995 for an overview), varying from lectures to field trips and role-plays. Tung (1982) Black and Mendenhall (1989) and Mendenhall, Dunbar and Oddou (1987) provide some guidance towards the choice of training methods. In general we can say that the larger the cultural novelty, the higher the degree of interaction with host-country nationals and the larger the job novelty, the more rigorous and intensive pre-departure training should be. Early (1987) showed, however, that even 6-8 hours of training could make quite a difference in performance, the intensity of adjustment needed and the extent of cosmopolitan perspective. This was true for both documentary and interpersonal training, although the latter was preferred by the participants.

Appraisal and compensation
There is a surprising lack of research on appraisal and compensation of international managers. Literature on expatriate appraisal (see for instance Dowling and Schuler, 1990; Oddou and Mendenhall, 1991) identifies the variables that influence an expatriate's performance (environment, task and personality factors) and points to the constraints in appraising managers on assignment. In most cases, the final appraisal of the expatriate is done in the parent country, where the appraisers have little or no knowledge of local circumstances, and the context of the performance may be lost. In view of the geographical and communicative distance between the expatriate and the appraiser, local management is often called in to give their opinion. They are supposed to be familiar with the expatriate's performance and be able to explain the local situation and environment-related factors. However, their comments are dictated by their local cultural background. Thus, a manager who is used to guiding and supervising a group through involvement and participation could receive a negative appraisal in a local culture where managers are expected to show strong leadership and be the ones who come up with ideas and initiatives. In such an environment, the appraisal will presumably be to the manager's disadvantage, although he may have made every possible effort and his performance would be termed excellent in the home country.

Most of the scarce literature on the compensation of international staff (Ackermann and Pohl, 1989; Brewster, 1991; Buckley and Brooke, 1992; Desatnick and Bennett, 1977; Dowling and Schuler, 1990; Ellison and Nicholas, 1986; Helms, 1991; Phatak, 1989; Reynolds, 1986) simply consists of a description of the different types of compensation systems (usually budget system, balance sheet/home net system, market system/local going rate system) and the different types of premium and allowances (mobility, hardship, housing, clubs, education, tax compensation, home leave). Several authors, however (Adler and Ghadar, 1990; Logger and Vinke, 1995, Edström and Galbraith, 1977b), point to the fact that especially when international transfers occur for management and organisation development reasons, overgenerous compensation packages are no longer appropriate. In this case international assignments are simple a part of the job that should not be rewarded extra. Toyne and Kuhne's (1983) study is one of the very few that takes a more strategic view and investigates the level of centralisation of the compensation and benefits programmes. Further, Harvey (1993a/b) makes a laudable attempt to develop a more comprehensive model for global compensation. Recent conference papers (e.g. Fenwick and DeCieri, 1995 and Thavanainen and Welch, 1995) also hold a promise for a more strategic view towards compensation and appraisal.

Conclusions

This brief review of the major research issues in international HRM in general and international transfers in particular leads to the identification of four major limitations, which we hope to overcome in this study.

First, the focus of most research is exclusively on expatriates in the limited sense of the word, that is parent-country nationals transferred to one of the subsidiaries. International human resource management research is rather ethnocentric in nature.[41] Furthermore, the vast majority of the studies involve American MNCs. Fortunately, there have recently been some studies focusing on multinationals from other countries, although many were Anglo-Saxon (e.g. Dowling and Welch, 1988 [Australia]; Hamill, 1989 [Great Britain]; Scullion [ibid.], 1991).[42] This is all the more important, because there is reason to believe that there are major differences between American, Japanese and European firms with regard to international HRM policies (see e.g. Cardel Gertsen, 1990; Hamill, 1989; Oddou et al, 1995; Peterson et al. 1996; Scullion, 1991; Stening and Hammer, 1992; Tung, 1988).

Second, there is a dearth of studies considering the interconnectedness, interrelatedness or integration of various personnel practices. Several authors have called for a more integrated approach (see among others Arvey et al, 1991; Baumgarten, 1995; Hendry, 1996; Tung and Punnett, 1993).

---

[41] A notable example is the publication of Barnett and Toyne (1991) who distinguish no less than 12 different groups of international personnel.

[42] Of course, many of the German studies discussed in the previous section focus on German MNCs.

Thirdly, most of the research in this field has an operational and practical flavour (Arvey et al, 1991; Ferner, 1994; Festing, 1996b; Gronhaug and Nordhaug, 1992; Ondrack and Saks, 1990; Wolf, 1994). Hardly ever is human resource management examined in a strategic sense, that is, is its relevance to and integration with the international corporate strategy considered. Boyacigiller (1990, 1991) pleads for a reorientation towards international transfers, in that decisions regarding international transfers should be tied to strategic decisions, and the emphasis should be on long-term organisational and management development. Ondrack (1985a/b) cites the study by Edström and Galbraith, which we discussed above, as a rare exception that does consider strategic issues and calls for more research in this tradition. Unfortunately, the situation has not changed very much since (oral communication by Ondrack during a conference at Cranfield, Sept. 1992). Fenwick, Welch and DeCieri (1993) lament that "early contributors such as [...] Edström and Galbraith (1977) [...] proposed concepts that, while incorporated in the work of Doz and Prahalad and Bartlett and Ghoshal appear to have been overlooked during the 1980s where research focused primarily on functional and operational aspects [...]" (1993:20). Macharzina (1995) comments: "Looking at work in the field of expatriation, we clearly notice a lack of comprehensive and higher level analyses, in which for instance the strategic orientation of the company forms the starting point that could explain decisions with regard to expatriation and expatriate management" (1995: 273, *our translation*). The German literature on international transfers is, as we have seen above, in general somewhat more strategically oriented than the Anglo-Saxon literature. Although many of the German studies also focus on operational issues, they include at least some observations on the organisational functions of expatriation. A review by Festing (1996a) showed, however, that since the middle of the 1980s most of the German literature has also focused on more operational issues.

Very recently, some studies have tried to build conceptual frameworks of the field of strategic IHRM (Adler and Bartholomew, 1992a; Kamoche, 1996; Milliman, Von Glinow and Nathan, 1991; Schuler, Dowling and DeCieri, 1993; Taylor, Beechler and Napier, 1996; Welch, 1994a; Welch and Welch, 1994). So far not much has been done, however, to empirically test the relationship between strategy and IHRM. Although Edström and Lorange (1984) provided some case study evidence, Caligiuri and Stroh's (1995) and Festing's (1996a/b) studies have, to our best knowledge, been the only ones to provide a systematic empirical test of the link between international strategy and IHRM.

This brings us to a *fourth* and final limitation in the field of international HRM, and especially strategic IHRM: the lack of empirical research. Dowling and Schuler (1990:162) indicate three reasons for this lack of international research.[43] First, the field of international management has been regarded as a marginal academic area by many management researchers. This would apply even more to international HRM, as the field of HRM itself is still considered to be in a stage of adolescence (Laurent, 1986). Second, international research is invariably more costly than domestic research. Finally, international research poses additional methodological problems.[44] On the operational level, we find a larger amount of empirical work. Very often, however, data analysis is limited to a simple descriptive frequency analysis (see e.g. Derr and Oddou, 1991; Groenewald and Sapozhnikov, 1990; Tung, 1981, 1982, 1988) and little effort is made to systematically test predefined hypotheses. A similar limitation is also signalled by Schuler and Florkowski (1996) when they discuss the state of knowledge in IHRM. A harmful possible consequence of this lack of sound empirical work is myth building based on a limited number of publications (see Harzing, 1995b; 1996b and 1997a for examples of this).

In this research project, we hope to overcome the limitations signalled above. Referring to the first limitation, this study *is* limited to PCNs, as they are considered most important for the focus of this thesis: control mechanisms. Our study does remedy part of the first limitation, however, as in addition to American and Japanese MNCs, MNCs from no less than seven European countries, are included in the empirical part of the study. To remedy the second limitation discussed above, subjects such as selection and training will be included into the analysis as alternatives to international transfers. The subject of our study is strategic in focus. Control and coordination are fundamental necessities in achieving the strategic goals of any organisation. When considering the international transfer of managers as a control mechanism, we link international human resource management with international corporate strategy. Starting from the other end - international transfers - it is important to recognise the strategic functions of international transfers. When considering a cut-back in the number of expatriates, because they become more and more expensive and because qualified local personnel becomes more and more available, one should not forget that international transfers also fulfil two other strategic functions, i.e. management development and organisation development. The current study explicitly draws all three functions of expatriation into the analysis. As the empirical part of this study involves the statistical testing of a large number of hypotheses derived from a comprehensive literature review, by means of a survey administered in 22 different countries, the fourth limitation (lack of empirical research) is clearly overcome.

---

[43] According to them, the lack of empirical research in international management is general and not limited to IHRM.

[44] An overview of these problems is given in Chapter 3.

Conclusion

In this section, we provided an introduction into the final building block of this thesis: international transfers. We discussed different staffing policies and offered a number of hypotheses on the factors that influence the choice for either PCNs, HCNs or TCNs. We also discussed the organisational functions of international transfers and showed that there is a reasonable amount of consensus about the different functions of expatriation, but that it is less clear in which circumstances the various reasons are most important. Some hypotheses were offered on this subject. The final subsection briefly reviewed research on international transfers and signalled four limitations that this study hopes to overcome. In the next chapter, we will combine the three building blocks discussed so far. First, we will discuss control issues in *multinational* organisations and second, we will consider the role of international transfers as a control mechanism in more detail.

2. Integration, configurations and performance

In the previous chapter, we discussed the three theoretical building blocks of this thesis: control mechanisms, multinational companies and international transfers. In this chapter, we will integrate these building blocks. First, in Section 1, we will discuss control mechanisms in MNCs and explore the headquarters and subsidiary characteristics that might influence the use of the various control mechanisms. Subsequently, Section 2 is devoted to the role of international transfers as a control mechanism in MNCs. In that section, we will discuss how international transfers can be used by headquarters to control subsidiaries in both a direct and an indirect way. In addition, the alternatives for international transfers in achieving indirect control by socialisation and networks are explored. Many of the hypotheses stated in the first two sections describe bivariate relationships, which might not fully capture the complexity of the object under study. Therefore, a final section, Section 3, constructs ideal-type configurations of headquarters and subsidiary characteristics and control mechanisms. MNCs conforming to an ideal type are hypothesised to show higher levels of financial performance.

1. CONTROL MECHANISMS IN MNCS

Introduction

In Chapter 1, we discussed organisational control mechanisms and the environment, strategy and structure of multinational companies. In this section we will combine these two elements and explore what can be deduced about the use of various control mechanisms in multinational companies. In doing so, we will take a two-step approach. First we will review what "traditional" organisation theory has to say about the use of control mechanisms in different circumstances and draw conclusions from this with regard to MNCs. Subsequently, we will discuss a number of headquarters and subsidiary characteristics that are hypothesised to influence the use of the various control mechanisms.[45]

Control mechanisms in national and multinational organisations

Two organisational characteristics (size and interdependence) and two environmental characteristics (uncertainty and heterogeneity/complexity) are usually considered to have the largest amount of influence on the applicability of different control mechanisms in organisations. To start with *size*, one of the results from the Aston studies (see among others Pugh et al., 1968, 1969) was that the larger the organisation in terms of employees, the more important was standardisation and formalisation (our bureaucratic formalised control) and the less important was centralisation (our personal centralised control). The larger an organisation, the more likely it is that a centralised approach to control will generate top management overload (Blau and Schoenherr, 1971). To our best knowledge, no studies have been conducted to measure the effect of size on output control or control by socialisation and networks.

Concerning *interdependence*, the level of dependence of different parts of the organisation on each other for e.g. inputs, Thompson (1967) draws a parallel between different types of interdependence and different types of control. A small amount of interdependence (pooled interdependence) can be handled by standardisation (our bureaucratic formalised control). A moderate amount of interdependence (sequential interdependence) needs coordination by plan or schedules (our output control category). A large amount of interdependence (reciprocal interdependence) finally calls for mutual adjustment (categorised as one of the elements of our control by socialisation and networks). To a large extent these propositions have been confirmed in empirical research by Baumler (1971) and Van de Ven, Delbecq and Koenig (1976).

An *uncertain* environment - defined by its synonyms dynamic, unpredictable, unstable, turbulent or changing - most of all precludes standardisation, because there are no standard situations and furthermore standardisation would preclude the necessary flexibility (Child, 1984; Galbraith, 1973; Lawrence and Lorsch, 1967; March and Simon, 1958; Mintzberg, 1983). Therefore, our formalised bureaucratic control would be very inappropriate. Furthermore, in an uncertain environment personal centralised control is too slow and inflexible to cope with the necessary information processing (Galbraith, 1973; Child, 1984). Output control would only be feasible if plans and budg-

---

[45] In discussing the subsidiary and headquarters characteristics, we will draw from a variety of research streams. Birkinshaw (1994) distinguishes the Strategy-Structure Stream, the Headquarters-Subsidiary Relationships Stream, the MNC Process Stream and the Subsidiary Role Stream in the literature on MNCs. Elements of all four research streams will be incorporated in our discussion and hypotheses.

ets are stated in rather general terms and the requested reports are not too detailed. This leaves us with (elements of) control by networks or socialisation as the most appropriate control mechanism for uncertain environments (Burns and Stalker, 1961; Child, 1984; Galbraith, 1973; Lawrence and Lorsch, 1967; March and Simon, 1958; Mintzberg, 1983).

An environment is *heterogeneous* (also called diverse) if the organisation's customers or markets have different characteristics and needs. Complexity is seen by some authors (e.g. Khandwalla, 1977; Mintzberg, 1983) as a different environmental factor, and is then usually defined as technological complexity. For other authors (e.g. Child, 1984; Daft, 1992; Robbins, 1993), however, complexity is simply a result of diversity. Here we will take the second point of view and consider the effects of heterogeneity and complexity together. Various authors (e.g. Khandwalla, 1977; Lawrence and Lorsch, 1967; Mintzberg, 1983; Thompson, 1967) have argued that organisations operating in a heterogeneous/diverse environment necessarily have to differentiate the organisation, that is create separate homogeneous parts to deal with each different element in their environment. This differentiation is usually accompanied by more decentralised decision-making, simply because the information needed to make these decisions is located with employees at a lower level in the organisation. This decentralised decision-making is incompatible with both personal centralised control - which by definition presupposes centralised decision-making - and bureaucratic formalised control, where actions are largely pre-specified at a central level. Decentralised decision-making presupposes freedom of action, which is mainly compatible with output control and control by socialisation and networks. Hage, Aiken and Marrett (1971) posit the relationship between diversity and control mechanisms in even more direct terms. According to them, organisations that are more diversified and more differentiated will use coordination by feedback or mutual adjustment rather than "a system of programmed interactions". They furthermore argue that these organisations will rely heavily on socialisation. So, in general we can say that elements of our control by socialisation and network category will be the most preferred way of control in heterogeneous and complex environments, while output control would be a good second.

In sum, we can say that large size results in a lower use of personal centralised control and a higher use of bureaucratic formalised control, while a high amount of interdependence, uncertainty and diversity/complexity all lead to a larger use of either output control or control by socialisation and networks. What would be the consequence of these observations for multinational companies? Multinationals are undoubtedly large, which would result in a low use of personal centralised control, but a larger amount of bureaucratic formalised control. By definition multinationals operate in heterogeneous/complex environments, because of the large geographical spread of their activities. Furthermore, the international environment *per se* is already more dynamic/uncertain/unpredictable than the domestic environment. Concerning interdependence in multinational companies, we can consider the different subsidiaries to represent the different organisational parts. We can then say that while some multinationals (particularly the multidomestic type) would have to deal only with pooled or sequential interdependence, the global and in particular the transnational type of multinational, with its integrated network structure, will certainly be characterised by reciprocal interdependence. So for multinational companies in general, three of the characteristics - large size, high diversity/complexity, large uncertainty/unpredictability - lead in the same direction, that is a more extensive use of output control and in particular control by socialisation and networks. This would be even more so for trans-national and global companies, which are in addition characterised by larger interdependence.

As our study focuses on a comparison *between* MNCs, however, these general indications do not provide us with enough information for a system-atic comparison. Therefore, in the next two subsections, we will deal with particular headquarters and subsidiary characteristics that might explain dif-ferences in the type of control mechanisms that are used by headquarters in respect of their subsidiaries. What can be concluded at this stage is that we would expect that, in MNCs in general, the more indirect means of control (output control and control by socialisation) dominate over the more direct ways of control (personal centralised and formal bureaucratic control). There-fore:

Hypothesis 2-1: MNC headquarters will use indirect control mechanisms to a larger extent in respect of their subsidiaries than direct control mechanisms.[46]

Headquarters characteristics and control mechanisms

In this section, we will discuss a number of headquarters characteristics that are assumed to influence the control portfolio in use by a particular head-quarters. In Chapter 1, we dealt with the influence that the country of origin of headquarters might have. Now, we will look at the type of organisational model that the MNC applies, the MNC's size and international experience and the complexity/diversity of the environment in which the MNC operates.

---

[46] This and the following hypotheses in this chapter are formulated in general terms, that is, we do not differentiate according to the different functional areas to be coordinated, such as fi-nance, marketing, production, personnel. An explanation and motivation for this choice is given in Section 2 of Chapter 3.

Organisational model
In the previous chapter, we identified three main types of international companies: multidomestic, global and transnational. The multidomestic firm is
characterised by a decentralised network structure, in which subsidiaries operate rather autonomously and differentiate products and policies for the local
market. The global firm operates in a much more integrated and centralised
way. Subsidiaries have less freedom of action and the MNC's strategy is focused on achieving efficiency with standardised products. The transnational
firm combines integration and responsiveness and is characterised by an integrated network structure in which subsidiaries can play a strategic role. What
would be the consequence of these different models for the application of the
various control mechanisms? Let us first look at the total level of control that
is exercised. When reviewing the descriptions of the various MNC types, it
should immediately become clear that multidomestic MNCs would exercise a
lower level of control over their subsidiaries than global or transnational
MNCs. To our best knowledge, Roth, Schweiger and Morrison (1991) are the
only ones who investigated this empirically. They found indeed that global
firms had higher levels of formalisation, centralisation and integrating mechanisms (among others: committees and task forces, direct personal contacts)
than multidomestic firms. The difference for shared values was not significant, however. Global and transnational MNCs are assumed to have broadly
comparable levels of control as both types of firms are highly integrated.
Therefore:

> Hypothesis 2-2: Subsidiaries of multinationals that apply a multidomestic organ-
> isational model will experience a lower level of control than subsidiaries of multi-
> nationals that apply either a global or a transnational organisational model. No
> difference in the level of control will be found between subsidiaries of global or
> transnational MNCs.

As subsidiaries from multidomestic companies should have a high level of
freedom to decide upon their own actions, we would expect that *if* any control
is exercised, headquarters would choose one of the more indirect ways of
control: output control or control by socialisation and networks. Also Bartlett
and Ghoshal (1989, 1992a) saw socialisation as the dominant control mechanism for multidomestic MNCs. Therefore:

> Hypothesis 2-3: The dominant type of control mechanisms that will be used in re-
> spect of subsidiaries of multidomestic MNCs will be output control and control by
> socialisation and networks.

We argued above that transnational and global firms would have broadly
comparable total levels of control, but how about the composition of the con-

trol portfolio? As the more informal control mechanisms have received the largest amount of attention, we will start here. Quite a number of authors have argued for the extensive use of informal control mechanisms (our *control by socialisation and networks*) in transnational firms. Egelhoff (1993) discusses the information-processing implications of transnationalism. Transnational strategies that aim to realise global efficiency, local responsiveness and world-wide learning simultaneously pose significantly greater information-processing requirements, both between headquarters and subsidiaries and among subsidiaries. Egelhoff distinguishes four specific information-processing implications that are very important. Of these four, especially the third: "the Use of Non-routine-Reciprocal Information-Processing Mechanisms will need to be Significantly Expanded" is important for our argument. This expansion is necessary in order to respond to the variety of changing opportunities the transnational strategy seeks to exploit. Egelhoff suggests various horizontal information-processing mechanisms that are able to perform this role (incidentally following Galbraith, 1973 in this): e.g. direct contact, task forces, integrating roles and teams. All these mechanisms have been classified in our control by networks and socialisation category in Chapter 1.

In various contributions, Hedlund argued that informal control would be more applicable in transnationals. In his 1986 publication Hedlund describes a heterarchical (his term for transnational) firm. One of the characteristics of this type of firm is that integration is achieved primarily through normative control. Hedlund and Ridderstrale (1992) comment that to prevent the N-form corporation (yet another term for a transnational type of firm) from breaking down or falling apart, control mechanisms will be used that are more subtle and focused on the lateral dimension. Socialisation and informal communication between employees will be the key mechanisms. International task forces are also important. Hedlund (1993) observes four developments in the practice of multinational management that suggest that hierarchies are giving way to heterarchies. Two of them have special relevance for our argument. First, Hedlund sees less formal control systems gaining in importance. In this respect he distinguishes "the design of systems for information flows and mechanisms to encourage shared goals, consensus on strategies and generally a strong corporate culture" (Hedlund, 1993:214). Second, because of changing organisational structures (one of the other points) and changing control systems, lateral communication is becoming increasingly important (see also Hedlund, 1994). Remarkable is the almost similar wording of White and Poynter (1990) when describing elements of their horizontal organisation (their name for a transnational company). According to them, this horizontal organisation is held together "by a flexible horizontal network, accompanied by lateral decision processes and, underlying it all, a common set of shared premises upon which decisions are based and actions assessed" (White and Poynter, 1990:98). In both these descriptions we clearly recognise elements of our control by network and socialisation category.

Macharzina (1992) describes a transnational type of firm in the following way: "For companies operating on an international scale, these developments require a strategic orientation that allows them to reach internal efficiency and local responsiveness at the same time. In these kind of international companies, sometimes called integrated networks, subsidiaries occupy a position equal to that of headquarters" (Macharzina, 1992:77, *our translation*). According to him, relying on the more formal and centralised control mechanisms is dysfunctional in these types of firms as they limit flexibilisation. More subtle control mechanisms should be used as these preserve flexibility and foster a common corporate culture.

Martinez and Jarillo (1989) suggest that changes in the international environment and international competition (from multidomestic and global to transnational) have resulted not only in changing strategies and structures for multinational companies, but also in a change in the combination of coordination mechanisms used by multinational companies. Coordinating mechanisms in multidomestic and global multinationals were mainly limited to structural and formal mechanisms, which comprise the first three categories we distinguished in Chapter 1 (personal centralised control, formalised bureaucratic control and output control). The complexity and uncertainty of a transnational environment, however, has forced multinational firms to adopt what Martinez and Jarillo call "more informal and subtle coordination mechanisms". In this category, they distinguish three different mechanisms. First, "micro-structural arrangements", also called lateral relations, that supplement the formal organisation structure. In the examples we easily recognise the already often-referred-to mechanisms distinguished by Galbraith (1973): teams, task forces, committees, individual integrators and integrative departments. Second, "informal communication channels supplementing the formal information system". These informal communication channels consist of direct contact between managers, regardless of their location (headquarters or subsidiaries) or hierarchical position. Third, "the development of a strong organisational culture that includes both a deep knowledge of the company's policies and objectives and a strong share of organisational values and beliefs" (Martinez and Jarillo, 1989:508). We clearly recognise the different sub-categories of our control by socialisation and networks as distinguished in Chapter 1: "socialisation", "informal lateral or horizontal exchange of information" and "formalised lateral or cross-departmental relations".

Finally, Schreyögg (1993) claims that in transnational firms bureaucratic control is not possible since rules have to be formulated "inaccurately and loosely" [*our translation*]. The alternative is socialisation. Transnational companies would need a common corporate culture and mutual adjustment. Therefore:

> Hypothesis 2-4: Subsidiaries of multinationals that follow a transnational organisational model will experience higher levels of control by socialisation and networks than subsidiaries of multinationals that apply a global organisational model.

In addition, some authors have discussed the application of *personal centralised control* in MNCs. Bartlett and Ghoshal (1989, 1992a) claim that centralisation is the dominant control mechanism in global companies. Gerpott (1990) suggests that centralisation will be highest for global strategies, lowest for multidomestic strategies and in between for "hybrid" (transnational) strategies. Welge (1987b) contends that within integrated global structures there will be less room for autonomy for subsidiaries. We would indeed expect personal centralised control to be rather high for global companies as they are characterised by a centralised hub structure in which headquarters takes the most important decisions. In the integrated network type of structure that characterises the transnational, subsidiaries can have a more strategic role, which would make centralisation of decision-making less feasible. In addition, global companies are not spread as much geographically (Porter, 1986b) as multidomestic and transnational firms, which would make centralisation of decision-making at headquarters level much easier. Therefore:

> Hypothesis 2-5: Subsidiaries of multinationals that follow a global organisational model will experience higher levels of personal centralised control than subsidiaries of multinationals following a transnational organisational model.

Concerning *bureaucratic formalised control,* few previous studies are available. Some of the authors above contrast informal control with bureaucratic and claim the latter to be less applicable in transnationals. A more focused motivation can be found in Macharzina and Wolf (1996). They refer to the fact that global companies try to sell standardised products, which would make a high level of standardisation a logical choice. Transnationals are much more differentiated and have to act in very flexible way. This would make standardisation and formal procedures infeasible. Therefore:

> Hypothesis 2-6: Subsidiaries of multinationals following a global organisational model experience higher levels of bureaucratic formalised control than subsidiaries of multinationals that follow a transnational organisational model.

Combining hypotheses 2-5 and 2-6, we can conclude that global companies are predicted to apply a relatively high amount of direct control (see Chapter 1 for the distinction between direct and indirect control). The level of *output control*, finally, would not be expected to differ substantially between the two organisational models. As described above, output control and planning and budgeting are rather indirect forms of control that are likely to be applied to a relatively high extent in both organisational models. Therefore:

> Hypothesis 2-7: Subsidiaries of MNCs that follow a global organisational model will not differ from subsidiaries of MNCs that follow a transnational organisational model in the level of output control they experience.

Size

Since the Aston studies, the influence of the size of the company on the application of particular control mechanisms, usually centralisation and formalisation, has received a lot of attention. As described above, among organisation theorists there is a consensus that a large size leads to more formalisation and less centralisation. Unfortunately, results in the international context are not always consistent. Some MNC researchers look at the increased risk that is associated with a larger size and therefore predict an increasing level of centralisation. Others refer to the difficulty of directly controlling a large enterprise, and predict a negative relationship between size and centralisation. Empirically, a positive relationship between size and centralisation has been found by Garnier (1982) and Yunker (1983). Hedlund's (1981) results are based on six firms only, but the two firms with the highest level of centralisation were large firms, while the two firms with the lowest level of centralisation were small firms. Mixed results were by found Gates and Egelhoff (1986), where decisions in the area of marketing were more centralised in larger firms, while decisions in the area of finance were more decentralised. Picard (1979) found a negative relationship when surveying MNCs. Gencturk and Aulakh's (1995) study seems to support Picard, when we look more closely at the terms in use. These authors investigated the use of process and output control in American firms. Process control was defined as monitoring; a high level of monitoring meant a high level of process control. Output control was defined as the level of influence of headquarters. If this level were low, there would be a high level of output control. So defined, these different control mechanisms resemble surveillance (high process control) and centralisation (low output control), which are both elements of our personal centralised control. That these measures were very much related was also shown by their intercorrelation which was quite high (-0.67, 0.000). Gencturk and Aulakh found that a large size is associated with lower use of process controls (surveillance) and a higher use of output controls (autonomy).

A number of studies have investigated domestic firms in a number of different countries. Replicating the original Aston studies Hickson et al. (1974) found a positive relationship between size and centralisation for British and Canadian firms, but a insignificant relationship for American firms. Another replication in Britain, Japan and Sweden (Horvath et al, 1981) found a negative relationship for the first country and a positive for the latter two. No significance levels were included in this study, however. Finally, Seror (1989) found a negative correlation between size and centralisation for American firms, but a positive one for Japanese firms. In view of the mixed conclusions above, we conclude that in general an MNC's size will not be systematically related to the level of centralisation of decision-making. Differences were found between various countries, however. Therefore, we will, if allowed by the number of responses per country, investigate whether the relationship between size and centralisation is constant across the various countries included in this survey. As a general hypothesis, however, we will put forward:

> Hypothesis 2-8: There will not be a significant relationship between the size of an MNC and the level of personal centralised control that headquarters exerts over its subsidiaries.

The theoretical and empirical results concerning *formalisation* are more consistent with the consensus among organisation theorists. Hulbert and Brandt (1980) found size of the company to be a major factor leading to formalisation and the use of bureaucratic control procedures. Wolf (1994)[47] found a higher level of standardisation for larger firms. The studies that investigated domestic firms in various countries (Hickson et al, 1974; Horvath et al, 1981; Seror, 1989) all found a positive correlation between size and formalisation. Therefore:

> Hypothesis 2-9: There will be a positive relationship between the size of a multinational and the level of bureaucratic formalised control that headquarters exerts over it subsidiaries.

Few previous studies have investigated the influence of size on our two other control mechanisms: *output control* and *control by socialisation and networks*. Wolf (1994) found a higher level of shared values ("Homogenität der Führungskräftewerte") for larger firms. If we interpret his "Berichtswesen" as output control, then we can also see a positive influence of size on this control mechanism. Egelhoff (1988a) also found a insignificant positive relationship between firm size and output control. This positive influence would be expected, as both mechanisms influence behaviour only indirectly (see Chapter 1). Larger firms will realise that direct personal centralised control will no longer be feasible and that they will have to rely on indirect mechanisms to

---

[47] It should be noted that Wolf's study deals with control in the area of personnel management only. With regard to many relationships, however, Wolf has been one of the very few researchers to investigate them. We have therefore interpreted his findings as applicable to control in general.

achieve control. Although bureaucratic formalised control was also judged a direct type of control, larger firms are unlikely to get away from the pressures of bureaucratisation. In view of the argument above, we would expect, however, that the correlations between size and both output control and control by socialisation and networks would be stronger than the correlation between size and formal bureaucratic control. Therefore:

Hypothesis 2-10: There will a positive relationship between the size of a multinational and the level of both output control and control by socialisation and networks that headquarters exerts over its subsidiaries.

And:

Hypothesis 2-11: The relationship between size and bureaucratic formalised control will be weaker than the relationship between size and both output control and control by socialisation and networks.

Extent of multinationality

Although the extent to which an MNC is internationally oriented might be an important factor in explaining the type of control mechanisms it uses, not much attention has been paid to the subject so far. As with the other characteristics, most of the studies focus on *personal centralised control*. In this respect Garnier (1982), Goehle (1980), Hedlund (1981) and Picard (1979) hypothesised a positive relationship between the size of foreign operations and centralisation. As some of these authors argue: as the foreign involvement increases, so does a headquarters' dependence and risk, which would lead headquarters to centralise decisions. Only in Garnier's study was the relationship confirmed; the other studies found insignificant or inconclusive results.

As a counterpoint, we might offer the studies by Egelhoff (1988a) and Gencturk and Aulakh (1995). Egelhoff found a significant negative relationship between centralisation and the size of foreign operations. Gencturk and Aulakh (1995) report that an increase in international experience (measured as the number of countries in which products are sold and the time expired since the first foreign sales) is associated with higher output controls (autonomy) and lower process controls (surveillance). A negative relationship would be expected, since, as Youssef (1975) indicates, direct control becomes less appropriate as the MNCs become more experienced and committed overseas. Although MNCs might want to centralise decision-making and exert close personal surveillance in the early ages of international expansion, they will realise that this is not a feasible option when the level of multinationality increases. Therefore:

Hypothesis 2-12: There will be a negative relationship between the level of multi-nationality that an MNC portrays and the level of personal centralised control that headquarters exerts over its subsidiaries.

Unfortunately, very few studies investigated the effect of the level of multina-tionality on other control mechanisms. Concerning *standardisation*, Wolf (1994) found a strong negative relationship with all of his three measures of internationalisation. As he indicates when formulating his hypothesis, a lower level of standardisation could be expected because the varied environment that accompanies a high level of multinationality precludes standardisation. As we support this reasoning, we will put forward the following hypothesis:

Hypothesis 2-13: There will be a negative relationship between the level of multi-nationality that an MNC portrays and the level of bureaucratic formalised control that headquarters exerts over its subsidiaries.

According to Egelhoff (1988a), the size of foreign operations and the number of foreign subsidiaries are negatively related to performance control (*output control*). He explains this negative relationship by the information overload that can be created by the large number of reports that would need to be proc-essed. On the other hand, reports, budgets and overall plans can give a more aggregate and indirect level of control than the previously discussed personal centralised control and bureaucratic formalised control. As Egelhoff indi-cates, these reports can be dealt with by staff groups on a routine basis and only serious exceptions have to be dealt with by higher-level management. In our view, output would therefore probably be more suitable for highly inter-nationalised companies than the more direct forms of control: personal cen-tralised control and bureaucratic formalised control. Consequently, we will put forward the following hypothesis:

Hypothesis 2-14: There will be a positive relationship between the level of multi-nationality that an MNC portrays and the level of output control that headquarters exerts over its subsidiaries.

To our best knowledge, the level of *control by socialisation and networks* has not been systematically related to the level of multinationality before. Wolf (1994) found a positive relationship between the level of multinationality and shared values which countered his expectations, as he expected the level of shared values to be lower since a higher level of multinationality means more diversity. The positive relationship reversed to a negative one, however, when various control factors were included. Next to shared values, our control by socialisation and networks also includes other elements (formal and informal networks), however. Although we expect the level of shared values and possi-bly also informal communication to be lower at a higher extent of multinationality, we would expect the more formal networks to form an excellent control mechanism of last resort, especially since all other control mechanisms seem less applicable in this context. Therefore:

Hypothesis 2-15: There will be a positive relationship between the level of multi-nationality of an MNC and the level of control by socialisation and networks that headquarters exerts over its subsidiaries.

Complexity/heterogeneity

Organisation theorists conclude that complexity/heterogeneity should lead to decentralised decision-making and would therefore not be compatible with our *personal centralised control*. In an international setting, there is some support for this contention. Egelhoff (1988a) found that foreign product diversity (number of products or product lines) is negatively related to centralisation. The same result was found by Picard (1979), while Garnier (1982) found both a significant positive and a significant negative result in two different samples. Wolf (1994) also found a significant negative correlation between diversification and centralisation. The negative relationship between complexity and personal centralised control can be motivated in various ways. First, a high level of complexity/heterogeneity would soon lead to an information overload if headquarters managers had to take decisions centrally. Second, as Garnier (1982) indicates, in firms with many products, dependence on each product is lower. This leads to a lower risk, more decentralisation and more autonomy for subsidiaries. Therefore:

Hypothesis 2-16: There will be a negative relationship between the level of complexity/heterogeneity at headquarters level and the level of personal centralised control that headquarters exerts over its subsidiaries.

Concerning *bureaucratic formalised control*, Wolf (1994) found a negative correlation between standardisation and the level of diversification. To our best knowledge, no other studies have investigated this relationship. A negative relationship would seem highly plausible, however, since a high level of diversity would be a forceful hindrance to both standardisation and formalisation. Therefore:

Hypothesis 2-17: There will be a negative relationship between the level of complexity/heterogeneity at headquarters level and the level of bureaucratic formalised control that headquarters exerts over its subsidiaries.

As with the level of multinationality, Egelhoff (1988a) found a negative relationship between foreign product diversity and performance control (*output control*). As we indicated above, we are not completely convinced by his underlying motivations. We mentioned that domestic studies led us to expect a higher level of output control and especially control by socialisation and networks in a situation of high complexity and diversity. The latter is a very flexible type of control mechanism that would seem ideally suited for heterogeneous and complex environments. As the argument is stronger for control by socialisation and networks than for output control, we will offer a hypothesis for the former type of control mechanism only.

Hypothesis 2-18: There will be a positive relationship between the level of complexity/heterogeneity at headquarters level and the level of control by socialisation and networks that headquarters exerts over its subsidiaries.

Conclusions

This section has investigated a number of headquarters characteristics that might influence the use of various control mechanisms. Of course, these characteristics might be interrelated. Larger firms would for instance in general be expected to show a higher level of heterogeneity/complexity than smaller firms do. In addition, firms following a transnational organisational model might be more internationally oriented than firms following a global organisational model. Some of these interrelationships will be discussed in Section 3, where we will try to build configurations of international firms. In the empirical part of this book, we will also try to assess which of the characteristics discussed at both headquarters and subsidiary level have the highest explanatory power in clarifying the use of a particular control mechanism. In the next section, we will focus our attention on various characteristics at subsidiary level that might influence the use of the various control mechanisms.

Subsidiary characteristics and control mechanisms

In the previous section, we discussed control mechanisms in multinational companies on an aggregate or macro level, across the entire MNC. Although some companies might not differentiate their control mechanisms across various subsidiaries, many are likely to do so. Subsidiaries take up different positions in the company network and not all subsidiaries are equally important for headquarters. In addition, the local environment may vary across subsidiaries, as might their responsiveness to this environment. Finally, the specific country in which the subsidiary is located, or rather the cultural difference between this country and the country of headquarters, might influence the type of control mechanism that is used. In this section, we will therefore investigate the influence of various subsidiary characteristics on the type of control mechanism that is used by headquarters towards this particular subsidiary. Characteristics that will be discussed in this section are size, age, interdependence, local responsiveness, subsidiary role and function, uncertainty of the subsidiary's environment and cultural distance.

Size

As for the size of the parent company, the relationship between the size of the subsidiary and *personal centralised control*[48] has received quite a lot of attention. Unfortunately, the results are just as mixed as for headquarters level. A negative relationship between size and personal centralised control was found by Cray (1984), Hedlund (1981) and Picard (1979), while a positive relationship was found by Halsberghe and Van Den Bulcke (1982). Mixed results were reported by Gates and Egelhoff (1986) and insignificant results were found by Garnier (1982) and Goehle (1980). Wolf (1994) found a significant negative relationship only when relative size was measured.

These contradictory empirical results could be explained by the equally contradictory theoretical motivations. As Hedlund (1981:52) explains:

> From a theoretical standpoint, one can detect two conflicting forces at work. On the one hand, increased size means that the subsidiary can build up its own resources and become less dependent upon management. On the other hand, a very large subsidiary is of great importance to the whole company and may therefore require a lot of attention.

Hedlund concludes that a curvilinear relationship might be most likely. As with the size of the parent company, contradictory results might also be due to a different pattern of relationships across countries. In a domestic but cross-cultural setting, Hickson et al. (1974) found size to be positively related to autonomy for American firms, negatively for Canadian firms and unrelated to autonomy for British firms. In the comparative domestic study by Horvath et al. (1981), size was negatively related to centralisation for British firms, positively for Swedish firms, while no significant relationship was apparent for Japanese firms. In view of these very mixed findings, we conclude that in general a subsidiary's size will not be systematically related to the level of personal centralised control. As differences were found between various countries, we will, if allowed by the number of responses, investigate whether the relationship between size and centralisation is constant across the various countries included in this survey. As a general hypothesis, however, we will put forward:

> Hypothesis 2-19: There will not be a significant relationship between the size of a subsidiary and the level of personal centralised control that headquarters exerts over this subsidiary.

---

[48] Please note that we have already formulated a hypothesis about the expected higher level of expatriates for larger subsidiaries. As we will discuss in Section 2, expatriation can serve both as an alternative to centralisation and as a facilitator of informal control.

Although in general size is expected to be related to a higher level of *bureaucratic formalised control*, we should not forget that in this study we look at the extent of bureaucratic formalised control that is exercised by headquarters *towards* its subsidiaries. Although larger subsidiaries might be more formalised, this is likely to be a self-induced formalisation and not formalisation or standardisation forced upon them by headquarters. We have been able to find only two studies that relate subsidiary size to the level of bureaucratic formalised control exercised by headquarters. Of these two, Hedlund (1981) found, contrary to his expectations, a negative relationship between both the relative and absolute size of the subsidiary when measured as turnover and formality. Both relationships were only marginally significant (0.09 and 0.07). Wolf (1994) found no significant relationships for absolute size and a marginally ($p < 0.1$ and $p < 0.15$) significant, negative, relationship for relative size, measured as both employees and turnover. The theoretical arguments for the relationship between subsidiary size and bureaucratic formalised control could go both ways. On the one hand, larger subsidiaries might be in a better position to resist this rather direct form of control, but on the other hand a larger size might induce headquarters to standardise and formalise operations to a larger degree. Since, in our view, both arguments are equally plausible, we will not offer a specific hypothesis on this relationship.

For the relationship between subsidiary size and *output* control the number of empirical investigations is again limited. Egelhoff (1988a) found a significant positive relationship for manufacturing, while for marketing and finance the relationships were not significant. Wolf (1994) found a generally positive relationship for absolute size only. Further, Wolf found a significant positive relationship between both relative and absolute size and shared values. Due to a complete lack of previous research, he did not offer a hypothesis about this. In his discussion of the findings he refers to a control gap that could be filled by international travelling, a control mechanism that is not included in this survey. In our view, a control gap could indeed be a problem in large subsidiaries. Precisely because of their size, large subsidiaries are very important for headquarters. Headquarters would therefore be likely to prefer to have some level of control over these subsidiaries. As the discussion above showed, however, centralisation and formalisation are probably less feasible for large subsidiaries. Output control could fill part of this gap, but we consider it more likely that the even more flexible and less oppressive control by socialisation and networks would be used to fill this control gap. We would therefore expect that headquarters would exert a relatively large extent of control by socialisation and networks towards larger subsidiaries. Therefore:

Hypothesis 2-20: There will be a positive relationship between the size of the subsidiary and the level of control by socialisation and networks that headquarters exerts over this particular subsidiary.

Age

The age of the subsidiary has also received a relatively large amount of attention by MNC researchers, especially where the relationship with *personal
centralised control*[49] is concerned. Fortunately, the empirical results are
somewhat more homogeneous than the ones we discussed in the previous
section. Although Garnier (1982), Goehle (1980) and Picard (1979) all found
insignificant results and Gates and Egelhoff (1986) found a significant negative relationship for the finance area only, Hoffman (1988), Youssef (1975),
Van den Bulcke and Halsberghe (1984) and Wolf (1994) all found support for
a negative relationship. This negative relationship seems very logical. Headquarters will tend to supervise young subsidiaries more closely and centralise
decision-making because the new investment brings specific uncertainties,
which have already been eliminated in older subsidiaries. Also younger subsidiaries probably do not have the same amount of qualified manpower that
older subsidiaries have, so are less likely to be left taking decisions on their
own. Therefore:

Hypothesis 2-21: The age of the subsidiary is negatively related to the amount of
personal centralised control that headquarters exerts over this particular subsidiary.

Concerning the other control mechanisms, the state of empirical research is
nearly non-existent. Although Wolf (1994) investigated the relationship between age and standardisation and shared values, no significant results were
found. Egelhoff (1988a) found a negative relationship between age and output
control only in the finance area. We believe that the "control mechanism" that
is most affected by the age of the subsidiary is given with the level of expatriation, as was discussed in the first chapter. However, the fact that two *personal* types of control are expected to be negatively related to subsidiary age
would lead us to expect that it might be the more *impersonal* types of control
(bureaucratic formalised control and output control) that are more prominent
in older subsidiaries. Therefore:

Hypothesis 2-22: The age of the subsidiary is positively related to the amount of
bureaucratic formalised control and output control that headquarters exerts over
this subsidiary.

---

[49] Please note that we have already formulated a hypothesis about the expected higher level of
expatriates for younger subsidiaries. As we will show in Section 2, expatriation can serve both
as an alternative to centralisation and as a facilitator of informal control.

Interdependence

In contrast to size and age, interdependence is an ambiguous concept. Before we discuss any possible impacts of this factor on the application of various control mechanisms, we will therefore first explore the exact meaning of this concept. In this study, we would like to distinguish three different levels of interdependence. First, *in*dependence, that is, the subsidiary is not or is hardly dependent on headquarters and is operating very much as a stand-alone company. This is the way in which subsidiaries in the so-called multidomestic MNCs would function. Second, *de*pendence, that is, the subsidiary is dependent on headquarters, which is claimed to be typical of subsidiaries in global MNCs. Finally, actual *inter*dependence: the subsidiary, headquarters and other subsidiaries all form part of an interdependent network, that is, they are in a sense all dependent on each other. This then is assumed a typical description of the function of subsidiaries in a transnational company. For the sake of clarity, these three different levels of interdependence are visualised in Figure 2-1. Interdependence will be used as a general term to indicate both *de*pendence and *inter*dependence. *Inter*dependence will be used when we refer to the interdependent network idea, in which subsidiaries are also dependent on each other.

Figure 2-1 Independence, dependence and interdependence in MNCs

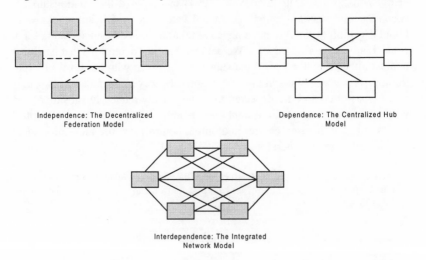

Independence: The Decentralized
Federation Model

Dependence: The Centralized Hub
Model

Interdependence: The Integrated
Network Model

In addition, we can also differentiate between input and output interdependence. Subsidiaries that depend on either headquarters or other subsidiaries for their inputs would be input-dependent. Subsidiaries that sell a large portion of their output to either headquarters or other subsidiaries would be output-dependent. Unfortunately, most authors do not distinguish between these different types of dependence and simply talk about increasing interdependence. Therefore, we will first discuss the influence of an increasing level of interdependence in general and then move to a more differentiated approach in which we will discuss both *de*pendence and *inter*dependence and input and output dependence separately.

That an increasing interdependence should lead to a higher total level of control is assumed, explicitly or implicitly, in many publications. Andersson and Forsgren (1995a/b) for instance assume the extent of subsidiary em-beddedness to be positively related to the amount of control exercised by headquarters. The study by Martinez and Jarillo characterises subsidiaries concerning their interdependence in relation to headquarters and other sub-sidiaries and found that the higher the amount of interdependence, the higher the total amount of control exercised. In a discussion about different control mechanisms in relation to interdependence, Hennart (1991) argues that in-creasing interdependence doesn't have to lead to increased centralisation as there are other ways to control subsidiaries, such as socialisation and output control. What he does argue implicitly is that increased interdependence should lead to increased control levels in one form or another. Many of the "centralisation" studies that will be discussed below also adhere to the posi-tive relationship between interdependence and control levels, as they (implic-itly) regard centralisation as the only control mechanism available. That an increasing level of interdependence should lead to higher control levels is easily comprehended. High levels of interdependence increase both the im-portance of subsidiaries for headquarters and the level of risk involved. Con-sequently, a higher level of control will be induced. Therefore:

Hypothesis 2-23: There will be a positive relation between the extent of interde-pendence of a subsidiary with the MNC as a whole and the total amount of control that is exercised by headquarters over that particular subsidiary.

Not all control mechanisms, however, will be equally affected by an increas-ing interdependence. Various authors have focused on the effect of interde-pendence on the level of centralisation (an element of our personal centralised control) and have generally found this relationship to be positive. Picard (1979) forms an exception to this case as he found a significant negative rela-tionship between interdependence and centralisation. In Hedlund's (1981) study, the two firms with the lowest level of interdependence also showed the lowest level of centralisation. Garnier (1982) found both affiliate sales to headquarters and affiliate purchases from headquarters to be strongly related to centralisation. In fact, these two variables were the only ones that showed consistent and very strong relationships with centralisation across the three samples discussed in his study. Welge (1982) also found the dependence of a subsidiary on the parent company to be the most important factor in deter-mining the level of centralisation. In their conceptual article, Baliga and Jae-ger (1984) hypothesise a positive relationship between interdependence and the level of centralisation. Gates and Egelhoff (1986) found mixed results: the relationship was negative for financial decisions and positive, but not signifi-cant, for marketing and production decisions. The negative relationship found by Picard (1979) is explained by Welge (1987b) by the fact that Picard fo-cused on marketing decisions. According to Welge (1987b:39): "the more a subsidiary delivers to sister units and/or to the parent company, the less im-portant is the marketing function for this subsidiary and the more decision-making authority can be granted and is granted in reality". Martinez and Ricks (1989) found a strong positive relationship between subsidiary depend-ence on headquarters and headquarters influence over subsidiaries. In Fors-gren and Pahlberg's (1992) study of the relationship between division man-agement and subsidiaries in Sweden, resource *in*dependence is related to autonomy. Finally, Quester and Conduit (1996) argue that the greater depend-ence of a parent company on its foreign operations, the greater the risk to the parent company and the stronger the tendency to centralise all decisions. In view of the observations above, we formulate the following hypothesis:

Hypothesis 2-24: There will be a positive relation between the extent of interde-pendence of a subsidiary with the MNC as a whole and the amount of personal centralised control that is exercised by headquarters over that particular subsidiary.

Fewer empirical data are available on the relationship between interdepen-dence and bureaucratic formalised control. Consistent with his hypothesis, Hedlund (1981) found a positive correlation between cross-shipments of goods and the level of formality of headquarters-subsidiary relationships. Mascarenhas (1984) found a positive, though not significant, correlation be-tween manufacturing interdependence and impersonal control mechanisms (standard operating procedures, reports, plans and schedules). Finally, Macharzina (1993) found a strong positive relationship between interdepend-ence and standardisation of both policies and processes in all functional de-partments of 69 German MNCs. Although the empirical evidence for a posi-tive relationship is not overwhelming, no contradicting results were found, so we will put forward the following hypothesis:

Hypothesis 2-25: There will be a positive relation between the extent of interde-pendence of a subsidiary with the MNC as a whole and the amount of bureaucratic formalised control that is exercised by headquarters towards that particular sub-sidiary.

In Mascarenhas's (1984) study, impersonal control mechanisms also included reports, plans and schedules, so that the positive relationship could be applied to our output control as well. Unfortunately, the only other study we have been able to find that reports on this relationship is Egelhoff (1988a). Egelhoff used nine measures of dependence to measure the influence on the level of output control for marketing, manufacturing and finance. Only one of the 27 correlations was significantly positive. In view of these inconclusive data, we will assume that output is not systematically influenced by dependence levels and that other control mechanisms are responsible for the higher overall control level with increasing dependence.

Concerning our final control mechanism: control by socialisation and networks, only three previous studies are available and their results are not very consistent. In their conceptual study, Baliga and Jaeger (1984) prescribe an extensive use of cultural control in situations characterised by a high amount of interdependence. In the study already referred to above, Mascarenhas (1984) found a significant positive relationship between personal communication and system-sensitivity on the one hand and interdependence on the other hand. System-sensitivity is defined as "the ability of subunit members to foresee the impact of other subunits of actions taken in one subunit and thereby to undertake appropriate behavior that avoids suboptimalization. This system-sensitivity is acquired by a process of socialisation as a function of the recruitment process, training programmes and international transfers" (Mascarenhas, 1984:95). Both personal communication and system-sensitivity would fit into our control by socialisation and networks category. On the other hand, Wolf (1994) found a significant negative relationship between interdependence and shared values, the socialisation element of our control by socialisation and networks. In view of the limited and contradictory evidence, we will not offer a hypothesis on this control mechanism, assuming that the other control mechanisms are responsible for the higher overall control level with increasing interdependence.

The studies above all referred to either interdependence in general or to *de*pendence from headquarters. We might expect that the management of *inter*dependence forms an additional challenge. Specifically, we would expect that where headquarters-dependent subsidiaries can more easily be managed by personal centralised control and bureaucratic formalised control, subsidiary-dependent subsidiaries would rather be managed by the more informal control by socialisation and networks. As subsidiary-dependent subsidiaries are less directly dependent on headquarters, they are likely to resist the more direct control mechanisms, leaving the more informal and flexible control by socialisation and networks as an alternative. Some support for this argument is found in the studies by Gupta and Govindarajan (1994) and Wolf (1994). Gupta and Govindarajan distinguish four different types of subsidiaries, with different levels of lateral interdependence with peer subsidiaries. In general, these subsidiaries' scores on lateral integration (our formal networks), corporate-subsidiary and inter-subsidiary communication and socialisation were positively related to their level of subsidiary dependence. Wolf (1994) found the level of shared values to be higher when sister subsidiaries were the subsidiary's main partners than when headquarters was the subsidiary's main partner. Therefore:

> Hypothesis 2-26: Subsidiary-dependent subsidiaries will experience a higher level of control by socialisation and networks than headquarters-dependent subsidiaries.

Finally, we promised to make a distinction between input- and output-dependent subsidiaries. We would expect output-dependent subsidiaries to experience a higher total level of control. Subsidiaries that sell a relatively high proportion of their output to other subsidiaries or headquarters are important nodes in the company network. If this type of subsidiary did not function according to plan, this would have a far greater impact on the overall company performance than when this happens for a subsidiary that just purchases part of their input from other subsidiaries or headquarters. Headquarters and subsidiaries could miss one of their many customers, but would be in serious trouble if they were confronted with a failing supplier, since companies are likely to have more customers than suppliers. Overall, an output-dependent subsidiary would therefore be more important strategically and would create higher risks that have to be controlled. Therefore:

> Hypothesis 2-27: Output-dependent subsidiaries will experience a higher level of total control than input-dependent subsidiaries.

Local responsiveness
Local responsiveness is a very important concept in the studies on MNCs that we described in the first chapter. This concept can be measured at both headquarters level and at the level of the individual subsidiary. At headquarters level responsiveness is incorporated into the strategy concept, where we assume companies that follow either a multidomestic or a transnational strategy to be more locally responsive than companies that follow a global strategy. In addition, subsidiaries might differ in the extent to which they (are allowed to) respond to the local market. Not every subsidiary of a multidomestic company will be equally locally responsive, for instance. We will therefore also discuss the possible influence of a subsidiary's extent of local responsiveness on the type of control mechanism that is used by headquarters towards this particular subsidiary. Unfortunately, there is only one previous study (Martinez and Jarillo, 1991) that deals explicitly with the concept of local responsiveness in relation to different control mechanisms.

Martinez and Jarillo (1991) studied the relationship between various subsidiary roles (see also the next section) and the amount of control exercised by headquarters towards a particular subsidiary. Concerning the type of control, they only distinguished between formal and subtle control mechanisms. The formal control mechanisms distinguished by Martinez and Jarillo include all our control mechanisms except for control by socialisation and networks, which is represented by Martinez and Jarillo's subtle mechanisms. As Martinez and Jarillo presented their results only for a clustering of subsidiaries on both interdependence and local responsiveness, we cannot deduce specific information on the effect of local responsiveness on the various control mechanisms. What can be said, however, is that local responsiveness seems to be negatively related to the total level of control exercised by headquarters. This is of course very logical, as in order to be locally responsive, a subsidiary should not be strictly controlled by headquarters. We will therefore put forward the following hypothesis:

Hypothesis 2-28: There will be a negative relation between the extent of local responsiveness of a subsidiary and the total amount of control that is exercised by headquarters over that particular subsidiary.

From Martinez and Jarillo's data, we can deduce that local responsiveness is negatively related to both the formal and the subtle control mechanisms. We would expect, however, that local responsiveness would most of all influence the extent of personal centralised control and bureaucratic formalised control that is exercised. These two control mechanisms are both direct types of control, which would involve more interference in the subsidiary's affairs and would be resisted by the relatively powerful locally responsive subsidiaries. Output control and control by socialisation and networks are more indirect and less interfering ways of control and are therefore assumed not to be negatively related to local responsiveness. In other words, the lower level of control exercised towards locally responsive subsidiaries will mainly be due to a lower level of personal centralised control and bureaucratic formalised control. Therefore:

Hypothesis 2-29: There will be a negative relationship between the extent of local responsiveness of a subsidiary and the amount of personal centralised control that is exercised by headquarters over that particular subsidiary.

And:

Hypothesis 2-30: There will be a negative relationship between the extent of local responsiveness of a subsidiary and the amount of bureaucratic formalised control exercised by headquarters over that particular subsidiary.

Subsidiary roles

It was only after the empirical part of this study had been concluded that we realised - partly by literature that became available only then - the possible importance of the subsidiary's strategic role for the type of control that is used by headquarters towards subsidiaries. Researchers in the subsidiary role research stream (see Footnote 45) have been very active recently (see Birkinshaw and Morrison, 1995 for an overview). Various writers (e.g. Birkinshaw, 1997; Birkinshaw, Jonsson and Hood, 1995; Birkinshaw and Morrison, 1995; Delaney, 1996; Doz and Prahalad, 1986; 1991; Ghoshal and Bartlett, 1990; Ghoshal and Nohria, 1989; Forsgren, 1990; Hedlund, 1986; Jarillo and Martinez, 1990; Martinez and Jarillo, 1991; Nohria and Ghoshal, 1994; Prahalad and Doz, 1987; Taggart, 1996a/c; Theuerkauf, 1991)[50] clearly suggest that many MNCs - and especially MNCs that are long established internationally - assign different strategic roles to different subsidiaries. As Blackwell et al. (1991), Edwards, Ferner and Sisson (1996) and Gupta and Govindarajan (1991) argue, this might have a considerable influence on the type of control mechanisms that are used with regard to various subsidiaries. Research by Govindarajan and Gupta (Govindarajan and Gupta, 1985; Gupta and Govindarajan, 1984) has indicated that in the case of diversified multi-business firms, aligning control systems to the differentiated strategic roles of business units had significant implications for business unit performance.

Unfortunately, we did not include any specific questions relating to the subsidiary's strategic role in the empirical part of our study. However, we can use the level of interdependence and local responsiveness to characterise subsidiary roles, as was done by Martinez and Jarillo (1991). Martinez and Jarillo characterise subsidiaries with regard to their level of integration with HQ and other subsidiaries and their level of responsiveness to the local environment, following the framework described in their earlier publication (Jarillo and Martinez, 1990). Control mechanisms were divided into groups: formal and informal/subtle control mechanisms. Formal control mechanisms comprise three of our four control mechanisms: personal centralised control, bureaucratic formalised control and output control, while informal/subtle control mechanisms embody the three elements of our control by socialisation and networks. Martinez and Jarillo formulated several hypotheses concerning the total amount of control exercised towards subsidiaries. This total level of control is hypothesised to be highest for high interdependence/high responsiveness subsidiaries (called *active subsidiaries*), intermediate for high interdependence/low responsiveness subsidiaries (called *receptive subsidiaries*) and lowest for subsidiaries having the reverse score (called *autonomous sub-*

---

[50] It must be said, though, that more than a decade earlier Peccei and Warner (1976) had already come to this conclusion.

sidiaries). Their empirical data - obtained from 50 subsidiaries of European, American and Japanese MNCs in Spain - indeed showed that autonomous subsidiaries experienced the lowest level of control. Receptive subsidiaries, however, experienced a higher level of total control than active subsidiaries. However, since the active subsidiaries in their sample scored medium on both interdependence and local responsiveness as opposed to the predicted high level for both characteristics, the hypothesis regarding the difference between active and receptive subsidiaries could not be fully tested. They suggest that active and receptive subsidiaries might actually require the same level of co-ordination, since coordination seems to be dependent mainly on an increasing level of integration.

Two other publications (Ghoshal and Bartlett, 1988 and Ghoshal and Nohria, 1989) describe subsidiary classifications that can be reinterpreted in terms of Martinez and Jarillo's classification above (see Figure 2-2 for an overview of the different types of subsidiaries). In a study about creation, adoption and diffusion of innovation by subsidiaries of MNCs, Ghoshal and Bartlett (1988) describe three different types of subsidiaries. Some subsidiaries created innovations but did not adopt or diffuse any, others created and adopted innovations, but did not diffuse them, while the third group performed all three functions. In our view, the first group - that only creates innovations - would be comparable to the autonomous subsidiary as described above, since it is very much a stand-alone company. The third group of subsidiaries - performing the creation, adoption and diffusion tasks - clearly resembles the active type, which is highly integrated but also performs key tasks on its own. The second group of subsidiaries would conform to the receptive subsidiary if it were not for the fact that they not only adopt, but also create innovations, although their level of innovation creation is lower than for the two other groups of subsidiaries. Concerning control mechanisms,[51] the largest amount of autonomy is found in the "autonomous" group, while the lowest amount of autonomy is found in the "receptive" group. Normative integration is by far the highest in the "active" group and very low in the "autonomous" group. Headquarters-subsidiary communication is lowest in the "autonomous" group and higher in both the "receptive" and "active" group. Overall, the lowest amount of control can be found in "autonomous" subsidiaries, while the level of control in "active" subsidiaries is only slightly higher than in "receptive" subsidiaries.

---

[51] Please note that Ghoshal and Bartlett do not refer to control mechanisms, but to organisational attributes and include slack resources and intra-subsidiary communication in the picture.

Figure 2-2 Comparison of subsidiary types from three different studies: Martinez and Jarillo, Ghoshal and Bartlett, Ghoshal and Nohria

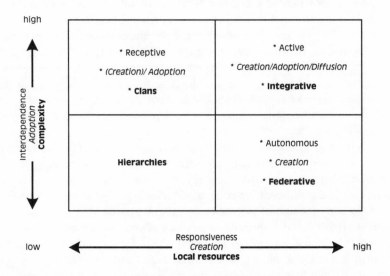

The second study, by Ghoshal and Nohria (1989), distinguishes four types of subsidiaries based on the level of environmental complexity and local resources. Higher environmental complexity is predicted to lead to higher interdependence and is therefore easily reinterpreted as interdependence in the terms of Martinez and Jarillo. The second variable, local resources, can be expected to be correlated to local responsiveness as locally responsive subsidiaries are likely to have a higher level of local resources. Ghoshal and Nohria distinguish hierarchies (no comparable term in Martinez and Jarillo's study) with low complexity and low local resources and integrative ("active") subsidiaries with a reverse pattern. Clans ("receptive subsidiaries") have a high level of environmental complexity but a low level of resources, while the reverse pattern is taken by federative ("autonomous") subsidiaries. The highest total level of control is found in integrative subsidiaries and both hierarchies and federative subsidiaries experience a very low level of control. However, as the integrative subsidiaries in Ghoshal and Nohria's sample score far higher than any of the other subsidiaries on both the level of environmental complexity and local resources, they are not completely comparable to Martinez and Jarillo's active type, which scored only medium on the comparable dimensions of interdependence and responsiveness. Concerning the *types* of control mechanisms, integrative subsidiaries scored higher on both socialisation and formalisation and lower on centralisation.

What can we deduce from these three studies? First of all, all studies clearly predict the lowest level of control for the "autonomous" type of subsidiary, characterised by a low level of interdependence and a high level of local responsiveness. Therefore:

Hypothesis 2-31: Subsidiaries that are characterised by a low level of interdependence and a high level of local responsiveness ("autonomous" subsidiaries) will experience a lower level of total control than both "receptive" (high interdependence/low local responsiveness) and "active" (high interdependence/high local responsiveness) subsidiaries.

It is not clear, however, how the control levels of "active" and "receptive" types of subsidiary should be compared. In Ghoshal and Bartlett's study both had approximately the same level of total control. In Martinez and Jarillo's study, the active type had a lower level of control than the receptive type, while in Ghoshal and Nohria's study the reverse was true. However, as we have seen above, Martinez and Jarillo's type was "under-active", while Ghoshal and Nohria's type was "over-active". We would therefore expect that:

Hypothesis 2-32: If "active" subsidiaries have a level of interdependence comparable to that of "receptive" subsidiaries, and a level of local responsiveness comparable to that of "autonomous" subsidiaries, their total level of control will equal the level of control for receptive subsidiaries.[52]

No far-reaching conclusions can be drawn concerning the specific *types* of control mechanisms that are used in the active and receptive subsidiaries respectively. The Ghoshal and Bartlett study, however, found autonomy lowest in receptive subsidiaries and the Ghoshal and Nohria study found centralisation higher in receptive subsidiaries than in active subsidiaries. A high level of personal centralised control in receptive subsidiaries would be logical, since these subsidiaries are usually simple executors of decisions of headquarters. We will therefore put forward the following tentative hypothesis:

Hypothesis 2-33: "Receptive" subsidiaries will experience a higher level of personal centralised control than "active" subsidiaries.

---

[52] Please note that this hypothesis could not have been deduced from the previous two sections separately since interdependence is hypothesised to be positively related to total control levels, while local responsiveness is hypothesised to be negatively related to total control levels. Active subsidiaries will require a relatively high level of control because of the added complexity of *combining* interdependence and local responsiveness.

As only one study is available on the level of bureaucratic formalised control in different types of subsidiaries and there are no studies at all on output control, no hypotheses will be offered on these control mechanisms. Concerning control by socialisation and networks, however, both the Ghoshal and Bartlett and the Ghoshal and Nohria study suggest that elements of this type of control would be used most in active subsidiaries. A high level of control by socialisation and networks could compensate for a lower level of personal centralised control and would be more appropriate for active subsidiaries that have to grapple with the added complexity of both high interdependence and high local responsiveness. Therefore:

Hypothesis 2-34: "Active" subsidiaries will experience a higher level of control by socialisation and networks than "receptive" subsidiaries.

In addition to the level of interdependence and responsiveness, in the empirical part of this study subsidiaries are also typified with regard to their function (assembly, production, sales, service, country headquarters and R&D). We will not offer a detailed discussion of the possible impact of the function of a subsidiary on the level or type of control exercised by headquarters, especially since no previous studies have investigated this relationship. What we would expect, however, is that in sales subsidiaries the dominant control mechanism would be output control and that the total level of control exercised towards these subsidiaries would be rather low. These subsidiaries are usually not of strategic importance for headquarters and do not constitute a large risk. Output control signalling exceptions (lower than average sales, for instance) would be sufficient. Therefore:

Hypothesis 2-35: In comparison with to subsidiaries with other functions, sales subsidiaries will experience a rather low level of total control. The dominant control mechanism that is used by headquarters in respect of these subsidiaries will be output control.

Further, traditional organisation theory usually indicates that R&D departments are characterised by high levels of autonomy and low levels of formalisation. Activities are controlled by more informal and subtle control mechanisms such as socialisation and informal communication. Creativity simply cannot flourish in an environment that is strictly regulated, and leaves researchers with a low level of autonomy. In an international context, the study by Ghoshal and Bartlett shows that local autonomy, normative integration and intensity of headquarters-subsidiary communication are all significantly positively related to the creation of innovations by subsidiaries. Therefore:

Hypothesis 2-36: Compared to subsidiaries with other functions, subsidiaries with an R&D function will have lower levels of personal centralised control and bureaucratic formalised control and higher levels of control by socialisation and networks.

Uncertainty

The level of uncertainty or change in a subsidiary's environment is a characteristic that has often been related to a more or less extensive use of a particular control mechanism. As has been the case for many characteristics, most researchers have focused on the relationship between uncertainty and centralisation of decision-making only. The results were not always consistent. Hedlund (1981) and Gates and Egelhoff (1986) predicted a negative relationship between competitive climate change and centralisation of decision-making. Hedlund's results were in the expected direction but not significant, while Gates and Egelhoff found positive relationships between change and centralisation of decision-making in the field of marketing, manufacturing and finance, although only the first relationship was significant. Baliga and Jaeger (1984), Negandhi (1987) and Quester and Conduit (1996) have argued that turbulent, dynamic and unpredictable environments would lead to decentralisation of decision-making, but did not offer empirical testing. Ghoshal and Nohria (1989) hypothesise a negative correlation between centralisation and environmental complexity, but the way in which they describe and operationalise environmental complexity (local competition and technological dynamism) conforms more to what we would call uncertainty/dynamism. This negative relationship was confirmed at a very high level of significance (p < 0.001), although the relationship was stronger for technological dynamism than for competition. In view of the observations above, we will put forward the following hypothesis:

> Hypothesis 2-37: There will be a negative relation between the level of uncertainty in the subsidiary's environment and the level of personal centralised control that headquarters exerts over the subsidiary.

Ghoshal and Nohria also hypothesised and found a positive relationship between environmental complexity and formalisation. This runs counter to the finding of organisational theorists as described in the first section. We should not forget, however, that in these studies the focus is on formalisation *within* an organisation, while our focus is on the level of formalisation that headquarters exerts towards its subsidiaries. On the other hand, in our opinion, it does not seem very likely that headquarters would impose formalisation and standardisation of decision-making in a given subsidiary if this subsidiary's environment is very volatile. Therefore:

Hypothesis 2-38: There will be a negative relationship between the level of uncertainty in the subsidiary's environment and the level of bureaucratic formalised control that headquarters exerts over this subsidiary.

Again no previous studies are available for the relationship between uncertainty and output control and although output control might be an alternative to personal centralised control and bureaucratic formalised control, we do not think it would be the best alternative. In our view, the best alternative would be control by socialisation and networks as this is the most flexible type of control, which would be very appropriate in changing environments, as is also argued by organisation theorists. Ghoshal and Nohria (1989) also hypothesised and found a positive relationship between environmental complexity and socialisation (one element of our control by socialisation and networks), although the relationship was much stronger for technological dynamism than for competition. Therefore:

Hypothesis 2-39: There will be a positive relationship between the level of uncertainty in the subsidiary's environment and the level of control by socialisation and networks that headquarters exerts over this subsidiary.

Cultural distance[53]

Although the amount of cultural distance between headquarters and the subsidiary in question might be an important factor influencing the type of control mechanism that is used, very little previous research is available in this field. Baliga and Jaeger's (1984) study, which was already referred to in previous sections, offers a prescriptive scheme of the type of control and delegation that would be appropriate to subsidiaries in various circumstances. In addition to interdependence and environmental uncertainty, cultural proximity was also included as a subsidiary characteristic that should influence the type of control mechanism used. In situations of rather low interdependence, a low cultural proximity (a high level of cultural distance) should lead to a preference for a bureaucratic control system (comprising both our bureaucratic formalised control and output control) and a high cultural proximity (a low level of cultural distance) to cultural control (the shared values element of our control by socialisation and networks). Cultural control would require more time and resources and would be more difficult to establish when cultural difference between headquarters and subsidiaries is high. A comparable rec-

---

[53] We did not include geographical distance as a subsidiary characteristic. Most of the concept of geographical distance is assumed to be captured in cultural distance and the nationality of headquarters and subsidiary. This is confirmed by Wolf's (1994) findings. When he recalculated the correlation coefficients between cultural distance and the various control mechanisms controlling for geographical distance, the resulting coefficients were nearly identical to the original ones.

ommendation is given by a second prescriptive study. Rosenzweig and Singh (1991) hypothesise a positive relationship between cultural distance and the reliance on formal mechanisms of control and argues for a kind of cultural control with cultural proximity. If headquarters and subsidiaries are from similar cultures, formal control might not be necessary as a high degree of shared values fills the gap. Rosenzweig and Singh do not define what they mean by formal control, but we assume that it comprises both our bureaucratic formalised control and our output control category. Only two empirical studies were available in this respect. Garnier (1982) found a positive, but not significant, correlation between "perception of differences in executives' attitudes and values" and the level of centralised decision-making. This finding is supported by Wolf (1994), although again the results were not statistically significant. If we interpret "Berichtswesen" as output control, Wolf (1994) also gives some support for a negative correlation between cultural distance and output control. No significant relationships were found between standardisation and cultural distance and shared values and cultural distance in this study.

Both prescriptive studies offered a very limited motivation for their arguments. Although we would agree that cultural difference probably makes the achievement of shared values more difficult, this would not necessary imply a reliance on bureaucratic formalised control or output control. The alternative of centralised decision-making is not included in the Rosenzweig and Singh study and is not related to cultural difference in Baliga and Jaeger's study. Further, the tentative empirical results by Garnier and Wolf do not support the theoretical prescriptions. Regardless of what was discussed above, however, we would expect that the most important way in which headquarters tries to control subsidiaries in a culturally distant subsidiary is by employing home-country nationals in top positions. A hypothesis on this relationship was already offered in Chapter 1. Related to this, however, we would conclude that since there is a positive relationship between cultural distance and direct personal control by expatriates, MNCs seem to prefer a direct personal type of control in culturally distant countries. This conclusion is also supported by the empirical results of Garnier and Wolf. This would then mean that impersonal types of control will probably be less prominent in subsidiaries located in culturally distant countries. Therefore:

Hypothesis 2-40: There will be a negative relationship between the level of cultural distance between headquarters and a given subsidiary and the level of both bureaucratic formalised control and output control that will be exerted by headquarters over this subsidiary.

Conclusion

This section has investigated a number of subsidiary characteristics that might influence the use of various control mechanisms. These characteristics might of course be interrelated. Larger firms would for instance in general be expected to be older and show a higher level of local responsiveness. Output-dependent subsidiaries would also be likely to be larger and older than input-dependent subsidiaries. Some of these interrelationships will be discussed in Section 3, where we will try to build configurations of international firms. In the empirical part of this book, we will also try to assess which of the characteristics discussed at both headquarters and subsidiary level have the highest explanatory power in clarifying the use of a particular control mechanism.

Conclusions

The aim of Section 1 has been to discuss the use of different control mechanisms in MNCs. To do this, we first reviewed what "traditional" organisation theory had to say about the use of control mechanisms in different circumstances. A first conclusion that could be drawn from this review was that multinational companies, in view of their characteristics (large size, uncertain and complex environment and high interdependence), would probably be prone to use more output control and especially control by networks and socialisation and less personal centralised control and formalised bureaucratic control. In two subsections, we subsequently discussed a number of headquarters and subsidiary characteristics that could explain differences in both the level and the composition of control mechanisms used in various circumstances. Some of these headquarters and subsidiary characteristics will be included in the configurations that will be discussed in Section 3. In the next section, however, we will first add the third building block of this book into the picture, and discuss the role that international transfers can play as a control mechanism in MNCs.

2. INTERNATIONAL TRANSFERS AS A CONTROL MECHANISM IN MNCS

Introduction

In the previous section, we combined two of the theoretical building blocks of this thesis: control mechanisms and multinational companies. In this section, we will add the third building block: international transfers. We will show how international transfers can be used as a control mechanism in multinational companies. First, we will try to delineate what we mean by socialisation and informal network communication. Second, we will discuss the influence of international transfers on two elements of our control by socialisation and networks: socialisation and informal networks. International transfers, however, are not the only means to facilitate socialisation and informal networks. We will therefore discuss alternative ways to achieve the same goal. In doing so, we will focus on management development and formal networks. In addition to influencing control by socialisation and informal networks,[54] international transfers can also be seen as a form of personal centralised control. The role of international transfers in this type of control will be briefly discussed. A final section offers a number of hypotheses on the role of international transfers and its alternatives in achieving the various types of control.

Socialisation and informal networks defined

Socialisation

Socialisation is defined as the process by which a new member learns the value system, the norms, and the required behaviour patterns of the society, organisation or group that he or she is entering. Socialisation builds organisational commitment, which is defined by Buchanan (1974) as: "a partisan, affective attachment to the goals and values of an organisation, to one's role in relation to goals and values, and to the organisation for its own sake, apart from its purely instrumental worth" (Buchanan, 1974:533). Buchanan views commitment as consisting of the following three components: "identification - adoption as one's own the goals and values of the organisation, involvement - psychological immersion or absorption in the activities of one's work role, and loyalty - a feeling of affection for and attachment to the organisation' (ibid.).

Van Maanen and Schein (1979) (see also Van Maanen, 1985) identify six dimensions that can be used to characterise socialisation processes. Each of these dimensions is represented with its counterpart. Together they form a continuum on which there is a considerable range between the two poles. The six dimensions are:

- *Collective vs individual socialisation processes.* Management training courses for a specific group of managers are an example of the first; apprenticeship programmes of the second.
- *Formal vs informal socialisation processes.* In a formal socialisation

---

[54] In this section, we will discuss the influence of international transfers on control by socialisation and *informal* networks. The *formal* network aspect of control by socialisation and networks is not likely to be directly influenced by international transfers. Formal networks can, however, be an alternative to international transfers in realising control by socialisation and in particular control by informal networks.

process, the individual(s) to be socialised is/are separated from other organisational members and put through an explicitly defined programme. Informal socialisation occurs when the newcomer is put among more experienced organisational members and is socialised through trial and error.

- *Sequential vs random socialisation processes.* Sequential socialisation processes are characterised by a sequence of specified steps leading to a specified result. In random processes the result is more or less known; the way to get there is unknown, ambiguous or constantly changing.
- *Fixed vs variable socialisation processes.* Fixed processes have a timetable, which gives the newcomer a clear idea when he or she can expect a new career step, while in variable processes people just get a promotion when they are "ready".
- *Serial vs disjunctive socialisation processes.* In a serial process newcomers can look to experienced colleagues as a role model. In disjunctive processes, there are no such role models (for instance the first women to enter managerial ranks).
- *Investiture vs divestiture socialisation processes.* Investiture processes build on the characteristics that the newcomers bring with them. Divestiture processes try to change newcomers and mould them into an organisational model.

These dimensions mainly focus on the socialisation of newcomers into an existing organisational culture. Of course, this is also relevant for international managers being transferred to other locations. Expatriates (parent-country nationals) are socialised into the parent company culture before they are sent to different subsidiaries. Although this can be and often is called control by socialisation, this kind of control is not the focus of this thesis. We will argue that this kind of control can even be equated with or at least seen as a direct substitute for personal centralised control. Control by socialisation in the context of this book has a slightly different meaning. The focus is not so much on the socialisation of individual expatriates, but more on the role these expatriates have in ensuring a common corporate culture across the different subsidiaries. In order to be able to transfer corporate culture, however, expatriates have be socialised into this culture as well. Even if subsidiary managers were completely socialised into the corporate culture, however, they would still regularly need information from either headquarters or other subsidiaries to take their decisions. In addition, this is where informal information networks, another element of our control by socialisation and networks, come in. We will discuss how international transfers can facilitate these informal networks. First, however, we will discuss the use and functioning of these networks in more detail.

Informal network communication

Since Mintzberg's (1973) now almost classic work, it is generally accepted that management is a job characterised by brevity, variety and fragmentation, with only occasional attention to the strategic aspects of a manager's task. Communication is of utmost importance in performing the manager's job. An overwhelming amount of this communication is conducted orally (in Mintzberg's study managers spend 80% of their time communicating orally; mail and reports were given only cursory attention). The importance of oral communication as a source of information for managers has been confirmed in a study on the information sources utilised by headquarters executives in multinational companies (Keegan, 1974). Human sources accounted for 67% of the information received. Documentary sources such as reports and letters were clearly much less important. Keegan also cites some other studies in other contexts reaching the same results.

But then, if we accept that oral communication is of prime importance, we would expect that with (recent) developments in the field of teleconferencing and video-conferencing, added to the already existing simple telephone conversations, face-to-face contacts and therefore international transfers and travelling would become less important. De Meyer (1991) strongly suggests, however, that this is not the case. He refers to studies in the 1960s and 1970s that showed that telephone communication patterns, which are oral but not face-to-face, are strongly related to the pattern of face-to-face communication. "Other than calls for simple exchanges of data, one only calls the people one knows well and sees fairly often. Thus the telephone complements but does not substitute for face-to-face communication." His own research in fourteen multinational companies shows that the same goes for recent innovations such as video- and teleconferencing. All managers who had experience with these systems admitted that they could make a valuable contribution to effective communication, but only after a certain level of confidence between the partners had been established. A preceding "handshake across the table" was seen as essential for the effective use of these systems and, for instance, electronic mail. However, even the effect of the "handshake" waned over time. Therefore, periodic face-to-face contact remained necessary. Intensive use of electronic media can bring down the necessary frequency of face-to-face contacts, but their necessity never disappears.

In the previous section, we noted that control by socialisation is not completely effective without network communication. Socialisation, on the other hand, can also facilitate network communication. De Meyer (1991) identifies several means to improve communication, of which socialisation was used most by the companies he studied. The use of temporary assignments was the most important tool used to achieve socialisation. In the next section the role of international transfers in achieving control by socialisation and informal networks will be discussed in more detail.

International transfers and control by socialisation and informal networks

The importance of international transfers to achieve control by socialisation and informal networks is emphasised by various authors. Most of them, however, tend to concentrate on one of the two elements: socialisation or creation of informal information networks. Therefore, these two elements will be discussed separately. After doing so, we will also discuss four different types of international managers and their contribution to control by socialisation and informal networks.

Socialisation

Numerous authors (see Bartlett and Ghoshal, 1987b; Daniels and Radebaugh, 1989; Derr and Oddou, 1993; Edström and Galbraith, 1977b; Horng, 1993; Jaeger, 1983; Kenter, 1989; Kobrin, 1988; Kuin, 1972; Kumar, 1993; Macharzina, 1993; Merchant, 1996; Pausenberger and Glaum, 1993; Rall, 1989; Robock and Simmonds, 1983) point to the fact that international transfers can foster socialisation in the company culture, either for the internationally transferred manager or for the company as a whole. Below we have included some typical quotations:

> Another reason [other than management development] why sufficient scope for international job rotation should be maintained is the need for what I would call "corporate acculturation". (Kuin, 1972:91)

> Where operations are in different countries and managers have different cultural and language backgrounds, control through programmes of "corporate acculturation" and "people transfer" can be important and effective. (Robock and Simmonds, 1983: 505)

> Philips found that the most effective way to manage complex flows of information and knowledge was through various socialisation processes: the transfer of people, the encouragement of informal communication channels that fostered information exchange, or the creation of forums that facilitated inter-unit learning. (Bartlett and Ghoshal, 1987b:50)

> Such integration was typically the result of a high degree of organisational socialisation and was achieved through extensive travel and transfer of managers between headquarters and the subsidiary, and through joint-work in teams, task forces, and committees. (Ghoshal and Bartlett, 1988:371)

Frequent transfers of managers among foreign operations develops increased knowledge and commitment so that fewer procedures, less hierarchical communication and less surveillance are needed. (Daniels and Radebaugh, 1989:545)

Informal information networks

Edström and Galbraith (1977b) were probably the first to recognise the function of international transfers as network builders. Extensive transfers create a network of informal contacts that can be used in collecting the information necessary to support local discretion. Edström and Galbraith also refer to Likert's (1967) linking pins and Lawrence and Lorsch's (1967) and Galbraith's (1973) integrators in this respect. It is no coincidence that the latter were classified under our control by socialisation and networks category in Chapter 1.

The creation of informal information networks through international transfers[55] is identified by, among others, Ondrack (1985a/b), Egelhoff (1988), Evans (1991), and Bartlett and Ghoshal (1995). *Ondrack* (1985a/b) conducted a study in which he tried to relate Perlmutter's classifications of multinational firms (see Chapter 1) to various patterns of international HRM, among which the functions of international transfers distinguished by Edström and Galbraith (see Chapter 1). Regiocentric and geocentric firms were hypothesised to make greater use of international transfers for management and organisation development (socialisation and creation of informal networks) than polycentric and ethnocentric firms. The sample of eight companies consisted of five regiocentric and three polycentric firms. The regiocentric firms did indeed transfer managers (parent-, host- and third-country nationals) for management development, while only one polycentric firm did this and then only for parent-country nationals. Transfer for organisation development occurred in only two of the regiocentric firms (for parent-, host- and third-country nationals). However, the value of international transfers in creating an international network (and socialisation) was recognised by all regiocentric firms. The high costs of transfers were the main reason to use substitutes such as international meetings and training programmes for organisation development purposes.

---

[55] Welch and Welch (1993) correctly indicate that international transfers can also damage networks if the wrong people are transferred or if people are re-transferred before they have built up their networks. Therefore, the use of expatriates may not always be the best choice. Although this is an important proviso, the general idea is still that international transfers can be used to facilitate informal information exchange. Another important proviso in this respect is made by Marschan, Welch and Welch (1996b), who indicate that language capabilities might be among the most important barriers to or facilitators of informal communication networks. They indicate that, despite modern communication methods, distortion in information exchange between individuals in different MNC units caused by language differences remains an important problem.

That *Egelhoff* (1988a) points to the role of international transfers in creating an informal information network is not surprising. His whole work is built on the information-processing perspective. The informal networks that international managers will be likely to maintain with previous co-workers can provide a considerable addition to the information-processing capability between various parts of the company. Increasing the number of transfers therefore increases the information-processing capability in a multinational company.

Evans (1991) also signals the influence of international mobility on the development of a "network of personal relationships based on long-term trust through which important horizontal initiatives get planned and implemented". He calls it the nervous system of the organisation and makes one important additional remark in this respect. According to him, network theory and research show that this nervous system requires a large number of loose ties (knowing someone who knows someone who knows someone) to function. However, these can be based on a relatively small number of strong ties between key people in the organisation. This could mean that the potential impact of this nervous system could extend far beyond the managers who were actually transferred to the organisation as a whole.

Bartlett and Ghoshal (1995) describe how Ikea realised control by socialisation and informal networks:

> Throughout the 1980s, Kamprad [Ikea's founder] led week-long training sessions on Ikea's history, culture, and values. Then, the company assigned the ambassadors who attended the sessions to key positions world-wide. By the early 1990s, more than 300 cultural agents were serving as nodes in a personal communication network that could collect and transmit information without the distortion that more formal information systems often introduce.[56] (Bartlett and Ghoshal, 1995: 141)

In a non-international setting, various authors have come to the same conclusion. Bush and Frohman (1992) argue that networking is reinforced by the transfer of managers across departmental barriers. Studies by Baty, Evan and Rothermel (1971) and Pfeffer and Leblebici (1973) indicate that personnel flows are one mechanism of (interorganisational) information transfer and communication. Kerr and Jackofsky (1989) argue that management development (MD) (including career pathing, mentoring/coaching and training) influences three components of the strategy implementation process: flexibility, communication and cohesion. Flexibility is influenced, because multiple perspectives and the ability to react rapidly to changing circumstances and new

---

[56] One might of course wonder whether the level of distortion in informal communication would be smaller by definition.

opportunities are built through the various MD activities. Communication is improved, because informal communication networks are built through career pathing. Cohesion, finally, is affected, because MD works as a socialisation mechanism. Training can be used for direct socialisation, mentoring provides role models for socialisation and career pathing "homogenises managers' experiences and reduces the tendency to identify with divisions and subcultures rather than the total organisation." These three components bear a great resemblance to the elements discussed above. So again, we see that international management theory can learn a lot from existing theories. What the discussion by Kerr and Jackofsky also does, however, is to bring up the question of whether international transfers (similar to career pathing in their discussion) are necessary to provide control by socialisation and informal networks. Do not other mechanisms provide the same results in a less expensive way? It is to this question that we will turn next. Before doing so, however, we will take a brief look at the different transfer archetypes and their role in achieving control by socialisation and informal networks.

Transfer archetypes
From the above discussion it should have become clear that it is not just *any* transferred international manager who provides effective control by socialisation and informal networks. In a study that, to our best knowledge, is the first attempt to characterise different types of expatriates, Borg (1988, Borg and Harzing, 1996) distinguishes four transfer archetypes that crystallised after ten years: naturalised, locally oriented, unsettled and cosmopolitan-oriented. The naturalised managers were those who remained in the foreign country or left the company during or after the first assignment. About half of the managers in this category left the company after an average time of eight years. The locally oriented managers returned home after just one assignment and are quite happy to stay there. This group had the lowest exit rate (16%). Unsettled managers were those who completed two or more assignments abroad and were then repatriated to their country of origin. They are unsettled as to whether they wish to stay at home or accept assignment and whether to stay with the company at all. Nearly one third of them had left the company at the end of the period of investigation. In the cosmopolitan-oriented category were those who took up several assignments abroad and remained there (or left the companies as cosmopolitans, about 19% of them). This cosmopolitan type can be considered as part of a professional mobile cadre of expatriates.

A comparable classification, though somewhat different in focus, is given by Black and Gregersen (1992). They distinguish expatriates who go native (Borg's naturalised type), expatriates who leave their heart at home (Borg's local type), expatriates who see themselves as free agents (Borg's unsettled type) and expatriates who see themselves as dual citizens (Borg's cosmopolitan type). Their distinction is based on the form of expatriate allegiance: either to the parent firm, to the local operation, to both or to neither of them. The cosmopolitans or dual citizens are the types of expatriates who are most likely to provide effective control by socialisation and informal networks, because of their international orientation, their frequent transfers (which foster socialisation and the creation of an international network) and their dual allegiance. The cosmopolitans remaining in the company, however, accounted for less then one fifth of the total cohort studied by Borg. He therefore argues that many managers have to be sent out because international transfers function as a way to identify professional expatriates (cosmopolitans). This would make the international transfer option even more expensive. Therefore, it high time that we consider the alternatives.

Alternatives to achieve control by socialisation and informal networks

Both the article by Kerr and Jackofsky and some of the other articles referred to above implicitly raised the question of whether international transfers are necessary to provide control by socialisation and informal networks. Do not other mechanisms provide the same results in a less expensive way? In Ondrack's (1985a/b) study, some respondents said that transfer for organisation development (more or less equivalent to control by socialisation and informal networks) had been abandoned because of the rising costs of international transfers. International meetings and training programmes were used as a substitute for organisation development transfers.

Furthermore, there are increasing signs that barriers to mobility - especially the problem of dual-career couples - become more and more important, leading to a decline in willingness to accept an assignment abroad (Forster, 1992; Kilgore, 1991; Kusters, 1994; Levolger, 1995; Punnett et al, 1992; Scullion, 1992; Welch, 1994b). Therefore, alternatives to international transfers would be very welcome. International transfers have indeed various functional alternatives, which will be discussed below: recruitment and selection, training and development, formal networks and appraisal, and compensation practices.

Recruitment and selection
Various authors indicate that selection is one of the major tools for developing and promoting corporate culture (see e.g. Evans and Lorange, 1989; Ferner, Edwards and Sisson, 1995; Schneider, 1988). Candidates can be carefully screened to fit into the existing corporate culture. There are indeed several ways in which recruitment/selection can help to achieve control by socialisation and informal networks. First, multinational companies can attempt to attract recruits who are to some extent pre-socialised by their education or family background (an approach sometimes called "buying values" instead of

"making values" (McDonald and Gandz, 1992), though in fact to achieve strong socialisation both will probably be necessary). An international orientation and/or experience for instance increases the chance that the newcomer has an open attitude to other cultures and is comfortable in dealing with diversity and different ways of handling things. This international orientation and/or experience can be the result of and measured by:

- participation in student exchange programmes;
- completion of a practical period abroad;
- being a child of parents with different nationalities;
- being a child of a father/mother who has been an expatriate;
- foreign language capability;
- completion of courses with an international content;
- living/schooling in a multiracial environment;

and to a limited extent even by:

- spending holidays in different countries;
- frequent relocation within the home country.

Although the last does not give a person international experience, it will preclude the development of strong "super-local" roots.

Sometimes attendance of certain schools and universities can provide an important kind of pre-socialisation. This will probably be more important in, for instance, Great-Britain (Eton and Oxbridge) or France (Grandes Ecoles) than it is in the Netherlands. What is particularly important is that these institutions not only pre-socialise their students, but also are very strong network builders.

Selecting people who already have some affinity with the corporate culture is very important, because it removes the necessity of radical re-socialisation (a divestiture socialisation process), which can be very difficult (Jaeger 1982). This can result in a reluctance to hire people who have (extensive) previous work experience in other companies and would be to some extent socialised into another company culture. So we see that firms relying on a strong corporate culture to achieve integration have a preference for hiring recently graduated university students. Of course an extreme example of this is Japanese firms, where entry into the organisation is usually only possible just after leaving university (Ishida, 1986; Pucik, 1991; Rhoen, 1995; Sano, 1996), but many large Western companies also rely on hiring a cohort of young graduates every year. Of course the hiring of a group of like-minded recruits (and their subsequent introduction and training together) promotes the building of informal networks between them.

Finally, a company relying on a strong corporate culture will generally recruit people for long if not life-time careers in the company (Baliga and Jaeger, 1984; Doz and Prahalad, 1984; Hedlund, 1993; Hennart, 1991; Kuin, 1972; Leksell, 1981). This works in two ways to promote socialisation. For the company, it justifies investment in socialisation processes, because the costs (which can be very high) can be recouped over a long time. For the employees, long-term employment gives them a greater personal stake in integrating themselves personally and completely into the organisation. Because of the recruitment of young graduates and the long-term employment policy, these companies will also rely very much on the internal labour market. The consequence for selection is that employees are selected as much for their potential as for their current capabilities and that they are not recruited for one specific function, but rather for non-specialised career paths. Of course, long-term employment also promotes the building of informal networks, because employees know they will have to rely on them for a long time.

The discussion above has (implicitly) focused on the socialisation of parent-country nationals before they are internationally transferred. The same ideas would also be valid for the recruitment and selection of host and third-country nationals. However, recruitment and selection of host-country nationals is not normally directed from headquarters. Therefore, although the recruitment/selection instrument might be useful in giving a head-start in the socialisation of potential expatriates, it is not likely to be a very strong instrument in promoting an overall corporate culture with a high level of shared values between headquarters and subsidiaries. The next instrument, training and development, might be a better option in this respect.

Training and development
Training is recognised as an important means for socialisation (Child, 1984; De Meyer, 1991; Derr and Oddou, 1993; Evans, 1989; Hennart, 1991; Kerr and Jackofsky, 1989; Mascarenhas, 1984; Ondrack, 1985a/b; Pazy and Zeira, 1983; Robock and Simmonds, 1983). We can distinguish on-the-job training - which can be a very effective socialisation mechanism, because the employee has direct role models to follow - and formal management training programmes. Here we will concentrate on the latter. Formal training programmes can, provided that they are to some extent company-specific, be an effective way to directly transfer the organisational goals and values to a whole group of people at the same time (thereby being a collective process of socialisation) (Wanous, 1980). Management trainees in large (multinational) companies usually follow a whole series of one- or two-week training courses. This shared experience in addition creates informal networks.

In multinational companies, however, these training programmes can provide an important impetus to achieve shared values and facilitate network building between headquarters and subsidiaries. Training programmes can be attended by people of different nationalities and from all parts of the company. The composition of the group can even have been meticulously thought out by the central personnel department. More important than the actual content of the training programme is the fact that employees with different nationalities and perspectives are brought together and can learn from each other. Furthermore, these training programmes (not forgetting the social events attached to them) create an informal international network of people within the company. Relationships built up during an intensive management training programme lasting several weeks are often durable. Therefore, in this way not only are individual competencies, such as the ability to service specific computer networks, built, but training also serves to build organisational competencies. Of course, these training activities do not have to be limited to a group of young management trainees. Company seminars and conferences can be organised for everyone to attend.

Formal networks
Equally or even more effective than a formal management training programme, is the option of forming formal networks. International task forces or project groups of employees of different backgrounds and nationalities can be constructed to work on a company problem (either real or constructed for the purpose of instruction). The Philips Octagon programme (Van Houten, 1989), in which a team of eight young high-potential managers of different backgrounds and nationalities are brought together to work on an actual company problem, is an excellent example. This programme lasts six to eight months and "its purpose is to broaden the scope of understanding of the company, to increase appreciation of the interdependence of functions and disciplines, and to provide a cross-cultural forum for working together and exchanging ideas" (Van Houten, 1989). Of course, this intensive cooperation also gives a very strong impetus to informal network building. The managers who have worked together in Octagon programmes are very likely to consult each other in the future.

Ghoshal et al. (1994) showed that what they call lateral networking mechanisms (joint work in teams, task forces and meetings) have significant positive effects on the frequency of both subsidiary-headquarters and inter-subsidiary communication. In our terminology, this would mean that the use of formal networks has a positive impact on control by informal verbal networks.

Appraisal and compensation
The instruments described above can be reinforced when the system of appraisal and compensation is aligned with them. The attitudes fostered by long-

term employment and the international perspective acquired by company training programmes will be hard to sustain when the system of appraisal and compensation is based on short-term profits for one single country. On the other hand, changing the reward system in isolation will not bring about the required change in attitude (Lawler, 1981).

In companies relying intensively on control by socialisation and informal networks, we would expect a system of appraisal and compensation with the following characteristics (Evans, 1989; Pucik and Katz, 1986):

- appraisal based on achieving long-term objectives of the company as a whole;
- no explicit monitoring and limited direct feedback;
- rewarding the contribution to global performance, rather than performance in a single country (especially if different transfer prices make honest comparison difficult);
- emphasis on indirect, non-monetary rewards such as challenging opportunities and assignments.

Though some research has been done in this area (Lei, Slocum and Slater, 1990) we will not pursue this option further as it is believed to have a support function, rather than being a strong instrument in itself.

International transfers and the alternatives: substitutes or complements?
In previous sections, we discussed alternatives for international transfers in achieving control by socialisation and informal networks.[57] Are these alternatives possible substitutes for international transfers or are they to be viewed as complementary? As indicated before, selection and recruitment and appraisal and compensation are seen as having a supportive rather than a direct influence. In addition, for host-country managers, these HRM functions are likely to be the responsibility of local HR managers (Rosenzweig and Nohria, 1994), so that their potential for corporate-wide integration is rather low.

Management training, however, is a very serious alternative to international transfers, because it provides many opportunities for both socialisation and network building. Compared with international transfers it provides a greater opportunity for meeting a variety of other managers in an equivalent period of time. Combined with its lower cost, this was the main reason for

---

[57] In addition to serving as a possible alternative to international transfers to achieve control by socialisation and informal networks, management training and formal networks can also be an alternative to international transfers in order to 'internationalise' managers. In a study by Derr and Oddou (1993) international task forces and in-company seminars ranked first and second in the list of nine alternative methods to foster internationalisation that would become both more important and more frequently used in future.

companies to use management training as a substitute for international transfers (Ondrack, 1985a/b). Management training does have the additional advantage that it can prepare would-be expatriates for foreign assignments in that it increases their sensitivity to cultural differences (both through the content of the training if it is aimed at this subject and through the contact with different nationalities). As discussed in Chapter 1, research has shown that pre-departure cross-cultural training reduces the likelihood of expatriate failure. So in this way training can also be an important complement of international transfers in increasing the effectiveness of the latter. International task forces or project teams have all the advantages of management training in fostering socialisation and, in particular, network building, but in addition can also provide solutions to important company problems.

Although there is no hard evidence on this, several authors (Bartlett and Ghoshal, 1989; Evans, 1991; Robock and Simmonds, 1983) suggest that international transfers would probably be the strongest alternative in providing socialisation and network building for expatriates themselves. Evans, for instance, sees "career and mobility management" as a stronger "glue mechanism", providing more "inter-unit cohesion" than project groups and training. When transferred internationally, the employee is immersed into the local culture and situation completely, has no way to escape and is dependent on his collaboration with people with different cultural backgrounds and perspectives to achieve results. This gives the best opportunity to provide a long-lasting multidimensional attitude. The contacts last longer and will be more intensive, which will give a better opportunity for long-lasting informal networks.

For subsidiary managers themselves, however, the direct influence of the participation in management training programmes or international task forces on the level of cultural integration and informal networking would probably be stronger than the indirect effect of expatriate presence in subsidiaries. Therefore, a high level of shared values between a given subsidiary and headquarters and an intensive informal information network can probably be achieved in a more direct and less expensive way than by international transfers. This does not mean, however, that international transfers have become useless. First, they can provide an important support function in achieving control by socialisation and informal networks, and second, they can fulfil a number of other functions, as discussed in Chapter 1. In an effective multinational company, we would therefore expect the use of both management training and task forces, and international transfers to achieve control by socialisation and informal networks.

International transfers and personal centralised control

In Chapter 1, we distinguished four different control mechanisms. We explained how international transfers facilitate control by socialisation and informal networks. In this section, we will show that international transfers can also be used to effectuate personal centralised control.

Several authors suggest that sending expatriates (parent-country nationals) to subsidiaries can have the same result as centralising decisions at headquarters. Hennart (1991), for instance, criticises the way autonomy is usually measured in multinational companies, namely as the locus of decision-making. If decisions are made at headquarters, subsidiaries are said to have little autonomy. However, is this autonomy of decision-making necessarily larger if decisions are made at subsidiaries? Decisions made by a perfectly socialised parent-country manager may be indistinguishable from those made at headquarters. No real autonomy exists for the subsidiary if expatriate managers make the decisions, because they are likely to act and make decisions in accordance with the parent company, being influenced as they are by many years ongoing process of socialisation and acculturation in the parent organisation. The result is, as Egelhoff (1988a) points out, that to some extent staffing with parent-country nationals leads to the same result as centralising more decision-making at the parent level. Of course, there are some differences. Although decisions made by parent-country expatriates are more likely to be in favour of headquarters in case of conflicting goals than is the case when decisions are made by host-country nationals, this is not necessarily true for each and every expatriate. Borg's (1988) naturalised expatriates would rather choose local interests and his cosmopolitans should value both perspectives equally. Furthermore, parent-country expatriate managers are more likely than headquarters executives to pay at least some attention to local conditions and demands, because they are confronted with them daily. We can therefore conclude that international transfers can indeed effectuate personal centralised control, if not through a quasi-centralisation of decision-making, than certainly through direct supervision (see Chapter 1) by expatriates.[58]

Earlier in this section we alluded to the argument that international transfers can be another way to achieve personal centralised control, exactly because parent-country expatriates are socialised into the company's ways of doing things. How do we then distinguish between these different types of

---

[58] Some authors (e.g. Edström and Galbraith, 1978) even see a role for expatriation in preserving bureaucratic control. In their description of this process they indicate that control remains largely impersonal and bureaucratic, but that expatriates make sure that company policy is applied. In our view, this would still mean that the 'expatriate extension' of bureaucratic control is direct and personal, thus resembling personal centralised control. The role of expatriates in bureaucratic formalised control will therefore not be further explored.

control? The difficulty of making this distinction probably led Baliga and Jaeger (1984) to combine two of the control mechanisms: personal control and control by socialisation into one type of control: cultural control (see also Chapter 1). We did not and do not choose to do so for two principal reasons. The first reason is that personal centralised control can exist without international transfers and socialisation. The second and more important reason is that, as explained before, our control by socialisation and informal networks is a much broader mechanism than the simple indoctrination of parent-company expatriate managers. These two remarks then give clues to distinguishing the two types of control. They have a common element, the socialisation of parent-company expatriate managers, which can facilitate the execution of both these control mechanisms. Both control mechanisms, however, have elements that go beyond this socialisation process.

Testing the role of international transfers and the alternatives as control mechanisms in MNCs

In this section, we have shown that a large number of authors claim that international transfers can be used to facilitate both socialisation and the construction of informal information networks. The way in which this process actually works, however, is hardly ever explained, nor indeed is the role of international transfers in this type of coordination "proved" empirically. Most of the authors simply refer to Edström and Galbraith (1977b) to substantiate their argument. Edström and Galbraith analysed the international transfer of managers in four multinational companies. One of these multinationals transferred a far greater number of managers than its direct competitor, despite their being of the same size, operating in the same industry and having nearly identical organisation charts. Edström and Galbraith hypothesised that in this multinational transfer of managers was being used to socialise managers and create informal verbal international information networks. So far, however, only two very recent case study research projects (Ferner, Edwards and Sisson, 1995; Welch, Fenwick and DeCieri, 1994) have attempted to test this hypothesis empirically. The first studied an international accounting and management consulting firm and concluded with regard to international transfers: "These transfers were seen [...] as a way for individuals to build up networks of contacts and to absorb the international ethos and practices of the firm: part, therefore, of what Edström and Galbraith (1977b) refer to as an international 'control strategy based on socialisation'" (Ferner et al, 1995:353). The second studied two Australian organisations operating in the global environment and concludes "they both rely heavily on transferring staff in order to facilitate coordination and control" (Welch et al, 1994:473). It is interesting to see that both studies in this respect refer to Edström and Galbraith (1977b) only, which once again confirms that - at least in the Anglo-Saxon world - this is believed to be the only study that has been done on this subject. Although these studies provide some preliminary ideas on the validity of Edström and Galbraith's hypothesis, a firm conclusion is hampered by the usual generalisation problems associated with case studies.

Some of the "German" studies discussed in Chapter 1 did empirically investigate the various roles of international transfers. Within the coordination role, however, the emphasis was mostly on a rather direct form of control (comparable to our personal centralised control). In addition, data were usually gathered at headquarters. The mere fact that a headquarters personnel manager scored a predefined statement referring, in one way or another, to control by socialisation and informal networks higher than 1 or 0 (no importance at all), does not prove beyond doubt that international transfers do indeed perform this function. It would have been more convincing if they had thought of this function spontaneously.

To remedy these problems, we tried to find a more quantitative and in a sense depersonalised way to test the hypothesis that international transfers serve to achieve control by socialisation and informal networks.[59] In the first part of this research project, the characteristics of both headquarters and subsidiaries on the composition of the control portfolio are studied. One of the control mechanisms that is studied is control by socialisation and networks. If subsidiaries with a large proportion of internationally transferred managers have a higher amount of control by socialisation and informal networks, we may conclude that international transfers indeed achieve control by socialisation and informal networks. As international transfers are hypothesised to influence the socialisation and informal network elements of control by socialisation and informal networks, but not necessarily the formal network element, this leads to the following hypotheses:

> Hypothesis 2-41: Subsidiary scores on the socialisation element of control by socialisation and networks will be positively related to the proportion of expatriate managers in the (upper-level) workforce.

And:

> Hypothesis 2-42: Subsidiary scores on the informal network element of control by socialisation and networks are positively related to the proportion of expatriate managers in the (upper-level) workforce.

---

[59] In this section we will describe the two ways of measurement that will be used in the empirical part of this book , which focuses on the subsidiary as the unit of analysis and uses the subsidiary managing director as respondent. Three other ways that rely on the questioning of a large number of expatriates and subsidiary managers individually are described in Harzing (1994).

Another, more direct, way of measuring the effect of international transfers on control by socialisation and informal networks is to ask subsidiary managers to rate the importance of the various organisational functions of international transfers in their subsidiaries. As discussed in Chapter 1, the main organisational functions of international transfers as defined by Edström and Galbraith (1977a) are "position filling", "management development" and "organisational development". Organisation development, defined as the development and reinforcement of both an informal communications network and a common corporate culture, comes very close to our definition of control by socialisation and informal networks. This way of measurement has some of the same drawbacks as those signalled above in the "German" studies, in that transfer functions are predetermined and managers are likely to attach at least some importance to each of the alternatives. An advantage of our study, however, is that subsidiary managers are probably more likely to be able accurately to indicate the functions of expatriation than headquarters managers, since the latter will not experience them daily, while the former will. If international transfers do indeed fulfil a role in the achievement of control by socialisation and informal networks, the organisational function referring to this (organisational development) should be rated as having more than a marginal importance. Further, since respondents are likely to give some importance to any alternative, organisational functions referring to control by socialisation and information networks should not be rated much lower than organisational functions referring to position filling and management development. Therefore:

Hypothesis 2-43: Organisation development (improving information channels and transfer of corporate culture) will be seen as an equally important function of international transfers as position filling and management development.

We indicated various alternatives to international transfers in achieving control by socialisation and informal networks. The most important of these alternatives were deemed to be management training and formal networks. As indicated above, for the expatriate manager himself, international transfers would probably be most effective in achieving socialisation and informal networks. When looking at the subsidiary as a whole, however, the *direct* effect of participation of subsidiary managers in international management training programmes and formal networks will probably be more influential than the *indirect* effect of the presence of expatriates in the subsidiary. Therefore:

Hypothesis 2-44a: Participation of subsidiary managers in international management training programmes is more strongly related to the level of shared values between subsidiaries and headquarters than the extent of expatriate presence in the upper-level workforce.

Hypothesis 2-44b: Participation of subsidiary managers in formal networks is more strongly related to the level of shared values between subsidiaries and headquarters than the extent of expatriate presence in the upper-level workforce.

And:

Hypothesis 2-45a: Participation of subsidiary managers in international management training programmes is more strongly related to the level of informal communication between subsidiaries and headquarters than the extent of expatriate presence in the upper-level workforce.

Hypothesis 2-45b: Participation of subsidiary managers in formal networks is more strongly related to the level of informal communication between subsidiaries and headquarters than the extent of expatriate presence in the upper-level workforce.

Although the alternatives to international transfers will be related to both elements of control by socialisation and informal networks, we would expect management training to be more strongly related to socialisation and formal networks to informal networks. There are various reasons for this assumption. First, international management training programmes often have an explicit socialisation aspect in that a major element of the training is the transfer of corporate values. Although participation in formal networks may lead to a higher level of shared values, this is more a by-product than a major objective. Further, the more informal and "away-from-work" atmosphere of training programmes provides more opportunities for informal socialising. Although this may also build strong informal communication networks, these networks may not so much be work-related. Participation in international task forces or committees is much more related to direct company problems. Informal communication networks established in formal networks are more likely to be used in other work settings as well. Therefore:

Hypothesis 2-46: Participation of subsidiary managers in international management training programmes will be more strongly related to the level of shared values between subsidiaries and headquarters than participation in formal networks.

And:

Hypothesis 2-47: Participation of subsidiary managers in formal networks will be more strongly related to the level of informal communication between subsidiaries and headquarters than participation in management training programmes.

In sum, we would therefore expect the level of shared values between subsidiaries and headquarters to be most strongly influenced by the participation of subsidiary managers in international training programmes. Second in importance would be the participation of subsidiary managers in formal networks, while the third place would be taken by the level of expatriate presence in the subsidiary in question. Regarding the level of informal communication between subsidiaries and headquarters, participation of subsidiary managers in formal networks would be the most important determinant, while participation of these managers in international management training and the level of expatriate presence in the subsidiary in question would occupy a second and third place.

Conclusions

In this section, we have added the third building block of our theoretical framework: international transfers, and explained how these can function as a control mechanism in MNCs. In doing so, we first attempted to get a clearer picture of what is meant by socialisation and network communication. We then discussed the general claim that international transfers can be used to achieve control by socialisation and informal networks and explained why not each type of international manager is equally effective in realising this goal. Subsequently, various alternatives to achieving control by socialisation and informal networks were discussed: recruitment and selection, training and development, formal networks, and appraisal and compensation. Of these, training and development and formal networks were judged the most important. An aspect of expatriation that was already alluded to in Chapter 1 when discussing the level of centralisation in Japanese MNCs is the direct control effect of expatriates. We explained how international transfers can be used to effectuate personal centralised control.

Finally, we offered some hypotheses about the relationship between international transfers and the alternatives on the one hand, and control by socialisation and informal networks on the other hand. Compared to the first part of this chapter, this section offered comparatively few hypotheses. This reflects the fact that very little is known about either the functioning of international transfers as a control mechanism or the relationship between international transfers and the alternatives such as management training and formal networks. In the empirical part of this book, we will try to explore the situations in which either international transfers or the alternatives have the largest influence.

3. CONFIGURATIONS AND PERFORMANCE IMPLICATIONS

Introduction

In Section 1, we discussed various headquarters and subsidiary characteristics that might influence both the level of control and the composition of the control portfolio. In Section 2, we added another variable that could influence the level of both control by socialisation and networks and personal centralised control: the number of international transfers. Above, we have indicated that many of the independent variables might be intercorrelated, introducing the problem of multicollinearity. Therefore, in the empirical part of this book we will try to establish the relative importance of each of these independent variables in explaining the use of each of the control mechanisms by using linear or logistic regression models.

The possible intercorrelation between the independent variables can also be seen in a more positive light. If many of the headquarters and subsidiary characteristics vary together, we might be able to construct configurations of characteristics that are likely to occur together, thus reducing the level of complexity. This section will therefore be devoted to configuration analysis. First, we will discuss the usefulness of the configuration approach in general, and in international management studies in particular. Subsequently, three configurations of MNCs that integrate many of the variables discussed in this and the previous chapter will be constructed. An implicit or explicit assumption of the configuration approach is that companies that conform more closely to one of these configurations (ideal types) will outperform other companies. We will therefore discuss some general issues related to performance measurement. A final subsection then offers some hypotheses on the relationship between configurations and performance.

The use of configuration analysis

In this section we will discuss the underlying ideas of the configuration approach and evaluate its use in both national and international management research. In a first subsection we introduce some fervent advocates and opponents of the approach in management research in general and distinguish two different approaches towards constructing configurations: typologies and taxonomies. In a second subsection, we will summarise the current state of configuration research in the field of international management and discuss the problems associated with it.

Configuration analysis in a national context: advocates, opponents, typologies and taxonomies

Following Meyer et al. (1993) the term "organisational configuration" is used to denote a multidimensional constellation of conceptually distinct characteristics that commonly occur together. Although its origins can be traced to Weber (1947), Woodward (1958), Burns and Stalker (1961) and Lawrence and Lorsch (1967), configuration analysis has achieved large-scale popularity in the late 1970s with important contributions by Miles and Snow (1978), Mintzberg (1979) and Miller and Friesen (1977, 1978).

Miller (1981, 1986, 1996) has become one of the most fervent advocates of configuration analysis. In his award-winning[60] article, Miller (1986) describes two alternative approaches to researching the relationship between strategy and structure, the main focus of his academic work. One approach would be to take one or two elements of strategy at a time and relate them to individual organisational variables. This would mean having to formulate numerous bivariate or well-defined multivariate hypotheses. According to Miller: "Any coherent theme might be obscured by the mist of atomistic speculation" (Miller: 1986:235). A further shortcoming of this approach is that associations among variables are studied out of the context in which they occur. The configurational approach on the other hand has one prime assumption: elements of strategy, structure and environment will often configure into "a manageable number of common, predictively useful types that describe a large proportion of high-performing organisations" (Miller: 1986:235). The predictive usefulness of these configurations (also called "gestalts", or "archetypes", or "generic types") lies in the fact that they are composed of mutually supporting characteristics. The presence of one or more of these characteristics can thus lead to the reliable prediction of the remaining elements.

Many other authors (see e.g. Doty and Glick, 1994; Meyer et al, 1993; Veliyath and Srinivasan, 1995) join Miller in describing configurations as a excellent way to describe parsimoniously a complex organisational reality. Meyer et al. (1993) go even further and claim that: "Discovering and invoking configurational patterns, types and categories is [...] fundamental to social theory and research. Configurations allow people to order and make sense out of their worlds by sorting things into discrete and relatively homogeneous groups. Indeed, systematic classification and the explanation of rationales for classification are "tantamount to the codification of the existing state of knowledge in a discipline" (Tiryakian, 1968)" (Meyer et al, 1993:1179).

---

[60] The article was awarded the *Strategic Management Journal* 1995 Best Paper Prize.

The configuration approach is not accepted without criticism, however. In an article written on the occasion of winning the *Strategic Management Journal* 1995 Best Paper Prize for his article "Configurations of Strategy and Structure" (1986), Miller reports of a friend who, being unaware of the identity of author, described the article in question as: "the worst manuscript I've seen in a long time". Once enlightened about the author, he added: "It is simplistic in its obsession with a few types, it is dogmatic in style, and it contains not one shred of empirical evidence. Reputable academics will hate it." Another colleague gave Miller a working paper with the title: "Miller, Mintzberg and McGillomania"[61] in which he claimed that strategic and structural elements combine in many more ways than those Miller discussed and that not all organisational changes involve quantum leaps between discrete configurations.

In his 1996 article, Miller responds that the configurations he proposed were not exhaustive but merely illustrative of important relationships. In his view this will inherently be the case for any typology. The point is that by identifying some common configurations and showing the consistency of their components, the researcher can go beyond the approach of "one variable at a time". According to Miller, this does not mean that configurations are discrete or that companies can only change by making one giant leap from one configuration to another. "[...] empirically derived configurations overlap along many dimensions and are usually connected on a snake like data surface. Order is reflected by the few dimensions it takes to describe the surface vs the many that are used to describe a company" (Miller, 1996:506).

A similar point is also put forward by Meyer et al. (1993). They report that critics of the configuration approach claim that classification schemes over-simplify reality and do not reflect the complexity of organisational life. Although Meyer et al. agree with this critique, especially in the cases where only one or two dimensions are used to classify firms, they do signal an important trade-off. Adding dimensions might indeed provide a better description of reality, but they also make configurations more complex and cumbersome. Meyer et al. say that: "It would be naive to think that the perfect taxonomy is one that perfectly replicates reality. Even if such a taxonomy could be constructed, its specificity would defeat its purpose to generalise and abstract" (Meyer et al., 1993:1182).

As Doty and Glick (1994) indicate, the most severe criticism brought forward is that typologies are classification systems rather than theories. As the critics see it, typologies can be used to cluster organisations into categories, but cannot contribute to useful theory building. Doty and Glick, however, argue that typologies are not the same as classification systems. "Classification schemes and taxonomies refer to classification systems that categorise

---

[61] A reference to the university at which both Miller and Mintzberg had been working.

phenomena into mutually exclusive and exhaustive sets with a series of discrete decision roles" (Doty and Glick, 1994:232). Typologies on the other hand refer to "conceptually derived interrelated sets of ideal types". The problem is that many researchers have interpreted typologies as classifications even if originally they were not defined in this way. In an earlier publication, Doty et al. (1993), refer to Mintzberg's and Miles and Snow's configurational theories and indicate that most researchers have interpreted these configurations as classification schemes rather than as ideal types. They indicate that Miles and Snow explicitly stated that they were presenting the "pure" form of each configuration (1978:30). Similarly, Mintzberg explicitly stated that his organisational forms composed "a typology of ideal or pure types" (1979:473).

As Meyer et al. (1993) discuss, considering configurations as classification schemes also introduces problems in performance analysis. If configurations are used as categories, every member in a given category is predicted to be equally effective, regardless of whether the particular organisation resembles the configurational characteristics almost completely or only very marginally. Following Drazin and Van de Ven (Drazin and Van de Ven, 1985; Van de Ven and Drazin, 1985), Meyer et al. plead for a more complex measure of fit. Organisations should not be fitted into a limited number of categories based on arbitrary decision rules. Fit is considered good to the extent that an organisation is similar to a conceptually identified ideal type along multiple characteristics of this ideal type. The larger the deviation from this ideal type, the lower the performance of a firm will be. In Chapter 5, we will indicate in detail how the level of fit or deviation is measured in our study.

Above, we have referred to different approaches in forming configurations: typologies and taxonomies. Typologies are developed conceptually, while taxonomies are empirically derived from a given data set. The taxonomy approach is inductive, focuses on internal validity, but is weak in its generalisability. The typology approach is deductive. The resultant configurations can be applied in a variety of different circumstances and are not dependent on particular industry contexts. Meyer et al. (1993), however, refuse to make such a clear-cut distinction. According to them, all useful typologies are grounded in empirical experience. On the other hand, although taxonomies might have been constructed by applying statistical techniques to empirical data, all useful taxonomies will be theoretically grounded. For one thing, the characteristics used to form groups will have to be selected based on existing theory. Meyer et al. therefore prefer to see typology and taxonomy as equally valuable, complementary approaches to representing configurations.

The same argument is put forward by Ketchen, Thomas and Snow (1993). In their article, they use both the inductive and the deductive approach. The

deductive approach performed better with regard to consistency and identifying and predicting performance differences. According to the authors, however: "cycling through the approaches might enhance understandings in ways
not possible through the use of a single configurational approach" (Ketchen,
Thomas and Snow, 1993:1307).

The different types of configuration analysis have been associated with different problems. The taxonomy approach has been very popular in the strategic groups' literature (see e.g. Cool and Schendel, 1987; Dess and Davis,
1984; Fiegenbaum and Thomas, 1990). Criticism of this approach has focused on the lack of theoretical significance, the arbitrary and narrow selection of variables and the unreliable or unstable results (Miller, 1996). According to Miller, a major problem with most taxonomies is that they do not
generate any insights beyond the specific sample out of which they are derived. Further, cluster analysis, widely used by taxonomists, has been severely
criticised (Ketchen and Shook, 1996) as relying too much on researcher
judgement. In addition, cluster analysis' sorting ability is claimed to be powerful enough to provide clusters even if no meaningful groups exist. Although
both Miller (1996) and Ketchen and Shook (1996) provide recommendations
that might remedy these problems, they require an amount of time and ex-
pense that will not always be available.

Although typological approaches are not plagued by the above-mentioned
problems, they have one major drawback: many typologies have never been
tested empirically, so it remains doubtful whether they are indeed a useful
way to structure organisational reality. In the first large-scale empirical test of
Mintzberg's typology, Doty et al. (1993) failed to find any support for this
very popular typology.[62] First, ideal-type configurations were not associated
with a unique contextual configuration, not even when the possibility of a
time lag was included. Since typologies are considered effective organisational forms, this might be due however to the fact that less effective organisations might dilute the hypothesised relationship. However, this possibility
was ruled out as well: organisations that had a higher internal consistency on
Mintzberg's design parameters were not more effective than organisations
with a lower consistency. In addition, organisations that had a better fit with
their environment were not found to be more effective than organisations with
a worse fit with their environment. Miles and Snow's typology was tested in
the same article and fared much better. Configurational fit based on Miles and
Snow's theory predicted 24% of the overall variation in organisational effectiveness. Fit among contextual, structural and strategic factors is therefore
concluded to be a relatively powerful predictor of organisational effective-

---

[62] It is interesting to note that the authors started out their study with the firm conviction of
finding a confirmation of Mintzberg's typology.

ness. That this study provides the strongest support for the Miles and Snow typology so far is partly attributed to the fact that earlier studies (e.g. Conant et al., 1990; Zajac and Shortell, 1989) treated the ideal types as classification schemes, in which marginal members are predicted to be as effective as organisations resembling the configuration characteristics completely.

What can we conclude from the above analysis concerning the usefulness of configuration analysis as a way to advance theory? First, although a combination of both approaches might be useful, the typological approach would probably be the best starting point in forming configurations. Doty and Glick (1994) provide a very convincing argument for the usefulness of the typology approach in generating new theories. They start with the criteria that theories must meet in order to be considered good theories. Although they acknowledge that there are no concise, unanimously accepted definitions of theory, they claim that theory-building experts seem to agree that there are at least three primary criteria that theories must meet: a) constructs must be identified, b) relationships among these constructs must be specified, and c) these relationships must be falsifiable.

Doty and Glick show that configuration analysis meets each of these criteria. Typologies contain two different kinds of constructs. The first is the ideal type or configuration, a complex construct that is a combination of multiple unidimensional constructs. These unidimensional constructs are the building blocks of traditional theoretical statements. In configuration theory, these "first-order" constructs are the dimensions that are used to describe each ideal type. Unlike the more traditional theories, however, typological theories do not highlight the hypothesised relationships between each of the unidimensional first-order constructs and the dependent variable(s). Instead, typological theories focus on the internal consistency among the first-order constructs *within* the ideal type. They further explain why this internally consistent pattern results in the specified level of the dependent variable(s) (usually performance or efficiency). This relationship between similarity to the ideal types of organisations and the dependent variable is the relationship that should be falsifiable, according to the third criterion. It can be falsified by measuring the deviation between real organisations and an ideal type and then using this deviation to predict the dependent variable.

Considering the discussion above, configuration analysis, and in particular the typological type of analysis, is thought to be an extremely valid and useful way to advance theory building. One might wonder, however, whether configuration analysis in an international context has provided additional ideas or problems. The next subsection will therefore take stock of the current state of configuration research in the field of international management.

Configurational analysis in an international context: mixed results
The interest in configurational analysis in an international context is of a rather recent date. In the early nineties, Macharzina and Engelhard (1991) discuss the state of international business theorising. According to them, in order to make any progress in this field, researchers need to adopt a helicopter perspective and get away from looking at tiny fragments. Drawing on organisation theory and referring to Miller and Friesen, they call for the application of the Gestalt approach in international business research. Although Macharzina and Engelhard refer mainly to international business research, the Gestalt approach might even be more applicable to international management research, since the latter's focus on the internal functioning of the organisation relates even more closely to organisation theory.

In a later publication, *Macharzina* (1993) made an effort to apply configuration theory in his study on the use of control mechanisms in MNCs following various international strategies. Macharzina justifies the need for the use of configurations in the following way:

> In view of the large number of empirically investigated univariate relationships between variables assumed to influence coordination and specific coordination mechanisms, we run the risk of not seeing the wood for the trees. Although we can identify a large number of statistically significant, but isolated relationships between independent variables and coordination mechanisms, these do not necessarily combine to a coherent whole. To solve this problem we have tried to extract distinct clusters of relationships between independent variables and coordination mechanisms to identify integrated and mutually independent configurations. (Macharzina, 1993:97 [*our translation*]).

Macharzina attempted to construct these configurations empirically, by means of cluster analysis. Unfortunately, the results of this attempt did not provide a very clear-cut pattern. One of the four clusters that was found did not provide a clear structure at all and was removed from further analysis, while two other clusters were very similar on many of the characteristics included. The study also did not provide much support for the necessary fit between strategy and control mechanisms, since two clusters of firms that followed different strategies had very similar control portfolios.

The study by *Bartlett and Ghoshal* (1989, 1992a), which has been used extensively in Chapter 1 for the description of the environment, strategy, structure and processes of MNCs, can also be seen as a typology. In Chapter 1, we have shown that a number of later studies have provided some empirical support for the Bartlett and Ghoshal typology. In view of the observations discussed in the previous section, however, the typology is a starting point for further research rather than a well-developed configuration analysis in itself. Although Bartlett and Ghoshal indicated that in some industries one organisational model would be more successful than another, they did not perform specific performance analyses.[63] In addition, the typology was used as a classification device, rather than as a set of ideal types as discussed above. Since Bartlett and Ghoshal's typology was discussed extensively in Chapter 1, we will not discuss it any further at this point. Elements of their typology will be used, however, in the construction of our own set of configurations.

Roth, Schweiger and Morrison (1991) examined the impact of international strategy on organisational design and the influence of organisational design on effectiveness at the business unit level. Two ideal profiles of what Roth et al. called implementation variables were constructed for two types of strategy: global and multidomestic. Control mechanisms (called administrative mechanisms) were a major part of these ideal profiles. Application of these control mechanisms was consistently hypothesised to be lower for multidomestic strategies than for global strategies. The top five performers of each strategy type were indeed found to differ significantly in their use of control mechanisms, conforming to the predictions of the conceptually derived ideal types. Further, for the remaining firms, there was a significant positive correlation between the level of fit with the empirically constructed ideal type and performance.

Some of the studies described above under subsidiary roles could also be regarded as configurations studies. As these studies have not been categorised in this way by the authors themselves, discuss only a limited number of characteristics and have been duly incorporated into the hypotheses stated in that section, we will not discuss them any further at this point. What does merit our attention is a follow-up study by *Ghoshal and Nohria* (1993) that tries to test empirically the relationship between the environment (classified in terms of integration/responsiveness) and an MNC's governance (control) mechanisms. Four patterns of control mechanisms are distinguished. First, structural uniformity in which all subsidiaries are managed in the same way. A strong and uniform governance mechanism is used for the whole company. A second pattern is called differentiated fit. Companies following this pattern differentiate their governance mechanisms according to the subsidiary context. The third pattern combines differentiated fit with a dominant overall governance mechanism and is called integrated variety. A final pattern shows neither differentiation nor a strong governance mechanism.[64] As a general description of the fit between environment and governance mechanisms, the typology is not very successful. Out of the 41 firms investigated, only 17 fall in the predicted

---

[63] Even if they had wanted to use their typology in this way, this would not have been feasible given the limited sample size.

[64] Ghoshal and Nohria's subsequent analysis is not completely consistent with this typology. In the structural uniformity category we find firms with a high level on either one (as suggested by the typology), two or all three governance mechanisms. The same goes for firms in the integrated variety category.

categories. What the study does show is that these 17 firms in general outperform the firms that have a misfit. There are two major problems associated with this study, however. First, the typologies are treated as simple categories, which means - as we have discussed above - that firms that comply marginally to a certain typology (marginal members) are predicted to be as effective as full members. A difference of just a few percentage points for several firms might have resulted in another classification and - given the rather small sample size - possibly in other conclusions. Further, Ghoshal and Nohria do not pay any attention to possible country-related performance differences. The percentage of American firms in the fit category (65%) is larger than in the sample as a whole (49%). Since, in terms of profitability measures such as return on sales, return on assets and return on equity, American firms have consistently been shown to have higher performance levels than European firms - for many other possible reasons besides a fit between environment and governance mechanisms - the difference in performance might in reality even be a country effect instead of a fit effect.

Birkinshaw and Morrison (1995) identified a three-fold typology of subsidiary roles and then explored the ways in which these subsidiaries differed on control mechanisms, interdependencies, value-chain activities, specialised capabilities and performance. No predefined typologies were suggested concerning these characteristics, however. Although some interesting differences appeared with regard to the configuration of value-chain activities (specialised contributors and world mandate subsidiaries had a more international value-chain configuration), and some of the measures of interdependencies, no significant differences appeared with regard to specialised capabilities and all but one of the seven measures of control mechanisms. Performance varied between the different subsidiary types, in the sense that specialised contributors had a significantly lower performance than the two other types. No effort was made, however, to relate performance to the fit with ideal profiles, since the quality of the findings precluded the identification of a meaningful ideal profile.

Finally, *Wolf* (1994, 1996b) and *Macharzina and Wolf* (1996) identified patterns of strategic orientation of both MNCs and subsidiaries and accompanying levels of certain control mechanisms. The strategic orientations that were used have been identified in Chapter 1 and are broadly similar to the ones we use in this thesis. The control mechanisms have been repeatedly discussed in Sections 1 and 2 of this chapter. In a subsequent empirical test (Wolf, 1996b), little support was found for these ideal profiles. Only one of the control mechanisms, value homogeneity, conformed reasonably to the ideal profile. Considering the results of various research projects, Wolf has become rather sceptical about the chances of discovering MNC gestalts. The reasons for this scepticism lie more in the practical than in the conceptual area, however. First, Wolf (1996b) wonders whether databases of future empirical research projects carried out by (international) business scholars will be large enough to distil archetypes that are significantly different from each other.[65] Two other problems identified by Wolf weigh heaviest for the taxonomic approach. According to Wolf, "taxonomists are chained to empirical performance analyses in such a way that they look to what degree the empirically derived configurations vary with respect to performance measures" (Wolf, 1996b:12-13). The problem is that performance is dependent on a whole array of factors and that there is little consensus about the best performance measures. Finally, as identified above, the use of cluster analysis, the favourite statistical tool of taxonomists, has been severely criticised.

In sum, configuration research in the field of international management is still very weakly developed. Most studies are based on a few characteristics only, use simple dichotomous categories and/or fail to find empirical support for their configurations. Part of this lack of development might indeed be due to the problems identified by Wolf. The problems associated with cluster analysis are less relevant in our case, however, since our focus will be on typologies rather than taxonomies. The problem of low response rates, on the other hand, could be a very important hindrance in our analysis. In Chapter 3, we will therefore describe how we have made every effort to maximise this response rate. The problem of finding adequate performance measures and explaining performance is also very relevant in the fit-performance analysis we plan to conduct. We will therefore pay due attention to this phenomenon. First, however, the next section will be devoted to the development and justification of our own configurations of multinational firms.

Configurations of multinational companies

In this section, we will define a typology of multinational companies that combines the description of MNC strategy, structure and process in Chapter 1 with many of the relationships discussed in Section 1 of this chapter. Although the approach will be typological, the description of the ideal types will be grounded as much as possible in available empirical studies. In the empirical part of this book, we will verify whether these configurational types do indeed differ on the characteristics described below.

A logical starting point for a typology would be either the external environment or a firm's organisational model (strategy/structure). Most of the

---

[65] This worry is not surprising given the low response rates of international mail surveys in general (see Harzing, 1996b, 1997b) and of Wolf's studies in particular. While his 1996 publication was based on the respectable number of 82 subsidiary observations, his 1994 study was based on data from 39 subsidiaries only.

(international) studies described above have used (international) strategy/structure as a starting point. Ghoshal and Nohria started out with the environment or more specifically the industry in which the company operated. Since the focus of this book is on control mechanisms and internal consistency, we chose the organisational model as our starting point. However, in the empirical performance analysis, we will investigate whether certain organisational models are related to higher performance in particular industries. Our configurations focus on internal fit, and are based on the concept of equifinality. There is no best strategy, structure, control mechanism, etc. Some combinations, however, when used as a consistent whole, will lead to higher effectiveness and performance. The implication of internal consistency for performance will be discussed in the next section. This section will be devoted to the description and motivation of the different configurations.

Table 2-1 summarises the characteristics of the three configurations that are distinguished in this study. As indicated above, the starting point of these configurations is the organisational models as discussed in the first chapter: multidomestic, global and transnational. The characteristics summarised in Table 2-1 have all been discussed in this chapter, but not all of them have been related to the three different organisational models.

To start with *headquarters characteristics*, we would expect multidomestic companies to be smaller in *size*, measured as either the number of employees or the level of total sales, than global and transnational companies. The rationale behind this is that multidomestic companies are less focused on achieving efficiency and cost leadership by economies of scale than global companies. Differentiation is their main source of competitive advantage and these companies will therefore usually be smaller than global companies. Although transnational companies will be less focused on achieving economies of scale than their global counterparts, it is assumed that their combined emphasis on efficiency, differentiation and world-wide learning requires a rather large company size. Following the same rationale, the same distinction goes for the average size of subsidiaries: subsidiaries of multidomestic companies will be smaller than subsidiaries of global and transnational companies.

Transnational companies will be likely to exhibit a higher level of *multinationality*, that is, be more internationally oriented, than global and multidomestic companies, since the foreign market will be more important for these companies than for the two other types of multinationals. Although multidomestic companies will have a relatively large number of foreign subsidiaries, these subsidiaries are likely to be rather small, so that the total level of employment abroad will not be as high as for transnational companies. Global companies will concentrate their subsidiaries in a limited number of countries and the home country will continue to be the dominant locus of investment for important value-chain activities. For both global and multidomestic companies, the home market is still a major source of revenue, while transnational companies have internationalised their sales to a larger extent to fully exploit opportunities abroad.

Table 2-1 Configurations of multinational companies

Organisational model	Multidomestic	Global	Transnational
Headquarters characteristics			
• Size of the company	relatively small	relatively large	relatively large
• Extent of multinationality	medium	medium	high
• Level of diversity of operations	medium	low	high
Subsidiary characteristics			
• Average size of subsidiaries	relatively small	relatively large	relatively large
• Average age of subsidiaries	relatively old	relatively young	average age
• Total level of interdependence	low	high	high
• Level of HQ dependence	low	high	medium
• Level of subsidiary dependence	low	medium	high
• Local responsiveness	high	low	high
• % autonomous subsidiaries	high	low	medium
• % receptive subsidiaries	low	high	medium
• % active subsidiaries	low	low	high
• % production subsidiaries	high	low	high
• % R&D subsidiaries	low	low	high
• % acquired subsidiaries	high	low	medium
Level and type of control			
• Total level of control	low	high	high
• Level of personal centralised control	low	high	medium
• Level of bureaucratic formalised control	low	high	medium
• Level of output control	medium	medium	medium
• Level of control by socialisation and networks	medium	medium	high
Level and type of expatriation			
• Extent of expatriate presence	low	high	high
• Type of expatriate control	--	more direct	more indirect

The level of *heterogeneity* or diversity of operations is assumed highest for transnational companies because of their three-dimensional competitive strategy and the fact that subsidiaries can take a strategic role in these companies. This is assumed to lead to higher levels of diversity within the company. Since global companies focus on standardised products that can be sold world-wide, their level of heterogeneity is assumed to be rather low. Multidomestic companies will take a middle position since their focus on differentiation will imply a certain level of heterogeneity. As their competitive strategy is less complex than that of the transnational company, their level of diversity will be somewhat lower.

Following the historical analysis in Chapter 1, subsidiaries of multidomestic companies are likely to be *older* than subsidiaries of global companies, simply because most of the multidomestic firms have a much longer history of international operation than the global firms that emerged mainly in the sixties and seventies. Another reason why subsidiaries of multidomestic companies are on average likely to be older is explained below, i.e. because acquisitions are more likely in multidomestic companies. Since most transnational companies will have grown out of either multidomestic or global companies, the age of their subsidiaries will most likely lie in between the age of subsidiaries of multidomestic and global companies.

The level of *interdependence* and *local responsiveness* for the various types of companies also follows directly from the description in the first chapter, and from Section 1 of this chapter. The level of interdependence will be lower for multidomestic companies, whose subsidiaries operate rather independently. Both global and transnational companies will have a high level of interdependence. For global companies, this means a high level of *de*pendence of subsidiaries on headquarters, while for transnational companies a high level of dependence *between* the various subsidiaries (see also Figure 2-1) will be present. Local responsiveness will of course be high for multidomestic companies, but also for transnational companies combining a high level of integration with a high level of responsiveness. Global companies will show low levels of local responsiveness as their focus is on integration.

As is done above, the two variables interdependence and responsiveness can be combined to depict different subsidiary roles: *autonomous*, *receptive* and *active* subsidiaries. Following the discussion in Chapter 1 and above, multidomestic companies will clearly have the largest number of autonomous subsidiaries, while global companies will have the largest number of receptive subsidiaries. Most of the active subsidiaries will be found in transnational companies, since these subsidiaries combine a high level of integration with the company as a whole with a high level of local responsiveness. Not all subsidiaries in transnational companies can or will be active, however. As Martinez and Jarillo (1991) indicate, the majority of subsidiaries in transnational companies will have receptive roles, and in view of their differentiated and flexible approach, some subsidiaries of transnational companies will have autonomous roles. The number of different subsidiary roles for different types of companies should be seen in relative and not in absolute terms. We do not therefore assume a one-to-one relationship between headquarters strategy and subsidiary strategy as is for instance done by Taggart (1996b).[66] The number of active subsidiaries will probably be very small in every type of company, since most subsidiaries will have either receptive or autonomous roles.

Concerning the different subsidiary types, we would like to make a distinction between the three different types of companies for the importance of *production* and *R&D subsidiaries* only. More production subsidiaries will be found in both multidomestic and transnational companies, when compared to their global counterparts. The rationale behind this is that the latter type of companies will concentrate their production in a limited number of locations and are less likely to produce products locally. Since subsidiaries in transnational companies are more likely to have strategic roles than subsidiaries in the other types of companies, we would expect subsidiaries with an R&D function, which can be considered to be particularly strategic, to occur more frequently in transnational companies.

The loosely coupled multidomestic structure explains why *acquisitions* are more likely to be found in this type of company. Acquired subsidiaries do not have to be completely integrated and can be left to operate rather independently. This would not be a viable option in global companies, which are therefore hypothesised to have a rather high number of greenfields. In addition, the focus on local responsiveness that is found in both multidomestic and transnational companies will increase the likelihood that local market knowledge or a local market position is bought through acquiring an existing company.

The summary of the *level and type of control* for the various types of companies follows directly from our discussion in Section 1 and will therefore not be discussed any further at this point. What does merit further attention is the *presence* and *role* of *expatriates* in the various types of companies. Expatriate presence is assumed lowest in multidomestic companies, because in this type of companies subsidiaries are rather autonomous. High expatriate presence is expected in both global and transnational companies. In global companies, the role of expatriates will lie mainly in the field of direct control; they act as an alternative for centralisation of decision-making. In transnational companies, on the other hand, expatriates will be mainly used to achieve control by socialisation and networks (indirect control).

---

[66] In his subsequent empirical analysis Taggart does not find strong support for this one-to-one relationship. In our view, this is entirely logical, since not every subsidiary can be expected to follow the same role given a certain headquarters strategy.

The main objective of this section has been to construct configurations of characteristics that can be used to summarise many of the relationships discussed earlier, and to simplify the complexity of MNC types. In the empirical part of this book, for each of these characteristics we will systematically test whether there are significant differences between MNCs following different international strategies. We will not investigate the interactions between the various characteristics themselves, although some of them are the subject of hypotheses in an earlier section of either this chapter or Chapter 1 (e.g. the positive relationship between *inter*dependence and control by socialisation and networks or the larger expatriate presence in larger subsidiaries).

A second objective of the construction of these configurations is to be able to test whether firms that have a higher level of internal consistency outperform other firms. However, performance is an ambiguous concept and can be explained by a multitude of factors. In the next section, we will therefore first discuss the problems associated with the explanation of performance differences between firms.

Comparing performance between multinationals: determinants and measurement issues

Introduction

Explaining differences in performance between companies is a hazardous issue. Firstly, firm performance is determined by a multitude of different factors. Hansen and Wernerfelt (1989), distinguish two broad groups of factors that are considered important determinants of firm performance: "economic" and "organisational factors".[67] Associated with these two groups of factors are different streams of research. Researchers in the economic tradition, usually called industrial organisation economics, emphasise external market factors. According to Hansen and Wernerfelt (1989), the most important determinants in this field include: industry characteristics, the firm's position relative to its competitors (mainly relative market share) and firm's variables such as size and relatedly diversification. The second stream of research, which builds heavily on behavioural and sociological foundations, is usually referred to as organisation behaviour or theory. In this field of research, there is much less

---

[67] Although we will use the terms economic and organisational factors in the remainder of the book , these terms should not be interpreted too literally. When we subsume industry under the economic factor, this does not mean that we close our eyes to the social and cultural aspects of industries; it simply means that the factor industry has received most attention from researchers in the economic tradition, just as is the case with the influence of size, diversity and multinationality on performance. In order to enhance comparability with previous studies, we have therefore chosen to deal with "economic" and "organisational" factors separately, before they are combined in an integrated analysis at the end of this chapter.

agreement on which factors to include to explain differences in performance. Hansen and Wernerfelt select organisation climate or culture[68] as one of the most-used organisational factors. In addition, Hansen and Wernerfelt refer to the importance that internal organisation researchers attach to fit with the external environment. To this, we might add a focus on internal fit or consistency as repeatedly discussed above. Since the focus of this book is on the internal functioning of MNCs, the effects of both organisational culture and internal consistency on performance will be discussed in a separate section. Hansen and Wernerfelt, however, found that both "economic" and "organisational" factors are significant determinants of firm performance. More importantly, the effects are roughly independent so that both contribute to an explanation of part of the performance differences.[69] It is therefore desirable that we pay some attention to the "economic" factors as well. This will be done in the remainder of this section. First, however, we will turn to a second major problem in performance measurement: how exactly do we measure it?

Performance measurement: what to measure?[70]

The measurement of performance is by no mean an unambiguous issue. In a review on the subject Venkatraman and Ramanujam (1986) claim: "Although the importance of the performance concept [...] is widely recognised [...], the treatment of performance in research settings is perhaps one of the thorniest issues confronting the academic researcher today." Organisational performance can be measured across a wide variety of dimensions. A very broad distinction can be made between financial and non-financial or operational performance indicators (Venkatraman and Ramanujam, 1986).[71] An extensive summary of non-financial performance indicators can be found in Whitt and

---

[68] Although we are aware of the (subtle) differences between climate and culture (see e.g. Denison, 1996 and Koene, 1996 for a description), we choose to use them as interchangeable in the context of this study.

[69] Hansen and Wernerfelt found organisational factors more important in explaining performance differences than economic factors. They also refer to a study by Schmalensee (1985), however, in which almost all of the variance in performance was explained by differences between industries. Of course, the relative influence of 'economic' and 'organisational' factors might be highly dependent on the specific sample of firms that is studied.

[70] Although the operationalisation of the various concepts in this study is not discussed before Section 2 in Chapter 3, we will justify our choice of the specific performance indicators in this section. The reason for this is that our choice is closely related to the problems associated with performance measurement in an international context.

[71] A different distinction is made by Paauwe (1996). To further research on the link between HRM and performance, he proposes a multiple perspective on performance. In doing so he distinguishes three dimensions of performance: strategic, professional and societal, and indicates five measuring units: quality of output, quantity of output, time, financial and behaviour, resulting in 14 different performance indicators (no indicator is supplied for the professional/financial intersection). Although the paper is focused on HRM, the same basic scheme could be adjusted for other areas.

Whitt (1988) and Gosling (1988). Some examples of these indicators are: commitment to quality, market growth, employee morale, market share, customer awareness, cost of downtime production flexibility, safety etc. These performance indicators might be very useful in studies with a very clearly delineated goal, e.g. measuring the impact of a training programme on employee morale or customer awareness. They are less suitable as a summary of overall firm performance, however.[72] Further, most of these indicators are for internal use only and are hard to come by for an outsider.

Financial performance indicators can also take numerous forms. Ketchen, Thomas and Snow (1993) mention some 35 financial measures that have been used to measure the performance of strategic groups. Most of these indicators refer either to profitability or to growth. Popular profitability measures are return on sales (ROS) and measures of return on investment (ROI) (return on assets (ROA) or return on shareholder equity (ROE), for instance). Growth indicators include sales growth and the growth versions of ROS and ROI. Most studies that investigate performance differences between firms use ROS, ROA, ROE or a combination of these indicators. ROA is used by Hansen and Wernerfelt (1989) and Haar (1989), while Rugman (1983) uses ROE. Geringer, Beamish and daCosta (1989) prefer ROS, but also include ROA and would have liked to include ROE as well. Lee and Blevins (1990) also use ROA, ROS, ROE and ROI, but add a growth measure (sales growth). The same is done by Roth and Morrison (1990), who combine ROI with sales growth. In addition to various other financial performance measures (e.g. current ratio, acid test, cash flow to debt), Soenen and Van den Bulcke (1988) use ROA and ROE, but net sales margin instead of ROS. Blaine (1994) also combines ROE and ROA with a pre-tax measure of performance: operating margin. In nearly all of these articles, performance indicators are collected for a five- to ten-year period.

Comparing performance in an international context introduces two major difficulties that influence the type of performance measures that can be used. First, in order to make valid comparisons, performance indicators should be collected for at least a five-year period, so that peculiarities of one single year do not distort the overall picture. Further, publicly available performance indicators are vastly preferable to questionnaire-collected performance indica-

---

[72] An exception to this might be net value added per employee as used by de Jong (1996) to compare the productivity of large European companies. Unfortunately, this measure suffers from vulnerability to exchange rate fluctuations. The lower value added per employee and the lower growth of value added of British companies is used by de Jong to support his claim of superiority of the Rhineland model over the Anglo-Saxon model. However, this difference might very well be due to the drastic devaluation of the pound sterling in relation to the ECU, the common measurement unit used in this study, in September 1992 when England decided to leave the EMS.

tors.[73] The latter are likely to be inexact, especially when collected at subsidiary level, and many respondents will be either unable or unwilling to provide them. Using annual reports for all of the companies included in the survey over a five-year period might be an option. Given the fact that performance was only one of the many aspects discussed in this book, this was considered a too time-consuming option, however. Furthermore, most companies are likely to distribute only their latest annual reports. We therefore relied on the publicly available performance data of the world's largest 500 firms as published yearly by Fortune.[74] In order to compare companies from different countries, financial data in the Fortune Global 500 are converted to a common currency (the US$). Unfortunately, the exchange rate between the dollar and many other currencies has fluctuated considerably over the period in question. Differences in performance indicators for non-American firms over various years will therefore be due to a combination of "real" differences and exchange rate fluctuations. Fortunately, this does not introduce any problems for the ROS, ROE and ROA indicators, since converted figures appear in both the numerator and the denominator of the formula that is used to calculate the indicator. Any exchange rate fluctuations will be cancelled out in this way. Growth measures, however, are calculated by dividing the value of a given indicator for one particular year by its equivalent for the previous year. In this case, a growth in sales might be completely due to a depreciation of the dollar to the currency of the country in question, while a decline in sales (a negative growth rate) in a given year might simply be due to an appreciation of the dollar. As filtering out this exchange rate influence would again require a too large time investment, we decided not to use growth measures in our analysis.[75]

Leaving out growth measures altogether leaves us with four regularly used performance measures: return on sales, return on equity, return on assets and operating margin. The choice between ROS and the alternative sales measure

---

[73] Of course, as Venkatraman and Ramanujam (1986) indicate, gathering data from *both* primary *and* secondary sources would be preferable, since this gives an opportunity to assess method convergence across different data sources and hence increases confidence in the operationalisation of constructs.

[74] In addition, 1994 annual reports were requested from all companies included in the survey and were provided by nearly all of them. These annual reports were used for companies that were not included in one or more of the yearly Fortune listings.

[75] Only two of the above studies included growth indicators. Lee and Blevins did indeed use annual reports, which is logical since the explanation of performance difference out of a limited number of variables was the sole purpose of their study. Roth and Morrison asked CEOs to rate their business unit's performance, since secondary data were not available. As the pre-test indicated that executives would be hesitant to disclose actual performance data, seven categories were included (negative, 0-5%, 5-10% etc.), which of course leads to a considerable loss of specificity. The fact that no performance differences were found in this study is therefore not surprising.

operating margin brings us to another major problem in comparing firm performance across countries. Both Soenen and Van den Bulcke (1988) and Blaine (1994) used a pre-tax sales measure. Although the former did not justify their choice, Blaine indicates that differing tax rates between countries might confound national differences in firm performance. Lower scores on the profitability measures in some countries might be due to differences in tax rates. Including a pre-tax indicator would solve this problem. Unfortunately, pre-tax figures are not publicly available, introducing the same problem as above, a time-consuming search in numerous annual reports. Further, in both studies differences between countries on the pre-tax measures were just as large as on the after-tax measures (ROE and ROA). Also, in Blaine's study an adjustment for tax differences considerably reduced the national differences in ROA, but increased them for ROE. Finally, as indicated by Blaine, differences in tax rates are not the only factor that can confound an international comparison of performance. Differences in accounting practices between countries concerning, for instance, depreciation, consolidation method, and foreign currency gains/loss will also influence these differences. It would be next to impossible, however, to adjust performance indicators for these measures.[76] Since pre-tax figures are not publicly available, we prefer to use ROS as a sales measure. ROA and ROE will be used as measures of return on investment. Following Blaine's example, however, we will adjust the three measures to reflect differences in corporate tax rates.

Country of origin and "economic" factors explaining performance differences between MNCs

Above we indicated that, in addition to organisational factors, differences in "economic" factors might also explain performance differences between firms. Three of the economic factors identified by Hansen and Wernerfelt (1989), industry, size and diversification, were also included in our study. In addition, many researchers in the field of international business, an area dominated by economists, have investigated the influence of multinationality on performance. Since multinationality is one of the headquarters characteristics included in our study, we will review the performance effects of this factor as well. Finally, many investigators of MNC performance have found the country of origin to be an important differentiating factor in firm performance. Although country of origin is clearly not an economic factor - it can have political, social, cultural, legal as well as economic aspects - we will

---

[76] Although Blaine does not attempt to make adjustments other than for different tax rates, he does indicate the likely impact of differing accounting practices. The overall effect of the difference in practice would be an increase in the various indicators for the USA and a decrease for the two other countries included in the survey.

discuss its effects in this section, simply because regarding it as an organisational factor would be an even worse choice. This section will therefore discuss the following factors that might explain performance differences: country of origin, industry, size, multinationality and diversification.

Country of origin Quite a number of researchers have investigated differences in performance between firms from different countries. Since the firms included in these samples were nearly always the largest companies in the respective countries, most of the studies concerned multinationals. Buckley, Dunning and Pearce (1978) found the nationality effect on growth and profitability to be significant. They did not give any details, however, about the specific countries that were found to host either high- or low-performing firms. Rugman (1983) compared the performance of American and European MNCs over a period of ten years (1970-1979). Performance was measured as ROE. American firms outperformed European firms by a considerable margin. Average ROE was 8.36% for European firms and 12.95% for American firms. Soenen and Van den Bulcke (1988) took a slightly different approach and compared performance levels of Belgian MNCs with Belgian subsidiaries of European and American firms over a five-year period (1979-1983). Concerning profitability (measured as ROE, ROA and net sales margin), American subsidiaries outperformed both European subsidiaries and Belgian companies although the difference was larger for the latter. Geringer, Beamish and daCosta (1989) included the largest 100 American and the largest 100 European MNCs in their study on the impact of diversification strategy and internationalisation on performance. In addition to the influence of these two variables, which will be discussed below, the authors found large differences in performance between American and European firms. Over a five-year period (1977-1981) ROS was 5.16% for American and 1.52% for European firms, while ROA was 6.82% for American versus 2.05% for European firms. Haar (1989) studied the ROA of the 50 largest American, European and Japanese companies over the 1980-1985 period. Again ROA of American companies was found to be highest with 5.8%, while Japanese and European firms had ROA percentages of 1.5 and 2.4 respectively. In the regression analysis, however, nationality was only significant when past profitability (1975-1979) was excluded as a predictor variable. Lee and Blevins (1990) examined American, Japanese, Korean and Taiwanese firms in the 1980-1987 period and once again American companies consistently outperformed their foreign rivals, regardless of whether performance was measured as ROE, ROA, ROI or ROS. Only for the sales growth variable did Korea perform better. Brown, Soybel and Stickney (1994) compare American and Japanese firms on a number of financial statement ratios for the years 1985-1988. Since American firms turn over assets other than inventory more quickly than Japanese firms, they have a significantly higher ROA. This difference increases over the years. Finally, Blaine (1994) concludes that in spite of the vast differences in the approaches used in previous studies it seems safe to say that American firms consistently outperformed similar Japanese and European firms during the period under study (1970-1987). Therefore, we will put forward the following hypothesis:

> Hypothesis 2-48: MNCs from different countries will differ significantly on the performance indicators included in the study. Specifically, American firms will outperform both European and Japanese firms on all the performance indicators included in our study.

Blaine's own study over the 1985-1989 period partly contradicts previous findings, however. Using a pre-tax sales measure, he finds that German firms have lower operating margins than American firms, while Japanese companies have approximately the same operating margins as American firms. The American "advantage" for ROA is lost when the figures are adjusted for differences in tax rates. Concerning ROE, the higher level of ROE for German companies becomes significant when adjusting for tax rates. Since most of the divergence with regard to previous studies is due to the fact that Blaine offers measures adjusted for tax differences, we will offer the following additional hypothesis:

> Hypothesis 2-49: When adjusted for different tax rates, the difference in performance between MNCs from different countries will no longer be significant. More specifically, American firms will no longer outperform both European and Japanese firms on all the performance indictors included in our study.

Given these large differences in performance between countries, especially when performance measures are not corrected for tax differences, researchers should be extremely careful to attribute performance differences to a specific independent variable in studies where multiple countries are involved. Above, we suggested that the higher performance levels for "fit" companies in the Ghoshal and Nohria (1993) study might be due to the fact that a disproportionate number of "fit" companies were of American origin. A more serious example of a possible misinterpretation of performance indicators can be found in a recent *Management International Review* article by Peterson et al. (1996). Peterson et al. try to relate the level of "best practices" in expatriate management to corporate performance in a sample of American, European and Japanese firms. Finding no significant overall relationship, they try to relate each of the individual best practices to performance and find - to their considerable surprise - that the importance of foreign language proficiency, encouragement of foreign language lessons for the expatriate overseas and a system in place for assignees to meet someone with local experience are all *negatively* related to one or more of their performance indicators. As the authors (or at least one of the reviewers) should have realised, both European and especially Japanese firms combine a high adherence to expatriate management "best practices" (as indicated in their own findings and e.g. Tung, 1982, 1987) with a rather low level of financial performance, while the reverse (low adherence to best practices, high financial performance) is true for American firms. This study thus offers a crystal-clear example of why statistical association does not always imply a causal influence. In particular, the very strong and very significant negative relationship between encouragement of foreign language lessons - which they had previously shown to be significantly different between the USA on the one hand, and Japan/Europe on the other hand - and all of the four performance indicators should have rung a bell.

Size Size is one of the elements that is included in the economic model of firm performance put forward by Hansen and Wernerfelt (1989). According to the authors, size is most often interpreted as a source of organisational costs or as a source of inefficiencies. In their empirical analysis they indeed found a significant negative correlation between firm size (measured as the natural logarithm of total assets) and performance. Buckley et al. (1978) found a significant negative relationship between size (measured as total sales) and growth. The relationship between size and profitability was also consistently negative over the period of investigation 1962-1972, but did not achieve significance. Kumar (1984) found a significant negative relationship for both growth and especially profitability. Rugman (1983) and Haar (1989) did not find a significant relationship between size and performance when using total sales as an indicator of size. As three studies found a negative relationship and the two others did not offer contradictory evidence, we will put forward the following hypothesis:

> Hypothesis 2-50: The size of an MNC will be negatively related to its performance.

Diversification As indicated by Datta, Rajagopolan and Rasheed (1991), "the relationship between diversification and performance has been one of the most extensively researched areas in the discipline of industrial organisation, strategic management and finance" (ibid.:529). In their review on the subject, they distinguish three broad conceptualisations of diversification: the degree of diversification, the type of diversification strategy and the mode of diversification. Our main focus will be on the influence of the type of diversification strategy on performance, a research area that originated in the field of strategic management, and within the field of diversification has been the most extensively researched area so far. The primary focus of research in this tradition is testing the hypothesis that firms following a strategy of related diversification will outperform firms that pursue unrelated diversification. The rationale for this hypothesis is provided in the seminal work by Rumelt (1974, 1982) who claims that, unlike unrelated diversification, related diversification permits the core skills of the company to be transferred. In addition, synergistic advantages are more easily realised when pursuing a strategy of related diversification. The hypothesis could be accepted in Rumelt's own study. As Datta et al. (1991) indicate, however, for each subsequent study that found support for the hypothesis, there is one that failed to find evidence that firms pursuing related diversification strategies outperformed unrelated diversifiers (although no support was found for the opposite either). The result is that: "after almost 25 years of fairly intense research and investigation, very little can be said with certainty on the diversification-performance relationship" (Datta et al.:545) As the authors of one of the studies that did find support for the hypothesis, Geringer et al. (1989) indicate, studies on diversification strategy have always been confined to single-nation studies. It would therefore be interesting to test the original hypothesis in a multiple-country study:

> Hypothesis 2-51: MNCs employing a related diversification strategy show higher performance levels than MNCs that employ an unrelated diversification strategy.

Multinationality The history, intensity of research activity and the state of knowledge concerning the relationship between multinationality and performance resembles that between diversification and performance rather closely. Its starting point lay in the early 1970s, when Vernon (1971) showed that MNCs had a higher return on assets than firms that were purely domestic. However, subsequent empirical research has shown very mixed results, with some studies confirming Vernon's findings, while others found an inconclusive relationship between multinationality - measured as the percentage of foreign sales - and performance, and yet others found a clear negative relationship (see Ramaswamy, 1992 and Sullivan, 1994b for an overview of studies in this field). As concluded by Grant (1987): "Despite rapid advances in the theory of multinational enterprise and a burgeoning empirical literature on the causes and consequences of overseas direct investment, understanding of how multinational expansion affects firm performance remains limited" (Grant, 1987:79).

Theoretically, there is a broad consensus about the positive impact of multinationality and performance (Daniels and Bracker, 1989; Grant, 1987; Ramaswamy, 1992). Grant summarises the reasons for expecting this positive relationship under four headings: returns to intangible assets, market power conferred by international scope, capacity to undertake risky investments and broadening of investment opportunities. A less abstract list of reasons is given by Daniels and Bracker who mention cost savings, access to technological and other resources, tax deferment or reduction, sales expansion and the extension of products' life cycles. In view of the general acceptance of the positive relationship between multinationality and performance, we will put forward the following hypothesis:

Hypothesis 2-52: A higher level of multinationality will be positively related to performance.

Our research does add to previous research in that it provides a test of the relationship in a multi-country study and uses a more sophisticated operationalisation of the concept of multinationality (see Chapter 3).

Industry A final "economic" aspect that will be included in the analysis of performance differences is the industry in which a company operates. Many of the studies above paid no attention to industry differences, and sometimes did not even include the industry distribution in their sample description. Buckley et al. (1978), however, found industry effects significant for both growth and profitability. This was only the case for the American firms in their sample, however. For non-American firms, nationality of the parent had a higher explanatory power. No details are given as to which industries are either high or low performers. Kumar's (1984) study also found a significant explanatory power for industry. Again, no indication is given as to which industries are either high or low performers. Haar (1989) also found industry to be a significant explanatory factor, especially when past performance was excluded as a predictor variable. The industries included in Haar's study were nearly the same as the ones included in our sample except for the fact that Haar's study the paper and pharmaceutical industry are found in the miscellaneous category, while Haar's study also includes metal manufacturing and industrial and farm equipment. The following individual industry dummies were significant in the regression analysis: chemicals, metals, motor vehicles and industrial equipment. Unfortunately, the size and sign of their influence is again not revealed. Hansen and Wernerfelt (1989) also find industry to be a significant factor in explaining performance differences. However, once more in this study no additional information is given on the specific influence of individual industry. Hansen and Wernerfelt refer to a study by Schmalensee (1985), however, in which industry differences (measured as industry ROA) explained almost all (at least 75%) of the variance in business unit performance. We will therefore put forward the following general hypothesis:

Hypothesis 2-53: There will be significant differences in performance between industries.

Performance implications: "organisational" factors

In this section, we will look at the "organisational" factors that could explain performance differences between firms. As discussed above, corporate culture is often seen as an important determinant of performance. In the first part of this section, we will therefore review various national and international studies that try to relate corporate culture to performance. As already mentioned in Chapter 1, implicit in most of the discussions on multinational companies is that the transnational company should be seen as an ideal type that is most suited to today's international competitive environment. Although Ghoshal and Nohria (1993) explicitly qualify this general idea, by claiming that it was never the intention of the writings by Bartlett and Ghoshal to portray one ideal type of company, they nevertheless indicate that more and more industries will face "transnational" requirements. We will therefore also explore the evidence related to performance consequences of various organisational models.

As discussed in previous sections, an important idea that underlies much of the research in the field of organisation studies is that external and internal fit lead to better performance. In the second part of this section we will therefore offer some hypotheses regarding the effect of both external and internal fit on performance in multinational companies, following the configurations as described above.

Performance consequences of corporate culture and the transnational organisational model

As indicated in the previous section, organisation climate or culture is one of the most-used organisational factors to explain differences in performance between companies. Many of these studies (e.g. Hansen and Wernerfelt, 1989; Posner, Kouzes and Schmidt, 1985; see Koene, 1996:29-32 for a more extensive overview) relate specific elements of corporate culture to a multitude of performance indicators. In view of the fact that the culture-performance relationship is only one of the many aspects that is investigated in this book, we will focus only on studies that relate the strength of corporate culture to financial performance.[77]

In a national context, Denison (1990) found culture strength to be positively related to organisational performance (measured as ROI and ROS) but negatively to future performance. These results are confirmed by Gordon and DiTomasso (1992) who find a strong corporate culture to be positively related

---

[77] Although a strong corporate culture is usually regarded as beneficial for a company, there are some obvious disadvantages, such as groupthink (Janis, 1972; Gerrichhauzen, 1991) and loss of flexibility (Welch and Welch, 1997).

to short-term performance. Calori and Sarnin (1991) found cultural intensity and homogeneity to be positively related to firms' growth, a more future-oriented variable. In a later study, Denison and Mishra (1995) also found cultural consistency to be strongly positively related to return on assets. The relationship with sales growth was somewhat weaker, however.

In an international context Ghoshal and Nohria (1989, Nohria and Ghoshal, 1994) find a strong positive relationship between the level of shared values between headquarters and subsidiaries and ROA, growth in ROA and sales growth. In Wolf's (1994) study shared values is the only control mechanism that is positively related to all of the performance (both financial and non-financial) indicators included in the study. The relationships that are found are strong and very significant. We will therefore put forward the following hypothesis:

Hypothesis 2-54: The level of shared values between headquarters and subsidiaries will be positively related to the overall performance of the MNC.

Although, as indicated above, many publications implicitly assume that the transnational company is best equipped for today's competitive environment, very few studies have empirically investigated the performance consequences of various organisational models. Roth and Morrison (1990) did not find any significant differences in performance between the various strategies included in their study (multifocal, global integration and locally responsive), although overall the multifocal strategy scored slightly better than two other strategies. Brinkgreve (1993) found that the transnational companies in his sample had nearly twice the ROA of non-transnational companies. Their sales growth was also slightly higher (12.5% vs 10.5%). The same result was found when transnational industries were compared with non-transnational industries. None of the differences was significant at the 5% level, however. Because of the general appeal of the argument and the fact that there are some slight empirical indications confirming it, we will put forward the following hypothesis:

Hypothesis 2-55: Companies following transnational models will outperform companies that follow either multidomestic or global models.

In addition, we would expect to see a different magnitude of performance differences *between* countries for firms following different international strategies. More specifically, differences between countries will be smaller for firms that follow a global or transnational strategy than for firms following a multidomestic strategy. Following Blaine (1994:126-127), the logic behind this argument is as follows. First, the creation of global markets and industries, as documented by many of the authors discussed in the previous chapter (e.g. Hout, Porter and Rudden, 1982; Prahalad and Doz, 1987; and Bartlett and Ghoshal, 1989), creates identical environmental threats and opportunities for similar firms in all nations. Second, firms in similar environmental contexts are assumed to adopt similar strategies and structures. Third, as performance is assumed a function of the fit between a firm's structure and environment, firms that adopt similar organisational responses should earn similar rates of return. Therefore, in general, similar firms headquartered in different nations should earn comparable rates of return. As Blaine correctly indicates, however, not all firms are global in nature. Although the global convergence effect might be present for highly integrated global and transnational firms, it will be much weaker for multidomestic firms that compete locally, focus on national responsiveness and are less globally integrated.

> Hypothesis 2-56: Performance differences between countries will be smaller for firms that follow a global or transnational model than for firms following a multidomestic model.

Performance consequences of configurational fit

Having discussed the possible impact of shared values and the type of organisational model on performance, we will now deal with the effect of configurational fit on performance. The focus will be on internal fit, that is, the fit between organisational model and processes within an MNC. In Chapter 1, however, we discussed the most likely MNC strategies and structures for the various industries included in this study. We would expect companies that have an external fit, that is, have the type of organisational model that fits the industry, would be more effective than companies that have a misfit. Therefore:

> Hypothesis 2-57: The closer the fit between industry and organisational model, the higher the performance.

Concerning internal fit, Miller (1982:137) suggests that there "is little doubt, based on empirical evidence that the integrity of the alignment among structural elements is an important determinant of performance". Above we discussed three ideal profiles of multinational companies that summarised most of the characteristics that had been discussed previously. Each of these ideal types showed a particular combination of characteristics that are hypothesised to occur together. Not all of these characteristics, however, are assumed part of an ideal profile with performance consequences. Performance consequences are hypothesised to be mainly the result of a fit between organisational model on the one hand and control mechanisms on the other hand, both at headquarters and at subsidiary level. The ideal profile of control mechanisms for various headquarters organisational models is summarised in Table

2-1. This same ideal profile is hypothesised to apply to the different subsidiary strategies or roles. Active subsidiaries, for instance, will have the same ideal profile for control mechanisms as transnational companies. We will therefore put forward the following hypotheses:

Hypothesis 2-58: The closer the fit between the organisational model applied by headquarters and the control mechanisms used towards its subsidiaries, the higher the performance of the MNC as a whole.

And:

Hypothesis 2-59: The closer the overall fit within an MNC between subsidiary roles and the control mechanisms used towards these subsidiaries, the higher the performance of the MNC as a whole.

Very few authors have investigated the influence of configurational fit in an international context. Above, we referred to the study by Ghoshal and Nohria (1993) and signalled the limitations of this study. The fact that researchers in the field of international management embrace this study very enthusiastically in itself indicates the lack of empirical studies in this field. Contrary to his expectations, Wolf (1994) did not find a positive correlation between adherence to an ideal profile and performance. He did find a negative correlation, however, between a lower than ideal use of the various control mechanisms for a given organisational model and performance. In a later article Nohria and Ghoshal (1994) link the idea of differentiated fit (different use of control mechanisms for different subsidiaries) and shared values and show that companies that combine these two control strategies outperform all other firms. This connects the idea of configurational fit discussed here and the importance of shared values as discussed above. We will therefore put forward the following hypothesis:

Hypothesis 2-60: Multinationals that combine a high level of control by socialisation and networks (shared values) with a fit at subsidiary level will outperform other multinationals.

Conclusions

In this section, we have integrated many of the variables discussed in previous sections into three distinct configurations of MNCs. Before doing so, however, we explored the relevance of configuration analysis in both a national and an international context. A final aspect that was added in this section was performance. Explaining performance differences between firms is a hazardous enterprise, since there are a multitude of factors that could influence performance. These factors are often divided into two categories: "economic" and "organisational". Some of the economic factors were discussed, as was the problem of choosing the right performance indicators. In a final section, we focused on the organisational factors that could explain differences in performance between companies: the strength of the corporate culture, the type of organisational model that an MNC uses, and the extent of configurational fit between organisational model and control mechanisms at both headquarters and subsidiary level. In Chapters 4 and 5 we will test the hypotheses that have been put forward in this and the previous chapter. First, however, in Chapter 3, we will focus on the design and methodological aspects of our study.

3. Research design and methodology

The two previous chapters provided the theoretical background for our study. This chapter will be devoted to a description of the research design and methodology. In a first section, we will discuss the problems associated with cross-cultural research. Section 2 then deals with the choice of the research method and the operationalisation of the variables included in this study. A more detailed description of the manner in which the mail survey, the research method selected to collect our data, has been organised can be found in Section 3. A final section describes the sample and investigates whether it can be considered representative for the population of MNCs in general.

1. CROSS-CULTURAL RESEARCH

Introduction

We will discuss cross-cultural research and the specific problems associated with it. The next section discusses the role of contingencies, choice and culture in cross-cultural research in general and in this study in particular. A subsequent section reviews the different types of management studies involving culture as identified by Adler (1983a, 1984a). Our study is shown to be a combination of the comparative and geocentric type of research. The methodological issues associated with this type of research are subsequently discussed.

The role of contingencies, choice and culture in cross-cultural research

In this section, we will briefly discuss various factors of influence in cross-cultural research. We can distinguish three major influences on organisations in general and the application of control mechanisms in an international context in particular: contingency, choice and culture.[78] We do not intend to give

---

[78] This discussion is based on Harzing and Hofstede (1996). A more extensive description of the model and an application to organisational change processes can be found in Harzing (1991).

an exhaustive overview of research in any of these three areas. Our main objective is to show that all three are relevant for our study on control mechanisms in multinational firms.

Contingency

Contingency theories of organisation postulate that the circumstances in the environment dictate organisation members' patterns of perceptions and preferences. Classical contingency theories, developed in the 1950s and 1960s (such as Burns and Stalker, 1961 in Britain; Lawrence and Lorsch, 1967 in the USA) at least implicitly assume that these patterns will be universal across national boundaries. The universality assumption is explicit in the "culture-free hypothesis" of US authors Harbison and Myers (1959). According to them, there is a general logic in the development of management methods applicable to both industrialised and industrialising countries. This logic of industrialisation prevails irrespective of the cultural setting, though Harbison and Myers admitted that cultural factors could influence the process and slow it down.

A subsequent and mitigated version of the "culture-free hypothesis" was formulated in Britain as part of the "Aston" studies of organisational structure by Hickson et al. (1974:74). They argued that not so much organisational structures themselves, but *context-structure relations* are stable across societies: "Even though Indian organisations might turn out to be less formalised [...] than American organisations, bigger Indian units would still be more formalised than smaller Indian units [...]." Their version of the culture-free hypothesis therefore assumes a cumulative effect of contingency and (national) culture. Although contingency theory has received some criticism (see e.g. Miller, 1981; Schoonhoven, 1981), its less deterministic successor, neo-contingency theory (see below), is widely accepted in both academic and textbook literature. The majority of studies described in the previous chapters either explicitly or implicitly use a (neo-)contingency perspective.

Choice

Child (1972), originally a member of the Aston research team, broke away with a fundamental criticism of contingency. He stressed the importance of "strategic choice". Organisational structure is not simply determined by the environment: managers do have some freedom of choice. Child's article recognised that there will be constraints on this choice. These constraints, however, may be relatively unimportant for various reasons. First, organisational structure does not necessarily have a strong effect on organisational performance. Managers can live with "non-ideal" structures without this having a dominant effect on their organisation's performance. However, even if managers do consider structure important for performance, they can choose to satisfice: that is trade off some potential gain in performance for a congenially structured organisation. They can also try to modify the environment or choose another environment to operate in, in order to retain a preferred structure. Finally, the contingency perspective itself has to accommodate choice when environmental demands are conflicting and there is no single best choice possible. The concept of strategic choice gave an impetus to the development of the neo-contingency theory: although organisations are still thought to be influenced by their contextual contingencies, the relationship is less deterministic and the outcome less predictable than in the traditional contingency theory.

Culture

The recognition of basic differences between organisations in different parts of the world, by anybody familiar with such organisations, is much older than organisation theory itself. A concern with national culture arose in the management literature in the 1960s (Farmer and Richman, 1965; Oberg, 1963; Webber, 1969), but the message that organisation principles are culturally dependent remained revolutionary throughout the 1970s and 1980s (Adler et al, 1989; Brossard and Maurice, 1976; Cooper and Cox, 1989; Hofstede, 1980a/b; Kelley, Whatley and Worthley, 1987; Kelley and Worthley, 1981; Laurent, 1983; Osigweh, 1989; Sorge, 1977, 1983; Steers, 1989; Tayeb, 1988).

Child and Tayeb (1983) distinguish between theories that treat cultures as "ideational systems" and those that treat them as "adaptive systems". Ideational theories look upon cultures as sets of ideas, values, shared symbols, and meanings. The adaptive system tradition regards cultures as total ways of life by which communities have survived and adapted in their ecological settings. This tradition draws attention to the expression of culture in the forms taken by artefacts and institutions. Of course, these two approaches are in fact faces of the same coin (Sorge, 1995). The nature of a society's institutions can be regarded as the expression of its dominant value orientation. In this view, institutions reflect the choices - which might also be pragmatic rather than value-oriented - that have been made within societies among alternative structural arrangements to cope with problems such as maintenance of social order, the promotion of economic and technical development, the allocation of people to productive activity, and the distribution of material benefits in relation to services performed and personal need. These institutions in turn can reinforce the existing national value systems.

Although, by now, the belief in the universality of management or organisational science has been discarded as a myth by many authors, (e.g. Adler, 1983b/c; Hofstede, 1980a/b, 1991; Laurent, 1983; Osigweh, 1989; Ronen, 1986), a relatively small proportion of management research focuses on cross-cultural or international issues. Adler (1983a) found that only 4.2% of the organisational behaviour articles published in American management journals focused on cross-cultural or international issues. Of these publications, nearly half focused on a single country. Two studies that replicated her findings could not find a significant increase in the number of cross-cultural articles (Godkin, Braye and Caunch, 1989; Peng, Peterson and Shyi, 1991).

Contingency, choice, culture and control mechanisms
Figure 3-1 links the three aspects of contingency, choice and national culture in their consequences for the use of various control mechanisms. National culture first determines the values of the decision-makers within the organisation. These values will in turn influence the choice decision-makers make between the various possible options. What options are seen as possible is constrained by contingencies and national culture (both directly and through the values of the decision-maker). Decision-makers can influence contingencies to some extent; they can for instance move to a different environment or opt for a different technology. Furthermore, the decision-makers' value system can influence the way contingencies are perceived. A highly uncertainty-avoiding decision-maker will probably perceive a change in the environment as more threatening than a low uncertainty-avoiding decision-maker.

Figure 3-1 Contingency, choice, culture and control mechanisms

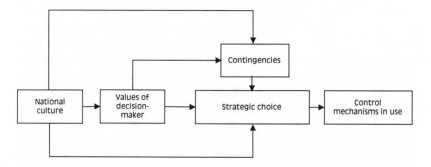

To make matters even more complex, national culture will also influence the occurrence of the various contingencies. Culture might for instance have an influence on the type of organisational model applied by headquarters, one of the contingency factors identified in this book as influencing the type of control mechanisms applied. Culture can therefore act as an independent variable in itself, but also as a moderator variable in the relationship between contingencies and control mechanisms. As Child (1981) indicates, this moderator effect will be particularly strong in micro-level processes of organisations relating to authority, style, conduct, participation and attitudes, and less pow-erful in macro-level issues such as formal structure and strategy.

A comparable point is made by Rosenzweig (1994), who provides a classi-ficatory scheme for management science theory, which is reproduced in Table 3-1. The variables included in a study can be either technical or social in na-ture. Since purely technical systems are not dependent on human behaviour, the relationship among technical variables is stable across countries and can therefore be generalised from one country to another. The same is not true for social systems, in which the relationships among variables often differ from country to country. A second distinction Rosenzweig makes is between closed and open systems. In closed systems, the focal variables interact with each other without being influenced by the external environment, while open sys-tems do interact with the external environment and might be dependent on it. Combining these two variables results in Table 3-1. Only theories in the first quadrant can be generalised across nations without questioning, while theo-ries in the fourth quadrant are severely restricted in their international gener-alisability. Our study falls in quadrant four, since it deals with an open social system.

Table 3-1 Types of management systems (Rosenzweig, 1994:32)

	NATURE OF FOCAL VARIABLES	
OPEN OR CLOSED SYSTEM	Technical	Social
Closed System	I	II
Open System	II	IV

Sometimes one of the constraining factors included in Figure 3-1 can be so strong as to leave the decision-maker practically no choice at all. Tayeb (1988) gives an example of the dominating influence of culture:

> In some countries the influence of cultural characteristics may override the influ-ence of contingency factors in shaping their organisations. For instance, mistrust and close direct supervision and control are prominent among Iranian cultural characteristics. In the Iranian study we found that some of the managers who had been educated in American and European universities were aware of the 'merits' of decentralisation of decision making in their organisations as an 'appropriate' re-sponse to their changing environment, but they were reluctant to apply such an ap-proach in their own companies. They did not trust subordinates' abilities and in-tentions to carry out their tasks "properly". (Tayeb, 1988:5-6)

The importance of contingency, choice and culture in our study
(Neo)-contingency theory is one of the most important foundations of our study. Most of the headquarters and subsidiary characteristics as discussed in Chapter 2 can be considered as contingency factors. Some of these character-

istics resemble the contingency factors included in the traditional organisation studies: age, size, interdependence, uncertainty and heterogeneity, although the specific operationalisation of these variables might differ in this study to reflect its international character. Others are specific to the study of MNCs: the extent of multinationality of the MNC, the local responsiveness of subsidiaries, subsidiary roles and the organisational model followed by headquarters. The two latter characteristics are also used in a more advanced configurational analysis, in which an adherence to an ideal-type combination of organisational model and control mechanisms is hypothesised to lead to better performance. Further, in the empirical analysis of the use of international transfers as a control mechanism, we hope to discover contingency factors that might explain their differential use.

The concept of choice is an important underlying factor in our study. We have already referred to the importance of strategic choice in Chapter 1, when we discussed the environment-strategy-structure-process paradigm. Strategic choice is very difficult to operationalise and measure, however, especially when using a survey method of data collection as was done in this study. We will therefore not pay specific attention to the concept of choice in the remainder of this thesis. Since we can only measure culture, contingencies and outcomes, we must keep in mind, however, that any relationship between culture and outcomes and contingencies and outcomes is mediated by strategic choice.

As already indicated above, our study can be classified in quadrant four of Rosenzweig's classification of management science theories, so that results found cannot be assumed universally applicable. Culture is therefore explicitly included as one of the independent variables in this study. Since culture is only one of the many independent variables in our study, however, we had to make a number of simplifications. Although we realise that national borders are not necessarily equivalent to cultural borders, for the sake of simplicity we equate nation with culture in this study. In the two previous chapters, we have offered some hypotheses on the influence of country of origin on the application of various strategies and in particular various control mechanisms. In addition, although some sophisticated treatises are available on the possible heterogeneity of culture *within* a nation (Boyacigiller et al., 1996; Enz, 1986), for the sake of simplicity we assume nations culturally homogeneous. Cultural distance between headquarters and subsidiary country is included as an independent explanatory factor in the application of control mechanisms, and especially in the use of international transfers as a control mechanism.

In addition, culture (or nation) is also included as an indirect or moderator variable in this study. Firstly, different countries might have different "endowments" of contingency factors. Differences in the application of control mechanisms related to different contingencies might in fact be country-of-origin differences, because of different contingency endowments across countries. In principle, multivariate statistical analysis should be able sort out these different influences, although much depends on the sample sizes that are realised for the different countries included in this study. Secondly, culture (or nation) might act as a moderator variable in some of the contingency/outcome relationships. In Section 2 of Chapter 2, we reviewed previous research that showed that some of these relationships are not constant across nations. In the empirical chapters we will therefore systematically analyse whether specific contingency/outcome relationships hold across nations. Again, however, the feasibility of this type of analysis is heavily dependent on the sample size for the different countries included in this study. Efforts to increase response rates and hence sample sizes are described in Section 3, while the sample itself is described in Section 4. For now, however, we will proceed with our discussion of cross-cultural research.

A typology of management studies involving culture

Adler (1983a, 1984a) provides a typology of management studies involving culture in which she delineates six approaches to researching cross-cultural management issues. Table 3-2 summarises the characteristics of these six different approaches. Parochial studies are studies originally designed and conducted in one culture by researchers from that particular culture. The overwhelming majority of this type of studies is American. Adler (1983b) published a review of over 11,000 articles published in 24 management journal between 1971 and 1980 and found approximately 80% of the publications to be studies of the USA conducted by Americans.[79] *Parochial* studies ignore culture and assume that their results are universal. Parochial studies usually do not assume that their culture is "better"; they simply ignore the fact that cultures might differ. *Ethnocentric* studies try to extend their theories to other cultures and in this sense there is often a flavour of cultural superiority in these studies. Theories of one culture are imposed on another culture. *Polycentric* research is in fact a collection of individual domestic studies conducted in various countries around the world. Polycentric studies are often descriptive in nature, using an inductive and often qualitative approach.

---

[79] A small sample of five years of articles in one American and two European international business/management journals (JIBS, MIR and IBR) showed the same American dominance in the field of international mail surveys. More than 80% of the *international* mail surveys originated from the USA.

Table 3-2 Types of cross-cultural management research (adapted from Adler 1983a:30-31)

Title	Approach to Similarity and Difference	Type of Study	Primary Question	Main Methodological Issues
PAROCHIAL RESEARCH	Single culture studies	Assumed similarity	Domestic management studies	What is the behaviour of people like in work organisations? Study is only applicable to management in one culture and yet it is assumed to be applicable to management in many cultures	*Traditional methodologies:* All of the traditional methodological issues concerning design, sampling, instrumentation, analysis and interpretation without reference to culture
ETHNOCENTRIC RESEARCH	Second culture studies	Search for similarity	Replication in foreign cultures of domestic management studies	Can we use home country theories abroad? Can this theory which is applicable to organisations in Culture A be extended to organisations in Culture B?	*Standardisation and translation:* How can management research be standardised across cultures? How can instruments be literally translated? Replication should be identical to the original study, with the exception of language
POLYCENTRIC RESEARCH	Studies in many cultures	Search for difference	Individual studies of organisations in specific foreign cultures	How do managers manage and employees behave in country X? What is the pattern of organisational relationships in country X?	*Description:* How can country X's organisation be studied without either using home country theories of models and without using obtrusive measures? Focus is on inductive methods and unobtrusive measures

COMPARATIVE RESEARCH	Studies contrasting many cultures	Search for both similarity and difference	How are the management and employee styles similar and different across cultures? Which theories hold and which do not?	*Equivalence:* Is the methodology equivalent at each stage in the research process? Are the meanings of key concepts defined equivalently? Has the research been designed such that the samples, instrumentation, administration, analysis and interpretation are equivalent with reference to the cultures included?
GEOCENTRIC RESEARCH	International management studies	Search for similarity	How do multinational organisations function?	*Geographic dispersion:* All of the traditional methodological questions are relevant with the added complexity of geographical distance. Translation is often less of a problem since most MNCs have a common language across all countries in which they operate. The primary question is to develop an approach for studying the complexity of a large organisation. Culture is frequently ignored.
SYNERGISTIC RESEARCH	Intercultural management studies	Use of similarities and differences as a resource	How can the intercultural interaction within a domestic or international organisation be managed? How can organisations create structures and processes which will be effective in working with members of all cultures?	*Interaction models and integrating processes:* What are effective ways to study cross-cultural interaction within organisational settings? How can universal and culturally specific patterns of management be distinguished? What is the appropriate balance between culturally specific and universal processes within one organisation? How can the proactive use of cultural differences to create universally accepted organisational patterns be studied?

Comparative studies explicitly focus on similarities and differences between cultures. They are truly cross-cultural in a sense that they compare organisations in different cultures for the phenomenon under study. They lie between ethnocentric studies that focus on culture-general aspects and polycentric studies that focus on culture-specific aspects of a given phenomenon. Although either the culture-general or the culture-specific element may dominate in a particular study, comparative studies do not start with the idea of a dominant or superior culture. Comparative studies are accompanied by a host of methodological issues that will be discussed in detail in the next section. Most studies discussed in previous chapters can be classified as *geocentric* research, research that focuses on the functioning of MNCs. Although Adler (1983c) indicates that it is the combination of multiculturalism and geographic dispersion that distinguishes multinationals from domestic organisations, most of the studies in the field of international business focused on geographic dispersion, often ignoring cultural differences. A final research approach, the *synergistic* approach, focuses on the *interaction* between different cultures. The recently flourishing research stream on multicultural work groups is an excellent example of research in this field (see e.g. Milliken and Martins, 1996; Thomas, Ravlin and Wallace, 1996; Watson, Kumar and Michaelson, 1993).

Our study has elements of both the comparative and the geocentric type of research. Since the focus of our study is on control mechanisms in *multinationals*, the geocentric approach is clearly applicable. Unlike many other studies that follow this approach, however, cultural differences are not ignored in our study and are indeed an integral element of the research design. The population of our study has been constructed in such a way that systematic comparisons across countries are possible. The synergistic approach would be ideally suitable for a more detailed study on how international transfers can be used to socialise subsidiary employees. In our study, however, the focus in this respect is on testing empirically the claim that international transfers *can* help to achieve control by socialisation and networks, not on explicating *how* they do this. As our research has elements of both comparative and geocentric research, we are confronted with two major methodological issues: equivalence and geographic dispersion. Geographic dispersion mainly influences the method of data collection and the practical issues associated with collecting data in geographically distant countries. These issues will be discussed in Sections 2 and 3. Equivalence will be discussed in the next subsection, where we discuss methodological problems in cross-cultural research or comparative research.

Methodological problems in cross-cultural research

As indicated in the previous subsection, comparative or cross-cultural research is accompanied by a multitude of methodological problems. Most of these problems can be subsumed under the heading equivalence.[80] Since the overview of methodological issues given by Adler (1983a, 1984a) incorporates most of the issues discussed by other authors (see e.g. Brewster et al., 1996; Cavusgil and Das, 1997; Douglas and Craig, 1983; Green and White, 1976; Harpaz, 1996; Hines, 1993; Hofstede and Spangenberg, 1986; Mullen, 1995; Nasif et al., 1991; Rosenzweig, 1994; Sekaran, 1983; Singh, 1995; Wright, Lane and Beamish, 1988), we will take this overview as our starting point. However, as our study combines the comparative and the geocentric approach, not all of the problems associated with cross-cultural research will be equally important for our purpose. Although our respondents come from different cultures, they are to some extent socialised into a common professional culture. We will therefore discuss a selection of the numerous issues distinguished by Adler under seven headings: culture, research topic, sampling, translation, measurement and instrumentation, administration and data analysis. For each of the issues, we will indicate how we have resolved them in our own study.

Culture

Many of the issues subsumed under this heading have already been discussed above. We indicated that although we realise that cultures might not be equated with nations, for the sake of simplicity we will assume this equivalence in this study. In addition, cultures are assumed homogeneous, which might stretch reality a bit. As recommended by Adler, however, culture is included as a specific independent variable. Other issues mentioned by Adler are the definition of culture and the mental programming of the researcher. Most criticisms of cross-cultural research begin with the conclusion that culture is not adequately defined (Nasif et al, 1991). This might sound rather strange since a more than 40-year-old article by Kroeber and Kluckhohn (1952, cited in Adler, 1984a) had already catalogued more than 100 different definitions of culture. The problem is therefore not so much that there is no definition of culture, but that to date there is no definition that is commonly agreed upon. In Section 2, we will discuss the definition and operationalisa-

---

[80] Although the need for various forms of equivalence is now well recognised in articles about the methodological aspects of cross-cultural research, few studies actually take care of these issues. In a review article on international marketing studies, Aulakh and Kotabe (1993) show that in the 1985-1990 period only 30% of the studies attempted to ascertain translation equivalence. This figure was 22% for metric equivalence and 52% for sampling equivalence. Only for sampling equivalence had these figures improved over the previous period (1980-1984).

tion of culture used in this study. A second problem identified by Adler, the mental programming of the researcher as a cultural being, could not be remedied in this study. Academics from different countries commented upon the questionnaire used (see Section 2). The construction of a multicultural research team, however, was not considered feasible. The main reasons for this were the simple lack of time and means available in a doctoral study, which started as an individual initiative and was executed without much institutional support.

Research topic

Adler indicates that "at the highest level of abstraction, the research topic (i.e. the research question or theory being tested) should be identical across cultures" (Adler, 1984a:45). Most importantly, concepts should be conceptually and functionally equivalent (see also Harpaz, 1996; Hines, 1993; Nasif et al., 1991; Rosenzweig, 1994; Sekaran, 1983; Singh, 1995). Do concepts used in the study have the same meaning in the cultures under study and are they equally important in these different cultures? As Sekaran (1983) indicates, this might not be a critical issue in organisational research, since researchers study comparable work settings in different cultures. Since our study focuses on MNCs that are confronted with a high degree of international exposure and is limited to developed countries, conceptual and functional conceptual equivalence might be even less of a problem. On the other hand, although many of our concepts measure factual issues (see Section 2), it is not at all unlikely that the "vaguer" concepts such as strategy and especially control are perceived differently in different countries. We believe, however, that at the highest level of abstraction the basic concepts will be relevant, important and broadly identical in all countries. On a more detailed, operational level, specific interpretation could vary across countries. This will be discussed under the heading measurement and instrumentation.

Sampling

Sampling issues in cross-cultural research include the size of the sample, selection of cultures and representative versus matched samples (Adler, 1983a/ 1984a, Harpaz, 1996; Nasif et al., 1991; Sekaran, 1983). According to Brislin et al. (1973), the number of countries included should be large enough to randomise the variance on non-matched cultural variables. This means that two- or three-country studies should be treated as pilot studies, rather than full-blown cross-cultural studies. We included nine HQ countries in our study, in order to remedy the problems of previous research in the field of control mechanisms in MNCs that focused on a limited number of countries only.

Many cross-cultural studies rely on convenience samples[81] and the opportunistic availability of access to particular countries (e.g. the location of a sabbatical leave, the location of an annual meeting of a professional association or the residence of friends and relatives) (Adler, 1984a). As Roberts (1970) indicates, the selection of cultures should be based on the *theoretical* relevance of these cultures for the research question. In our study we included MNCs from nine different headquarters countries: USA, Japan, UK, France, Germany, Finland, Sweden, Switzerland and the Netherlands. The selection of countries was based on their economic importance, the presence of a reasonable number of MNCs and on their cultural characteristics. Countries from the Anglo-Saxon, Germanic, Latin European and Nordic clusters (see Ronen and Shenkar, 1985) are present in our sample. Japan, which forms a cluster of its own in most culture studies, has also been included. Countries from the Latin American, Far Eastern, Arab and Near Eastern cluster have not been included, because these countries did not host enough full-blown MNCs. In our sample of subsidiary countries, representatives from the Latin American and Far Eastern cluster were added to the clusters above. No countries from the Arab and Near Eastern cluster were included, mainly because a non-favourable response to a female researcher was expected. Eastern European countries were also excluded, because they did not host enough full-blown subsidiaries.

A final issue to be considered is the selection of either representative or matched samples. Representative samples are samples that resemble the total population of a given country. Matched samples are samples in which research objects are matched on as many characteristics as possible, except for the variables under study. Hofstede's (1980a, 1991) well-known study on cultural values used matched samples. Respondents were matched on as many characteristics (e.g. age, employer and function) as possible except for national culture. In our case, the choice of a matched sample was obvious: we wanted to compare MNCs across countries and therefore did not want to include a cross-section of different types of businesses.

Translation

An important issue when conducting a non-domestic mail survey is the language of the questionnaire. If the decision is taken to translate the questionnaire, literal accuracy can be achieved by using qualified translators and back-translations. As most cross-cultural researchers indicate (see e.g. Adler,

---

[81] That sampling issues are by no means problematic in cross-cultural studies alone is shown in an article by Mitchell (1985) which evaluates the validity of correlation research conducted in organisations. Of the 126 articles reviewed, 80% relied on convenience samples. In addition, half of the studies did not report response rates and only 10% compared respondents with non-respondents.

1983a; Brewster et al., 1996; Harpaz, 1996; Hines, 1993; Hofstede, 1980a; Nasif et al., 1991; Sekaran, 1983), however, equivalence of meaning is more important than literal equivalence. Excellent guides are available for the translation of research instruments (see e.g. Brislin, 1986). In this study, however, it was decided to use English-language questionnaires only. Although this choice was mainly dictated by budget constraints, there were also other valid reasons.

Firstly, it was assumed that managing directors of a subsidiary of an MNC would have at least a working knowledge of English. They might not be able to write English or speak it fluently, but they should be able to respond to an English-language questionnaire. This is also assumed by Adler (1983a, 1984a), who indicates that, in geocentric studies, translation is frequently not an issue, since most multinationals have a common language. Also Albaum, Strandskov and Erickson (1989) showed that translation might not be necessary when a population understands, to a greater or lesser degree, the language of the researcher. In their sample of Danish students, different languages (English/Danish) did not lead to substantially different responses. As might be commented, however, not all multinationals will have English as their company language and not all nationalities are equally fluent in English. Further, although people from e.g. Latin American countries might have a working knowledge of English, the fact that a questionnaire is in English might be the deciding factor not to participate in a survey.

This brings us to a second problem. We cannot assume that a managing director in, for instance, Italy reads Italian. It might be an expatriate from a US company who "manages" with English. A solution for this might be to include a questionnaire in both English and the host country's language. A disadvantage of this option, however, is that it would almost double the costs for both printing and postage and might give a bulky impression at first sight. More importantly, however, a managing director in Italy might be able to read neither English nor Italian if he or she is an expatriate from Germany or France and the company language is German or French. As translation would therefore probably introduce more problems than it would solve, it was decided to use English-language questionnaires only. Retrospectively, however, we think that it might have been a good idea to use a more differentiated approach and for instance include a Spanish-language questionnaire with the letters sent to three of our Latin American countries (Brazil is Portuguese-speaking) and Spain.

Measurement and instrumentation

Measurement and instrumentation issues include two major problems that might be relevant to our study: the need for conceptually equivalent items and metric equivalence. The problem of conceptually equivalent items is related to the conceptual equivalence of the research question discussed above. Although at an abstract level concepts might be equivalent across cultures, their specific meaning might be different. Aggressive behaviour and marital satisfaction might be meaningful constructs in many countries, but different questionnaire items should be used in measuring them, since the specific content of the concepts might differ across countries. To a lesser extent, the same might be applicable to some concepts used in our study. Because of the multitude of cultures included and the assumed homogenising influence of the professional position of the respondents, we chose not to differentiate questionnaire items across cultures, however.

Metric equivalence means that the psychometric properties of data from different cultural groups must exhibit the same coherence and structure. Subjects in the study must respond to the measurement scales used in the same way (Mullen, 1995). According to Mullen, there are two threats to metric equivalence in cross-cultural research: inconsistent scoring across populations and scalar inequivalence. Although some research has been done on the applicability of Likert scales and the semantic differential across countries (Albaum et al., 1987), we cannot simply assume that respondents in all countries are equally familiar with different scale formats. A lack of scalar equivalence or response-set bias might be due to the fact that respondents interpret scales in different ways. Personality characteristics such as social desirability, acquiescence, evasiveness or humility might not be distributed equally over different cultures. Asian people for instance are often said to avoid extremes (Kotabe et al., 1991; Lee and Green, 1991; Lincoln and Kalleberg, 1985), which results in a tight clustering of answers around the mean. For some instruments, such as the Job Description Index (Drasgow and Kanfer, 1985) and the Organisational Commitment Questionnaire (Riordan and Vandenberg, 1994), metric equivalence across different sub-populations has been empirically verified. However, we cannot simply assume that this will be the case for other instruments.

Metric equivalence can only be assessed after the data have been collected. Several approaches have been suggested to assess measurement equivalence, such as comparing scale reliability and factor scoring across countries, the optimal scaling of data and multiple group LISREL. Where appropriate, these approaches will be used in the empirical part of this book to assess metric equivalence of our research instruments.

Administration

In the administration or data collection phase, it is first important to assess the appropriateness of various research methods in different countries. Punnett and Shenkar (1994) propose a contingency model that specifies the fit between specific contextual variables (values, education, economic development, language, political system and religion) and various research methods (surveys, interviews, secondary, experiments and observations). Education, economic development and language are indicated to have a high impact on the applicability of surveys. Written surveys are usually only feasible if respondents are literate (in the language of the survey) and have a certain level of education. Language has already been dealt with above and education is hardly an issue in our population, since most respondents will have either professional or university-level education. Given the countries included in the survey, the level of economic development will not be too much of a problem either, although the mail service may be less reliable in Latin America and some Southern European countries.

The timing of data collection is also identified as an important issue (Adler, 1983a, 1984a; Nasif et al. 1991; Sekaran, 1983). Not too much time should elapse between the collection of data in the different countries, since otherwise data might not be comparable. As will be described in Section 3, in our study questionnaires were sent within a three-month period, so that difference in timing was not a problem.

Another issue to be considered in this phase is the response to the research administrator. As Adler (1983a, 1984a) indicates, subjects from different cultures might react respectfully, indifferently or in a hostile way to characteristics such as sex, race, origin, status, and citizenship. As indicated above, an expected negative response to the sex of the researcher was one of the main reasons for not including Arab and Near Eastern countries in our population. A major issue in cross-cultural research is a respondent's response to foreigners. There is some evidence that domestic surveys generate higher responses than foreign surveys (Jobber and Saunders, 1988; Teagarden et al., 1995). As indicated above, a multinational research team was not considered feasible. However, as will be described in Section 3, we tried to add a certain amount of local content to our study by constructing an international committee of recommendation.

Data analysis
We can be brief about data analysis. Since cross-cultural studies are complex, appropriate statistical analysis is needed. Univariate or bivariate statistics are only a starting point and multivariate techniques such as multiple regression, factor and cluster analysis are needed to explore fully the complexity of the object under study. Fortunately, many studies nowadays apply multivariate techniques, although as indicated in Chapter 1 many studies in the field of IHRM even resort to simple frequency analyses. The empirical part of this study will explore the data collected with both univariate/bivariate and multivariate techniques.

Conclusions

In this section, we discussed various issues related to cross-cultural research. First, the role of culture was investigated and contrasted with other influences such as contingency factors and strategic choice. Both contingency factors and culture were indicated as playing a role in our study. Second, six approaches to researching cross-cultural management issues were discussed. Our study combines elements of the comparative and geocentric approach and therefore has to cope with the methodological issues associated with both types: equivalence and geographical distance. The methodological problems associated with equivalence were discussed. Geographic dispersion influences the method of data collection and the practical issues associated with collecting data in a variety of geographically distant countries. These practical problems will be discussed in Section 3. The next section discusses the choice of the research method and the operationalisation and pre-testing of the variables.

2. CHOICE OF RESEARCH METHOD, OPERATIONALISATION AND TESTING

Introduction

In this section, we will first explain our choice of data collection. A survey method was deemed the best choice. Various alternatives: personal, telephone, mail, fax and email surveying are discussed and compared. A subsequent section discusses the level of data collection and justifies our choice of the key informant approach towards data collection. The limitations of this approach and possible remedies are discussed. A finally section discusses the operationalisation of the variables used in our study and describes the way we pre-tested our questionnaire.

Choice of research method

Researchers in the field of control mechanisms in MNCs have so far focused on a rather limited number of headquarters and/or subsidiary countries (Picard, 1980; Hedlund, 1981; Garnier, 1982; Gates and Egelhoff, 1986; Martinez and Ricks, 1989; Martinez and Jarillo, 1991; Gencturk and Aulakh, 1995). Many studies focused on American MNCs only and included one or two subsidiary countries. Only two studies included Japanese companies (Negandhi and Welge, 1984; Gupta and Govindarajan, 1994). If European multinationals were included at all, the results could not be differentiated between the various European companies because the number of MNCs per European country was simply too small (Gates and Egelhoff, 1986; Ghoshal and Nohria, 1989, 1993; Wolf, 1994) or because only one European country was included (Negandhi and Welge, 1984). In addition, only two studies investigated differences between industries (Gates and Egelhoff, 1986; Ghoshal and Nohria, 1993), which is very unfortunate as different industry distributions across countries might explain many of the differences found between these countries. Most studies therefore had to conclude that their results could not be generalised.

In view of these earlier experiences, we decided to build our population of firms in a very systematic way, including a comparable proportion of firms in eight different industries, MNCs headquartered in seven European countries, the USA and Japan, and subsidiaries in 22 countries spread over six cultural clusters (Anglo-Saxon, Germanic, Scandinavian, South European, Latin American and Asian). In addition, we also wanted to be able to analyse at the level of the individual multinational firm in order to investigate whether companies differentiate their control mechanisms for different subsidiaries. More recently, various authors (e.g. Hedlund, 1986; Prahalad and Doz, 1987; Ghoshal and Nohria, 1989; Forsgren, 1990; Ghoshal and Bartlett, 1990; Martinez and Jarillo, 1991; Theuerkauf, 1991; Nohria and Ghoshal, 1994) clearly suggest that many MNCs - and especially MNCs that are long established internationally - now assign different strategic roles to different subsidiaries. As Blackwell et al. (1991), Edwards, Ferner and Sisson (1996) and Gupta and Govindarajan (1991, 1994) argue this might have a considerable influence on the type of control mechanisms that are used with regard to various subsidiaries.

In order to be able to perform analyses at all these different levels, the final sample would have to be reasonably large. Since for most of the data secondary sources were not available,[82] this meant that a survey would be the only feasible method of investigation. Of the three traditional survey methods; mail, interview and telephone surveys, the latter two were discarded very soon. With regard to telephone surveying, even for a relatively small sample and high participation rates, the high costs of international telephone calls would have exceeded the available budget.[83] In addition, language problems

---

[82] One should not conclude too quickly, however, that secondary data are not available. Harzing (1997a, 1998a) shows that in the field of MNC staffing policies interesting results can be achieved by a creative use of secondary data.

[83] The estimated cost of a completed questionnaire for one of the Latin American countries would lie around 600 Dutch guilders (30 minutes for the interview including possible recalls and an assumed participation rate of one in three). Even for European countries, the cost would lie around 100 Dutch guilders per completed questionnaire. Our final choice, a mail survey, cost less than 30 Dutch guilders per completed questionnaire.

would become more serious as some potential respondents might be able to read but not speak English. Finally, time-zone differences would drastically limit the hours available for telephoning. Interview surveying would multiply the problems associated with telephone surveying.

In addition to these two traditional survey methods, two relatively new ones have become available: surveying by fax or email. Sending questionnaires by fax would be much cheaper than telephone surveying, since the questionnaire could be faxed within 5 minutes. On the other hand, response rates might be (much) lower and reminders might be necessary so that part of the cost advantage would be lost. Further, although not as time-consuming as telephone calls, faxing some 1500 questionnaires would take quite a lot of time. To our best knowledge, only one study (Tse et al., 1994) has tested the use of fax surveying. They found that response rates for questionnaires sent by fax were lower than for questionnaires sent by mail, but that the response speed was higher. Since response speed was not an issue in our case and costs would still be higher than for mail surveying, we discarded this option as well. Because of the smaller size of the population (see Section 3), fax reminders were sent to the potential respondents of the pilot study. The fact that this did not provide *any* additional responses confirmed our choice not to use this method.

Electronic surveying has been a serious option, however. Its vast advantages are its negligible costs and its speed of delivery. In addition, email surveying could reduce data entry time and costs, because the transformation of returned questionnaires into data readable by a statistical programme could be automated. Because of the very low costs[84] of email transfer and the limited amount of time involved in sending out the email questionnaire, the population could easily be doubled or tripled or even further increased to ensure reasonable response rates. Further, especially in less-developed countries, email is a faster and more reliable method of data transmission than mail. Finally, email would be an environmentally correct option, an advantage not to be underestimated. Several studies have investigated the use of email for data collection (Kiesler and Sproull, 1986; Parker, 1992; Schuldt and Totten, 1994; Sproull, 1986) and with the exception of one (Parker, 1992) found response rates for email surveys to be somewhat (Kiesler and Sproull, 1986; Sproull, 1986) or considerably (Schuldt and Totten, 1994) lower than for mail surveys. Not surprisingly, response speed was higher for email surveys. In addition, Kiesler and Sproull (1986) found that email respondents made fewer

---

[84] When questionnaires are sent from a university that has a permanent Internet connection, there are no additional costs at all.

item completion mistakes and gave less "socially desirable" answers.[85] Sproull (1986) also found that email surveys produced more extreme answers.

As also indicated by Sproull (1986), however, there are two important issues that could hinder email surveying: the respondent's access to email and their willingness to respond to surveys via email. Although email systems are widespread nowadays and would certainly be expected to be present in the world's largest companies, it is by no means certain that the highest in command in an organisation would use email. Although there are no quantitative data available on this issue, it is our impression that a sizeable minority of managers do not even use a computer. This would then drastically limit the number of potential respondents. More importantly, even if we were to find potential respondents that *do* use email, it would be questionable whether they would be willing to respond via email. The problem of data security should not be underestimated, since email messages can easily be intercepted. Further, as many email users will be able to confirm, the presence of junk mail has increased drastically over the past few years.[86] In an article written some five years ago, Parker claims: "The electronic-mail medium does not deliver a disagreeable volume of junk mail - at least not yet. Certainly it does not convey many questionnaires to subscribers." We think few people would agree with this claim nowadays. The presence of junk mail and the increasing number of questionnaires sent by email puts the email surveyor in an even worse position than the mail surveyor. While a mail survey usually attracts at least a glance and has to be physically destroyed, email surveys can be deleted without being read and with no more than a mouse click. We fear that a potentially tremendous opportunity for cost- and time-effective surveying has fast become an unattractive option. In sum, the two limits: access to email and willingness to respond were judged too important to make electronic surveying a feasible option.

Mail surveying therefore remained as the best option. Two major problems are associated with mail surveying when compared to the more personal research methods. First, questions or terms may be misinterpreted by respondents. We will discuss how we have tried to prevent these problems. Second, response rates in mail surveys, and in particular in international mail surveys, are usually rather low. In Section 3, we will discuss the efforts we have made to improve response rates and indicate how the mail survey was actually prepared and executed. In Section 4, we will deal with the possible non-response

---

[85] The authors explain this by the fact that social context is considerably reduced in electronic communication, making it impersonal and anonymous. This will lead respondents to be relatively unconcerned with social norms and the impression they give others. Any subscriber to electronic news groups will confirm this observation.

[86] The same phenomenon has occurred with facsimile transfers. A sizeable proportion of faxes sent nowadays fall in the category of unaddressed advertising.

bias in the sample. Now, we will first move to the level and approach of data collection we chose in our mail survey.

Level and approach of data collection

Although we justified our choice of a mail survey as the way to collect our data in the previous subsection, the level of data collection is still open. Since the focus of our study is on control mechanisms that are applied by head-quarters in respect of their subsidiaries, two levels of data collection are feasible: headquarters and subsidiaries.[87] Although some of the best-known studies on control mechanisms in MNCs (Egelhoff, 1988a/b; Ghoshal and Nohria, 1993) collected data at the level of headquarters, we have chosen data collection at the level of the subsidiary. The reasons that led to this choice will now be discussed.

Justification of data collection at subsidiary level
In Chapter 2, we discussed several headquarters and subsidiary characteristics that might influence the composition of the control portfolio. At subsidiary level, a larger number of characteristics were identified than at headquarters level. Furthermore, as will become apparent in the next subsection, all but one (organisational model) of the headquarters characteristics could be identified by means of secondary data collection. Many of the characteristics at subsidiary level, however, could only be collected from respondents. Although managers at headquarters level might be aware of some of the subsidiary characteristics, it is unlikely that they are as well informed about these characteristics as subsidiary managers, who usually have only one subsidiary under their supervision and experience the subsidiary's operations on a daily basis.

Even if headquarters managers are aware of the situation in a number of different subsidiaries, their estimate of, for instance, the application of the various control mechanisms might be biased. Headquarters managers are more likely to describe intended control strategies, while subsidiary managers will be more likely to describe actually realised control strategies. In other words, headquarters managers will be likely to describe how the application of the various control mechanisms *should be*, while subsidiary managers are more informed about how control mechanisms are applied in practice.

---

[87] Although we recognise the growing importance of divisional and regional headquarters in MNCs (see e.g. Forsgren and Holm, 1995; Forsgren, Holm and Johanson, 1995; and Schütte, 1996), we did not explicitly include this level of analysis in our study. We feel that this level merits a separate analysis and thought it would unwise to introduce yet another variable in an already rather complex research design. However, as can be seen in Section 4, approximately one third of our sample of subsidiaries had a function as country headquarters.

Even if we assume that headquarters managers are totally informed and aware of the actual situation, they might be more likely to be subject to a social desirability bias. The transnational ideal and the use of more subtle control mechanisms have been extensively described in the more professional journals such as *Harvard Business Review*, and in management abstract services. Either consciously or unconsciously, headquarters managers might describe their organisation in terms of ideal types that conform to the current management hypes. On the level of separate questions, few headquarters managers would like to admit that they give subsidiaries a very low level of autonomy and that managers in subsidiaries do not share the values espoused at headquarters. In our opinion, although they might want to portray their organisation in a positive light, subsidiary managers are more likely to be honest about these issues.

It was therefore decided that the subsidiary level was to be the main level of data collection. The only variable that could cause problems in this respect is the organisational model followed by headquarters, since subsidiaries might not be fully informed about this. Below we will discuss how we tried to resolve this issue. In addition to questionnaires sent to subsidiaries, we also sent questionnaires to both CEOs and corporate HR-managers at headquarters. As will be described in Section 4, the result is that for twenty companies information for some variables is available at both HQ and subsidiary level.

Having decided what the level of data collection would be, the next step was to identify the potential respondents at these levels. The choice of one key informant in the person of the managing director for subsidiaries and the CEO and HR manager at headquarters, was motivated by both budgetary/practical and substantial reasons.[88] To start with the latter, although at subsidiary level some questions might be more suited to, for instance, the HR or production manager, the managing director was assumed to be the person who would be best aware of the *overall* variety of characteristics that were probed in our questionnaire. Having more than one respondent per company would not be feasible in terms of the additional time and costs involved and the risk of incomplete questionnaires. At headquarters level, the same motivation applied although in this case we were able to separate the measurement of international HRM and strategy issues, since the relationship between the two was not an issue under study, and ask the questions to the most appropriate person. However, the key informant approach is certainly not without problems. These problems and potential solutions will be described next.

---

[88] Please note that the choice of a single respondent is very common. Reviewing the leading journal in the field of strategy, *Strategic Management Journal*, Bowman and Ambrosini (1997) note that the use of a single respondent is relatively widespread in strategy research, even for studies that focus on a far more limited number of countries and organisations than we do.

The key-informant approach: problems

There are two major problems associated with the use of so-called key informants: measurement error and common method variance. As indicated by Philips (1981), *random* measurement error may be increased since respondents are asked to make "complex social judgements" about their organisation. This may place unrealistic demands on them as respondents. Further, *systematic* measurement errors may distort key-informant reports, because of bias or simple ignorance. In her own study, Philips (1981) showed that both sources of measurement errors were important.

Common method variance can occur whenever variables in the study are collected from the same respondent. As Podsakoff and Organ (1986) indicate: "Because both measures come from the same source, any defect in that source contaminates both measures, presumably in the same fashion and in the same direction" (1986:533). This can lead to artefactual covariance between self-report measures of two or more different constructs. Two main sources that could account for this artefactual covariance are the *consistency motif* and the *social desirability problem* (Podsakoff and Organ, 1986). Respondents will usually try to maintain a consistent line in their answers. This consistent line may be based on lay theories respondents might have about the relationship between various organisational phenomena. This tendency is aggravated if different variables are operationalised with items that are similar in content. The possibility of the consistency motif cannot be ruled out completely in our study. However, we feel that the relationships between the variables in our study are rather complex and are not very likely to be subject of lay theories. Furthermore, we have made an effort to prevent the use of items that are similar in content as much as possible. The social desirability problem occurs because respondents might try to put themselves (or the organisation) in a favourable light. In our opinion, this tendency would be more important for questions that ask about individual characteristics than for questions about organisational characteristics. Furthermore, for most of our questions there are no obviously socially desirable answers. Even if some answers might be considered to put the organisation (or rather headquarters) into a more favourable light (e.g. giving subsidiaries more autonomy, differentiating products for local needs), as indicated above, subsidiary managers would be more likely to be honest than headquarters managers.

The key-informant approach: solutions

A solution to the problem of measurement error would have been to send the questionnaire to more than one potential respondent in each company. In view of the prevalent response rates in international research (see also Section 3), it is highly unlikely, however, that enough multiple responses would have been received. Furthermore, mailing more than one questionnaire to each company would have considerably increased costs of both printing and postage. How-ever, for one of the most critical and difficult-to-measure variables, the or-ganisational model followed by headquarters, measurement error can be as-sessed in the cases where more than one subsidiary has indicated this organ-isational model. In these cases, the consistency of subsidiary answers will be analysed. In addition, for about twenty companies, data are available at both HQ and subsidiary level (see also Section 4), so that consistency between HQ and subsidiary answer can be analysed. Finally, as will be discussed in the next subsection, for about half of the headquarters included in our sample, we compared a company's organisational model as derived from subsidiary re-sponses with the organisational model as espoused in either a company annual report or in professional or academic articles. In this way we combined Snow and Hambrick's (1980) self-typing measurement approach with their investi-gator inference and external assessment approach, thus increasing the likeli-hood of reliable and valid measurement.

The problem of common method variance could have been considerably reduced by having two respondents in each organisation answer different parts of the questionnaire (see e.g. Miller, 1987a/b and Miller and Dröge, 1986 for an example of this approach). Unfortunately, the problems as dis-cussed above with measurement errors would be magnified in this case. Where only a single respondent filled in the complete questionnaire for a par-ticular firm, instead of the desired two or more respondents, the data collected could still be useful. When spreading the measurement of key variables over several respondents in one firm, the risk of ending up with only a very small usable sample is very high. Although this approach might work very well in cases where firms have already agreed to participate, it creates too much of a risk in mail surveys.

Podsakoff and Organ (1986) suggest various procedures to reduce the same-source variance without resorting to different respondents: escalating the unit of analysis, separation of measurement, and scale reordering. *Esca-lating the unit of analysis* involves aggregating the data to a higher level (e.g. departments), so that the answers of part of the respondents can be used to estimate some of the variables and the answers of the remaining respondents to estimate the other variables. Although some of our analyses will be done at headquarters level, this usually involves measures collected at this same level. For the other cases the number of responses per headquarters is simply to small (see Section 4) to split the respondents into different groups. *Separation of measurement* refers to a separation of the collection of the data in time, place (work vs home) or medium (telephone vs written questionnaire). For various reasons, discussed above, this option was also not feasible in this study. A final procedure, *scale reordering*, involves rearranging the question-naire so that the dependent variable follows, rather than precedes, the independent variable. This should reduce consistency artefacts. Podsakoff and Organ themselves do not think this procedure will make much of a difference. In our opinion, if the independent variable precedes the dependent variable, consistency artefacts would be expected to increase instead of decrease. We therefore did not apply this procedure. In addition to these procedural variables, Podsakoff and Organ suggest various *statistical and post hoc remedies*: Harman's one-factor test, partial correlation procedure, elimination of social desirability and scale trimming. Where appropriate, these remedies will be applied in the empirical part of this thesis.

Conclusion

In this subsection, we discussed the level of data collection and the problems associated with the key informant approach to data collection. These problems are most important when dealing with subjective variables. In the next subsection, we will discuss how we have operationalised the variables included in our study. Fortunately, as will be shown below, we were able to find fairly objective measurements for many of our variables and to find supporting evidence for some variables that had to be measured in a more subjective way.

Operationalisation of variables and pre-test

Introduction

In this subsection, we will discuss the way in which we operationalised the variables used in our study. Before doing so, we would like to make some general remarks. Since low response rates frustrate useful conclusions in many international studies, generating a reasonable response rate, both for the sample as a whole and for the various subsamples, was a major aim in our study. Using data from 35 methodological studies, Jobber and Saunders (1993) showed that for industrial populations, the length of the questionnaire was an important predictor of response rates: the longer the questionnaire, the lower the response rate. We therefore tried to limit the number of questions to the absolute minimum. This meant, first, that no questions were asked on issues that could be verified using secondary data. However, another consequence was that we could not use ten-item scales to measure every construct in the study. Most constructs were therefore measured using two or three items.

Furthermore, we could not differentiate control mechanisms for various functional areas. Many studies found that decisions in the field of marketing, HRM, industrial relations, production, R&D and finance are centralised to different degrees. Decisions in the first three fields are usually more decentralised than decisions in the latter three fields (see Van den Bulcke, 1984 for an overview). In view of the size constraints, it was felt to be infeasible to include *both* different control mechanisms *and* different functional areas. Since most previous studies focused on one control mechanism (centralisation) for various functional areas, we decided to do the reverse and focus on various control mechanisms without differentiating across functions. Since the managing director was judged to be the person most knowledgeable on the variety of issues probed in the questionnaire, we decided, following Martinez and Jarillo (1991), to phrase the questions on control mechanisms in general terms. Focusing on, for instance, marketing or HRM could mean biased or missing data, since the managing director might not be aware of the control mechanisms used in these areas.

In the remainder of this section, we will discuss the operationalisation of our variables. In doing so, we will follow closely the order of the theoretical chapters, that is, we start with the building blocks: control mechanisms, MNCs and international transfers as discussed in Chapter 1. We then move to the headquarters characteristics and subsidiary characteristics as discussed in Chapter 2. The operationalisation of variables related to the role of international transfers as a control mechanism is discussed under the building block: international transfers. After the operationalisation of performance, a brief discussion on the pre-test of our questionnaire will conclude this section.

The building blocks

Control mechanisms After a review of the relevant literature, we identified, in Section 1 of Chapter 1, four main control mechanisms: personal centralised control, bureaucratic formalised control, output control and control by socialisation and networks. To measure these different control mechanisms empirically, we adapted and supplemented the questions that were used by Martinez and Jarillo (1991). Martinez and Jarillo's study is one of the very few that has measured control mechanisms at subsidiary level, making the questions very suitable for our purpose. In addition, they did not differentiate according to various functional areas, which also conformed to our approach.

Since Martinez and Jarillo only compared formal mechanisms with informal mechanisms, their questions on formal control mechanisms were not as differentiated as we would like them to be. Therefore, additional questions were constructed for the "direct supervision" aspect of personal centralised control and the "standardisation" aspect of bureaucratic formalised control. Martinez and Jarillo's questions were rather long (they were used in an interview setting) and were therefore slightly trimmed. We maintained their approach of stating alternatives, in the form of "some MNCs do this; others do something else". Phrasing the question in this way could reduce the social desirability effect, since it is indicated that both approaches are in use by (other) MNCs (see also Douglas and Craig, 1983). The 5-point Likert scale used by Martinez and Jarillo was converted into a 7-point scale in order to increase the possible variety in answers. In order to emphasise that we solicited information about the control mechanisms applied at the individual subsidiary, we added "towards your subsidiary" for every question. Finally, we made some slight adjustments in wording (e.g. multinational firm in every question instead of the variety of terms - firm, corporation, and company - used by Martinez and Jarillo). The final questions used are shown below.

Personal centralised control
- Centralisation aspect (reverse-scored): *In some multinational firms, (strategic) decision-making is largely centralised at headquarters; in other firms subsidiaries have a large amount of autonomy. In general, what is this subsidiary's autonomy to decide its own strategies and policies?*
- Direct supervision aspect: *In some multinational firms headquarters managers strive for a close personal surveillance of the behaviour of their subsidiaries. Other firms do not use this kind of direct personal supervision. Please indicate the degree of personal surveillance that headquarters' managers execute in respect of this subsidiary.*

Bureaucratic formalised control
- Standardisation aspect: *In some multinational firms, all subsidiaries are supposed to operate in more or less the same way. In other firms, such standardised policies are not required. In general, what is the degree of standardisation that headquarters requires from this subsidiary?*
- Formalisation aspect: *Some multinational firms have written rules and procedures for everything and employees are expected to follow these procedures accurately. Other firms do not have such strict rules and procedures, or if they have, there is some leniency about following them. Please indicate the kind of rules and procedures that headquarters imposes on this subsidiary.*

Output control
- Output evaluation aspect: *Some multinational firms exert a high degree of output control, by means of a continuous evaluation of the results of subsidiaries. Other firms exert very little output control beyond the requirement of occasional financial reports. Please indicate the degree of output control that headquarters exerts over this subsidiary.*
- Planning aspect: *Some multinational firms have a very detailed planning, goal setting and budgeting system that includes clear-cut (often quantitative) objectives to be achieved at both strategic and operational level.*

Other firms have less developed systems. Please indicate the type of planning/goal setting/budgeting that headquarters uses in respect of this subsidiary.

Control by socialisation and networks

- Socialisation aspect: *Some multinational firms attach a lot of value to a strong "corporate culture" and try to ensure that all subsidiaries share the main values of the firm. Others do not make these efforts (or, having made them, have had no success). To what extent do the executives in this subsidiary share the company's main values?*

- Informal communication aspect: *Some multinational firms have a very high degree of informal communication among executives of the different subsidiaries and headquarters. Other firms do not foster that kind of informal communication and rely exclusively on formal communication channels. Please indicate the level of informal communication between this subsidiary and headquarters/other subsidiaries of the group.*

- Formal networks aspect: *Some multinational firms make extensive use of committees/task forces/project groups, both temporary and permanent, made up by executives from different subsidiaries and headquarters. To what extent have this subsidiary's executives participated in these kinds of groups in the past couple of years?*

Following Martinez and Jarillo (1991), other studies in this field and our discussion in Chapter 1, the various control mechanisms are regarded as additive, so that scores for the different control mechanisms can be summed to display the total level of control. Subsidiaries experiencing a relatively high level of all four control mechanisms are thus considered to be more strongly controlled by headquarters than subsidiaries that experience high levels of control on only one or two of the four control mechanisms or medium levels on all four. In addition, we included two questions related to the role of international transfers as a control mechanism. First, we asked respondents about the application of the direct type of expatriate control in their subsidiary. Retrospectively, we wish we had included direct expatriate control as one of the functions of international transfers, rather than as one of the control mechanisms. Second, we included one of the two major alternatives to international transfers to realise the informal communication and socialisation aspects of control by socialisation and networks, namely international management training. The other major alternative, formal networks, has already been included above.

- Direct expatriate control: *In some multinational firms, parent-country nationals are assigned to subsidiaries to ensure that headquarters poli-*

cies are carried out. Others do not send out expatriates or do it for other reasons. Please indicate the degree to which headquarters uses expatriates to directly control this subsidiary's operations.

- International management training: *Some multinational firms make extensive use of international (as opposed to purely national) management training programmes. In these programmes executives from different subsidiaries and headquarters follow courses that deal mostly with the transfer of company-specific knowledge. What has been the participation of this subsidiary's executives in these kinds of training programmes in the past couple of years?*

Multinational companies In Section 2 of Chapter 1, we described the environment, strategy and structure of MNCs. Three main types of MNC were derived from a review of relevant literature: global, multidomestic and transnational. In the empirical part of this book, industry will be used as a proxy for the international environment. The industries included in our population are assumed to be spread over the global, multidomestic and transnational type of environment. Subsidiary managers were asked to indicate the industry in which the subsidiary was operating. If the subsidiary was operating in more than one industry, they were asked to indicate the industry that generated the largest percentage of its sales.

Since no questions were readily available to measure the organisational model of MNCs, we created our own questions, based on the characteristics of the different types of firms as described in Bartlett and Ghoshal (1989, 1992a). Nine statements were constructed that measured aspects of organisational structure, the role of subsidiaries, the dominant competitive strategy etc. Respondents were asked to indicate the extent to which they agreed with the various statements. The introduction emphasised that we sought their opinion about the MNC overall, not about the specific subsidiary. The nine statements are reproduced below:

- *Our company's strategy is focused on achieving economies of scale by concentrating its important activities at a limited number of locations.*
- *Our company can be adequately described as a very loosely coupled and decentralised federation of rather independent national subunits.*
- *In our company, a typical subsidiary's main function is to deliver company products and carry out headquarters' strategies.*
- *Our company can be adequately described as an integrated and interdependent network of different but equivalent subunits, in which headquarters does not a priori play a dominant role.*
- *Our company not only recognises national differences in taste and values, but actually tries to respond to these national differences by con-*

sciously adapting products and policies to the local market.

- *In our company subsidiaries regularly act as a strategic centre for a particular product or process; in other words, subsidiaries regularly perform a role as "centre of excellence".*
- *In our company, there are not only large flows of components and products, but also of resources, people and information among company's subsidiaries.*
- *Our company's competitive position is defined in world-wide terms. Different national product markets are closely linked and interconnected. Competition takes place on a global basis.*
- *Our company's competitive strategy is to let each subsidiary compete on a domestic level as national product markets are judged too different to make competition on a global level possible.*

In the questionnaire, the main concepts appeared in bold. Although some questions aimed specifically at measuring a certain type of company (global: 1, 3, 8, multidomestic: 2, 4, 9; transnational: 4, 6, 7), we did not create scales. Equally important as the score on these three key questions would be the relative position on the other questions. Following their conceptual description, transnationals would be expected to score "in between" on, for instance, economies of scale, differentiation and both global and local competition. Multidomestic companies on the other hand would be expected to score high on their own key questions and low on the key questions for global companies and vice versa. In addition, global companies would be expected to score low on the network statement, since headquarters plays a dominant role in global companies. In the empirical part of this book, responses to these questions will therefore be factor-analysed to discover any underlying constructs.

International transfers Concerning international transfers, we measured both the level and the function of expatriation for the subsidiary in question. Three questions were used to assess the presence of expatriates in a given subsidiary. These questions asked respectively for the nationality of the managing director, the number of top five jobs held by expatriates and the total number of expatriates working in the subsidiary.

Concerning the functions of international transfers, we maintained the basic classification of Edström and Galbraith (1977a): position filling, management development and organisation development. Since these concepts might not be completely clear to the respondents, each of the concepts was operationalised using two specific questions that captured the main elements of the concept as summarised in Table 1-7.[89] Respondents were asked to indicate the importance (on a scale from of very little importance to of utmost importance) of the following functions of expatriation. They were told that they could skip the question if there were no expatriates in their subsidiary's workforce.

- *Transferring specific technical or management knowledge from HQs or other subsidiaries to this subsidiary.*
- *Improving information and communication channels with HQs or other subsidiaries of the group.*
- *Ensuring a homogeneous corporate culture throughout the company as a whole.*
- *Filling positions for which no local personnel are available in this country.*
- *Training the expatriate in question for future positions at other subsidiaries.*
- *Training the expatriate in question for future positions at headquarters.*

Headquarters characteristics
Four headquarters characteristics were identified: organisational model, size, extent of multinationality and complexity/heterogeneity. Above, we indicated how we operationalised the organisational model. In this section, we will discuss the operationalisation and measurement of the other characteristics.

Size Three measures were used to operationalise the size of an MNC: the number of employees, total world-wide sales, and total world-wide assets. Although these measures will probably be highly correlated, they have a slightly different focus. In particular, size measured by the number of employees might differ from the two other measures. The natural logarithm of the number of employees was used as the final measure of size. As indicated by Miller and Dröge (1986), this logarithmic scale is used to normalise this variable, which might otherwise be badly skewed. Since the same might be true for sales and assets, we will also use transformed versions of these variables in the empirical part of this thesis. All three measures are derived from secondary sources: either the company's annual report or the Global Fortune 500 listing. Data from the last available year (usually 1994) are used.

Extent of multinationality. As indicated by Ramaswamy (1992), most studies investigating the effects of multinationality are limited in their conceptualisa-

---

[89] As indicated above, direct expatriate control was included with the questions on control mechanisms, since we realised only after the data had been gathered that it would have been more suitable to include it as a function of expatriation.

tion of multinationality. Of the 15 studies reviewed in his article, 13 used foreign sales as the only measure of multinationality. The same point was made by Sullivan (1994b), who reviews 17 articles and finds that all but one use one single measure (foreign sales) to operationalise multinationality. Both studies provide a more multidimensional concept of multinationality, including - next to foreign sales - measures such as foreign assets, number and dispersion of subsidiaries and international experience. Although Sullivan's operationalisation has been subject to criticism (see Ramaswamy, Kroeck and Renforth, 1996 and a subsequent reply by Sullivan, 1996), it is comforting to see that after more than 20 years of contradictory results on the effects of multinationality, there is at least some discussion about a more sophisticated operationalisation of the construct. Unfortunately, as for the measurement of performance, operationalisation of the construct is very dependent on the actual data available. We therefore propose a six-item operationalisation of the construct, where the choice of items was based on both the operationalisations by Ramaswamy and Sullivan and the availability of data.

The six different measures that are used to operationalise the extent of multinationality all have a slightly different focus. First, the percentage of *foreign sales* (sales abroad/total sales) gives an indication of the importance of the foreign market in relation to the home markets. Some firms, however, generate high levels of foreign sales mainly by exports, which reduces their commitment abroad. To measure this commitment abroad we also included the percentage of *foreign employees* (employees abroad/total employees). A related measure is the *number of foreign subsidiaries*. These two measures are not interchangeable, however, since a firm can have a high percentage of foreign employees spread over a limited number of subsidiaries, which would drastically reduce their international exposure. The number of subsidiaries abroad can also include a high number of relatively small and less important sales subsidiaries. We therefore included the *number of manufacturing subsidiaries* as a fourth measure of international exposure. Even when a firm has a high percentage of foreign employees and a large number of (manufacturing) subsidiaries, these employees and subsidiaries might be concentrated in a limited number of countries, which would again limit the firm's international exposure. A fifth measure of internationality is therefore the *number of countries* in which the MNC owns foreign subsidiaries. A sixth and final measure is more related to the extent of international experience and indicates the time elapsed since the *first foreign subsidiary* was founded.

The advantage of all of these measures is that they can be found in secondary sources, although information on e.g. the percentage of foreign sales and the number of countries is more readily available than information on the percentage of foreign employees and the number of manufacturing subsidiaries. The main source for these data was companies' annual reports. In addition, we also consulted the *Directory of Corporate Affiliations* (NN, 1996), Stop-ford's *Directory of Multinationals* (Stopford, 1992) and Kepos' *International Directory of Company Histories* (Kepos, 1995).

Heterogeneity/complexity. In Section 1 of Chapter 2 a company was defined facing a heterogeneous environment if the organisation's customers or markets have different characteristics and needs. A firm's level of heterogeneity/complexity in this sense is broadly comparable to its level of diversification. Following Varadarajan and Ramanujam (1987), we chose to measure the level of diversification by the number of different SIC (Standard Industrial Classification) categories an MNC operates in. Two different types of diversification can be distinguished in this respect: narrow-spectrum and broad-spectrum diversification.[90] Narrow-spectrum diversification means that firms operate in different 4-digit SIC codes, but that all their areas of operations are located within one or two 2-digit SIC codes (e.g. 2024: ice cream and frozen desserts; 2032: canned specialities; 2052: cookies and crackers and 2067: chewing gum, which all fall under the 2-digit code: food and related products). Broad-spectrum diversification means that firms operate in different two-digit SIC codes, but that within a 2-digit SIC code their activities are not very differentiated. SIC codes for all of the MNCs included in our sample were collected from the *Directory of Corporate Affiliations*. We counted both the number of different 2-digit SIC codes and the number of different 4-digit SIC codes in which the MNC operated.

Headquarters characteristics at subsidiary level In the questionnaires we sent to subsidiaries, respondents were asked to supply various headquarters characteristics: country, number of employees, turnover and year of foundation. These characteristics were used for identification purposes only, since more reliable data for these measures were available from secondary sources.

Subsidiary characteristics

Country of location, size and age The 22 countries to which the questionnaires were sent were indicated on the questionnaire and the respondent was

---

[90] Many studies looking at the type of diversification strategy used either Rumelt's (1974) or Wrigley's (1970) classification schemes, distinguishing either four or eight different categories. As Datta et al. (1991) indicate, fitting firms into these schemes involves considerable subjectivity. They cite a study that found that even informed executives were unable to classify consistently firms using the Rumelt scheme. Since the use of multiple raters (a combination of researchers and industry experts) was considered infeasible in this study, we chose the more objective approach of classifying firms according to their SIC codes. This, however, limits the comparability of our study to previous research.

asked to tick the country of location of the subsidiary. The size of the subsidiary was operationalised using two questions that asked for the total workforce of the subsidiary and its volume of turnover. Since in many questionnaires the currency and/or the actual turnover were illegible, we decided to use only the number of employees as an indication of size. For HQ size, the natural logarithm of the number of employees was used as the final measure of size.

Data on the age of the subsidiary were collected by asking the respondent to indicate the year of foundation of the subsidiary. Since the time that the subsidiary has been under the reign of headquarters might be as important for the type of control used as the actual age of the subsidiary, we also asked the respondent to indicate the year in which the subsidiary was acquired by its current owner (if applicable).

Interdependence Following many of the studies discussed in Chapter 2 and Martinez and Jarillo's study referred to above, interdependence was operationalised using a relatively objective measure: the percentage of intracompany sales and purchases. However, in our discussion about interdependence we made a distinction between *de*pendence and *inter*dependence. The first refers to the *de*pendence of subsidiaries on their headquarters, while the second refers to the *inter*dependence between various subsidiaries. *De*pendence corresponds to the centralised-hub organisational model that was indicated to be typical of a global company, while *inter*dependence fits the integrated network model, typical of the transnational company. In the configurations of MNCs discussed in Section 3 of Chapter 2, we also indicated that global companies would be expected to have high levels of *de*pendence, while transnational companies would be characterised by high levels of *inter*dependence.

In our questions on intra-company sales and purchases, we therefore asked respondents to differentiate between their purchases from and sales to headquarters and subsidiaries. Four questions were constructed that asked for the percentage of purchases from or sales to either headquarters or subsidiaries in relation to total purchases or sales. As respondents would not be likely to know the exact percentages, six answer categories were included: 0%, 1-25%, 26-50%, 51-75%, 76-99% and 100%.

Local responsiveness As we discussed in Section 1 of Chapter 2, Martinez and Jarillo's study is the only one that deals with the influence of the amount of local responsiveness of a subsidiary on the level and type of control mechanism that is used towards this subsidiary. We therefore used a slightly adapted version of the questions originally constructed by Martinez and Jarillo to measure local responsiveness. Since their question about the percentage of value added was not well understood in the pre-test, we decided to substitute this question with a question about marketing. The questions used are reproduced below. In the questionnaire, the main concepts appeared in bold. As for interdependence, six answer categories were created.

- *Please give your best estimate of the percentage of R&D incorporated into products sold by this subsidiary that is actually performed by this subsidiary.*
- *Please give your best estimate of the percentage of company products sold by this subsidiary that have been manufactured (to any degree) by this subsidiary.*
- *Please give your best estimate of the percentage of company products sold by this subsidiary that have been created or substantially modified for this market.*
- *Please give your best estimate of the percentage of marketing for company products sold by this subsidiary that is consciously adapted to local circumstances.*

Subsidiary role Since the subsidiary role as defined in our study is composed of a combination of the level of (inter)dependence and local responsiveness, no additional questions were necessary for this variable. The function of the subsidiary was measured with a simple tick-box question that asked respondents to indicate whether their subsidiary fulfilled the following functions: sales/distribution, service, assembly, production, R&D or country headquarters. Of course, more than one answer was possible.

Uncertainty Uncertainty in the subsidiary's environment as discussed in Section 1 of Chapter 2 was operationalised using Miller and Dröge's (1986) measures, which reflect the degree of change and unpredictability with regard to competition, consumers, the market and technology. Their scale was based on earlier studies by Miller (1983) and Khandwalla (1974, 1977). Some slight changes in wording were made to simplify the English for non-native speakers (e.g. outdated instead of obsolete, twice a year instead of semi-annually). The questions used are reproduced below:

- *How often should this subsidiary change its marketing practices in order to keep up with the market and competitors?*
- *Please indicate the rate at which products/services in this industry are becoming outdated.*
- *To what extent is the production/service technology in this industry subject to change?*
- *How difficult is it to forecast demand and consumer tastes?*
- *How predictable are the actions of your competitors?*

As in the original, 7-point Likert scales were used, with markers such as rarely (e.g. every five years) vs extremely frequently (e.g. twice a year) at the end of the scales.

Cultural distance Nearly one hundred different culture dimensions were identified by Lytle et al. (1995). In our study, culture was operationalised using Hofstede's (1980a, 1991) dimensions: power distance, uncertainty avoidance, masculinity/femininity and individualism/collectivism.[91] Although Hofstede's work has been the subject of considerable criticism (see Harzing and Hofstede, 1996 for a summary), it has gradually become a classic and part of "normal science" (Kuhn, 1970). Successive Social Science Citation Indexes list a total of more than 1000 citations of it from 1981 through 1996. Replications (see e.g. Hoppe, 1993; Lowe, 1996b; Punnett and Withane, 1990; Søndergaard, 1994) have largely found the same differences as the IBM study did. Further, the cultural clusters found by Hofstede conform to the clusters found in many other studies (see Ronen and Shenkar, 1985). A considerable advantage of Hofstede's study is the large number of countries included (all of our headquarters and subsidiary countries were part of Hofstede's study) and the convenient quantification of the various cultural dimensions. Several alternative approaches (Laurent, 1983; Triandis, 1983; Trompenaars, 1993) lose out on either the number of countries included or the lack of any empirical verification.

The cultural distance between each headquarters and each individual subsidiary was calculated using an adjusted version of the Kogut and Singh (1988) formula:

$$CD_s = \sum_{i=1}^{4} \left\{ \left(I_{is} - I_{ih} \right)^2 / V_i \right\} / 4$$

where I_{is} stands for the score for the ith cultural dimension of the subsidiary country in question, I_{ih} stands for the score for the ith cultural dimension of the headquarters country in question, V_i is the variance of the index of the ith cultural dimension, and CD_s is the cultural difference of the subsidiary country from the headquarters country. The scores on each of the four dimensions for the countries included in our survey can be found in Hofstede (1980a).

Performance data
In Section 3 of Chapter 2, we justified our choice of return on sales (ROS), return on assets (ROA) and return on equity (ROE) as performance indicators. The data needed to calculate these ratios were taken from the 1995 Global Fortune 500 list and company 1995 annual reports, where necessary.

---

[91] Hofstede's fifth dimension, Confucian dynamism, was not included since data for this dimension were not available for most of the countries in our study.

We will use both the five-year (1990-1994) average and the most recent year as performance indicators. A five-year-average rate masks peculiarities of single years, but last year's figures could logically be expected to be most related to the independent data that were either collected by questionnaire in 1995 or from 1995 annual reports.

Performance was also measured at subsidiary level. However, since we expected that many respondents might be hesitant to supply exact performance data (see also Roth, Schweiger and Morrison, 1991), we asked them to evaluate a subsidiary's performance in relation to other subsidiaries in the group. Respondents were asked to indicate both the relative sales growth and the relative profitability over the past five years.

Pre-test of the questionnaire

Since most of the variables were operationalised using either existing scales or objective measures, a large-scale pre-test was deemed to be too cost-and time-intensive. In the pilot mailing (see Section 3) respondents were invited to note down any difficulties they had in answering the questions. Two of the four respondents used this opportunity. Most remarks involved questions that were not completely clear. These questions were adjusted. In addition, all four respondents had difficulty in answering the questions about cultural dimensions at headquarters and subsidiaries. These questions were therefore deleted from the final questionnaire and substituted by the objective cultural distance indicator as described above. The questionnaire was also sent to all of the committee members (see Section 3), academics in 20 different countries. In general, the questionnaire was very well received. However, quite a number of recommendations were made concerning the wording of questions and scale markers. In addition, some questions were thought to be too difficult to answer for subsidiary managers. Most of the recommendations were included in the final version of the questionnaire and a number of questions (mainly concerning HQ characteristics) were deleted.

Conclusions

This section discussed the choice of research method, the level of data collection, the operationalisation of variables and the pre-testing of the questionnaire. After comparing various survey methods, a mail survey was judged the best way of data collection. Further, a deliberate choice was made to collect our main data at subsidiary level, since respondents at this level were thought to give more truthful and reliable answers. A key-informant approach was chosen as the best method of data collection. The limitations of this approach and its possible remedies have been duly discussed. A final section then discussed the operationalisation of the variables used in our study. Many variables were operationalised using either existing scales or objective measures. In our opinion, this limited the necessity of a large-scale pre-test. This section thus discussed a number of substantive choices. In the next section, the focus will be on the procedural aspects of international mail surveys.

3. MAIL SURVEY PROCESS

Introduction

Section 1 discussed the general methodological problems associated with cross-cultural research. In addition, international or cross-cultural research in general, and international mail surveys in particular, are accompanied by a number of practical problems. These problems remain largely undescribed, either consciously or unconsciously, in virtually all books and articles.[92] Also, "Literature concerned with response rates from industrial samples drawn from multiple countries is nearly absent" (Dawson and Dickinson, 1988:492), so that international researchers often do not have the slightest idea of what response rates to expect when sending questionnaires abroad.

When it comes to the more practical and mundane issues such as the collection of addresses, the design of questionnaires, the choice of incentives and other ways to maximise response, the international researcher has to rely on a handful of articles that give fragmented information about a very limited number of countries (Angur and Nataraajan, 1995 about the use of incentives in India; Ayal and Hornik, 1986 about source effects in Israel and the USA; Dawson and Dickinson, 1988 about incentives and response rates in the UK, West Germany, Canada, USA, Japan and France; Jobber and Saunders, 1988 about source effects in Britain and the USA; Jobber, Mirza and Wee, 1991, about the use of incentives in Singapore, Malaysia and Thailand; and Keown, 1985 about incentives and response rates in Hong Kong and Japan).

This paucity of articles on international mail surveys is all the more surprising since there is a simply overwhelming number of publications available on virtually every imaginable aspect of mail surveys in a domestic setting: number of questions, questionnaire length, the colour of the questionnaire, user-friendly questionnaire formats, ticking versus circling answers, the researcher's name (native or non-native American), anonymity, deadlines, type of outgoing postage, type of return envelope, pre-contacts, follow-ups, offer of results, personalisation, topic interest, auspices of the survey, numerous types of incentives, colour of the signature on a covering letter, response rates

---

[92] For a rare exception, see Mintu, Calantone and Gassenheimer (1993) who discuss their mail survey experience in the USA and Philippines.

of left- or right-handed respondents, use of hand-written postscripts and many, many more.[93] The field has even generated a substantial number of reviews on factors affecting response rates to mail surveys which together cover hundreds and hundreds of articles (see e.g. Church, 1993; Fox, Crask and Kim, 1988; Harvey, 1987; Jobber, 1986; LaGarce and Kuhn, 1995; Yu and Cooper, 1983). Further, Diamantopoulos, Schlegelmilch and Webb (1991) used these and other reviews to draw up an exhaustive checklist of potential influences on mail survey response and queried both researchers and respondents about the influence of each factor. They conclude that: "the results of the present study show a high degree of congruence in the perceptions of researchers and respondents with regard to the influences associated with mail-questionnaire response in an industrial setting" (1991:338). In addition, the process of receiving and responding to a mail survey has been examined phenomenologically (Helgeson, 1994) and attempts have been made to build models to predict response rates (Jobber and Saunders, 1986, 1993).

The contrast between the maturity of this field of research in a domestic setting and the virtual absence of articles in an international setting is striking. To paraphrase Laurent (1986): while cross-cultural or international research as such may slowly be outgrowing its infancy, research on the way international research is or should be conducted is in an early embryonic stage. As Yeung (1995) indicates: "We often have only a vague idea on how a piece of research or finding has come about in its published form" (Yeung, 1995: 313-314). Therefore, we will give some insights into how we solved the practical problems that we encountered when preparing our survey. An important aspect of this was the devising of various incentives to increase response rates. We will show the results of these incentives in terms of response rates and discuss the major differences in response rates across countries.

Practical issues in international mail surveys

This section will describe the practical issues that were encountered during the preparation of our international mail survey. The mail survey involved mailing questionnaires to CEOs and HR managers at the headquarters of 122 MNCs and to the managing directors of some 1650 subsidiaries of these mul-

---

[93] No separate references are included for these various aspects, since most of the studies have been included in the review articles. It must be said, however, that virtually all of these studies have been done in the field of (consumer) marketing or public opinion surveying and have appeared in either marketing journals or journals such as *Public Opinion Quarterly*. Few of the results seem to have found their way into organisation studies. In a review of 303 articles in the field of organisation studies with regard to their research design Grunow (1995) comments: 'If they describe the 'realized project' as 'ex post design', they don't even offer insight into *practical* problems of doing organizational research.'

tinationals in 22 different countries. A pilot mailing was sent to 96 subsidiaries in 12 different countries at the beginning of June 1995. For the final
mailing questionnaires were sent out in two batches: one in October 1995 and
one in January 1996.[94] Reminders for the first batch were sent in January
1996, about three months after the original mailing. Reminders for the second
batch were sent in March 1996, about six weeks after the original mailing.
Below we will discuss the issues that had to be solved *before* sending out
questionnaires: building the database of addresses, ensuring personalisation
and local content, designing the questionnaire and postcards and devising
incentives to increase response rates.

Building the database of addresses
As indicated in Section 2, in order to improve the external generalisability of
our study, we decided to build our population of firms in a very systematic
way, including a comparable proportion of firms in eight different industries,
MNCs headquartered in seven European countries, the USA and Japan, and
subsidiaries in 22 countries spread over six cultural clusters (Anglo-Saxon,
Germanic, Scandinavian, South European, Latin American and Far Eastern).
In addition, we also wanted to be able to analyse at the level of the individual
multinational firm in order to investigate whether companies differentiate
their control mechanisms for different subsidiaries.

The result was that we could not simply copy addresses from the first
available address book with, for instance, foreign-owned subsidiaries in the
US. Therefore, our starting point was an address book that included the
names and addresses of the 500 largest MNCs and their subsidiaries in some
80 countries (Hoopes, 1994). As only about one third of the 1400 addresses
that we selected from this book included the names of the managing directors
and personalisation is usually thought to be important to achieve reasonable
response rates (see below), it was decided to fill this gap by searching for
these names in other address books. In doing so, we noticed that many of the
addresses we had copied from the original book were incorrect and so it was
decided to check every address on the list against other (even more recent)
sources. Some of the original addresses could not be checked, or turned out to
be holding companies or very small representative agencies. Therefore, additional addresses of some 400 subsidiaries of the selected MNCs in the predetermined industries/countries were collected to substitute for the discarded

---

[94] There were two very mundane reasons for sending out the questionnaire in two batches. First,
very little help was available to prepare the envelopes for mailing (labelling, packaging etc.).
Sending the questionnaires out in two batches allowed me to spread this very boring work over a
longer period. Second, sending out the questionnaires in two different years meant that the costs
could be divided over two yearly budgets. To make sure that we did not overload the university's mail department, the mailing of the two batches was also spread over three days.

addresses. All in all this process took about two months of full-time work. In total, we used about forty different books.[95]

Only after we had collected and checked most of the addresses did we request (and receive) annual reports for all 122 MNCs included in our population. These annual reports were mainly requested to get financial and historical information about the company. In addition, however, many annual reports turned out to contain a complete directory with name and address information for the companies' (major) subsidiaries. Annual reports might therefore be an excellent starting point to collect addresses, especially since they are likely to be more up to date than address books. Addresses were checked once more against this source and another 200-250 addresses were added. Even though the most recent address books were used, addresses were at least a year old before the questionnaires were actually sent out and 12.5% of the questionnaires came back undeliverable (see Table 3-3). This is by no means abnormal in international mail surveys. Shipchandler, Terpstra and Shaheen (1994) had 26.1% returns, while Schlegelmilch and Robertson (1995) indicate that about 20% of the entries in printed directories become invalid each year. Casson, Loveridge and Singh (1996) found nearly 21% of the addresses of the Fortune 500 list used in their study to be inaccurate or out of date. Further, one should not forget that actual postal returns are a conservative estimate of undeliverables. The fact that 25% of the undeliverables only became apparent in the reminder already indicates that postal services are not always reliable. Finally, the fact that a questionnaire has arrived at the company in question does not guarantee it will reach the addressee in person. In our own survey we tracked down several cases in which a manager would have been happy to cooperate, but never received our mailings. Since we mailed a postcard and two questionnaires, it is highly likely that these were purposefully intercepted by gatekeepers.[96]

A related problem is whom to address the questionnaire to. In our case the managing director was the most appropriate person as he/she was most knowledgeable about the issues we requested information on. Further, in most address books only the names of managing directors are available. We therefore decided to send the questionnaire to a named individual, followed by the job title: managing director. Especially in subsidiaries of MNCs, however, it is highly likely that the managing director will be rotated frequently. In fact,

---

[95] For example the Kompass and Dun and Bradstreet addresss books for each country for which they were available, Graham and Trotman's *Major Companies of Europe and Far East and Australasia* and many country-specific address books, e.g. *Handbuch der Grossunternehmen* and *Handbuch der Mittelständischen Unternehmen* for Germany.

[96] Wright, Lane and Beamish (1988) found that in their study almost 25% of the letters sent by courier were not received by the person they were addressed to, even though they had been signed for at the organisation.

we had several returns indicating that Mr So-and-so was no longer working for the subsidiary and had returned to headquarters. An alternative for future studies might therefore be to include the name, but to add a line saying "or his/her representative/successor".

Personalisation and local content

Although the results on this particular aspect of mail surveys are not completely consistent, personalisation is usually thought to increase response rates (see e.g. Dillman, 1978; Fox, Crask and Kim, 1988; Harvey, 1987; Jobber, 1986; LaGarce and Kuhn, 1995; Yu and Cooper, 1983). Letters were therefore mail-merged to prepare personalised addresses and salutations. A handwritten signature was also included. To increase the feeling of being addressed personally both the announcement postcard (see below) and the questionnaire included a scanned photograph of the researcher before a wall of relevant international books. In the pilot survey, half of the 96 questionnaires included photographs. Only four responses were received in the pilot survey, but three of them were questionnaires with photographs. Although these numbers are too small to draw any definitive conclusions, it was decided to give photographs the benefit of the doubt in the final mailing.

As the pilot survey elicited a very low response rate (less than 4%), several additional measures were envisaged to increase response rates. One of these was an international committee of recommendation. Although there is no consistent evidence to prove that domestic surveys generate a higher response than foreign surveys (Ayal and Hornik, 1986; Jobber and Saunders, 1988; Teagarden et al., 1995), it was hypothesised that addressees would be more likely to respond if a local university had endorsed the project. Academics at local universities in the 22 countries were therefore contacted with the request to act as a member of an international committee of recommendation. A description of the research project was included in each case. Fortunately, none of them refused, although no representative could be found for Venezuela or Mexico. The names of these people were included on both the announcement postcard and the questionnaire under the heading: "Committee of recommendation"[97]. In addition to increasing the "local content" of the survey, this committee was though to increase the perceived importance of the project.

---

[97] The final committee consisted of the following members (in alphabetical order). Prof. John Dunning, Rutgers University, USA; Prof. Paul Evans, INSEAD, France; Dr. Anthony Ferner, University of Warwick, United Kingdom; Dr. Carlos Garcia Pont, IESE, Spain; Prof. Gunnar Hedlund, Stockholm School of Economics, Sweden; Prof. Martin Hilb, Hochschule St. Gallen, Switzerland; Prof. Geert Hofstede, IRIC, The Netherlands; Dr. Jorma Larimo, University of Vaasa, Finland; Prof. Christian Maroy, Université Catholique de Louvain, Belgium; Dr. Aahad Osman-Gani, Nanyang Business School, Singapore; Prof. Jaap Paauwe, Erasmus University, The Netherlands; Prof. Victor Prochnik, Federal University of Rio de Janeiro, Brazil; Prof. Gordon Redding, University of Hong Kong, Hong Kong; Prof. Marino Regini, IRES Lombardia,

Questionnaire and postcards

A second modification to the pilot mailing was the addition of an announce-ment postcard as response rates (see e.g. Dillman, 1978; Fox, Crask and Kim, 1988; Harvey, 1987; Jobber, 1986; LaGarce and Kuhn, 1995; Yu and Cooper, 1983), response speed and data quality (Murphy, Dalenberg and Daley, 1990) usually increase with pre-contacts.[98] In the final mailing, respondents received a postcard – which briefly explained the nature of the study and indicated four typical questions to which the survey might give an answer - about a week before the questionnaires were due to arrive. This postcard included both the committee of recommendation and the photograph.

The questionnaire was carefully designed to be easy to complete. It had only six open-ended questions that asked for factual data (year of foundation, number of employees, etc.).[99] All the other questions used tick boxes. Since questionnaire length is found to be an important factor in explaining response rates in an industrial population (Jobber and Saunders, 1993), the total num-ber of questions was limited to 56, spread over six pages. Though results on the effect of coloured questionnaires on response rates are inconsistent (Greer and Lohtia, 1994; Gullahorn and Gullahorn, 1963; Jobber and Sanderson, 1983; Matteson, 1974, Pressley and Tullar, 1977; Pucel, Nelson and Wheeler, 1971), the questionnaire was printed on pale yellow paper for greater recog-nition. Both the committee of recommendation and the photograph were printed on the questionnaire. On the back of the questionnaire's last page, the return address (an international business reply number) was printed in such a way that respondents could return the questionnaire by folding it in three and taping/stapling it. Neither postage nor envelope was needed.

A response card, including the respondent's name and address, was in-cluded with the questionnaire. Respondents could use this response card to indicate that they did not want to participate in the survey (about 10% used this opportunity) or to indicate that they had sent back the questionnaire anonymously[100] by separate post.

Italy; Dr. Oscar Risso Patrón, Universidad Argentina John F. Kennedy, Argentina; Prof. Arndt Sorge, Humboldt Universität, Germany; Prof. Bill Roche, University College Dublin, Ireland; Prof. Danny Van Den Bulcke, Universiteit Antwerpen, Belgium; Prof. Yoko Sano, Keio Univer-sity, Japan; Prof. Udo Wagner, Universität Wien, Austria; Dr. Steen Scheuer, Copenhagen Busi-ness School, Denmark; Dr. Denice Welch, Norwegian School of Management, Norway.

[98] Interestingly, the only study that found a decrease of response rates when prenotification was used was conducted outside the USA (UK, Jobber and Sanderson, 1983). Another study, con-ducted in Denmark (Albaum and Strandskov, 1989), found that prenotification did not have any effect on response rates. Again, there might be a difference in the usefulness of this tactic across countries.

[99] A large number of open-ended questions usually leads to a decrease in response rates (Jobber and Saunders, 1993).

[100] Anonymity was shown to be positively related to response rate in industrial populations (Jobber, 1986; Jobber and Saunders, 1993).

Incentives

A third modification to the pilot mailing was the choice of a different incentive. In the pilot survey we promised half of the addressees that the first five respondents would get a copy of my recently edited book on International HRM (Harzing and Van Ruysseveldt, 1995). Only one of these 46 questionnaires was returned, while three of the questionnaires without this incentive were returned. Although again these numbers are too small to draw any definitive conclusions, the incentive certainly does not seem to have resulted in a dramatic increase in response rate. On second thoughts, it was rather "ethnocentric" (viewed from the academic profession) to think that managers would be as motivated as researchers by the idea of receiving a book. Kalafatis and Tsogas (1994) reported significantly lower response rates for a comparable incentive: the inclusion of an academic or trade article. As an explanation, they argue that: "the realisation that the data to be provided may eventually be published in a peer journal deters recipients from completing the questionnaire. The reasons for such behaviour have not been investigated but could be related to a perceived breach of confidentiality or a feeling of increased sense of responsibility in providing 'correct' or factual data" (Kalafatis and Tsogas, 1994:141). In addition to failing to give a positive incentive, the promise of a book could therefore also have given a negative incentive. Further, the book incentive could have missed its goal, as promised incentives are less effective than enclosed incentives (Church, 1993; Harvey, 1987; Jobber, 1986; Yu and Cooper, 1983).

In search of an appropriate incentive for the final mailing, numerous options have been reviewed. Pens and the like were discarded very soon, because they had been used so many times before that the novelty would have worn off. Monetary incentives have been shown to be very effective in increasing response rates both in mail surveys (Armstrong and Yokum, 1994; Church, 1993; Fox, Crask and Kim, 1988; Harvey, 1987; Jobber, 1986; London and Dommeyer, 1990; Yu and Cooper, 1983) and in interviews (Goyder, 1994). There are several problems attached to monetary incentives, however. First, what currency do you use in international surveys? Paper money is preferable to coins, because it is less bulky, lower in weight and generally has a more aesthetic appeal. Using local currencies would in this case be problematic, as for many countries the smallest denomination available in notes is much larger than the US$. In the Netherlands, for instance, the smallest denomination is worth approximately $6, which would make the incentive far too expensive. Using US$ in all countries could be seen as offensive in some countries. Further, offering money might be considered as an insult in itself in some countries. Keown's survey (Keown, 1985) showed that response rates dropped to 0% in Hong Kong when a dollar was included. We therefore decided to discard the monetary incentive as well.

Serious incentive options have been: a lottery with electronic organisers as prizes and a sachet of flower seeds. The first was thought to appeal to a manager's sensitivity to technological gadgets, but was discarded because of the relatively high cost (offering only one for more than 1600 respondents was not considered to be much of an incentive), the fact that lotteries are illegal in some countries and the knowledge that promised incentives are in general less effective than enclosed incentives. The sachet of flower seeds was mainly meant to be symbolic. First, it would be connected to a flourishing relationship in the cover letter and second, respondents would be advised to sow the seeds. The company report that was promised would then be available by the time the seeds started flowering. Finally, we also discarded this option, however, mainly because of the Dutch image concerning soft drugs. The present might be misinterpreted or, worse yet, be intercepted at customs.

Finally, we decided to use a small and relatively cheap present: a bag of Pickwick tea for one. This tea-bag was attached to the cover letter next to a PS: Why don't you take a short break, have a nice cup of tea and fill out the questionnaire right now? It will only take 10-15 minutes. This incentive was hypothesised to catch the addressee's attention, prevent the questionnaire from being thrown away immediately, put the respondent in a pleasant mood and emphasise that it would not take too much time to fill out the questionnaire (just the time to drink a cup of tea). In the reminder, we elaborated on this theme by including instant coffee for the addressees that did not like tea. Even when using such a simple present, it should be verified, however, whether it is applicable cross-culturally. We checked whether tea is drunk in every country included in our survey (it was) and whether the colour of the tea-bag (green) did not have negative connotations in some countries (it did not). In spite of these precautions, we had not thought that even a bag of tea or a sachet of coffee could be regarded as an insult. A researcher from Hong Kong we consulted afterwards to ask for explanations of the low response rate in Hong Kong, suggested that Chinese CEOs might be concerned that the researcher would think that they were after the tea or coffee and would like to save face. On the other hand, we received some very positive reactions from both Western and Japanese respondents on this particular incentive.

Offer of the results
Although so far this has not been proven to increase response rates and has sometimes even reduced response rates (Jobber and Sanderson, 1985; Kalafatis and Tsogas, 1994; Kerin et al, 1981; Yu and Cooper, 1983), we thought it only fair to offer respondents the opportunity to receive a summary of the results and recommendations. Nearly 90% of the respondents indicated that they would like to use this opportunity. As mentioned above, respondents could also indicate this on the response card, while the questionnaire itself

remained anonymous. A professional-looking company report was mailed about three months after the last reminders had been sent out. Several firms contacted the researcher to order more detailed reports. Some subsidiaries also for asked additional copies to be sent to headquarters.

Mail survey results: response rates and timing of responses

All of the issues discussed in the previous section aim, either directly or indirectly, at improving response rates. In this section, we will therefore discuss the results of our survey in terms of response rates. We will briefly discuss typical response rates in international mail surveys, and quote some of the reactions of the respondents who declined to participate. Subsequently, detailed results on the number of questionnaires sent out for each country, the number of respondents in the first mailing and the reminder, the number of respondents who declined to participate and the number of undeliverable questionnaires will be given. Also some information will be furnished about the timing of the responses. Finally, response rates are shown to vary considerably across countries and nationalities.

Introduction
International mail surveys aimed at a managing director/CEO population have a history of very low response rates. For regular mail surveys without either a follow-up or a pre-contact by telephone, response rates typically vary between 6% and 16% (Dawson and Dickinson, 1988; Ghoshal and Nohria, 1993; Jobber, Mirza and Wee, 1991; Jobber and Saunders, 1988; Shipchandler, Terpstra and Shaheen, 1994; Wolf, 1994). Although reminders usually increase response rates a recent survey (Kopp, 1994) received only 8.8% response with two mailings.

Many of the firms that declined participation in this survey indicated that they had a corporate policy not to participate in mail surveys, since the number of questionnaires had simply become overwhelming, especially over the past five years. One American company even used standard response cards to deal with this issue! To quote some of the typical answers that were received from headquarters:

> Roughly 100 requests of this kind are received by (company name) *weekly* from all over the world. We had to decide not to answer anymore in order to set no precedent.

> (company name) admires the intent of your project and wishes you all success. (CEO name) is receiving many such requests and does not feel he can deal with them with the seriousness they require.

As you can imagine we do receive a number of similar requests and in order to organise our participation on a rational basis we normally limit our contribution to surveys which are quantitative in orientation and deal specifically with our particular business. Only in this way can we reduce the input to a manageable volume!

We wish we could say yes but because we receive so many requests to participate in surveys, questionnaires and research projects we have been forced to say no to all. We know you understand.

In recent times the increase in requests to participate in questionnaires and surveys has grown enormously and is now at a level where our staff are no longer able to cope with them without serious interference to their normal work. We have, therefore, been obliged to adopt, reluctantly, the policy of not becoming involved in questionnaires, surveys and returns - whatever their nature or extent - unless they are a statutory requirement.

We appreciate your interest in (company name) and wish it were possible to answer each of your questions for your thesis. Unfortunately, we receive many letters similar to yours, and because of limited time and manpower, it is impossible to respond favourably to every request. To be fair to all, it was decided that none be responded to in order to concentrate our efforts in providing our customers with quality products and service.

or simply:

Too many, too often.

Reading these responses, we even began to wonder why mail surveys to this population generated any responses at all. In view of the number of questionnaires most companies seem to receive, we have been impressed by the conscientiousness of most headquarters to deal with these issues. We received an answer from 56% of the CEOs in our sample (21% responding, 35% declining participation). For large Global 500[101] companies the questionnaire crisis seems to be particularly acute. From the largest 25 companies in our survey (ranking 1-37 on the 1994 Global 500), we received only two responses. Sixteen companies declined participation, leaving only seven that gave no response at all.

---

[101] Jobber and Saunders (1993) showed a general negative impact of using the Fortune or Times top 500 as a sampling frame as compared to, for instance, membership lists, readership lists and directories. This is undoubtedly because so many researchers rely on the top 500 firms. Unfortunately, this problem could not be circumvented because, for the testing of our hypotheses, we simply needed a sample of large MNCs.

Detailed Results of the survey

Table 3-3 shows the results of this survey with regard to the number of questionnaires that were sent out, the number that were undeliverable, the number that declined participation, the number that did not generate any response at all, the responses to the first mailing and the responses to the reminder.

Table 3-3 Distribution of responses in five categories across 22 countries

Subsidiary country		Unde-liver-able	No respon-se at all	Declined participa-tion	Response to first mailing	Response to re-minder	Total
Argentina	Count	5	26	1	3	1	36
	%	13.9	72.2	2.8	8.3	2.8	100.0
Austria	Count	5	30	4	5	3	47
	%	10.6	63.8	8.5	10.6	6.4	100.0
Belgium	Count	9	47	8	11	3	78
	%	11.5	60.3	10.3	14.1	3.8	100.0
Brazil	Count	9	50	3	10	5	77
	%	11.7	64.9	3.9	13.0	6.5	100.0
Denmark	Count	5	19	3	14	2	43
	%	11.6	44.2	7.0	32.6	4.7	100.0
England	Count	15	81	27	17	8	148
	%	10.1	54.7	18.2	11.5	5.4	100.0
Finland	Count	5	13	4	3	5	30
	%	16.7	43.3	13.3	10.0	16.7	100.0
France	Count	10	81	8	11	3	113
	%	8.8	71.7	7.1	9.7	2.7	100.0
Germany	Count	14	68	19	8	8	117
	%	12.0	58.1	16.2	6.8	6.8	100.0
Hong Kong	Count	11	50	2	3	1	67
	%	16.4	74.6	3.0	4.5	1.5	100.0
Ireland	Count	5	15	10	8	3	69
	%	12.2	36.6	24.4	19.5	7.3	100.0
Italy	Count	12	61	4	15	6	98
	%	12.2	62.2	4.1	15.3	6.1	100.0
Japan	Count	13	36	4	12	4	69
	%	18.8	52.2	5.8	17.4	5.8	100.0
Mexico	Count	8	54	2	4	6	74
	%	10.8	73.0	2.7	5.4	8.1	100.0
Netherlands	Count	10	46	23	18	7	104
	%	9.6	44.2	22.1	17.3	6.7	100.0
Norway	Count	4	16	3	11	2	36
	%	11.1	44.4	8.3	30.6	5.6	100.0
Singapore	Count	13	54	3	8	1	79
	%	16.5	68.4	3.8	10.1	1.3	100.0
Spain	Count	15	68	6	10	4	103
	%	14.6	66.0	5.8	9.7	3.9	100.0
Sweden	Count	8	34	9	8	3	62
	%	12.9	54.8	14.5	12.9	4.8	100.0
Switzerland	Count	10	25	8	11	3	57
	%	17.5	43.9	14.0	19.3	5.3	100.0
USA	Count	14	80	21	10	3	128
	%	10.9	62.5	16.4	7.8	2.3	100.0
Venezuela	Count	5	24	1	4		34
	%	14.7	70.6	2.9	11.8		100.0
Various	Count				2		
	%				100.0		
Total	Count	205	978	173	206	81	1643
	%	12.5	59.5	10.5	12.5	4.9	100.0

There are major differences between countries in the division of responses over the last five categories. First, there is a large number of responses in the first mailing in Denmark and Norway. Second, the large number of responses in the reminder for Germany, Mexico and Finland is remarkable. Overall around 28% of the responses were collected in the reminder, but for these countries, the percentages were 50%, 60% and 62.5% respectively! Even the difference in the percentage of respondents who declined participation is striking. For most countries, this number lies below the number of positive responses, but for England, Germany and the USA it is the other way round. Although the positive response rate for these countries is low to medium, respondents do make an effort to indicate that they do not want to participate. The Netherlands and Ireland combine a high positive response rate with a high number of respondents declining participation. Including the number of undeliverables, the result is that for Ireland only 36.6% of the sample gave no response at all. Low non-response rates (below 45%) were also obtained for Denmark, Finland, the Netherlands, Norway and Switzerland, while three of the four Latin American countries, Hong Kong and France had non-response rates above 70%.

Timing of responses and reminders
Due to longer mail delivery times, responses in international mail surveys will obviously come in more slowly. Even so, for the first mailing - sent in October - roughly 20% of the total amount of responses was received within a week, 50% within two weeks and 70% within three weeks. The remaining 30% trickled in over another six to seven weeks, the last response arriving approximately ten weeks after the questionnaires had been mailed. Almost exactly the same pattern emerged for the reminder of this first mailing. The responses to the second mailing sent out in January came in more slowly with only 10% in the first week, but recovered quickly in the second week, by the end of which 50% of the final amount of questionnaires had been received, as in the first mailing. After three weeks 70% had arrived. In the reminder to the second mailing respondents took even more time: only 10% after the first, 35% after the second and 60% after the third week. The somewhat slower response in the second mailing was probably because a large number of non-European countries were included in the second mailing. In general, one should be able to predict the eventual success of the mailing about three weeks after the questionnaires have been sent out.

Reminders included a complete set: letter, questionnaire and response card. Addresses that turned out to be incorrect or addressees who had indicated that they did not want to participate did not receive a reminder. In both cases, the reminders generated an additional response of around 40% (40.9% and 39.5% respectively) of the original response. As indicated above, around 28% of the responses were received through reminders. The timing of the reminders did not seem to make a difference in this case.

Response rates

Table 3-4 indicates the response rates per industry, headquarters country and subsidiary country. Response rates were calculated by dividing the number of positive responses to both the first mailing and the reminder by the number of deliverable questionnaires. This formula has become customary in international research, because of the high number of undeliverable questionnaires (Black and Porter, 1991; Dawson and Dickinson, 1988; Jobber, Mirza and Wee, 1991; Jobber and Saunders, 1988; Keown, 1985; Kotabe et al, 1991; London and Dommeyer, 1990; Murray, Wildt and Kotabe, 1995; Shipchandler, Terpstra and Shaheen, 1994). A Kruskal-Wallis test was performed to see whether response rates differ significantly between industries, headquarters countries and subsidiary countries. Response rates do not differ significantly between industries (chi-square 5.370, sig. 0.615). They do differ significantly, however, for both headquarters (chi-square 24.104, sig. 0.002) and subsidiary countries (chi-square 54.662, Sig. 0.000).

Table 3-4 Response rates for different industries and (headquarters and subsidiary) countries

Industry	Response rate (overall 20%)	Subsidiary country	Response rate (overall 20%)
		Hong Kong	7.1%
Computers	16.2%	USA	11.4%
Electronics	17.1%	Argentina	12.9%
Food and Beverages	18.4%	France	13.6%
Motor vehicles and parts	20.4%	Singapore	13.6%
Paper (products)	20.6%	Venezuela	13.8%
Chemical (products)	21.3%	Mexico	15.2%
Petroleum (products)	21.4%	Germany	15.5%
Pharmaceutical	23.8%	Spain	15.9%
		UK	18.8%
Country of location		Austria	19.0%
of headquarters	Response rate	Belgium	20.3%
		Sweden	20.4%
USA	14.3%	Brazil	22.1%
Japan	16.7%	Italy	24.4%
France	18.6%	Netherlands	26.6%
UK	19.7%	Japan	28.6%
Germany	21.8%	Switzerland	29.8%
Finland	24.0%	Ireland	30.6%
Sweden	24.6%	Finland	32.0%
Switzerland	30.4%	Norway	40.6%
Netherlands	31.5%	Denmark	42.1%

These response rates confirm the finding of various studies that response rates in Japan are higher than response rates in the USA (Daniel and Reitsperger, 1991; Jain and Tucker, 1995; Tung, 1982; Kriger and Solomon, 1992; Kopp, 1994; Ueno and Sekaran, 1992). They do not unambiguously confirm that response rates in Japan are higher than response rates in European countries (as found by Birdseye and Hill, 1995; Dawson and Dickinson, 1988; Jain and Tucker, 1995; Kopp, 1994; and Tung, 1982). Further, they certainly do not confirm the finding of many studies that response rates in the USA are higher than response rates in European countries (Banai and Reisel, 1993; Cullen, Johnson and Sakano, 1995; Dawson and Dickinson, 1988; Jain and Tucker, 1995; Jobber and Saunders, 1986; Kopp, 1994; Kwok and Arpan, 1994; Morris, Davis and Allen, 1994; Schlegelmilch and Robertson, 1995; Tung, 1982).[102] In all cases, however, questionnaires were sent from the USA.

The overall response rate of our survey (20%) compares favourably with most of the other studies aimed at a comparable population. As indicated above, most of these studies had response rates between 6% and 16%. It is very difficult to compare our response rates for individual countries with previous studies, however, since there are no studies that report response rates for more than a couple of countries included in our survey. There is one study that has not been mentioned yet, the Price Waterhouse Cranfield study (Brewster et al, 1994). The Price Waterhouse Cranfield study has so far been conducted in 14 (European) countries, 12 of which are included in our survey as well. As this is the only study that compares response rates in more than two or three European countries and in which surveys were not sent from the USA, it forms an excellent base for comparison (see Table 3-5).

In both surveys Scandinavian countries have the highest response rates, although in the Price Waterhouse Cranfield study top scorers are Sweden and Finland, while in our study this position is taken by Norway and Denmark. On average, however, the response rates for the Scandinavian countries are extremely comparable (33.8% for our survey, 34.5% for the Price Waterhouse Cranfield survey). For four large European countries (Germany, France, UK and Spain), response rates in both surveys are also very comparable. Major differences occur for Switzerland, the Netherlands, Ireland and Italy. In all cases response rates for our survey are (much) higher. Especially remarkable are the high response rates for Italy in our survey, as this country scored lowest in some other surveys (O'Neill et al, 1995; Talaga and Buch, 1992) and Italians are not renowned for their dutiful response to written requests.

---

[102] It must be noted that none of the studies referred to focuses explicitly on differences in response rates or draws any conclusions from them.

Table 3-5 Response rates of our survey compared with response rates of the Price Waterhouse Cranfield (PWC) study

Country	Response rates (%) our survey	Response rates (%) PWC[103]
Overall	20.0	18.5
France	13.6	13.0
Germany	15.5	14.0
Spain	15.9	14.0
UK	18.8	22.0
Sweden	20.4	40.0
Italy	24.4	10.0
Netherlands	26.6	15.0
Switzerland	29.8	16.0
Ireland	30.6	12.0
Finland	32.0	46.0
Norway	40.6	29.0
Denmark	42.1	23.0

In the Price Waterhouse Cranfield study, questionnaires were translated and adapted for different countries and sent out by local universities, so that the local content of the study was much higher than for our study. Response rates for nine out of twelve countries, however, were higher in our survey than in the Price Waterhouse Cranfield study.[104] Combined with the data on response rates in other international mail surveys, it therefore seems safe to conclude that response rates in our survey are very reasonable.

The fact that the highest response rates for headquarters country included countries that also scored high as a subsidiary country (e.g. Netherlands, Switzerland),[105] while the USA scored very low both as a headquarters and as a subsidiary country, led us to assume that it might be useful to look at the differences in response rates between *nationalities*. In this case, the response of, for instance, Dutch expatriates on assignment in Singapore would be headed under the "Dutch" response rate. As can be seen when comparing Table 3-5 and Table 3-6, for some countries the difference is remarkable. Japan's high response rate, for instance, is largely based on responses of non-Japanese expatriate managing directors. The 13.8% for Venezuela is entirely

---

[103] The Price Waterhouse Cranfield response rates for the individual countries had to be estimated from a bar chart (Brewster et al., 1994:238) and for some countries had to be averaged over several years. They might therefore not be completely exact.

[104] The fact that our overall response rate is only slightly higher than the Cranfield response rate is due to the fact that with the exception of Brazil and Japan all non-European countries in our survey had below average response rates.

[105] Individual top scorers (i.e. headquarters where around 50% of the subsidiaries responded) can also be found in the smaller European countries. These MNCs had a significantly higher percentage of foreign sales (p < 0.001) and foreign employees (p < 0.05) than the rest of the sample.

composed of foreign expatriates; no native Venezuelans responded. Not surprisingly, response rate also differed significantly between nationalities (chi-square 55.892, Sig. 0.000).

Table 3-6 Response rates for different nationalities

Nationality of Respondent	Response rate (%)	Nationality of Respondent	Response rate (%)
Hong Kongese	0	Spanish	18.4
Venezuelan	0	Swedish	19.6
Singaporean	4.8	Belgian	20.4
Mexican	6.5	British	22.3
Argentinean	9.1	Italian	25.8
Austrian	10.0	Dutch	27.4
American	11.6	Swiss	27.6
French	12.5	Finnish	28.0
German	13.4	Irish	32.4
Brazilian	14.3	Norwegian	38.7
Japanese	16.8	Danish	40.6

A k-means cluster analysis was performed to see whether response rate clusters with significantly different means could be formed. A three-cluster solution[106] resulted in the following clusters:

- *Low response rate* (mean 12.46%): respondents with Hong Kongese, Singaporean, Japanese, Argentinean, Brazilian, Mexican, Venezuelan, US, Austrian, French or German nationality.
- *Medium response rate* (mean 21.37%): respondents with Belgian, Italian, Spanish, Swedish or British nationality.
- *High response rate* (mean 30.66%): respondents with Danish, Finnish, Norwegian, Irish, Dutch or Swiss nationality.

Reasons for these differences in response rates could lie in the field of culture (either culture as such or cultural distance from the Netherlands), the number of questionnaires received by respondents (lower for smaller countries, lower for countries in which research is mainly conducted by case studies), the international orientation of different countries/nationalities (the more internationally oriented, the more willing to participate in an international survey), English-language proficiency (although e.g. French and Spanish respondents might be able to read English, they might be more likely to answer a questionnaire in their native language) or a different response to the different in-

---

[106] A four-cluster solution resulted in group means that were not significantly different for each group pair.

centives. For a more detailed discussion of the differences in response rates between countries and the possible explanations for this, refer to Harzing (1997b and 1998c).

Conclusions

We discussed the practical problems associated with international mail surveys and the way they were solved in our study. A final conclusion that can be drawn in this respect is that, as in domestic surveys (Dillman, 1978; Walker, Kirchmann and Conant, 1987), attention to many details that might seem unimportant at first sight is simply necessary to secure reasonable response rates. In our survey, these response rates were shown to vary considerably across countries and nationalities in a way that contradicts much of the earlier (American) research in this field. A more detailed description of the final sample of our study can be found in the next section.

4. DESCRIPTION OF THE SAMPLE AND NON-RESPONSE BIAS

In this section, we will give a detailed description of the final sample of our study at both subsidiary and headquarters level. We will include the number of respondents per industry, headquarters country and subsidiary country, the size and age of the company and the function of subsidiaries. Possible non-response bias will be investigated for each of these aspects.

Subsidiary sample

Subsidiary country, industry and headquarters country
Table 3-7 summarises the number of respondents by industry, subsidiary country and country of the location of headquarters. With regard to industry, the chemical, pharmaceutical and electronics industry have a higher number of respondents than average, while the number of respondents for the computer, petroleum and paper industry lies below average. As we have seen above, however, these differences are not due to differences in response rates, which are not significantly different across industries. Differences in the number of responses by industry are largely due to the different representation of industries in the population as a whole. Due to differences in the number of subsidiaries per firm, and the necessity to consider other characteristics, we have not been able to achieve a completely balanced spread of the subsidiaries across industries. The industry distribution in our sample, however, is representative of the population the questionnaires were sent to.

The number of questionnaires received per headquarters country varies considerably from a low of 16 for the Netherlands to a high of 55 for the USA. These differences largely result from a difference in the representation of the different headquarters countries in our population. Not all countries have an equally large number of MNCs, so that the number of subsidiaries included in the population varies considerably across headquarters countries. In this case, however, our sample is not completely representative of the population the questionnaires were sent to. In Section 3, we showed that response rates varied significantly across headquarters countries. Since some of the headquarters countries with a relatively low number of MNCs had response rates that were higher than average and vice versa, these differences in response rates make analyses and conclusions at headquarters level more feasible.

Table 3-7 Number of respondents by industry, subsidiary country and headquarters country

Industry	Number of respondents	Subsidiary country	Number of respondents
Electronics, electr. Equipment	41	Argentina	4
Computers, office equipment	26	Austria	8
Motor vehicles and parts	30	Belgium	14
Petroleum (products)	20	Brazil	15
Food and Beverages	34	Denmark	16
Pharmaceutical	46	Finland	8
Paper (products)	25	France	14
Chemical (products)	55	Germany	16
Various	10	Hong Kong	5
		Ireland	11
Country of location of headquarters	**Number of respondents**	Italy	21
		Japan	16
		Mexico	10
Finland	23	Netherlands	25
France	26	Norway	13
Germany	32	Singapore	10
Japan	38	Spain	14
Netherlands	16	Sweden	11
Sweden	41	Switzerland	14
Switzerland	31	UK	25
UK	25	USA	13
USA	55	Venezuela	4

The number of questionnaires received for the different subsidiary countries varies from 4 (Argentina and Venezuela) to 25 (UK and the Netherlands). Again, this difference is partly due to a difference in the representation of the different subsidiary countries in our population. Not all countries have an equally large number of foreign subsidiaries within their borders. As we have seen in Section 3, however, response rates also varied significantly between subsidiary countries, so that again our sample is not representative of the population the questionnaires were sent to. In the case of subsidiary countries, this is deemed not to be too much of a problem, since the spread of responses across countries is very reasonable. The large number of subsidiary countries included in our survey, however, implies that analysis at a subsidiary country level will not be feasible. Analysis at the level of the different cultural clusters is a possibility, however. The number of responses per cluster are respectively: Asian (Far Eastern + Japan): 31, Latin American: 33, Germanic: 38, Anglo-Saxon: 49, Latin European: 63 and Nordic: 73.

The total number of 287 subsidiary responses represents 104 different headquarters (85% of our population). The number of responses per headquarters varies from one to eleven. For 35% of the headquarters represented in the final sample, only one of the subsidiaries included in the mailing responded. Two, three or four responses per headquarters were received in respectively 20%, 15% and 15% of the cases, while for the remaining 15% of the headquarters we received five or more responses. If we aggregate the responses per headquarters (see Table 3-8), we see that the representativeness of our sample concerning industry and headquarters country is excellent.

Table 3-8 Number of firms per industry and headquarters country, population and sample; % of industry or headquarters country of total population or sample between brackets.

Industry	Population	Sample	Headquarters country	Population	Sample
Electronics	17 (13.9%)	15 (14.4%)	Finland	9 (7.4%)	6 (5.8%)
Computers	13 (10.7%)	12 (11.5%)	France	12 (9.8%)	12 (11.5%)
Motor vehicles	12 (9.8%)	11 (10.6%)	Germany	10 (8.2%)	9 (8.7%)
Petroleum (products)	16 (13.1%)	13 (12.5%)	Japan	22 (18.0%)	18 (17.3%)
Food and Beverages	16 (13.1%)	15 (14.4%)	Netherlands	4 (3.3%)	4 (3.9%)
Pharmaceutical	15 (12.3%)	13 (12.5%)	Sweden	10 (8.2%)	9 (8.7%)
Paper (products)	15 (12.3%)	11 (10.6%)	Switzerland	5 (4.1%)	5 (4.8%)
Chemical (products)	18 (14.8%)	14 (13.5%)	UK	11 (9.0%)	10 (9.6%)
			USA	39 (32.0%)	31 (29.8%)
			Europe	61 (50.0%)	55 (52.9%)

Concerning the representativeness of our sample compared to the population of MNCs as a whole, we can remark that nearly two thirds of the Global Fortune 500 companies operate in the industries included in our sample. Neither our population nor our sample is completely representative concerning headquarters countries. Although the percentage of American firms in our sample comes very close to the percentage of American firms in the Global Fortune 500, the percentage of Japanese firms in our sample is somewhat lower (17.3% vs 27%). Considerably higher is our percentage of European firms

(52.9% vs 32%). This imbalance was created on purpose, however, in order to be able to analyse our data at the level of the different European countries. It does mean, however, that our sample is not completely representative of the population of Global Fortune 500 firms in this respect. With regard to subsidiary countries, we can remark that six of the eight commonly distinguished cultural clusters are present in reasonable numbers in our sample. Further, the 22 countries represented in our survey include a majority of the developed Western countries and a selection of Asian and Latin American countries.

Size, age and subsidiary function

Table 3-9 summarises size and age characteristics for the sample, population and Global Fortune 500 firms. When we compare the sample average to the population average, we see that for most of the characteristics these averages lie very close together, so that the sample can be considered to be representative of our population. On average, MNCs in our sample are only slightly older and slightly larger (in terms of sales and employees) than the population of MNCs the questionnaires were sent to.

Table 3-9 Various sample characteristics compared with the population and Fortune 500 firms

Characteristic	Fortune 500 (1994)	Population (average)	Sample (average)	Sample lowest value	Sample highest value
Subsidiary size (empl.)	n.a.	1,458	828	4	12,000
Subsidiary foundation	n.a.	1956	1955	1711	1994
HQ size (employees)	24,267	77,116	83,463	4,024	692,800
HQ year of foundation	n.a.	1907	1902	1288	1991
Headquarters sales	$5.40 $*$10^9$	$23.95 $*$10^9$	$26.02 $*$10^9$	$1.62 $*$10^9$	$154.95 $*$10^9$

There is one characteristic, however, that differs significantly (t-value: 2.939, p < 0.01) between our responding and non-responding firms, which is the size of the subsidiary in terms of employees.[107] Subsidiaries that responded are on average much smaller than subsidiaries that did not respond. It must be said, however, that data for the number of subsidiary employees were available for only a subset of the subsidiaries in the population (1162 out of 1643). In spite

---

[107] This subsidiary size effect interacts with a subsidiary country effect. The two subsidiary countries that on average have the largest subsidiaries: USA (3779 employees) and Germany (2834 employees) also have a response rate that is (much) lower than average. If we exclude these two countries, the difference in size between responding and non-responding firms is no longer significant. This interaction could explain part of the low response rates for the USA and Germany, however. It is not unlikely that managing directors of larger subsidiaries receive more questionnaires and have a higher workload than managing directors of smaller subsidiaries, so that the response rate for the former would be lower.

of this non-response bias, however, there is a very reasonable spread across subsidiaries in their number of employees, so that hypotheses regarding size can be tested.

When we compare the characteristics of both our population and our sample to the Global Fortune 500 firms, we see that MNCs in our sample are considerably larger in terms of employees and sales. This is not surprising, since, within the pre-specified selection of headquarters countries, we selected the largest companies in each industry in our population. Our sample will therefore probably be more representative of the largest 150-200 MNCs. Table 3-10 gives a further breakdown of the number of subsidiary and headquarters employees and headquarters sales. This breakdown shows very clearly that although the sample can be considered representative of the largest 150-200 MNCs, it still shows a large spread in the number of employees and the level of world-wide sales.

Table 3-10 Breakdown of subsidiary and headquarters employees and headquarters sales

Subsidiary employees		Headquarters employees		Headquarters sales	
Category	%	Category	%	Category, milliards of $	%
< 50	16	< 25000	30	< 5	9
51-100	9	25001-50000	21	5-10	26
101-250	24	50001-100000	23	10-20	22
251-500	19	100001-250000	19	20-50	29
501-1000	12	> 250000	7	> 50	14
1001-5000	16				
> 5000	3				

Table 3-11 indicates the percentage of subsidiaries in the sample with a sales, service, assembly, production, R&D and country headquarters function.[108] We can see that most subsidiaries have a sales function and that a sizeable majority have a production function. Subsidiaries with an assembly function are found only in the electronics, computer and automobile industry. These industries also have a higher than average percentage of subsidiaries with a service function. More strategic functions, such as performing R&D and fulfilling the role of country headquarters, are reserved for approximately one third of the subsidiaries in our sample. Subsidiaries with these strategic functions are usually larger and older than other subsidiaries. Since we do not

---

[108] The percentages do not add up to 100% since a subsidiary normally has more than one function.

know the function of subsidiaries in our population, we cannot test for non-response bias concerning this characteristic.

Table 3-11 Percentage of subsidiaries in the sample with a certain function

Function	Sales	Service	Assembly	Production	R&D	Country HQ
% of subsidiaries in the sample with this function	84%	34%	12%	60%	28%	35%

A final characteristic of the subsidiaries included in our sample that we will discuss is the entry mode used by headquarters. All subsidiaries were wholly owned, since this was one of the conditions of inclusion in our population. Of the 287 subsidiaries included in our sample 193 (67.2%) were greenfields, i.e. they had been set up by headquarters itself. The remaining third were acquired by their current headquarters. Most of these acquisitions (around 60%) occurred in the last ten years.

Headquarters sample

In addition to the questionnaires sent to subsidiaries, questionnaires were also sent to CEOs and HR-managers at headquarters. The result is that for around 20 companies data are available at both headquarters and subsidiary level. Table 3-12 summarises the number of responses per industry and headquarters country.

Table 3-12 Number of responses of headquarters CEOs and HR-managers per headquarters country and industry; response rates between brackets

HQ country	CEO	HRM	Industry	CEO	HRM
Finland	1 (11%)	4 (44%)			
France	2 (17%)	- (0%)	Electronics	5 (29%)	7 (42%)
Germany	3 (30%)	4 (40%)	Computers	1 (8%)	1 (8%)
Japan	5 (23%)	6 (27%)	Motor vehicles & parts	2 (17%)	3 (25%)
Netherlands	3 (75%)	2 (50%)	Petroleum (products)	5 (31%)	2 (13%)
Sweden	3 (30%)	3 (30%)	Food and Beverages	4 (25%)	1 (6%)
Switzerland	- (0%)	1 (20%)	Pharmaceutical	1 (7%)	3 (20%)
UK	4 (37%)	3 (27%)	Paper (products)	2 (13%)	2 (13%)
USA	5 (13%)	2 (5%)	Chemical (products)	6 (33%)	6 (33%)
Total	26 (21%)	25 (21%)	Total	26 (21%)	25 (21%)

Since the total number of responses received is rather small, it is not surprising that response rates differ considerably and that the sample is not completely representative of the population the questionnaire was sent to. However, significant differences in response rates are only found for the different headquarters countries. When we compare this table with Table 3-4 (the number of *subsidiary* responses per headquarters country), we see that again the Netherlands has the highest response rate, while the USA scores very low. A domestic effect on response rates seems present at this level of analysis.

As can be seen in Table 3-13, the CEO and HRM samples are fairly representative of the total population in terms of size and age. Respondents and non-respondents do not differ significantly in this respect. As at subsidiary level, our sample is not representative of the average Global Fortune 500, but rather of the largest 150-200 MNCs.

Table 3-13 Size and age of headquarters samples compared with the population average

Characteristic	Fortune 500 (1994)	Population (average)	Sample (CEO)	Sample (HRM)
Headquarters size (employees)	24,267	77,116	77,975	73,143
Headquarters year of foundation	n.a.	1907	1919	1891
Headquarters sales	$5.40 *$10^9$	$23.95 *$10^9$	25.68*10^9	$18.25 *$10^9$

In view of the limited number of responses at this level and the unbalanced spread of the responses over countries and industries, the data collected at this level will not be systematically analysed. However, we will use the data on strategy and control mechanisms as a check on the data collected at subsidiary level. In addition, some of the data collected from HR-managers will be used in an illustrative way to compare our results on HRM practices to previous research in this field.

Conclusions

At subsidiary level our sample can largely be considered to be representative of the population the questionnaires were sent to. Response rates for various headquarters and subsidiary countries differed considerably, but the sample still represents a reasonable spread across countries, which facilitates external generalisability. The only other characteristic that is significantly different between responding and non-responding firms is the size of the subsidiary. Smaller subsidiaries are over-represented in our sample. In spite of this, there is still a considerable variety in subsidiary size in our sample, so that hypothesis testing concerning size should not pose any problems. The sample of CEO and HR-manager responses at headquarters level is reasonably representative of the total population, but the total sample sizes are so small that most conventional statistical analyses cannot be performed. Data at this level will therefore only be used in an illustrative way.

Concerning the characteristics discussed in this section, we showed that our sample is also largely representative of the Global Fortune 500 firms, although firms in our sample are larger than the average Global Fortune 500 firm. Our sample is probably more representative of the largest 150-200 MNCs.

In this chapter, we have discussed the research design and methodology of our study. In the first section, we reviewed the specific problems associated with cross-cultural research. Subsequently, Section 2 dealt with the choice of the research method and the operationalisation of the variables included in this study. A more detailed description of the way in which the mail survey - the selected method to collect our data - was executed, was presented in Section 3. The final section described the sample and investigated whether it can be considered to be representative of the population of MNCs in general. The next two chapters will test empirically the hypotheses put forward in Chapters 1 and 2 by means of the sample discussed in this chapter.

4. Results: Theoretical building blocks

In this chapter, we will discuss the empirical results concerning the three building blocks of our study: control mechanisms, multinational companies and international transfers. In each main section, we will first use scale or factor analysis if necessary to reduce questionnaire items to constructs to be used in further analysis. Subsequently, we will explore the cross-cultural equivalence of our data with some of the methods suggested in Section 1 of Chapter 3. Finally, any specific hypotheses put forward in the respective sections of Chapter 1 will be tested. Most of the hypotheses stated in that chapter are only indirectly related to our main research questions as described in the Introduction. However, by testing these hypotheses, we can provide an external validation of the empirical data that will be used in the next chapter to answer our main research questions. If most of the hypotheses, constructed after an extensive review of previous research, can be accepted, the confidence in the validity of our research instruments is considerably enhanced.

1. CONTROL MECHANISMS

Introduction

This first main section discusses the first building block of our thesis: control mechanisms. After a review of the relevant literature, we identified, in Section 1 of Chapter 1, four main control mechanisms: personal centralised control, bureaucratic formalised control, output control and control by socialisation and networks. We will discuss the reliability of the scales used to measure these various control mechanisms. A subsequent section investigates whether these scales can be considered cross-culturally equivalent. In the final section we will then test the hypotheses that have been put forward in Section 1 of Chapter 1 concerning the country-of-origin effect in the application of control mechanisms.

Table 4-1 *Spearman rho correlations between the various control items*

	Centra- lisation	Direct su- pervision	Expatriate control	Standar- disation	Formal- isation	Output evaluation	Planning	Sociali- sation	Informal commu- nication	Formal networks	Manage- ment Training
Centralisation	1.000										
Direct supervision	.485***	1.000									
Expatriate control	.182***	.188***	1.000								
Standardisation	.383***	.203***	.026	1.000							
Formalisation	.255***	.238***	.042	.579***	1.000						
Output evaluation	.107*	.196***	-.047	.270***	.331***	1.000					
Planning	.138*	.081	-.016	.269***	.341***	.539***	1.000				
Socialisation	.014	-.078	.030	.202***	.229***	.194***	.240***	1.000			
Informal communication	-.076	-.066	.021	-.034	-.015	-.470	.011	.380***	1.000		
Formal networks	.025	.063	-.032	.127*	.110	.028	.150*	.236***	.266***	1.000	
Management training	.012	-.025	-.090	.165**	.201***	.162**	.203***	.439***	.304***	.366***	1.000

*, **, *** Correlation is significant at the 0.05, 0.01 and 0.001 level respectively, all 2-tailed.

Scale reliability analysis

In Section 2 of Chapter 3, we discussed the different items that were used in the questionnaire to measure the various control mechanisms. In this section, we will investigate whether the scales thus defined can be considered reliable indicators of the various control concepts. As can be seen in Table 4-1, where items part of the same scale (see Chapter 3) are grouped together, these items always correlate more strongly with each other than with any of the other items. Although expatriate control correlates weakly with the two measures of personal centralised control, it is, as expected, a clearly separable type of control mechanism. We therefore decided to perform a scale analysis using the items as defined in Section 2 of Chapter 3.

However, since international management training correlates strongly[109] with each of the elements of control by socialisation and networks, it was decided to add this item to the scale to be constructed for control by socialisation and networks. Table 4-2 shows the Cronbach's alpha for the various control scales. For our main level of analysis, the subsidiary level, all alphas lie around 0.70, which is considered satisfactory.[110] As an illustrative comparison, we have added the Cronbach's alphas for the small sample of CEOs and HR-managers at headquarters. These managers also answered the questions about control mechanisms, but indicated their application to the company as a whole. For CEOs the alphas are broadly comparable, for HR-managers they are slightly higher for all four control mechanisms. We therefore conclude that the scales constructed to measure the different control mechanisms can be considered to be reliable indicators of the different control concepts in our study.

The HRM alpha for personal centralised control is a special case, since we combined direct expatriate control and centralisation. In the HRM sample, direct supervision correlated very weakly with centralisation, while the correlation between expatriate control and centralisation was quite strong. Apparently, HR managers see centralisation of decision-making and expatriation of parent-country nationals to ensure that headquarters policies are carried out as part of the same control mechanism, while this is much less the case for

---

[109] This correlation is not surprising, since in Section 2 of Chapter 2 we identified international management training as a major alternative to international transfers to achieve socialisation and informal communication.

[110] Not all scale reliabilities lie above 0.70, a value usually considered as adequate (Cortina, 1993). However, as Cortina indicates Cronbach's alpha is heavily dependent on the number of items. This can be illustrated with our data as well. Considering all control items together gives an alpha that is slightly above 0.70. However, the average item-total correlation for this solution is only 0.36, while the average item-total correlation for our control scales is 0.53. Therefore, considering the small number of items per scales, our scales are considered adequately reliable.

CEOs and subsidiary managers. This might very well be explained, however, by a different distribution in headquarters countries across these three samples. In the HRM sample, there are five times as many German and Japanese MNCs than French and American MNCs, while in the two other samples the percentages from both groups are broadly comparable (30% vs 27% and 25% vs 28%). As can be seen above, German and Japanese MNCs exercise a high extent of expatriate control, while French and American MNCs score very low on the use of this control mechanism. Again, this shows the danger of using small, unbalanced samples in international management research.

Table 4-2 Scale reliability (Cronbach's alpha)[111] for the various control scales

Source of data	Personal centralised control	Bureaucratic formalised control	Output control	Control by socialisation and networks
Subsidiaries	0.67	0.73	0.70	0.68
HQ CEOs	0.71	0.68	0.74	0.68
HQ HR-managers	0.73*	0.91	0.80	0.76

Our remark in Chapter 1 that different control mechanisms should be regarded as complements rather than substitutes is clearly confirmed by Table 4-3. Except for direct expatriate control, nearly all of the control mechanisms are positively correlated. Personal centralised control is most likely to be used together with bureaucratic formalised control, while bureaucratic formalised control is likely to be used with any of the other control mechanisms except for expatriate control. Output control also has bureaucratic formalised control as its most likely partner, while control by socialisation and networks is combined with either bureaucratic formalised control or output control but not personal centralised control. The relationship between direct expatriate control and personal centralised control will be further discussed in Chapter 5.

Evaluating cross-cultural equivalence

In this section, we will evaluate whether our measures for control mechanisms can be considered equivalent across the various countries included in the survey. We will first investigate a possible bias resulting from characteristics such as social desirability, acquiescence, evasiveness or humility that might not be distributed equally over different cultures. Secondly, we will assess the cross-cultural reliability of the scales constructed in the previous section.

---

[111] Standardised item alphas (the alpha values that would be obtained if all of the items were standardised and had a variance of 1) are slightly higher.

Table 4-3 Spearman correlations between the different types of control mechanisms

	Personal centralised control	Bureaucratic formalised control	Output control	Control by socialisation and networks	Direct expatriate control
Personal centralised control	1.000				
Bureaucratic formalised control	0.330***	1.000			
Output control	0.147*	0.361***	1.000		
Control by socialisation and networks	0.002	0.221***	0.182**	1.000	
Direct expatriate control	0.229***	0.042	-0.042	-0.039	1.000

*, **, *** Correlation is significant at the 0.05, 0.01 and 0.001 level respectively, all 2-tailed

Personality biases

Personality characteristics such as social desirability, acquiescence, evasiveness or humility might not be distributed equally over different cultures. As indicated in Section 1 of Chapter 3, Asian people are often said to avoid extremes, which would result in a tight clustering of answers around the mean. In our sample, respondents from both the Far Eastern and Latin American subsidiary-country cluster chose somewhat less frequently the end-values of the scales (1 and 7) than respondents from the other clusters. However, since for the other country clusters normally only 5% of the cases are found at these end-points of the scale, the relatively small sample size (30 and 33) of the Far Eastern and Latin American clusters could also explain this peculiarity.

Furthermore, a Levene test for the homogeneity of variance across subsidiary countries or country clusters showed that, except for expatriate control, the assumption of equal variance could not be rejected for any of the questions. The heterogeneity of variance for expatriate control is not surprising, since the extent of expatriate control is of course highly dependent on the presence of expatriates.[112] This presence of expatriates is very unequally distributed across subsidiary countries (see also Section 3). Many subsidiaries in

---

[112] Since expatriation can have other functions than direct control, there is no one-to-one linkage. However, a high level of expatriate control without the presence of expatriates would be impossible.

Scandinavian countries do not have *any* expatriates among their workforce and would systematically score this question with a 1. The result is that the variance of this variable can differ substantially across countries.

Scale reliability across countries

Above, we showed that our scales for personal centralised control, bureaucratic formalised control, output control and control by socialisation and networks could be regarded as reliable. In cross-cultural research, however, for a scale to be reliable, it must show this reliability across the different countries included in the survey. In this section, we will explore this cross-cultural reliability by two means. First, we will compare Cronbach's alpha across countries, and second, we will optimally scale data for the various countries.[113]

Table 4-4 Scale reliability (Cronbach's alpha) of the control scales across subsidiary-country clusters

Subsidiary country cluster	Personal centralised control	Bureaucratic formalised control	Output control	Control by socialisation and networks
Far Eastern	0.62	0.74	0.61	0.71
Latin American	0.66	0.77	0.67	0.69
Anglo	0.70	0.72	0.76	0.67
Germanic	0.63	0.66	0.67	0.61
South European	0.68	0.75	0.62	0.77
Nordic	0.71	0.73	0.69	0.63
Average	0.67	0.73	0.70	0.68

As 22 subsidiary countries were included in the survey, analysis on the level of each separate country would not be feasible because of the resultant small subsample sizes. Therefore, data have been grouped into the six cultural clusters as described in Section 1 of Chapter 3, so that the smallest sample size is 30 and the largest 73. Table 4-4 shows the scale reliability of the various control scales across subsidiary-country clusters. Although scales show slightly different levels of reliability across country clusters, they never fall below a reliability level of 0.6, which is considered satisfactory. Additionally, the difference in scale reliability between different country clusters is gener-

---

[113] Mullen (1995) recommends Multiple Group LISREL as the preferred approach for diagnosing measurement equivalence. Unfortunately, this approach needs rather large sample sizes. Although Mullen does not indicate the exact size of the samples needed, he indicates that they have to be larger than for the Optimal Scaling procedure that needs 25 or more observations, and preferably 50 or more. Since our subsample only barely meets *this* requirement, we chose to use a combination of two other techniques as recommended by Mullen as an alternative when multiple group LISREL is not possible.

ally rather small; two thirds of the alphas fall in a range of the average reliability +/-5%.

The second approach we used to assess measurement equivalence is optimal scaling (Mullen, 1995). To use this technique data are partitioned in mutually exclusive and exhaustive subsets (subsidiary country clusters in our case). SPSS 7.0's PRINCALS (non-linear principal components analysis) is then used to optimally scale the data. This reveals the structure of the respective underlying metrics in each subset. Scalar equivalence exists if the rank orders and distances between scale values are the same across subsets (Mullen, 1995).

Since this procedure is rather time-intensive, it was only applied to the scales with the highest and lowest reliability: personal centralised control and bureaucratic formalised control. Items for these scales were optimally scaled and, as recommended by Mullen, optimally scaled values (OSVs) were graphed against the raw scores and visually inspected. If the lines are parallel, the response patterns are similar and exhibit scalar equivalence. For each of the four items we tested, lines were virtually parallel. The only exceptions were cases where the end-points of the scales did not receive any responses (this occurred mostly in the Latin American and Far Eastern clusters). As described above, this might very well be a problem of sample sizes. We therefore conclude that scalar equivalence is acceptable.

Conclusions
In this section, we explored whether the scales that were constructed for the various control mechanisms exhibit measurement equivalence across countries. A slight bias was found in the answers of respondents in the Far Eastern and Latin American cluster. These respondents had a higher tendency to avoid the end-points of the scales than respondents from other country clusters. In spite of this, homogeneity of variance across country clusters could not be rejected for any of the variables included in the scales. Scale reliabilities across cultures were very similar and were all above an acceptable level. Optimal scaling signalled the same "avoidance of extremes" bias. Otherwise, scales were found equivalent. Since the identified bias might very well be a reflection of varying sample sizes, we conclude that, in general, our scales can be considered cross-culturally equivalent. Therefore, in the next section, we will proceed by testing the specific hypotheses that were formulated in Section 1 of Chapter 1.

Country of origin and control mechanisms: testing the hypotheses

In this section we will test each of the hypotheses that has been put forward in Section 1 of Chapter 1. First, we will look at the overall differences in the application of control mechanisms between industries, subsidiary countries and headquarters countries. Subsequently, we will test the hypotheses 1-1 to 1-8, which related to the differences between pairs of countries in the application of specific control mechanisms. A final subsection will summarise these findings and give an overview of the countries that are either high or low users of a particular control mechanism.

Differences in the application of control mechanisms between industries, subsidiary countries and headquarters countries
In Chapter 1, we indicated that we did not expect to find any significant differences in the application of the various control mechanisms between industries, and (except for expatriate control) between subsidiary countries.

Table 4-5 Kruskal-Wallis-Anova analysis of the differences in application of the various control mechanisms across industries

	Personal centralised control	Bureaucratic formalised control	Output control	Control by socialisation and networks	Direct expatriate control
Chi-square	7.079	5.008	3.664	11.683	8.91
Df	7	7	7	7	7
Assymp. Sig	0.421	0.659	0.818	0.111	0.276

Table 4-6 Kruskal-Wallis-Anova analysis of the differences in application of the various control mechanisms across subsidiary-country clusters

	Personal centralised control	Bureaucratic formalised control	Output control	Control by socialisation and networks	Direct expatriate control
Chi-square	6.507	6.340	10.564	1.859	43.663
Df	7	7	7	7	7
Assymp. Sig	0.260	0.275	0.061	0.868	0.000

As Table 4-5 and Table 4-6 indicate, this is indeed confirmed by our data.[114] No differences are found across industries, while for subsidiary-country clusters only the application of direct expatriate control differs significantly

---

[114] Although equal variance in the different country and industry samples could not be rejected (Levene test for the homogeneity of variance), the distribution of the various control scales was found to be non-normal (K-S Lilliefors normality test). We therefore used the non-parametric versions of the Anova analysis (Kruskal-Wallis Anova) and t-test (Mann-Whitney test) to test our hypotheses. Using non-parametric tests also helps to overcome the problems related to small (sub)sample sizes.

across countries. The difference in output control between subsidiary-country clusters is marginally significant. However, subsequent Mann-Whitney tests for each combination of country clusters found significant differences only between the Germanic cluster on the one hand and the Far Eastern, Anglo-Saxon and Nordic clusters on the other hand.[115] The same results were found when individual countries were used instead of subsidiary-country clusters. As indicated in Chapter 1, we *did* expect to find differences in the application of control mechanisms between MNCs headquartered in different countries. As Table 4-7 shows, considerable differences are indeed found across countries. With the exception of control by socialisation and networks, the application of all control mechanisms differs significantly across headquarters countries.

Table 4-7 Kruskal-Wallis-Anova analysis of the differences in application of the various control mechanisms across headquarters countries

	Personal centralised control	Bureaucratic formalised control	Output control	Control by socialisation and networks	Direct expatriate control
Chi-square	16.250	31.985	17.738	12.416	32.932
Df	7	7	7	7	7
Assymp. Sig	0.039	0.000	0.023	0.134	0.000

Testing the specific hypotheses
More interesting than these overall differences, are the differences between specific countries as formulated in hypotheses 1-1 to 1-8 (Chapter 1). Below, we will test each of these hypotheses. For the testing of some of these hypotheses, we will have to resort to single-item indicators, since previous studies focused on specific elements of, for instance, personal centralised control and control by socialisation and networks. At the end of this chapter, Table 4-23 summarises the results of the hypotheses that have been tested in this chapter.

Hypothesis 1-1 related to the difference in the level of autonomy between subsidiaries from American and Japanese MNCs. Subsidiaries of Japanese MNCs were hypothesised to have higher levels of autonomy than subsidiaries

---

[115] Unfortunately, there is no non-parametric procedure that can provide an overall *post hoc* analysis, so that we had to perform separate Mann-Whitney tests for each specific combination of country clusters. Using a parametric Anova analysis, the differences could be reproduced with the less conservative *post hoc* comparisons such as LSD, Duncan and Bonferroni. A Tukey HSD *post hoc* comparison finds only significant differences between Germany on the one hand and the Far Eastern and Anglo cluster on the other hand. No significant differences are found with the most conservative *post hoc* comparison, Scheffé's test.

of American MNCs. Although the difference was in the expected direction, it was only marginally significant (Z: -1.749, p = 0.08, 2-tailed).

The level of autonomy was also the subject of *Hypothesis 1-2* which related to the difference in the level of autonomy between subsidiaries from German MNCs on the one hand and other European and Japanese MNCs on the other hand. Subsidiaries of German MNCs were hypothesised to have lower levels of autonomy than subsidiaries of both other European and Japanese MNCs. The difference for both comparisons was in the expected direction and statistically significant (Germany-Japan, Z: -2.503, p = 0.012, 2-tailed; Germany-other European, Z: -2.943, p = 0.003, 2-tailed).

As a final hypothesis relating to autonomy, *Hypothesis 1-3* compared Sweden with both the other European countries and the USA and hypothesised that subsidiaries of Swedish MNCs will have higher levels of autonomy than subsidiaries of both other European countries and the USA. Although in both cases the difference was in the expected direction, it did not achieve significance (Sweden-other European, Z: -1.000, p = 0.318, 2-tailed; Sweden-USA, Z: -1.785, p = 0.074, 2-tailed).

Hypothesis 1-4 compared Japanese and American MNCs concerning the level of bureaucratic formalised control they exerted over their subsidiaries. Subsidiaries of American MNCs were hypothesised to experience higher levels of bureaucratic formalised control than subsidiaries of Japanese MNCs. The difference in our sample was in the expected direction and highly significant (Z: -3.802, p = 0.000, 2-tailed).

Hypothesis 1-5 also considered bureaucratic formalised control and hypothesised subsidiaries of both American and British MNCs to experience higher levels of bureaucratic formalised control than subsidiaries of French MNCs. The difference between American and French MNCs was in the expected direction and significant at the 0.05 level (Z: -2.308, p = 0.021, 2-tailed). The difference between British and French MNCs was in the expected direction, but narrowly missed the 0.05 significance level (Z: -1.952, p = 0.051, 2-tailed).

Output control was the subject of *Hypothesis 1-6*, which related to the difference in the application of this control mechanism between American and British MNCs on the one hand and other European and Japanese MNCs on the other hand. Subsidiaries of the former MNCs were hypothesised to experience higher levels of output control than subsidiaries of the latter MNCs. We tested this hypothesis using four pair-wise comparisons. Of these four comparisons, the difference between both American and British subsidiaries on the one hand and Japanese subsidiaries on the other was significant (USA-Japan, Z: -2.831, p = 0.005, 2-tailed; UK-Japan, Z: -2.936, p = 0.003, 2-tailed). The difference between American and UK subsidiaries on the one hand and European subsidiaries on the other was in the expected direction, but not significant (USA-Europe, Z: -1.522, p = 0.128, 2-tailed; UK-Europe, Z: -1.947, p = 0.051, 2-tailed). The reason for this lack of significance can be read from Table 4-8: one of the European countries, Germany, has a very high level of output control.

Hypothesis 1-7 stated that, in spite of the well-known use of clan control in Japanese companies, subsidiaries of Japanese *multinational* companies are likely to report a lower extent of shared values with headquarters than subsidiaries of American MNCs. Japanese MNCs are more likely to rely on socialised expatriates to supervise decisions taken at headquarters. This hypothesis is confirmed by our data. Subsidiaries of American MNCs report a significantly higher level of shared values with headquarters than subsidiaries of Japanese MNCs (Z: -2.891, p = 0.004, 2-tailed).

Hypothesis 1-8 related to both shared values and informal communication and compared subsidiaries of American MNCs with subsidiaries of French MNCs. The latter were expected to score lower on both elements of control by socialisation and networks. Again, our data confirmed this hypothesis; the difference between subsidiaries of American and French MNCs was in the expected direction and significant for both shared values and informal communication (Z: -3.376, p = 0.001, 2-tailed, Z: -2.091). Hypotheses 1-7 and 1-8 show that although the application of control by socialisation and networks did not differ significantly across countries (see Table 4-7), there are significant differences between countries for certain *elements* of control by socialisation and networks.

Summary and conclusions
Using a conservative 2-tailed significance level, four of the eight hypotheses we have tested could be accepted at a significance level of p < 0.05, while in many cases the level of significance was p < 0.01. For hypotheses 1-5 and 1-6, mixed support was found and hypotheses 1-1 and 1-3 could not be accepted. In all cases, the difference was in the expected direction. Using a 1-tailed significance level, which is acceptable since we predicted the direction of the difference in all cases, hypotheses 1-1 and 1-5 can be accepted as well, while only one of the two comparisons made for hypothesis 1-3 and one of the four comparisons made for hypothesis 1-6 fails to achieve the 0.05 significance level. Therefore, overall, our sample shows a considerable amount of confirmation for the hypotheses that have been derived from previous literature and thereby consolidates the knowledge in this field. An overview of all the specific hypotheses tested in this chapter can be found in Table 4-23.

The eight hypotheses above have only tested differences between specific country couples or clusters, since in constructing our hypotheses no studies could be found that had empirically tested differences in the application of control mechanisms among a large number of countries. Since our sample *did* provide this opportunity, we also performed an overall *post hoc* analysis of variance to see whether any significant differences occurred between the countries included in our survey.[116] Table 4-8 provides an overview of the countries that are either high or low users of a particular type of control mechanism. For each control mechanism, we indicated the two countries that were either the heaviest or the lightest users. If a third country came very close to the top or bottom two, it was added between brackets.

Table 4-8 Use of control mechanisms in subsidiaries of MNCs headquartered in different countries

Control mechanism	High use in subsidiaries of MNCs from:	Low use in subsidiaries of MNCs from:
Personal centralised control	Germany, UK	Switzerland, Sweden
Bureaucratic formalised control	UK, USA, (Germany)	Finland, Japan
Output control	UK, Germany, (USA)	Japan, Finland
Control by socialisation and networks	Switzerland, Sweden	France, Japan

From Table 4-8 we can conclude that subsidiaries of German MNCs experience a very high level of control. The only type of control mechanism for which German MNCs are not among the top two or three users is control by socialisation and networks. As already apparent from previous literature, the two Anglo-Saxon countries are heavy users of the impersonal types of control mechanisms (bureaucratic formalised control and output control), although the UK also scores high on personal centralised control. Subsidiaries of Finnish and French MNCs experience a rather low level of control. The same is true for subsidiaries of Japanese MNCs, but as we will see in Section 3, for them, direct expatriate control is a very important alternative to the other control mechanisms. Switzerland and Sweden are the heaviest users of the most informal type of control: control by socialisation and networks. That MNCs headquartered in these countries do not prefer the direct type of control is reflected in their very low use of personal centralised control. Further, although not shown in the table, their use of the other direct type of control, bureaucratic formalised control, is also below average.

In addition to testing the difference in the application of control mechanism across different industries and headquarters and subsidiary countries, we also performed an analysis at the individual headquarters level. For each of the headquarters included in the sample, we calculated the relative use of a

---

[116] Since there is no non-parametric test that provides this opportunity, we used the parametric Anova analysis to test for difference. Because of this, and because of the fact that not all of the differences are significant at a 0.05 level when a more stringent test than the LSD multiple range test is used, the results should be regarded as indicative only.

specific control mechanism, i.e. the use of this control mechanism by the company in question compared to the average use of this control mechanism in the sample. This was then compared to what was known about this company from either academic articles (e.g. Ghoshal and Nohria, 1993; Nobel and Birkinshaw, 1998; St. John, 1995), popular articles (e.g. Maljers, 1992; Taylor, 1991) or annual reports. Unfortunately, we cannot give a detailed overview of these comparisons since anonymity was promised to the respondents. What we can say, however, is that in the majority of the cases our results confirmed other descriptions of a given company. It is not surprising that the conformity was not complete, since the measures used in different publications are not identical. Ghoshal and Nohria, for instance, measure only one aspect of our control by socialisation and networks: socialisation.

Conclusions

In this section, we have discussed the empirical results concerning the first building block of our thesis: control mechanisms. We showed that the reliability of the scales used to measure the various control mechanisms is satisfactory. A subsequent subsection indicated that these scales could also be considered cross-culturally equivalent. In a final subsection we then tested the hypotheses that were put forward concerning the country-of-origin effect in the application of control mechanisms. As expected, no differences were found in the application of control mechanisms between industries and subsidiary countries (except for expatriate control). However, using a 1-tailed level of significance nearly all of the hypotheses on specific differences between headquarters countries could be accepted. These results considerably enhance confidence in the validity of the research instrument used to operationalise and measure our first building block. We will now turn to the second building block of this thesis.

2. MULTINATIONAL COMPANIES

Introduction

This second main section discusses the second building block of our thesis: multinational companies. In Section 2 of Chapter 1, we provided an introduction into the environment, strategy and structure of MNCs. As indicated in Section 2 of Chapter 3, the principal industry in which an MNC operates will be used as a proxy for the international environment. In Section 4 of Chapter 3 we gave an overview of the number of respondents in the various industries

(Table 3-7). Above, we showed that control mechanisms did not vary systematically according to industry.

Section 2 of Chapter 1 discussed the various classifications of MNCs used in the international management literature and gave a detailed description of one of these classifications. This led to the identification of three distinct organisational models for multinational firms: global, multidomestic and transnational. As indicated in Section 2 of Chapter 3, the organisational model of MNCs was, as were most of the other concepts, measured at subsidiary level. Subsidiary managers might not be fully informed of the organisational model applied by the MNC as a whole, and their opinions might be coloured by the specific circumstances of the subsidiary. We will therefore first consider the multi-rater reliability of the organisational model concepts. Since this multi-rater reliability is found to be acceptable, subsidiary scores are aggregated at headquarters level. Subsequently, the nine items measuring specific elements of the organisational models are reduced to three factors that could be interpreted as representing the different organisational models. Then the cross-cultural equivalence of the measures used to operationalise these different models is explored. A final section tests the hypotheses that have been put forward in Section 2 of Chapter 1 with regard to the country-of-origin and industry effect in the application of different organisational models.

Multi-rater reliability

The organisational model items were measured at the level of the individual subsidiary, but were in fact MNC-level variables. Using these variables in an organisational-level analysis presents the question of the validity of aggregating individual (subsidiary) scores to the organisational (MNC as a whole) level. Aggregation of data assumes within-group homogeneity *and* between-group heterogeneity of data (Klein et al, 1994). As Table 4-9[117] indicates, between-group heterogeneity (difference across headquarters[118]) is (highly) significant for each of the nine items that were used to measure the MNC models. [119]

---

[117] The distribution of the various organisational model items was found to be non-normal (K-S Lilliefors normality test). We therefore used the non-parametric versions of the Anova analysis.

[118] Only headquarters with more than one respondent were included in this test.

[119] Most variable names are self-evident (S for strategy/structure + an abbreviation of the main concept for the item in question). The statement 'in our company a typical subsidiary's main function is to deliver company products and carry out headquarters' strategies' was represented by SPIPELIN (subsidiaries are simple delivery pipelines of headquarters).

Table 4-9 Kruskal-Wallis-Anova analysis of the differences in the nine organisational model items across headquarters

	SDECENTR	SDIFFERE	SDOMESTI	SECOSCAL	SEXCELLE
Chi-square	117.865	124.639	129.846	110.481	97.090
Df	66	66	66	66	66
Assymp. Sig	0.000	0.000	0.000	0.000	0.000

	SFLOWS	SGLOBAL	SNETWORK	SPIPELIN
Chi-square	108.474	99.655	130.341	143.472
Df	66	66	66	66
Assymp. Sig	0.001	0.005	0.000	0.000

Below, within-group homogeneity (concordance between responses of different subsidiaries of the same headquarters) will be measured in two different ways. First, we will calculate Kendall's coefficient of concordance for all headquarters with two or more respondents, using the nine original items. Second, these nine items will be reduced to their underlying constructs and we will investigate whether different subsidiaries of the same headquarters indicate the same dominant factor.

Kendall's coefficient

Kendall's coefficient of concordance was used to assess multi-rater reliability. This coefficient measures the extent of within-MNC agreement and thus within-group homogeneity. Kendall's W ranges between 0 and 1, with 0 signifying no agreement and 1 signifying complete agreement. A corresponding chi-square statistic indicates the significance of Kendall's W. Statistics were calculated for each headquarters with two or more respondents.

Table 4-10 Multi-rater reliability of subsidiary respondents

	Number of subsidiary respondents			
	Two	Three	Four	Five or more
Average of Kendall's W	0.82	0.58	0.47	0.50
Range of Kendall's W	0.288 – 0.949	0.281 - 0.816	0.052 - 0.653	0.052 - 0.889
Percentage significant at 5%	0	47	47	13
Percentage significant at 1%	0	0	13	75
Percentage significant total	0	47	60	88
Number of firms	21	15	15	16

Following the approach taken by Finkelstein (1992), Table 4-10 summarises the average and range of Kendall's W and the percentage of significant results. For headquarters with two respondents, the average Kendall's W is relatively high, but none of the cases is significant at the 5% level. Lower Kendall's Ws and higher significance levels are found for headquarters with three or more respondents.

More problematic than the lack of significance for two respondent firms and the rather low average Kendall's Ws for the three+ respondent firms is the range of Kendall's Ws. Apparently, in some firms the level of agreement is very low. We must realise, however, that this is a rather strict test of within-company agreement. Normally, Kendall's coefficient of concordance is calculated for scales only (see e.g. Finkelstein, 1992; Hoeksema, 1995). Since, as indicated in Section 2 of Chapter 3, we will not construct scales for the organisational model concept, we tested all of the individual items together, thus reducing the possibility of internal compensation. In the next section, we will therefore suggest another alternative for measuring within-group homogeneity.

Dominant factor analysis
As indicated in Section 2 of Chapter 3, the items used to measure the MNC's organisational model were not meant to be part of scales, since the relative position on *each* of the items *might* be important in deciding upon the organisational model applied by a particular MNC. In this section, the nine items are therefore factor-analysed to discover any underlying constructs. If the exploratory factor analysis shows that the items do indeed represent three different organisational models, we can then investigate whether different subsidiaries within the same MNC indicate the same dominant organisational model for their headquarters.

Assumptions and criteria used in factor analysis In applying factor analysis, departures from normality, homogeneity of variance and linearity are only relevant to the extent that they diminish the observed correlations and would not be a hindrance to applying factor analysis. Only normality is necessary if a statistical test is applied to the significance of factors, which is rarely done (Hair et al., 1995). Some degree of multicollinearity is desirable, because the object is to identify interrelated sets of variables. The sample size, however, is an important issue to consider in factor analysis. According to Hair et al. (1995), a sample of fewer than 50 observations would not usually be factor-analysed and a sample size of 100 or larger is preferable. In relation to the number of variables, the general rule is to have at least five times as many observations as there are variables to be analysed, while a ten-to-one ratio would be more acceptable. Since our number of observations is 285 and the observation-to-variable ratio is nearly 32, the sample size offers no restrictions to factor analysis.

Various measures are available to test the appropriateness of a factor model for the data in question. First, a visual inspection of the correlation matrix of the variables included in factor analysis should reveal a substantial number of correlations larger than 0.30. A formal test for these inter-correlations is Bartlett's test of sphericity, which can be used to test the hypothesis that the correlation matrix is an identity matrix, which means that all diagonal items are 1 and all off-diagonal items 0 (Norusis, 1994). Second, the matrix of anti-image correlations (the negative of the partial correlation coefficient) should show a low proportion of large coefficients. This is so because if a group of variables shares common factors, the partial correlation between pairs of variables should be small. The Kaiser-Meyer-Olkin (KMO) measure of sampling adequacy is a formal test that compares the magnitude of correlation and partial correlation coefficients. Small KMO values indicate that factor analysis might not be applicable (Norusis, 1994). Kaiser (1974, cited in Norusis, 1994) uses the following guidelines to interpret the KMO measure: below 0.50: unacceptable, 0.50 or above: miserable, 0.60 or above: mediocre, 0.70 or above: middling, 0.80 or above: meritorious, 0.90 or above: marvellous. The Bartlett test and the KMO measure of sampling adequacy will both be used below to test the applicability of factor analysis to our data.

When deriving the factors important decisions relate to the extraction and rotation method and the number of factors to extract. In our case principal component analysis was used. The use of this method is widespread, since the application of its major alternative, common factor analysis, is accompanied by a number of complications. An oblique rotation, direct oblimin, was used instead of one of the more common orthogonal rotations (equamax, quartimax, varimax). Oblique rotation allows correlation between the extracted factors. Since we could expect e.g. a negative correlation between a factor representing a global model and a factor representing a multidomestic model, this type of rotation was deemed more appropriate. With regard to the number of factors to be extracted various criteria are available (Hair et al., 1995): latent root criterion (extract only factor with latent roots or eigenvalues greater than 1), *a priori* criterion (based on a theory to be tested), percentage of variance criterion and scree test criterion. A combination of these criteria will be used below to determine the number of factors to be extracted.

Application and interpretation of factor analysis Figure 4-1 indicates the rotated factor solution on the nine items used to measure MNC models. Bartlett's test of sphericity was highly significant (416.62459, p = 0.00000). KMO's measure of sampling adequacy was 0.67. Although not very high, it is considered acceptable for the application of factor analysis. Three factors were extracted that had an eigenvalue larger than 1. A three-factor solution also conforms to our *a priori* theoretical expectation of three organisational models. These three factors explained 58.4% of the variance. As indicated by Hair et al. (1995) it is not uncommon for the analyst in the social sciences to consider a solution that accounts for 60% of the total variance, and in some instances even less, as a satisfactory solution. A scree plot showed a very steep slope for the first three factors and a clear levelling off after these three factors. All four criteria therefore indicate that a three-factor solution would be a good solution.

Figure 4-1 Factor analysis of subsidiary responses on the nine items measuring MNC models, highest factor loadings in bold

Rotated Factor Loadings:

	Transnational	Global	Multidomestic
SEXCELLE	**.73829**	-.06054	-.03240
SFLOWS	**.70112**	.17908	.04331
SNETWORK	**.54783**	-.49289	.24226
SECOSCAL	.19658	**.71315**	-.10294
SPIPELIN	.03616	**.70355**	-.24792
SGLOBAL	.44896	26737	**-.69298**
SDOMESTI	.27349	-.21403	**.83695**
SDIFFERE	**.63347**	-.16534	.48151
SDECENTR	.24183	**-.66321**	.20178

Factor Correlation Matrix:

	Transnational	Global	Multidomestic
Transnational	1.00000		
Global	-.03303	1.00000	
Multidomestic	.08822	-.25258	1.00000

The actual interpretation of the three factors was led by the broad theoretical expectations about the relative position of the various organisational models on the nine items. This means that the usual criteria for accepting a factor loading as significant (> 0.30) are not applied in all cases. The first factor has been named transnational. It scores highest on three statements that can be considered typical for the transnational organisational model. Subsidiaries play a strategic role as centres of excellence; there are large flows of products, resources, people and information between subsidiaries; and the structure can be characterised as a network model of interdependent organisational units. Concerning the statement on economies of scale, simple pipeline roles for subsidiaries and the importance of domestic competition, this factor scores between the two other factors, which would also fit the description of the transnational model nicely. The relatively high scores on global competition, differentiation and decentralisation do not completely conform to what might be seen as typical for transnational companies, however. Global companies could be assumed to score highest on the first, while multidomestic companies could be assumed to score highest on the second and third. Since transnational companies would in all cases be expected to score second and the differences are not that large, the first factor is accepted as representing the transnational organisational model.

The second factor has been named global. It scores highest on two of the three statements that could be seen as typical for the global organisational model: the importance of economies of scales and the treatment of subsidiaries as delivery pipelines. As would be expected from the description of this model, it scores lowest and negative on the three statements typical of the multidomestic model: domestic competition, differentiation and decentralisation. Also, the negative score on the network statement is not surprising, since headquarters is expected to play a dominant role in global companies. Since the relatively low score on global competition is the only one that does not fit the global model completely and since the difference with transnational companies is not very large on this score, we decided to accept the second factor as representing the global model.

If the exploratory factor analysis indeed identified three broad constructs that can be related to the organisational models described in Chapter 1, the final factor would then be expected to represent the multidomestic model. As can be seen, it indeed scores highest on one of the statements that can be seen as typical of the multidomestic model: the level of domestic competition. In addition, it scores lowest on all three items that could be seen as typical of the global model, its logical antipode. The relatively high score for the network statement can probably be explained by the second part of the statement. Although multidomestic companies would not be expected to be *inter*dependent, subsidiary managers would be likely to agree that headquarters does not play a dominant role. In contrast to what might be concluded from the descriptions in Chapter 1, this factor scores lower on the statements on differentiation and decentralisation than the first factor. However, since the difference is not that large, the third factor is accepted as representing the multidomestic organisational model. The appropriateness of this interpretation is supported by the factor correlation matrix that shows that the global and the multidomestic factors are (significantly) negatively related, while the correlation between the transnational factor and the two other factors is small and insignificant, reflecting its middle position.

Comparison of dominant factors across subsidiaries of the same MNC Factor scores, composite measures for each factor, were calculated for each observation (subsidiary response). Subsequently, for each observation the dominant factor was identified. To be accepted as a dominant factor, the factor score for this factor had to be positive and higher than the two other factor scores, while the difference with the next factor score had to be at least 10% of the spread in factor scores for that particular factor. In this way, a dominant factor or headquarters organisational model was identified for each subsidiary observation (for 57, or 20% of the subsidiary observations no dominant model could be identified based on the criteria used above). Finally, for headquarters with two or more subsidiary responses, dominant organisational models were compared. Table 4-11 summarises the results of this comparison.

Table 4-11 Conformity in headquarters organisational model across subsidiary responses

	Number of subsidiary respondents			
	Two	Three	Four	Five or more
Percentage unanimous	76	40	60	31 (62)
Percentage two related strategies	19	47	27	50 (19)
Percentage two conflicting strategies	5	13	7	0
Percentage three different strategies	0	0	7	19
Number of firms	21	15	15	16

As can be seen in Table 4-11, in a large proportion of headquarters different subsidiaries identified the same dominant organisational model. The column with five or more respondents included three cases where only one of the six subsidiaries had a different opinion, and two cases where respectively one of the eight and one of the eleven subsidiaries identified a different organisational model. If we consider these cases as unanimous the number between brackets applies. If subsidiaries were not unanimous, the divergent subsidiaries usually selected a dominant model that was related to the model chosen by the other subsidiaries. Related models are global-transnational and multidomestic-transnational. In all cases the divergent subsidiaries selected the related model as the second dominant model.

Problematic would be a situation in which different subsidiaries chose clearly conflicting models: multidomestic and global, or even chose three different models. This would clearly indicate a lack of within-group homogeneity. Altogether, this occurred in eight of the 103 headquarters for which data were available. The subsidiary responses of six of these headquarters were excluded from the sample. All headquarters with three conflicting strategies and three of the five headquarters with two conflicting strategies were excluded. Their average Kendall coefficients were 0.21 (range 0.052 to

0.392) and none of these coefficients were significant. Two cases with conflicting strategies were maintained in the sample because of their high and significant Kendall coefficients (0.869 and 0.667). The final sample of subsidiary observations can now be considered to show both between-group heterogeneity and within-group homogeneity. We can therefore safely aggregate subsidiary responses to headquarters level in order to perform a definitive factor analysis on the nine items operationalising the MNC organisational model. This will be done in the next section.

Forming the organisational model constructs

In the previous section we investigated whether the assumptions for the aggregation of subsidiary data to the level of headquarters, between-group heterogeneity and within-group homogeneity had been met. With the exception of six headquarters, this was indeed shown to be the case. Data for 97 headquarters were therefore aggregated and factor-analysed for their underlying constructs. The first part of this section describes this process. In the second part, we will try to validate this factor analysis using secondary data about some of the MNCs included in the sample.

Factor analysis

Although the number of observations is considerably reduced by aggregation of the data, the number of observations is still close to the preferred 100 and the observations-to-variable ratio exceeds the preferred ten. Figure 4-2 reproduces the rotated factor solution on the nine items used to measure MNC models.

Bartlett's test of sphericity was significant (205.83514, p = 0.00000). KMO's measure of sampling adequacy was 0.71. Although not very high, it is considered acceptable for the application of factor analysis. Three factors were extracted that had an eigenvalue larger than 1. As indicated above, a three-factor solution also conforms to our broad theoretical expectation of three organisational models. These three factors explained 63.8% of the variance. As also referred to above, a solution that accounts for 60% of the total variance is considered satisfactory in the social sciences. A scree plot showed a very steep slope for the first three factors and a levelling off after these three factors. All four criteria therefore indicate that a three-factor solution would be a good solution.

The interpretation of the three factors was again led by the broad theoretical expectations of the relative position of the various organisational models on the nine items.[120] The first factor was labelled multidomestic since it scored highest on two of the three items that could be seen as typical for the multidomestic organisational model (decentralisation and domestic competition) and lowest and negative on the three key items of the global organisational model. The only scores that counter theoretical expectations are the score on differentiation, which is slightly higher for the second factor, and the high score for the network structure. However, for differentiation the difference is not that large and the multidomestic factor still scores positive. The high score for the network statement was already partly explained above. It is likely that subsidiaries of multidomestic companies have primarily reacted to the second part of this statement. Therefore, the first factor was accepted as representing the multidomestic organisational model.

Figure 4-2 Factor analysis of aggregated subsidiary responses on the nine items measuring MNC models; highest factor loadings in bold

Rotated Factor Loadings:

	Multidomestic	Transnational	Global
SDECENTR	**.81093**	.05360	-.27715
SDIFFERE	.43812	**.57898**	-.34690
SDOMESTI	.46538	.31136	**-.79014**
SEXCELLE	.14909	**.83454**	-.00057
SFLOWS	-.12255	**.76275**	.06215
SNETWORK	**.66334**	.42145	-.21657
SGLOBAL	-.21807	.11531	**.90354**
SECOSCAL	**-.72642**	.00727	.34352
SPIPELIN	**-.75248**	-.06493	.27961

Factor Correlation Matrix:

	Multidomestic	Transnational	Global
Multidomestic	1.00000		
Transnational	.15390	1.00000	
Global	-.36650	-.06144	1.00000

---

[120] Some items (e.g. SDECENTR) that were used in the first analysis to explain the 'global' factor were used in this analysis to explain the 'multidomestic' factor and vice versa, because in the first analysis they had a high negative (positive) loading on the global (multidomestic) factor, while in the second analysis they had a high positive (negative) loading on the multidomestic (global) factor.

Figure 4-3 Factor plot in rotated factor space

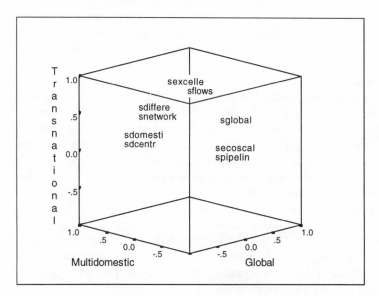

The second factor was interpreted to represent the transnational organisational model, since it scores highest on two of the three statements that could be regarded as typical of the transnational organisational model and relatively high on the third. Conforming to theoretical expectations, it scores "in between" for all of the other statements, except for differentiation for which it scores higher than the multidomestic factor.

If the exploratory factor analysis indeed identified three broad constructs that can be related to the organisational models described in Chapter 1, the third factor would then be expected to represent the global model. As can be seen in Figure 4-2, this factor indeed scores highest and positive on all three statements typical for the global organisational model and lowest and negative on all three statements typical for the multidomestic model. The negative score on the network statement also conforms to theoretical expectations, since headquarters plays a dominant role in global companies. The third factor was therefore concluded to represent the global organisational model. The appropriateness of this interpretation of the three factors is supported by the factor correlation matrix, which shows that the global and the multidomestic factors are (significantly) negatively related, while the correlation between the transnational factor and the two other factors is smaller and insignificant, reflecting its middle position.

In a graphical way, Figure 4-3 again shows that the transnational factor scores highest on two of the transnational's key characteristics: excellence and flows, and lower but largely positive on the key characteristics of the two other models. The multidomestic factor scores highest on two of the multidomestic's key characteristics, lower on the key transnational characteristics and lowest and negative on the key global characteristics, while exactly the reverse is true for the global factor.

External validation

Since factor analysis involves a number of subjective decisions, we have tried to validate the results of the factor analysis in terms of the dominant organisational model for each headquarters, using secondary data on the MNCs included in the sample. Using the same criteria as above, dominant organisational models based on factor scores were identified for each headquarters. Unfortunately, we cannot give a detailed overview of these results since anonymity was promised to the respondents. In Section 2 of Chapter 1, we described a number of firms that were identified, either in the popular press or in professional or academic literature, as actual or potential transnationals. Of the six companies that were included in both the description in Section 2 of Chapter 1 and in our sample, three were found to have the transnational model as their dominant organisational model, while for two others the transnational model was a close second.

As indicated in Section 3 of Chapter 3, annual reports were requested and received from all MNCs in our population. Before verification of the dominant organisational model based on factor scores, annual reports of the companies were read closely for indications of the application of particular organisational models. We were able to find such indications for 40 of the MNCs included in our sample and classified them as global, transnational or multidomestic. Comparing this classification with the dominant organisational model based on factor scores resulted in a similar classification in 32 cases. One MNC that was classified as global based on its annual report had a dominant transnational model another combined a global classification with a multidomestic model. The largest group of "misclassifications" (six cases) concerned MNCs that were classified as transnational but based on their factor scores had a multidomestic organisational model. Five of the cases in this group were companies in the food and beverages industry. Apparently, many firms in this industry are in a transition phase from multidomestic to transnational. In all but one of these eight "misclassifications", the classification based on the annual report was the second dominant model.

Although part of this external validation is based on a possible subjective judgement by the researcher, we feel that, overall, we can have reasonable confidence in the validity of the factor analysis performed in this section. What remains to be proven, however, is the cross-cultural equivalence of our measurements of MNC models. This will therefore be the subject of the next section.

Evaluating cross-cultural equivalence

In this section we will try to evaluate whether our measures for MNC models can be considered equivalent across the various countries included in our survey. We will first investigate the possible bias resulting from characteristics such as social desirability, acquiescence, evasiveness or humility that might not be distributed equally over different cultures. Secondly, we will assess the reliability across countries of the factor analysis performed in the previous section.

Personality biases

Personality characteristics such as social desirability, acquiescence, evasiveness or humility might not be distributed equally over different cultures. As indicated in Section 1 of Chapter 3, Asian people are often said to avoid extremes, which would result in a tight clustering of answers around the mean. No indications for this were found in the responses for the nine organisational model items. However, respondents from the Latin American subsidiary-country cluster chose somewhat less frequently from the lower end of the scales (1). The result is that, especially for the statement concerning flows, centres of excellence and network structure, means for the Latin American cluster are (significantly) higher than average.

However, this difference is likely to be caused by "true" differences and not by a cultural bias. Nearly two thirds of the subsidiaries in Latin America that responded to the survey are in the food, pharmaceutical or electronics industry, which - as we will see below - are rather transnational. Further, two thirds of the responding subsidiaries in this cultural cluster have their headquarters in the USA, Sweden or Switzerland, three countries with a high score on the transnational organisational model. It is therefore not surprising that Latin American subsidiaries agree more than average with the key statements of the transnational organisational model.

Furthermore, a Levene test for the homogeneity of variance across subsidiary countries or country clusters showed that, for only four of the nine statements, variance is not homogeneous. Three of these items are the three key transnational statements. Their heterogeneity of variance is mainly caused by the different responses in the Latin American cluster as discussed above. The remaining item concerns the importance of global competition. Heterogeneity of variance in this case is mainly caused by a different distribution of responses in the Asian cluster, which on average scores significantly higher on this item. Again, this might very well be a "true" difference rather than a cultural bias, since presence in the Asian market might be a prerequisite for global competition.

Equivalence of factor scores

Although Douglas and Craig (1983:263-269) suggest various ways to assess factor pattern similarity across countries, the assessments all rely on sub-samples that are large enough to perform separate analyses. In our case, how-ever, the largest subsample, the Nordic cluster, contains only 73 observations, while all other clusters have a smaller number of observations. Separate factor analyses for these clusters would not be feasible. Since the Nordic cluster approximates the sample size necessary for the appropriateness of factor analysis, a separate factor analysis was run for this cluster. Bartlett's statistic and the KMO measure of sampling adequacy were lower than for the total sample, but still acceptable. Figure 4-4 shows the factor loading plot for this cluster. Visual inspection of this factor plot reveals a considerable similarity to factor plot of the total sample (Figure 4-3) .[121]

Figure 4-4 Factor plot in rotated factor space for Nordic region subsidiaries

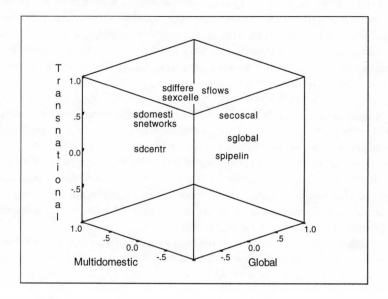

---

[121] We must realise that, especially in rather small samples, complete factor similarity is un-likely. Even in a comparison of four culturally rather similar countries (UK, USA, Australia and New Zealand), different factor scores were found in a domain where homogenising influences across countries were considered to be considerable (Norburn et al., 1990).

Concerning the organisational model followed by headquarters, we might also consider cross-cultural equivalence as the relevance of the different items for MNCs *headquartered* in different countries. Unfortunately, sample sizes are even smaller in this case, the largest being subsidiaries of MNCs headquartered in the USA (53). Again, a separate factor analysis was run for this subsample. Bartlett's statistic and the KMO measure of sampling adequacy were lower than for the total sample, but still acceptable. Figure 4-5 shows the factor loading plot for this cluster. Visual inspection of this factor plot also reveals a considerable similarity with the factor plot of both the total sample (Figure 4-3) and the Nordic region subsample (Figure 4-4). Therefore, although we cannot formally test their cross-cultural equivalence, at least we do not have any specific indications that the measures would *not* be cross-culturally equivalent.

Figure 4-5 Factor plot in rotated factor space for US headquarters

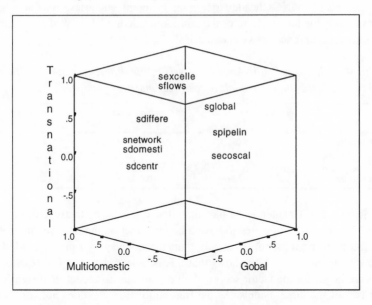

Country-of-origin and industry effect: testing the hypotheses

In this section, we will test each of the hypotheses that were put forward in Section 2 of Chapter 1. First, we will look at the overall differences in the application of the various organisational models between industries and headquarters countries. Subsequently, we will test hypotheses 1-9 to 1-12 that related to the differences between pairs of countries and groups of industries in the application of specific organisational models. In this section, we will also give a complete overview of the application of the three organisational models in the nine different headquarters countries and the eight different industries that have been included in our survey. Since none of the three organisational models seemed to be applicable to the petroleum industry, a final subsection reruns the factor analysis excluding this industry. Consequently, differences between industries and especially headquarters countries become more pronounced.

Differences in application of organisational models across industries and headquarters countries [122]

Since the distribution of both the original nine statements and the factor scores for two of the three organisational models was found to be non-normal (K-S Lilliefors test of normality), non-parametric tests were applied. We first tested for the overall difference in the application of the three organisational models across MNCs headquartered in different countries. As Table 4-12 shows, only the factor score for the multidomestic model showed a marginally significant difference between countries.

Table 4-12 Kruskal-Wallis-Anova analysis of the differences in application of the three organisational models across headquarters countries

	Global factor score	Multidomestic factor score	Transnational factor score
Chi-square	9.038	15.372	4.853
Df	8	8	8
Asymp sig.	0.339	0.052	0.773

In Section 2 of Chapter 1, we indicated that we expected the type of industry in which the MNC operates to have a larger effect on the relative application of the three organisational models than the country in which the MNC is headquartered. Table 4-13 shows that this is indeed the case. Chi-square values are larger for the factor scores of all organisational models and significant for two of the three models. As the transnational model does not contrast as sharply with other models as the global and multidomestic model, it is not surprising that differences between countries and industries are smallest for this model.

---

[122] For this section, we used the data that were aggregated at headquarters level. Using the data collected at subsidiary level would overstate the significance of the differences found. It must be noted, however, that in view of the relatively small sample sizes for both headquarters countries and industries (varying from 4 to 30 for headquarters countries and 11 to 15 for industries), it will be rather difficult to find significant differences.

Table 4-13 Kruskal-Wallis-Anova analysis of the differences in application of the three organisational models across industries

	Global factor score	Multidomestic factor score	Transnational factor score
Chi-square	23.849	14.048	10.957
Df	7	7	7
Asymp sig.	0.001	0.050	0.140

Hypothesis testing and country/industry overview
In Section 2 of Chapter 1 we formulated one specific hypothesis with regard to the difference in application of the three organisational models between MNCs headquartered in different countries and three hypotheses that focused on the difference between industries. At the end of this chapter, Table 4-23 summarises the results of the hypotheses that have been tested in this chapter.

Table 4-14 Relative application of different organisational models in MNCs headquartered in different countries; highest positive values in bold (standardised values)

HQ country	No. of firms	Global		Multidomestic		Transnational	
		total sample	-/- petro*	total sample	-/- petro*	total sample	-/- petro*
Finland	6	-.09	-.13	**.34**	**.29**	-.05	-.28
France	9	-.29	-.50	**.74**	**.95**	-.26	.35
Germany	9	**.52**	**.75**	-.68	-.65	-.15	-.27
Japan	18	**.22**	**.30**	.17	.19	-.09	-.21
Netherlands	3	.31	.40	-.48	-1.30	**.44**	**.53**
Sweden	8	-.19	.15	**.19**	**.32**	.15	.10
Switzerland	4	.48	.55	-.01	.10	**.73**	**.63**
UK	10	-.35	-.40	**.25**	**.48**	-.02	-.10
USA	30	-.11	-.14	-.28	-.15	-.01	**.41**
Total	97	.00	.00	.00	.00	.00	.00

* This score will be explained in the next section

According to *Hypothesis 1-9*, Japanese MNCs were expected to be more likely to apply multidomestic models than American MNCs. Although the difference in the application of this model was in the expected direction, the difference was not significant (Z: -1.533, p = 0.125, 2-tailed). A complete overview of the application of the different organisational models for MNCs headquartered in different countries can be found in Table 4-14. In some countries, MNCs have clearly dominant organisational models. A multi-domestic model prevails in Finnish, French and British MNCs. MNCs in these countries have a higher than average multidomestic factor score and a lower than average factor score for both other models. German MNCs also have a clearly dominant organisational model: the global model. MNCs from other countries have a higher than average score on more than one model. Japanese MNCs are most likely to apply either the global or the multidomestic model, while Dutch and Swiss MNCs score highest on the transnational model, but apply the global model as a close second. For Swedish MNCs, the multidomestic model seems to be the most likely choice, but this is closely followed by the transnational model. American MNCs take a special position: for none of the three models, their factor score does lie above average.

Hypothesis 1-10 predicted that firms in the electronics, computer, automobile, petroleum, chemical and pharmaceutical industry would be more likely to apply the global organisational model than firms in the other (food and paper) industries. This hypothesis can clearly be accepted (Z: -4.462, p = 0.000, 2-tailed). Since the multidomestic organisational model can in many respects be considered as the opposite of the global model, it is hardly surprising that *Hypothesis 1-11* can be accepted as well (Z: -3.464, p = 0.001, 2-tailed). This hypothesis predicted that firms in the food and paper industry would be more likely to apply a multidomestic model than firms in the other industries. Finally, *Hypothesis 1-12* concerned the application of the third organisational model: the transnational model. Firms in the food and pharmaceutical industry were hypothesised to be more likely to apply this model than firms in the other industries. The difference was in the expected direction and narrowly missed the 0.05 level of significance (Z: -1.924, p = 0.054, 2-tailed).

Table 4-15 Relative application of different organisational models in MNCs operating in different industries; highest positive values in bold (standardised values)

Industry	No. of firms	Global		Multidomestic		Transnational	
		total sample	-/- petro*	total sample	-/- petro*	total sample	-/- petro*
Electronics	13	**.38**	**.48**	-.07	-.10	.26	.29
Computer	11	**.50**	**.55**	-.51	-.50	-.27	-.42
Automobile	10	**.35**	**.35**	-.28	-.22	-.26	-.14
Petroleum	12	-.08	--	-.07	--	-.74	--
Food and beverages	14	-.85	-.89	**.69**	**.66**	.44	.40
Pharmaceutical	13	.01	.20	-.30	-.06	**.09**	**.22**
Paper	11	-.74	-.80	**.46**	**.69**	-.08	-.21
Chemical	13	**.53**	**.52**	-.05	-.01	.37	.26
Total	97	.00	.00	.00	.00	.00	.00

* This score will be explained in the next section

A complete overview of the application of the different organisational models in different industries can be found in Table 4-15. The computer and automobile industry clearly have the global model as their dominant model. Their factor score on this model is higher than average, while their factor scores for the two other models are lower than average. The electronics and chemical industry are divided between the global and transnational model. The multi-domestic model is clearly dominant for the paper industry, while the food and beverages industry has the highest score for both the multidomestic and the transnational model. No clearly dominant model can be deduced for the pharmaceutical industry, although the transnational model seems most likely. The petroleum industry is a special case, since it scores lower than average on each of the three organisational models. In addition, several of our respondents in this industry indicated that the statements used to determine the three organisational models were not applicable to the petroleum industry. We therefore decided to rerun the factor analysis, excluding the observations for the petroleum industry. The results will be reported in the next subsection.

The differences that are found in the application of the various organisational models between countries can largely be explained by a different industry distribution. Finnish MNCs operate mostly in the paper industry, while the automobile and the chemical industry are over-represented in the sample of German MNCs. The lack of a clearly dominant model for both Swedish and American MNCs could be explained by the fact that for these countries nearly all industries are represented in the sample. Consequently, the middling of diverging factor scores results in an overall factor score close to average.

To test the relative influence of headquarters country and industry on the application of the three organisational models, we performed a General Linear Model Manova analysis. The industry effect appeared to have significant explanatory power for all three organisational models, while the headquarters-country effect was only (marginally) significant for the multidomestic model.

Eliminating the petroleum industry

As indicated above, none of the three organisational models seemed to be applicable to the petroleum industry. Apparently, the statements we used to operationalise these models did not capture the characteristics important in this industry. Therefore, we decided to rerun the factor analysis, excluding the firms in the petroleum industry. Figure 4-6 shows the results of this analysis. Although the number of observations (85) was now somewhat lower than the recommended 100 and the observations-to-variable ratio was below ten (9.4), Bartlett's test of sphericity is still highly significant (178.83917, p = 0.00000) and KMO's measure of sampling adequacy is even slightly higher (0.73) than for the original solution. A three-factor solution explained 62.8% of the variance.

If we compare this solution with Figure 4-2, we see that most of the scores are fairly similar. In the earlier solution, two of the nine items did not score completely as expected: "differentiation" and "network". In this solution, the situation has improved for differentiation that now scores highest for the multidomestic factor. The network item still scores much lower than expected for the transnational factor.

The differences in the application of the three organisational models across headquarters and industries generally become more pronounced using this solution. Only the difference in the application of the transnational model across industries becomes smaller. This increased difference also becomes apparent when we look at the -/- petro columns in Table 4-14 and Table 4-15. Overall, the patterns become more pronounced, especially for headquarters countries. American MNCs, for instance, now have a clearly dominant or-ganisational model: the transnational model. The results of two of the hy-potheses we tested in this section also change slightly when we use this solu-tion. Hypotheses 1-9 and 1-12 become less significant (Z: -1.245, p = 0.213, 2-tailed and Z: -1.567, p = 0.117, 2-tailed, respectively).

Figure 4-6 Factor analysis of aggregated subsidiary responses (excluding petroleum industry) on nine items measuring MNC models; highest factor loadings in bold

Rotated Factor Loadings

	Multidomestic	Transnational	Global
SDECENTR	**.85940**	.02839	-.21738
SDIFFERE	**.57026**	.41281	-.23564
SDOMESTI	.51980	.20353	**-.74832**
SFLOWS	-.05084	**.83724**	-.01162
SEXCELLE	.30285	**.76233**	.15142
SNETWORK	**.72633**	.14630	-.11623
SGLOBAL	-.17624	.13612	**.87584**
SECOSCAL	**-.63686**	.05851	.46550
SPIPELIN	**-.69685**	-.21163	.40681

In spite of the more pronounced differences between headquarters countries, however, a General Linear Model Manova analysis without the petroleum industry showed that again the industry effect had a significantly larger ex-planatory power for all three organisational models than the headquarters country.

Conclusions

In this second section, we discussed the empirical results with regard to the second building block of this thesis: multinational companies. We showed that the multi-rater reliability of the items and factors used to measure the various organisational models was acceptable. Subsequently, subsidiary scores are aggregated to headquarters level and the nine items measuring organisational models were reduced to three factors that could be interpreted as representing the different organisational models. External validation of these models provided a reasonable level of support for them. A subsequent section then explored the cross-cultural equivalence of the measures used to operationalise these different models. A final section tested the hypotheses that have been put forward in Section 2 of Chapter 1 with regard to the country-of-origin and industry effect in the application of different organisational models. In this section, we also gave an overview of the relative application of these models across headquarters countries and industries. An overview of all the specific hypotheses tested in this chapter can be found in Table 4-23. Using a 1-tailed level of significance, three of the four hypotheses on specific differences between headquarters countries and industries could be accepted. All differences were in the expected direction. These results considerably enhance confidence in the validity of the research instrument used to operationalise and measure our second building block. We will now turn to our third and final building block: international transfers.

3. INTERNATIONAL TRANSFERS

Introduction

This third main section discusses the third building block of our thesis: international transfers. After a review of the relevant literature, we formulated a number of hypotheses concerning the use of PCNs (parent-country nationals) in various circumstances. The first subsection will test these hypotheses. A subsequent subsection investigates the functions of expatriation and tests the various hypotheses that have been put forward in this respect. In a final subsection, we will then discuss the results of the questionnaire sent to HR managers at headquarters. Since all questions used to probe expatriate presence in the subsidiary in question were factual, we will not assess cross-cultural equivalence of these measures as we did in the previous sections.

Test of hypotheses on expatriate presence

In this subsection, we will test the hypotheses put forward in Section 3 of Chapter 1. As indicated in Section 2 of Chapter 3, expatriate presence was measured using three questions that asked for the nationality of the managing director, the number of expatriates in top-5 positions and the total number of expatriates in the workforce of the subsidiary respectively. Since all hypotheses regard the presence of expatriates in top positions only, we will not use the third measure in this section. In this subsection, we will first discuss the hypotheses related to the influence of headquarters country, subsidiary country and industry. As will be shown, the results concerning these variables were considerably influenced by differences in response rates between expatriates and locals for certain countries and industries. We will therefore also test these hypotheses using the data of the population as a whole. A second subsection discusses the hypotheses regarding subsidiary and headquarters characteristics. Since many of the independent variables in this section might be interrelated, in a third subsection we will explore the relative influence of each of the independent variables.

Headquarters-country, subsidiary-country and industry effects

In Section 3 of Chapter 1, various hypotheses were formulated concerning the influence of headquarters country, subsidiary country and industry on the presence of expatriates. In this section, we will test these hypotheses, using both the nationality of the managing director and the number of expatriates in top-5 positions as indicators of expatriate presence. At the end of the chapter, Table 4-23 summarises the results of the hypotheses that have been tested in this chapter. As the distribution of the variables included in the analysis was non-normal (K-S Lilliefors test of normality), non-parametric tests were used.

Table 4-16 Nationality of the managing director

	Frequency	%	Valid %	Cumulative %
PCN	92	32.1	32.1	32.1
TCN	42	14.6	14.6	46.7
HCN	153	53.3	53.3	100.0
Total	287	100.0	100.0	

For the nationality of the managing director, we compare PCNs and HCNs only, since the number of TCNs is too small to base any firm conclusions on and the hypotheses contrasted PCNs with HCNs. What can be said with regard to TCNs is that most TCNs are found in Far Eastern and Latin American subsidiaries of American, Dutch and Swiss MNCs in the pharmaceutical and petroleum industry. As Table 4-16 shows, the majority of the managing directors in our sample have the nationality of the host country, while nearly a third are parent-country nationals. The percentage of TCNs is relatively high in our sample, since the response rate among TCNs was much higher than the average response rate.[123]

The average number of expatriates in top-5 positions is 1.33. As would be expected, there are large differences in this respect between subsidiaries headed by an expatriate, and subsidiaries headed by a local managing director. In the former case, the average number of top-5 expatriates is 2.53, while in the latter case it is only 0.51. In addition, there are, as we will see below, considerably large differences between countries and industries concerning the percentage of PCNs or HCNs as managing directors and the number of expatriates in top-5 positions. We will first discuss the results concerning the sample of subsidiaries that responded to our survey. Since differences in response rates of PCNs and HCNs between countries and industries could influence these results, we will also discuss the results of the population as a whole.

Results for survey sample Hypothesis 1-13 related to expatriate presence in top positions in subsidiaries from MNCs headquartered in different countries. German and Japanese MNCs were hypothesised to have the highest expatriate presence, American and British MNCs the lowest, while the other European countries were expected to score in between. A Kruskal-Wallis-Anova analysis for these three clusters of countries showed that the differences were indeed significant for both the nationality of the managing director[124] (chi-square: 17.141, p = 0.000, 2-tailed) and the number of expatriates in top-5 positions (chi-square: 18.574, p = 0.000, 2-tailed). Since there might very well be additional differences between the five countries included in the other European group, the average percentage of PCNs as managing directors and the average number of expatriates in top-5 positions were calculated for each headquarters country. Figure 4-7 shows these values for each headquarters country in relation to the average values in the total sample.

As we can see in Figure 4-7, Japan and Germany do indeed have a higher than average expatriate presence, while the UK and the USA score below average. However, the five other European countries differ considerably among themselves in their expatriate presence: the Netherlands and Switzerland score clearly above average, Sweden and France below average, while expatriate presence in Finnish MNCs lies around average.

---

[123] This is an interesting phenomenon. It might be concluded that TCNs, as truly international managers, are more likely to respond to international surveys.
[124] The dependent variable, nationality of the managing director, was recoded into 0 for HCN and 1 for PCN, so that the average value shows the percentage of PCNs as managing directors for each independent variable.

Figure 4-7 Percentage of PCNs as managing directors and number of expatriates in top 5 in different headquarters countries related to average in total sample; average total sample = 0

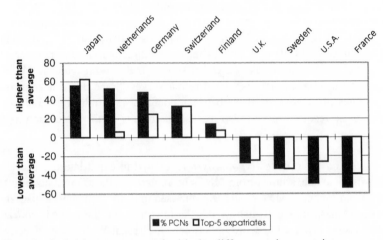

Hypothesis 1-14 was concerned with the differences in expatriate presence in different subsidiary countries. Subsidiaries in Asian and Latin American countries were hypothesised to have a higher expatriate presence than subsidiaries in the USA and in European countries. This hypothesis could be accepted at very high levels of significance for both the nationality of the managing director (Z: -6.294, p = 0.000, 2-tailed) and the number of expatriates in top-5 positions (Z: -5.858, p = 0.000, 2-tailed). Since the group of Europe and the USA includes 15 different countries, there might very well be additional differences between the countries included in this group. The average percentage of PCNs as managing directors and the average number of expatriates in top-5 positions were therefore calculated for each subsidiary country. Figure 4-8 shows these values for each subsidiary country in relation to the average values in the total sample. Countries with less than five observations were excluded.

As Figure 4-8 shows clearly, the Asian and Latin American countries do indeed have a very high expatriate presence. However, there are remarkable differences within the group of European countries. Germany has a very high expatriate presence, while Ireland and the Scandinavian countries have an extremely low expatriate presence. Most other countries score around average, especially with regard to the number of expatriates in top-5 positions.

Related to the influence of both headquarters and subsidiary country is the cultural difference between the two countries. *Hypothesis 1-15* indicated that expatriate presence would be positively related to cultural distance. Again this hypothesis could be accepted for both the number of expatriates in top-5 positions[125] (Spearman's rho: 0.204, p = 0.000, 2-tailed) and the nationality of the managing director (Z: -2.274, p = 0.023, 2-tailed).

Figure 4-8 Percentage of PCNs as managing directors and number of expatriates in top 5 in different subsidiary countries related to average in total sample; average total sample = 0

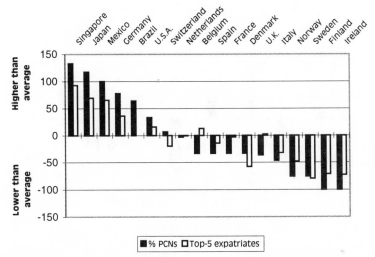

Finally, *Hypothesis 1-16* predicted a lower expatriate presence in non-global industries. Although the difference was in the expected direction it was only significant for the number of expatriates in top-5 positions (Z: -2.090, p = 0.037, 2-tailed). We therefore calculated the average percentage of PCNs as managing directors and the average number of expatriates in top-5 positions for each industry. Figure 4-9 shows these values for each industry in relation to the average values in the total sample.

Most of the global industries do indeed have a higher than average or an average expatriate presence, with the automobile industry as an extreme case. Contrary to the hypothesis, the computer industry has a lower than average expatriate presence, while the percentage of PCNs as managing directors in the paper industry is slightly *above* average. As we will see below, many of

---

[125] Since data were not normally distributed and the number of expatriates in top-5 positions was measured with an ordinal scale, Spearman correlation coefficients were used instead of Pearson correlation coefficients.

these and other observations that partly contradicted the hypotheses can be explained by differences in response rates of PCNs and HCNs in various countries and industries.

Figure 4-9 Percentage of PCNs as managing directors and number of expatriates in top 5 in industries related to average in total sample; average total sample = 0

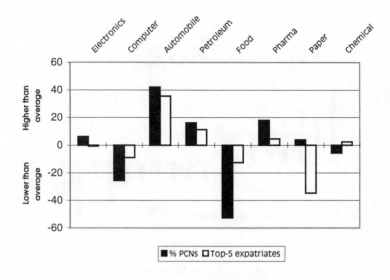

Results for population. Although most of the hypotheses that were formulated in Section 3 of Chapter 1 could be accepted, for a number of countries and industries the results did not completely conform to our expectations. However, if response rates differed between PCNs and HCNs for particular countries or industries, we might have an over- or under-representation of PCNs as managing directors and would to a lesser extent also overestimate or underestimate the number of expatriates in top-5 positions.[126]

In order to be able to compare response rates between PCNs and HCNs, we would need to be aware of the nationality of every managing director in our population. Since for non-respondents the nationality could not be deduced from the questionnaire, their nationality was determined based on their names (mostly both first and last names were available). A full justification of

---

[126] Since subsidiaries with a PCN as managing director usually have more expatriates in top-5 positions, an over-representation of PCNs would automatically lead to an overestimation of expatriates in top 5 positions.

why this research method could be valid in general can be found in Harzing (1995c). For this book, sufficient justification can be found in considering the number of successful classifications in a subsample of the original sample, namely the returned questionnaires. Out of 287 questionnaires returned, a verification was not possible in 69 cases, because the respondent preferred to remain anonymous, the respondent was not the same person the questionnaire was sent to, the respondent's name was unavailable or the respondent's name could not be classified in the first place. Out of the remaining 218 cases, 212 had been classified correctly. In six cases, the respondent turned out to be a TCN instead of a PCN or HCN. So in fact less than 3% of the cases was classified incorrectly.

As readers might be concerned about how the research method was used in practice, some specific examples will be given below. In many cases the choice was as simple as this: is Carlos Gonzales de Castejon Spanish or Swedish, is Mikko Tanhuanpää Finnish or German or is Diarmuid O'Colmain Irish or French? Of course, some combinations of headquarters and subsidiary countries proved to be more difficult than others. What about the difference between Swedish/Finnish/Danish/Norwegian names, between Singaporean and Japanese names, between German/Austrian/Swiss names, and last but not least, between American and British names? For the first three groups, assistance was sought from a Finnish, a Japanese and a German citizen, respectively. They were able to classify more than 70% of the names without having *any* doubts. Names that evoked any doubts remained unclassified.

The hard part involved American/British names, so we decided to call in the help of a larger number of people. A list of names was sent to two email lists - one with a dominant American audience and one with a dominant British audience - and subscribers were asked whether they could classify any of the names as either British or American. Apart from a sizeable number of reactions calling the research method preposterous, and casting doubts on the author's future academic career, no useful suggestions were received from American subscribers.[127] The British subscribers for the larger part did not seem to be bothered about the research method and were very helpful. For most of the names unanimous votes (varying from 5 to 10 reactions), were received; for some other names the votes were more mixed. It was decided to classify only the names with unanimous votes, while the others remained unclassified. In all, 80-85% of the names were classified by the author herself, sometimes helped by the fact that the same names would occur in different

---

[127] The American response is understandable, since the United States is a country that experienced large waves of immigration and in which names might say little about nationality. In a subsequent study, based on the same research method (Harzing, 1998e), American headquarters and subsidiaries were therefore removed from the sample.

country combinations, while another 10% were classified by "assistants". As indicated above, the names that could not be unambiguously identified remained unclassified.

Having thus identified the nationality of 90-95% of the respondents, we calculated response rates for HCNs and PCNs. Overall response rates for these two groups were very similar: 19.01% for HCNs and 18.79% for PCNs. Large differences occurred, however, for various countries and industries. Starting with the headquarters country, response rates for PCNs were (much) higher for Finland, the Netherlands and Switzerland, while response rates for HCNs were much higher for France and Sweden. If we calculate the percentage of PCNs for the population as a whole, which increases the sample size to about 1750,[128] Finland, the Netherlands, Switzerland and Sweden all score very similarly. These four countries now all score around average, which is what we predicted in Hypothesis 1-13. In the total population, France has a slightly higher percentage of PCNs than before, but still falls in the same group as the UK and the USA. Testing our original hypothesis with the data of the population as a whole now results in three groups that are all significantly different from each other at a 0.000 level of significance. However, a modification to Hypothesis 1-13 should be that not only British and American MNCs, but also French MNCs have a very low expatriate presence.

Turning to subsidiary countries, the response rates for PCNs were higher for almost all Asian and Latin American countries. However, calculating the percentage of PCNs for the total population still shows that expatriate presence in these countries is significantly higher than average. The unexpectedly high expatriate presence in the survey sample in Germany was due to a very low response rate of HCNs in this country. In the total population, the percentage of PCNs as managing directors is slightly *below* average. The high expatriate presence in the USA, on the other hand, is not due to response rate differences. In the total population, the percentage of PCNs as managing directors is even slightly higher for this country than in the survey sample. For all of the other countries, the percentage of PCNs as managing directors in the population as a whole is very comparable to this percentage in the survey sample. Our original hypothesis can still be accepted at a very high level of significance (Z: -9.935, p = 0.000, 2-tailed). However, a modification of Hypothesis 1-14 should be that subsidiaries in Asia, Latin America *and* the USA have a higher than average expatriate presence, while subsidiaries in Ireland and the Scandinavian countries have a lower than average expatriate presence (see Harzing, 1998a for a number of explanations for these differences). The

---

[128] This sample size is higher than the number of questionnaires that were actually sent out, since for various reasons some headquarters were excluded from the population after the 'naming exercise' had been executed.

result of these "corrections" with regard to headquarters and subsidiary country is that the hypothesis with regard to cultural distance can also be accepted at a higher level of significance (Z: -7.145, p = 0.000, 2-tailed).

Concerning the industry, we noted unexpected results for both the computer and the paper industry. The former had a lower than expected expatriate presence, while expatriate presence in the latter was higher than expected. Again, these "inconsistencies" are largely due to differences in response rates between HCNs and PCNs. In the computer industry the response rate for HCNs was 2.5 times as large as for PCNs, while in the paper industry the response rate for HCNs was only half that of PCNs. For the population as a whole, the percentage of PCNs as managing directors for the computer industry is only slightly below average, while for the paper industry it is considerably below average. For all other industries response rates did not differ between PCNs and HCNs. The result is that we can accept our Hypothesis 1-16 with a high level of confidence (Z: -5.403, p = 0.000, 2-tailed).

In sum, taking differences in response rate into account and testing our hypotheses on a larger number of observations allowed acceptance of all our hypotheses at an even higher level of significance. The observed differences between the survey results and the population results again illustrate the danger of working with small sample sizes.

Subsidiary and headquarters characteristics
In addition to the influence of the country of headquarters and subsidiary and the industry in which the subsidiary is operating, we identified a number of other subsidiary and headquarters characteristics that might influence the presence of expatriates in a given subsidiary. We will now test the hypotheses that were formulated about these characteristics.

Hypothesis 1-17 predicted that the percentage of PCNs in top positions in a subsidiary would be positively related to both the subsidiary's absolute size and its relative size. The absolute size of the subsidiary was measured by its number of employees, while the relative size was calculated by dividing the number of subsidiary employees by the number of employees of the MNC as a whole. This relative size varied from 0.0001 to 0.17 with a mean of 0.0135. The hypothesis with regard to absolute size could be accepted for both the number of expatriates in top-5 positions (Spearman's rho: 0.263, p = 0.000, 2-tailed) and the nationality of the managing director (Z: -2.315, p = 0.021, 2-tailed). Larger subsidiaries have a significantly higher expatriate presence. The average number of employees in a subsidiary headed by a PCN is 1276, compared to 600 for subsidiaries headed by an HCN. Although the result for relative size was in the expected direction, it was not significant. We therefore have to conclude that it is absolute, rather than relative size that might lead headquarters to increase expatriate presence in a particular subsidiary.

The older the subsidiary, the lower the expatriate presence will be. This was the purport of *Hypothesis 1-18*. The hypothesised relationship was significant for both the number of expatriates in top-5 positions (Spearman's rho: -0.118, p = 0.050, 2-tailed) and the nationality of the managing director (Z: -3.521, p = 0.000, 2-tailed). The average age of a subsidiary headed by a PCN is 32 years, while subsidiaries headed by an HCN are on average 47 years old.

Hypothesis 1-19 considered the effect of entry mode on expatriate presence. Greenfield subsidiaries were hypothesised to have a higher expatriate presence than acquisitions. Again the difference was in the expected direction and significant for both the nationality of the managing director (Z: -3.756, p = 0.000, 2-tailed) and the number of expatriates in top-5 positions (Z: -1.963, p = 0.050, 2-tailed). Greenfield subsidiaries have a PCN as a managing director in 46% of the cases, while for acquisitions only 21% of the subsidiaries have a PCN as managing director.

In *Hypothesis 1-20* we looked at the influence of a subsidiary's function on the level of expatriate presence. Subsidiaries with less "strategic" functions (sales and service subsidiaries) were hypothesised to have a lower expatriate presence than subsidiaries with an assembly, production, R&D or country HQ function. Although the difference was in the expected direction, it was not significant for the nationality of the managing director (Z: -0.645, p = 0.519, 2-tailed) and only marginally significant for the number of expatriates in top-5 positions (Z: -1.838, p = 0.066, 2-tailed).

Hypothesis 1-21 predicted that underperforming subsidiaries would "attract" a high expatriate presence. Of course, this hypothesis can only be truly tested by using a longitudinal approach. However, in a cross-sectional analysis we would expect subsidiaries headed by a PCN to perform below average. The hypothesis can be accepted for both the number of expatriates in top-5 positions (Spearman's rho: -0.137, p = 0.020, 2-tailed) and the nationality of the managing director (Z: -2.543, p = 0.011, 2-tailed). Since, for reasons explained in Section 2 of Chapter 3, our performance measure was subjective, we cannot rule out the possibility that PCNs simply have a more conservative estimate of a subsidiary's profitability. In order to explore this possibility, we tested whether underperforming subsidiaries headed by an HCN still attract a higher expatriate presence in terms of the number of expatriates in top-5 positions. Spearman's rho is only slightly lower (-0.128), but, because of the smaller sample size, no longer significant (p = 0.113, 2-tailed). Further, the relationship between profitability and the share of expatriates in the total workforce is significant for both the total sample and for subsidiaries headed by an HCN (Spearman's rho: -0.182, p = 0.002, 2-tailed and -0.172, p = 0.033, 2-tailed). It is therefore unlikely that the negative relationship that was found between profitability and expatriate presence is only due to respondents' bias.

As indicated in *Hypothesis 1-22*, we expected more internationalised MNCs to have a less ethnocentric personnel policy and therefore employ fewer PCNs in top positions in their subsidiaries. As indicated in Section 2 of Chapter 3, six different measures were used to operationalise the level of internationalisation. Since these six measures have different units of measurement, they were standardised before being subjected to a scale reliability analysis. This analysis revealed that the percentage of foreign sales had a very low item-total correlation and that its exclusion resulted in a more reliable scale. The final scale therefore consisted of five items that had a Cronbach's alpha of 0.71, which is considered acceptable. Since a lot of cases had missing values for one or more of the five items, it was decided to set three items as the minimum for a case to be included in the analysis. Since the scale reliability for any three-item combination was above 0.50, this was not deemed to be too much of a problem. The relationship between the level of internationalisation and expatriate presence was in the expected direction, but was very far from achieving significance. On second thought, however, the level of internationalisation of an MNC might also be expressed in its relative employment of third-country nationals. Employing TCNs means that managers are drawn from a world-wide pool, which can truly be considered as a geocentric staffing policy (see Section 3 of Chapter 1). Therefore an additional analysis was performed that compared the level of internationalisation of an MNC for subsidiaries headed by a PCN, an HCN and a TCN. As expected, the level of internationalisation of an MNC was highest when subsidiaries were headed by a TCN and lowest when subsidiaries were headed by a PCN. As predicted by, for instance, Adler and Ghadar's (1990) life cycle of international evolution, MNCs usually start with PCNs as managing directors of their subsidiaries, move to HCNs when they have more international experience and turn to a more geocentric personnel policy once they are highly internationalised.

Interaction effects
Above, we discussed the influence of both country/industry and various subsidiary and headquarters characteristics on the level of expatriate presence. However, many of these characteristics might be interrelated. In this section, we will therefore explore the unique effect of each of these variables.[129] Since

---

[129] Since the explanation of expatriate presence as such is not one of our main research questions, multivariate results are discussed in this chapter, rather than in the next, which deals with control mechanisms.

the effects observed above were similar for both measures of expatriate presence, this analysis will be performed for the nationality of the MD only.

Logistic regression: methodology. Since the nationality of the managing director is a binomial variable, a binomial logistic regression analysis was conducted that indicates the chance of having a PCN as a managing director. The nationality of the managing director is captured by a dummy variable which takes the value of 1 if the managing director is a PCN, and 0 if the managing director is an HCN. In the binomial logistic model, the probability of a PCN is explained by the variables industry, country of headquarters location, country of subsidiary location, cultural distance, subsidiary size, subsidiary age, entry mode, subsidiary function and subsidiary performance.[130] The regression coefficients estimate the impact of the independent variable on the probability that the managing director will be a PCN. A positive sign for the coefficient means that a variable increases the probability of a PCN. A negative sign indicates the reverse. The model can be expressed as:

$$P\ (Y) = 1/(1 + e^{-Z}),$$

where Y is the dependent variable (the selection/occurrence of a PCN in this case), Z is a linear combination of the independent variables

$$Z = \beta_0 + \beta_1 X_1 + \beta_2 X_2 + \ldots + \beta_n X_n,$$

where β_0 is the intercept, $\beta_1 \ldots \beta_n$ the regression coefficients and $X_1 \cdots X_n$ the independent variables.

The models were estimated with SPSS 7.0 using the maximum-likelihood method. Both full and reduced models, which included only the best predictor variables, were estimated. For the reduced models, a backward conditional elimination method was used, which removes variables that do not significantly improve the probability of the observed results. For both the full and reduced models, all variables were entered in one block, since there were no theoretical motivations for a stepped model.

Two methods will be used to assess the goodness of fit of the model. *First*, the null hypothesis that all ßs, except β_0 are zero is tested with the model's chi-square When the model's chi-square is significant, this null hypothesis can be rejected. The model's chi-square thus indicates whether the model performs better than a model containing only a constant. The higher and more significant the chi-square, the better the fit of the model. *Second*, the correct

---

[130] The level of internationalisation of the MNC was excluded as an independent variable. This variable was highly insignificant in the bivariate analysis. Since there were a lot of missing values for this variable, its inclusion would have meant a reduction of the already relatively small sample size by another 20%.

classification rate is investigated. The higher the correct classification rate, the better the fit of the model. This classification rate should be compared to the classification rate that can be achieved by chance. A chance model's classification rate is equal to $a^2 + (1-a)^2$, where a is the proportion of either one of the two instances of the dummy variable in the sample (the proportion of PCNs or HCNs in our case) (Morrison, 1974). Hair et al. (1995) suggest a minimum improvement of 25% in order to claim a well fitting model.

The importance of individual variables is assessed by the Wald statistic and by the partial correlation of each predictor variable with the dependent variable. A test that a specific coefficient is zero can be based on the Wald statistic. The partial correlation of each predictor variable with the dependent variable is indicated by R. R can range in value from -1 to +1. A positive value indicates that as the variable increases in value, so does the likelihood of the event occurring. If R is negative, the opposite is true. The higher R is (either positive or negative), the higher the explanatory power of the independent variable in question.

Since the independent variables industry, country of headquarters location, subsidiary country, type of subsidiary and entry mode are nominal variables, new variables are created to represent the different categories. Recoding was done by the deviation method, in which each category of the predictor variable except the reference category (the last category in this case) is compared to the overall effect. Coefficients for the different categories indicate how much the specific categories differ from the overall effect. Positive coefficients indicate that industries or countries are more likely than average to have a PCN as a managing director.

Logistic regression: survey results The first model converged after eight iterations. It has a high and highly significant model chi-square (142.959, p = 0.000), a very good sensitivity (its ability to predict PCNs, 80.95% classified correctly) and an excellent specificity (its ability to predict HCNs, 89.63% classified correctly). With an overall correct classification rate of 86.30%, it predicts significantly better than a chance model would. Model 1 results in an improvement over the chance model by nearly 64% $[0.863/(0.3836)^2 + (1-0.3836)^2]$. This improvement lies well above the 25% as suggested by Hair et al. (1995).

Of the independent variables, the variable "country of origin of headquarters" conforms broadly to our observations in the previous subsection. Japan and Germany are more likely to have a PCN as managing director, while subsidiaries of French and British MNCs are less likely to do so. As observed above, subsidiaries of Dutch and Swiss MNCs also have a higher than average likelihood of having a PCN as managing director. We should note, however, that the coefficients are significant for Japan and the UK only.

The results for industry paint a rather different picture from the one above. Taking the other variables into account, subsidiaries in two of the global industries, the automobile and computer industry, are significantly less likely to have a PCN as a managing director, while subsidiaries in the multidomestic paper industry are significantly more likely to do so. The fact that many subsidiaries in the two first industries have German or Japanese parents, are much younger than average (29 and 26 vs 41 years) and, for the automobile industry, are much larger than average (1933 employees vs 852) has confounded this effect in the previous bivariate analysis. For the paper industry, the reverse reasoning is applicable. Subsidiaries in the paper industry are more likely to have a Finnish, British or American parent, are older (51 vs 41 years) and smaller (514 vs 852) than average. Furthermore, 56% of the subsidiaries in the paper industry are acquisitions, while this goes for only 33% of the total sample. The high and highly significant likelihood of a PCN as managing director for the petroleum industry was concealed in the bivariate analysis by the fact that most subsidiaries in this industry have an American, British or French parent and are older and smaller than average.

For subsidiary countries, the results *do* conform to our observations above. Subsidiaries in the Latin American and Asian countries are more likely to have a PCN as managing director.[131] As also indicated above, Ireland and the Scandinavian countries have a lower than average likelihood of having a PCN as managing director. Interestingly, American subsidiaries no longer have a higher than average likelihood of having a PCN as a managing director. The bivariate results were biased by the fact that American subsidiaries have nearly three times as many employees as the average subsidiary in the sample. Surprisingly, cultural distance is not positively but negatively related to the likelihood of a PCN as MD. Further analysis showed that this reversal is due to the inclusion of the subsidiary country into the regression analysis. Apparently, the choice of a PCN is more related to the specific subsidiary country than to cultural distance between headquarters and subsidiary country.

All of the other subsidiary characteristics scored in the expected direction. In complete conformity to the results found in the bivariate analysis, only relative size and the function of the subsidiary were not significant. A reduced model confirms this observation. Using backward elimination, the type of subsidiary variable was eliminated first and the relative size variable second. Although the chi-square of the model decreases slightly, this decrease is not significant. The correct classification rate of the model (86.76%) is even slightly higher than for the first model.

---

[131] One exception is Argentina. Since the results for this country are based upon one observation only (a subsidiary that had an HCN as managing director), we can safely disregard this anomaly.

Logistic regression: population results In the previous subsection, we indicated that some of the results concerning industry, headquarters and subsidiary country (and therefore cultural distance) might be biased because of an over- or under-representation of PCNs in the sample. Fortunately, these data were available for the total population as well, so that we have an opportunity to verify the results concerning these variables. This model converged after six iterations. It has a high and highly significant model chi-square (422.082, $p = 0.000$), a reasonable sensitivity (its ability to predict PCNs, 55.79% classified correctly) and an excellent specificity (its ability to predict HCNs, 85.44% classified correctly). With an overall correct classification rate of 74.31%, it predicts significantly better than a chance model would. Model 3 results in an improvement over the chance model by nearly 40% $[0.7431/(0.3753)^2 + (1-0.3753)^2]$ This improvement lies well above the 25% as suggested by Hair et al. (1995).

The results concerning headquarters country are comparable to the ones in the survey sample. Japan and Germany have a higher and France and the UK a lower likelihood of having a PCN as managing director in their subsidiaries. The difference is that now this likelihood is significant for all these four countries.

Looking at the subsidiary countries, the results for the total population are very comparable to the results of the survey sample. The Argentinian anomaly has disappeared now that a larger number of observations are included. Using a larger number of cases, the influence of cultural distance on the likelihood of having a PCN as managing director is positive again, as predicted by our Hypothesis 1-15 and previous research. It is therefore likely that the negative influence in the smaller sample is due to a disproportionate influence of specific subsidiary countries. On the other hand, the cultural distance variable is not highly significant in the population sample and is excluded in a reduced model. Even larger sample sizes might be necessary to give a final verdict on this variable.

Finally, concerning the industry variable, results for the total population more closely conform to our observations above and to Hypothesis 1-16. However, in this case we feel that the smaller survey sample might give more relevant information, since it includes age, size and entry mode, which were all found to differ considerably across industries. We will therefore have to reconsider Hypothesis 1-16. Although subsidiaries in the automobile industry might have a higher and subsidiaries in the paper industry a lower than average percentage of PCNs, these differences are not due to the extent of "globalness" of the industry, but rather can be explained by the vast differences in size, age and entry mode of subsidiaries between these industries.

Conclusions

Using a conservative 2-tailed significance most of the specific hypotheses concerning expatriate presence could be accepted. However, taking differences in response rates between HCNs and PCNs into account, some modifications to the hypotheses for specific headquarters and subsidiary countries were suggested. French MNCs turned out to have a lower than average expatriate presence in their subsidiaries and within the group of European subsidiary countries Irish and Scandinavian subsidiaries turned out to have a lower than average expatriate presence. Concerning subsidiary characteristics, only relative size and the function of the subsidiary did not make a significant difference in the expatriate presence. Further, a high level of internationalisation of the MNC was shown to be more related to a high level of TCN presence than to a lower PCN presence.

The multivariate analysis confirmed many of the results of the bivariate analysis. Results concerning both headquarters and subsidiary country were very similar, both in the survey sample and in the population as a whole. Concerning subsidiary characteristics, again only relative size and the function of the subsidiary did not make a significant difference in the presence of expatriates. Serious differences occurred, however, concerning industry and cultural difference. It was shown that for some industries, the hypothesised and accepted industry difference was probably not due to the extent of "globalness" of the industry, but simply to large differences in subsidiary size, age and entry mode between industries. The influence of cultural distance on the likelihood of a PCN as managing director was positive in the bivariate analysis, negative in the multivariate analysis of the survey sample and positive in the multivariate analysis of the total population. For the time being, in view of the larger number of observations in the latter case and comparable results in previous studies, we accept the positive influence as more likely.

The differences in expatriate presence found in this section might be due to a different relative importance of the various functions of expatriation in different circumstances. In the next section, we will therefore test the hypotheses that have been put forward in this respect.

Test of hypotheses on functions of expatriation

In Section 3 of Chapter 1, we discussed various organisational functions of expatriation. Although different authors use different classifications, most of the functions mentioned in the literature could be subsumed under the three basic functions distinguished by Edström and Galbraith (1977a): position filling, management development and organisation development. Many studies also included a more direct form of control, which was classified under organisation development. In Section 2 of Chapter 3, we discussed the different questions that were used to measure the three functions of international transfers. We will add direct expatriate control, one of the control mechanisms, to these questions.[132] In this section, we will test the various hypotheses with regard to the functions of expatriation that have been formulated in Section 3 of Chapter 1. Before doing so, however, we will give a general overview of the importance of the various functions of expatriation.

Introduction

Table 4-17 shows the average importance of the various functions of expatriation, measured at both subsidiary and headquarters (HR-managers) level. It is not surprising that each of the functions is considered less important at subsidiary level, since the perceived importance of each of the functions was strongly related to the actual expatriate presence. In some of the subsidiaries that responded to these questions, expatriate presence was very low. In addition to this difference, there are a number of interesting similarities and differences in the rank order of the different functions at both levels. At both levels, knowledge transfer is seen as the most important reason for expatriation, while direct expatriate control is seen as least important. The importance of transfer for management development (MD) takes an intermediate position at both levels, However, two of the organisation development (OD) functions, the transfer of organisational culture and the improvement of information channels, are seen as relatively important at subsidiary level, while they are relatively unimportant according to HR-managers at headquarters. This difference might very well be explained by the fact that the subsidiary sample includes only some of the same MNCs as the headquarters sample. Furthermore, headquarters managers would consider the importance of certain functions for all MNC subsidiaries, while our subsidiary sample only includes a selection of them. In particular, subsidiaries in non-Western countries might be under-represented in our subsidiary sample. On the other hand, expatriates might not be sent out so much for OD-reasons, as indicated by headquarters managers, but the responses at subsidiary level might indicate that in actual practice this function is more important than expected at headquarters. Concerning position filling (PF), we find the exact opposite pattern: headquarters managers see this as the second most important reason for expatriation, while at subsidiary level it is seen as one the least important reasons. Again, this might be explained by differing samples. If we had included more non-Western subsidiaries, position filling might have been more important at subsidiary level as well. Another explanation could be that respondents at sub-

---

[132] As already mentioned in Chapter 3, we realised only after the data had been gathered that it would have been better to include direct expatriate control as a function of expatriation.

sidiary level are hesitant to judge their co-workers as less competent, as would be inherently implied by the "no qualified locals available" reason.

Table 4-17 Average importance on a scale of 1-5 of various functions of expatriation, measured at subsidiary and headquarters level

Function of expatriation	Subsidiary level			Headquarters level		
	N	Mean	Standard deviation	N	Mean	Standard deviation
OD-Direct expat control	210	2.26	1.24	25	2.73	1.00
OD-Transfer culture	212	2.67	1.15	25	2.88	.93
OD-Improve info channels	212	3.08	1.28	25	3.28	1.10
PF-Knowledge transfer	212	3.29	1.13	25	4.28	.79
PF-No locals	212	2.32	1.28	25	3.60	1.04
MD-Training for HQ	212	2.69	1.19	25	3.40	1.12
MD-Training for subsidiaries	212	2.59	1.16	25	3.36	.86

That these specific functions of expatriation can indeed be subsumed under three general functions is confirmed by the fact that correlations *within* the three groups are higher than between functions of *different* groups. At subsidiary level, however, we also find a relatively high correlation between two transfer (knowledge, culture) functions.

Headquarters country, subsidiary country and cultural distance
In the previous section we showed that subsidiaries of German and Japanese MNCs have a much higher expatriate presence than average. According to *Hypothesis 1-23* this would be mainly due to the fact that German and Japanese MNCs attach a higher importance to the organisation development function of expatriation than MNCs from other countries. At subsidiary level, this difference was in the expected direction and very significant (Z: -3.037, p = 0.002, 2-tailed). The difference was mainly due to the "direct expatriate control" and the "improvement of information channels" sub-functions. Expatriation for transfer of organisation culture was around average for Germany and below average for Japan. At headquarters level the difference was in the expected direction, but not significant. As was done for control mechanisms, Table 4-18 indicates headquarters countries for which particular functions of expatriation are either more or less important than average.[133] As indicated by Hypothesis 1-23, the organisation development function is most important for Japanese and German MNCs. Transfer for management development is very

---

[133] Since there is no non-parametric test that provides this opportunity, we used the parametric Anova analysis to test for differences. Because of this, and because of the fact that not all of the differences are significant at a 0.05 level when using a more stringent test than the LSD multiple range test, the results should be regarded as indicative only. The same qualification applies to Table 4-19.

important in Dutch, Swiss and also German MNCs. This is partly confirmed by a study by Levolger (1995:35), which finds management development the most important reason for international transfers in Dutch companies. The higher than average use of international management training (as a control mechanism) by Swiss and Dutch MNCs also fits this observation. Position filling is seen as most important in British and American MNCs.

Table 4-18 Importance of functions of expatriation in MNCs headquartered in different countries

Function of expatriation	High importance in MNCs from:	Low importance in MNCs from:
Organisation development	Japan, Germany	USA, France
Management development	Netherlands, Switzerland, Germany	Japan, Sweden
Position filling	UK, USA	Germany, France

In the previous section, subsidiaries in Asian and Latin American countries were shown to have a higher than average expatriate presence. For Latin American countries, *Hypothesis 1-24* assumes this to be a consequence of a higher than average importance for position-filling functions of expatriation. This hypothesis could be accepted at a relatively high level of significance (Z: -2.160, p = 0.031, 2-tailed). As Table 4-19 shows, however, position filling is also important for subsidiaries in Asian countries. Asian and Latin American subsidiaries also score highest on transfer for organisation development. Somewhat surprisingly, management development is also considered an important reason for expatriation in Latin American subsidiaries.

Table 4-19 Importance of functions of expatriation in different subsidiary regions

Function of expatriation	High importance in:	Low importance in:
Organisation development	Asia, Latin America	Nordic countries, Southern Europe
Management development	Anglo-Saxon countries, Latin America	Asia, Germanic countries
Position filling	Latin America, Asia	Anglo-Saxon countries, Southern Europe

Although we were not able to draw any definitive conclusions about this, cultural distance is generally considered to be related to a high expatriate presence. *Hypothesis 1-25* indicates that this would be mainly due to a higher importance of the organisation development function in culturally distant countries, while to a lesser extent position filling would also be more important. Management development, on the contrary, was hypothesised to be less important in subsidiaries in culturally distant countries. The statistical results support this hypothesis. Transfer for organisation development is significantly (p = 0.010) related to cultural distance, while the same is true for transfer for position filling at a lower level of significance (p = 0.051). The results for management development are in the expected direction, but not significant (p = 0.165).

Subsidiary and headquarters characteristics

As put forward in *Hypothesis 1-26*, the organisation development function is indeed found less important for older subsidiaries (Spearman's rho: -0.228, p = 0.001, 2-tailed). Also, as formulated in *Hypothesis 1-27*, expatriation for position filling is less important in acquisitions than in greenfields (Z: -1.940, p = 0.052, 2-tailed). Confirming *Hypothesis 1-28*, the size of the MNCs as a whole is positively related to the importance of international transfers for management development (Spearman's rho: 0.162, p = 0.019, 2-tailed). Finally, as put forward in *Hypothesis 1-29*, more internationalised MNCs do indeed place heavier emphasis on international transfers for management development (Spearman's rho: 0.269, p = 0.000, 2-tailed). Contrary to our hypothesis, these MNCs also place a heavy emphasis on position filling as a reason for international transfers, although this relationship is not significant (Spearman's rho: 0.099, p = 0.196, 2-tailed).

Conclusions

We explored the various functions of expatriation: position filling, management development and organisation development. At both subsidiary and headquarters level, knowledge transfer is seen as the most important reason for expatriation, while direct expatriation control is seen as least important. However, not all of the three general functions are equally important in MNCs from different headquarters countries or in subsidiaries in different subsidiary regions. In addition, the importance of these functions was found to vary in respect of subsidiary characteristics, such as age and entry mode, and headquarters characteristics, such as size and level of internationalisation. Using a conservative 2-tailed significance, most of the specific hypotheses that had been put forward in Section 3 of Chapter 1 could be accepted. In this section, we referred to some of the data that had been collected at headquarters level from HR-managers. In the next section, we will discuss these data in detail.

Results from HRM questionnaire

In Section 3 of Chapter 1, we briefly reviewed the major research issues in the field of international HRM in general and international transfers in particular. The results of the questionnaire sent to headquarters HR-managers allow us to draw tentative conclusions concerning some of these issues. In addition to the questions about control mechanisms and the functions of expatriation, HR-managers were asked to answer some questions about the number of (female) expatriates working for the company as a whole, the relative use of PCNs, HCNs and TCNs, and to indicate their agreement with a number of statements with regard to expatriate management. This section briefly discusses the results of the data gathered from these managers. Since the final sample is relatively small (25 respondents), most of the results should be regarded as illustrative.

Expatriate selection
Answers of HR-managers concerning the number of PCNs, HCNs and TCNs conform closely to what we have seen earlier. Table 4-20 summarises the average percentage of these different nationality groups from different data sources. Apart from the relatively high level of TCNs in the subsidiary survey sample, due to a very high response rate of TCNs, the data from different sources are very comparable. They suggest that HCNs are the most likely option for top positions in foreign subsidiaries, while the percentage of TCNs is still rather low.

Table 4-20 Percentage of HCNs, PCNs and TCNs in top positions, three different data sources

Source of data	% HCN	% PCN	% TCN
Subsidiary survey sample	53	32	15
Subsidiary population	60	36	4
HR-managers at headquarters	62	33	5

Data gathered from HR-managers also confirm the higher than average expatriate presence in German and Japanese MNCs and in the automobile industry. Further, as also discussed above, PCNs are used to a larger extent in Asia and Latin America than in the USA/Western Europe, most HCNs can be found in the Western world and the largest percentage of TCNs is found in Asia and Latin America. Further, it can be concluded that MNCs with a larger total number of expatriates (both in absolute and relative terms) employ a higher percentage of TCNs and a lower percentage of PCNs. Apparently, TCNs are considered when the expatriate pool has to be broadened.

Table 4-21 Scores (scale 1-5) of different HQ countries on problems related to expatriates and locals

HQ countries		Dual careers inhibit acceptance assignment	PCNs experience serious re-entry problems	High turnover among local employees	Attracting high calibre locals is difficult
USA, UK, France	Mean	3.80	3.40	2.20	1.80
	N	5	5	5	5
Japan, Germany	Mean	2.90	2.50	3.00	2.80
	N	10	10	10	10

One of the reasons for employing a high percentage of PCNs in top positions in subsidiaries could be that the MNC experiences problems in the employment of locals. Visa versa, a relatively high percentage of HCNs in top positions could be due to problems concerning expatriate management. In the HRM questionnaire various questions were asked about specific problems concerning either expatriates or locals. Table 4-21 summarises the average responses for a number of PCN- and HCN-related problems for the two clusters of countries identified above with either a higher (Japan, Germany) or a lower (USA, UK, France) than average use of PCNs. Although none of the differences is statistically significant, Japan and Germany score nearly one point higher on the two problems related to locals, while American, British and French MNCs score nearly a point higher on the two problems related to PCNs.[134]

In general, companies feel that there are no serious problems with regard to the number of parent-country nationals that are prepared to work abroad (Figure 4-10). There is, however, a *serious* lack of parent-country nationals having sufficient international management skills (see Figure 4-11).

Companies that feel that they lack home-country personnel with sufficient international management skills employ more third-country nationals in Western Europe. Also, these companies also employ more host-country nationals in Asia and Africa. It seems as if a lack of qualified PCNs leads companies to explore other options more seriously. Companies that send out expatriates for management development reasons report fewer problems with a lack of international management skills. This suggests that companies that take training and development seriously have a more internationally competent workforce.

---

[134] Of course, the direction of causality is very ambiguous. Do Japanese and German MNCs send out many expatriates because they have problems with locals or do they have problems with locals because they send out many expatriates?

Figure 4-10 There is a lack of PCNs who want to work abroad

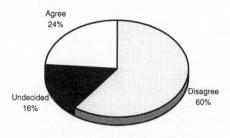

Figure 4-11 There is a lack of PCNs with sufficient international management skills

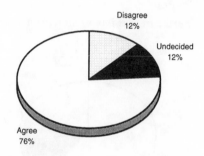

Female expatriates and dual-career couples

In the companies included in our survey the percentage of female expatriates varied from 0% to 30% of the total expatriate workforce. As can be seen in Table 4-22, the Scandinavian countries have the highest percentage of female expatriates, while Japan and Switzerland have the lowest. There is a perfect fit between the scores of the various countries on Hofstede's masculinity/femininity dimension and the percentage of female expatriates. Feminine countries have a much larger share of female expatriates than masculine countries. The industry distribution also confirms this picture. Traditionally male-oriented industries such as the computer and petroleum industry have a significantly lower percentage of female expatriates than more female-oriented industries such as the food and paper industry.

Table 4-22 The percentage of female expatriates in various countries and industries

High % of female expatriates:		Low % of female expatriates:	
Industry	HQ-country	Industry	HQ-country
Food and beverages	Finland	Computer	Japan
Paper	Sweden	Petroleum	Switzerland

The inability of the partner to continue his or her career is seen as an important reason to hesitate about accepting an assignment (see Figure 4-12). Although this is a problem for both male and female expatriates, companies with a high number of female expatriates report even larger problems in this respect. This is not surprising as female expatriates are even more likely to have a career-oriented partner. On the other hand, male partners might find it easier to get a job abroad than female partners. Interestingly, companies that report larger problems in finding home-country personnel with sufficient international management skills employ a larger number of female expatriates. As above, it seem as if necessity leads companies to explore non-standard options more seriously.

Figure 4-12 Partner's career is important reason to hesitate about accepting an assignment

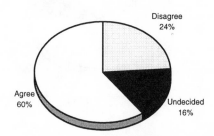

Repatriation

More than half of the companies included in our survey report that expatriates experience re-entry problems when returning from their foreign assignment (see Figure 4-13). Expatriate re-entry problems are less prominent in companies that maintain a centralised roster of all managerial employees. Furthermore, companies that attach high importance to management development as a reason for expatriation tend to have fewer repatriation problems. This is logical, as companies sending out expatriates for management development will have a more planned approach to career management.

Figure 4-13 Repatriates experience re-entry problems

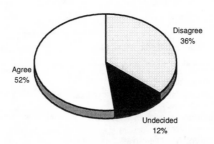

Conclusions

In this section, we discussed a number of conclusions that could be drawn with regard to prominent expatriate management issues by means of the data gathered from HR-managers at headquarters. Although, because of the small sample size, few statistically significant results could be reported, the data in general supported the conclusions in the previous section. In addition, some interesting descriptive results were found with regard to expatriate selection, dual career couples and repatriation.

4. CONCLUSION

This chapter has described the results concerning the three main building blocks of this thesis: control mechanisms, multinational companies and international transfers. No less than 40 specific hypotheses, based on an extensive review of previous research, were tested. Table 4-23 summarises the results of these hypotheses. For all but one of the hypotheses, the difference was in the expected direction. Using a 1-tailed level of significance, which is acceptable since we predicted the direction of the difference for each hypothesis, eight hypotheses were significant at the 0.001 level, eleven at the 0.01 level and another thirteen at the 0.05 level. Only eight hypotheses were not significant at a 0.05 level or better. Of these, three were significant at a more relaxed level of significance (0.10).

In addition to consolidating previous research, the acceptance of the majority of our hypotheses enhances our confidence in the validity of the research instruments used to measure the various concepts. In the next chapter, we will focus on the integration between the building blocks and discuss control mechanisms in multinational companies and the role of international transfers as a control mechanism. Furthermore, we will build configurations of multinational companies that integrate many of the variables used in this book and explore performance implications.

Table 4-23 Summary of the results of the hypotheses tested in this chapter; results contrary to hypotheses printed in bold

No.	Content of the hypothesis	Expected direction	Accepted 0.05 sign., 1-tailed	1-tailed sign.
1	Autonomy subsidiaries Japanese MNCs higher than subsidiaries American MNCs	Yes	Yes	*
2a	Autonomy subsidiaries German MNCs lower than subsidiaries European MNCs	Yes	Yes	**
2b	Autonomy subsidiaries German MNCs lower than subsidiaries Japanese MNCs	Yes	Yes	**
3a	Autonomy subsidiaries Swedish MNCs higher than subsidiaries European MNCs	Yes	**No**	n.s.
3b	Autonomy subsidiaries Swedish MNCs higher than subsidiaries American MNCs	Yes	Yes	*
4	Subsidiaries American MNCs higher BFC than subsidiaries Japanese MNCs	Yes	Yes	***
5a	Subsidiaries American MNCs higher BFC than subsidiaries French MNCs	Yes	Yes	*
5b	Subsidiaries British MNCs higher BFC than subsidiaries French MNCs	Yes	Yes	*
6a	Subsidiaries American MNCs higher OC than subsidiaries European MNCs	Yes	**No**	†
6b	Subsidiaries American MNCs higher OC than subsidiaries Japanese MNCs	Yes	Yes	**
6c	Subsidiaries British MNCs higher OC than subsidiaries European MNCs	Yes	Yes	*
6d	Subsidiaries British MNCs higher OC than subsidiaries Japanese MNCs	Yes	Yes	**
7	Subsidiaries American MNCs higher shared values than subsidiaries Japanese MNCs	Yes	Yes	**
8a	Subsidiaries American MNCs higher informal communication than French MNCs	Yes	Yes	*
8b	Subsidiaries American MNCs higher shared values than French MNCs	Yes	Yes	***
9	Japanese MNCs more multidomestic than American MNCs	Yes	**No**	†
10	Electronics, computer, motor, petroleum, pharmaceutical and chemical industry more global than other industries	Yes	Yes	***
11	Food and beverages and paper industry more multidomestic than others	Yes	Yes	***
12	Food and beverages and pharmaceutical industry more transnational than others	Yes	Yes	*
13*	Expatriate presence in subsidiaries from MNCs headquartered in different countries	Yes	Yes	***
14*	Expatriate presence in subsidiaries in different regions of the world	Yes	Yes	**
15*	Positive correlation between cultural distance and expatriate presence	Yes	Yes	**
16*	Expatriate presence in subsidiaries in different groups of industries	Yes	Yes	*
17a*	Positive correlation between absolute subsidiary size and expatriate presence	Yes	Yes	**

17b*	Positive correlation between relative subsidiary size and expatriate presence	Yes	**No**	n.s.
18*	Negative correlation between subsidiary age and expatriate presence	Yes	Yes	*
19*	Higher expatriate presence in greenfields than in acquisitions	Yes	Yes	*
20*	Lower expatriate presence in sales/service subsidiaries than other subsidiaries	Yes	**No**	n.s.
21*	Negative correlation between subsidiary performance and expatriate presence	Yes	Yes	**
22*	Negative correlation between internationalisation and expatriate presence	Yes	**No**	n.s.
23	Japanese and German MNCs higher than average importance control function	Yes	Yes	***
24	Latin American subsidiaries higher than average importance position filling	Yes	Yes	*
25a	Positive correlation between cultural distance and control function	Yes	Yes	**
25b	Positive correlation between cultural distance and position-filling function	Yes	Yes	*
25c	Negative correlation between cultural distance and MD function	Yes	**No**	†
26	Higher importance control function in younger subsidiaries	Yes	Yes	***
27	Position filling (no locals) less important in acquisitions than in greenfields	Yes	Yes	*
28	Larger MNCs attach higher importance to MD function	Yes	Yes	**
29a	Internationalised MNCs attach higher importance to MD function	Yes	Yes	***
29b	Internationalised MNCs attach lower importance to position-filling function	**No**	No	†

BFC = bureaucratic formalised control, OC = output control.

* These hypotheses were tested using two different measures of expatriate presence. If the direction of the difference was the same in both cases, the significance level was averaged over these two measures.

*** p < 0.001, ** p < 0.01, * p < 0.05, † p < 0.10, all 1-tailed.

5.   Results: Integration, configurations and performance

In the previous chapter, we discussed the empirical results regarding the three building blocks of our study: control mechanisms, MNCs and international transfers. The acceptance of the majority of our hypotheses enhanced the confidence in the validity of our research instruments. In this chapter, we will focus on the integration between the three building blocks. In Section 1, we will explore the application of control mechanisms in multinational companies. The influence of both headquarters and subsidiary characteristics on the level and type of control applied by headquarters in respect of their subsidiaries will be discussed. Section 2 probes into the role of international transfers as a control mechanism in MNCs. International transfers are shown to play a role as both a direct and an indirect control mechanism. A final section, Section 3, empirically tests three distinct configurations of MNCs that integrate many of the variables discussed in previous sections. In addition, this section also tries to explain performance differences between MNCs, using country-of-origin, "economic" and "organisational" factors as determinants.

1. CONTROL MECHANISMS IN MNCS

Introduction

In Chapter 4, we discussed the empirical data on both control mechanisms and multinational companies. In this section, we will combine these two elements and focus on control mechanisms in multinational companies. In Section 1 of Chapter 2, a review of the relevant literature revealed a number of headquarters and subsidiary characteristics that could explain differences in both the level and type of control mechanisms that are used in different MNCs. One of these, the country in which the MNC is headquartered, has already been discussed in Section 1 of Chapter 4, and was found to have a considerable influence on the control portfolio used by a particular MNC. In this section, the influence of the remaining characteristics will be investigated. As many of these characteristics might be interrelated, a fourth and final section will try to assess which of the characteristics discussed have the highest explanatory power.

Headquarters characteristics

In Section 1 of Chapter 2, we identified four specific headquarters character-istics that might influence the control portfolio: the organisational model ap-plied by the MNC in question, its size, and the extent of multinationality and heterogeneity of operations. These characteristics will be discussed below and any specific hypotheses that have been put forward will be tested.

In general, however, *Hypothesis 2-1* predicted that - when compared to national companies - the indirect control mechanisms (output control and control by socialisation and networks), would be used to a larger extent in MNCs than the direct control mechanisms (personal centralised control and bureaucratic formalised control). Since our sample includes MNCs only, this hypothesis cannot be truly tested. However, the mean level of indirect control (4.86) for our sample of MNCs is considerably higher than the mean level of direct control (3.35), which lends some credibility to our hypothesis.

Organisational models
In Section 2 of Chapter 4, we showed that the three distinct organisational models that were identified for MNCs in Section 2 of Chapter 1 could be identified in our empirical data as well. Since these constructs were measured at subsidiary level, the data had to be aggregated to headquarters level. For six headquarters, between-group homogeneity was judged inadequate, so that these headquarters were excluded from further analysis. Following the criteria discussed in Section 2 of Chapter 4, a dominant organisational model was identified for each headquarters. In this process, an additional six headquar-ters that did not show a dominant model were excluded from the analysis. As Table 5-1 shows, the global organisational model is most popular in our sam-ple, while the transnational model is least popular. The fact that the transna-tional model is the least prevalent model conforms to the findings of Leong and Tan (1993) and the general idea that the transnational model is an ideal type that has been realised by a minority of firms only. However, contrary to Leong and Tan's findings, the global model instead of the multidomestic one was the most prevalent model. Since industry distributions are not available for Leong and Tan's study, it is difficult to assess whether this difference should be seen as a result of increasing globalisation in the six years that have passed since their data collection, or whether it is simply an result of different industry distributions or construct measurements.

Table 5-1 Number of MNCs applying the different organisational models

		Frequency	%	Valid %	Cumulative %
Valid	Multidomestic	30	22.8	32.6	32.6
	Transnational	22	21.2	23.0	56.5
	Global	40	38.5	43.5	100.0
	Total	92	88.5	100.0	
Missing	System missing	12	11.5		
Total		104	100.0		

With regard to the characteristics of the different organisational models, *Hypothesis 2-2* predicted that subsidiaries from multidomestic MNCs would experience a lower level of control than subsidiaries from either global or transnational firms. The difference between global and multidomestic companies in the total level of control exerted over subsidiaries is significant at the 0.007 level (Z: -2.682, 2-tailed). The difference between transnational and multidomestic companies narrowly misses the 0.05 significance level (Z: -1.872, p = 0.061, 2-tailed). As predicted, there is no difference between global and transnational companies in the level of control exerted over subsidiaries (Z: -0.195, p = 0.845, 2-tailed).

Turning towards individual control mechanisms, *Hypothesis 2-3* predicted multidomestic companies to have output control and control by socialisation and networks as their dominant control mechanisms. Since these control mechanisms are more indirect and less obtrusive, they were hypothesised to fit the rather independent subsidiaries of multidomestic companies better than the more direct personal centralised control and bureaucratic formalised control. Both personal centralised control (t-value: -4.259, p = 0.000, 2-tailed) and bureaucratic formalised control (t-value: -2.326, p = 0.026, 2-tailed) are used significantly less in multidomestic companies than on average in our sample of MNCs. The application of control by socialisation and networks is also below average, but not significantly so (t-value: -1.219, p = 0.233, 2-tailed). For output control, the application in multidomestic companies lies around average (t-value: 0.034, p = 0.973, 2-tailed). Therefore, since personal centralised control and bureaucratic formalised control are used significantly less than average in multidomestic companies, while the application of output control and control by socialisation does *not* differ significantly from average, we can conclude that the latter two control mechanisms can indeed be considered as the dominant ones in multidomestic companies.

Hypotheses 2-4 to *2-7* compared the application of the four different control mechanisms for global and transnational companies. Subsidiaries from global companies were hypothesised to experience lower levels of control by socialisation and networks (Hypothesis 2-4), but higher levels of both personal centralised control (Hypothesis 2-5) and bureaucratic formalised control (Hypothesis 2-6). No difference was expected in the level of output control (Hypothesis 2-7). Hypothesis 2-7 can be accepted since the difference between transnational and global companies in the level of output control exerted over subsidiaries is far from significant (Z: -0.158, p = 0.874, 2-tailed). For the three other hypotheses, the difference was in the expected direction, but in none of the cases did the difference achieve statistical significance (Z: -1.413, p = 0.158, 2-tailed; Z: -1.267, p = 0.205, 2-tailed; Z: -1.347, p = 0.178, 2-tailed). This is not surprising, since aggregation of the data at headquarters level has drastically reduced the sample size. In general, however, we can conclude that there is a tendency for global firms to use the two direct control mechanisms suited to their centralised and integrated organisational model to a larger extent than transnational firms, while transnational firms have a higher application of control by socialisation and networks suited to their interdependent network structure, which allows a strategic role for subsidiaries.

Size of the MNC as a whole
The influence of size on the level of personal centralised control (or centralisation as it is called in most studies) has received quite a lot of attention in previous literature. Unfortunately, results were very mixed so that *Hypothesis 2-8* predicted no significant relationship between size and this type of control mechanism. The statistical results show a positive relationship between both measures of size (employees and total sales) and the level of personal centralised control that is exerted over subsidiaries. In neither of the two cases, though, is the relationship statistically significant. Since previous research found differences in the relationship between size and personal centralised control for various countries, we also investigated this relationship for each individual country. This exploration showed a positive relationship for Finland, Japan and the UK and a negative relationship for the Netherlands. Since sample sizes for individual countries were rather small, these relationships only acquired marginal, if any, significance. For the other five countries, correlation coefficients were very small and/or contradictory for the two measures of size.

A positive relationship between size and bureaucratic formalised control was predicted in *Hypothesis 2-9*. Although the correlation coefficient was in the predicted direction, it did not achieve significance for either of the two measures. Again, there are considerable differences between countries, however. Strong positive relationships (correlation coefficients varying from 0.444 to 0.687) are found for France, the UK and Switzerland, while negative relationships are found for Finland and Sweden (correlation coefficients varying from -0.300 to -0.657). Since sample sizes for individual countries were rather small, these relationships only acquired marginal, if any, significance. For the other four countries, correlation coefficients were very small and/or contradictory for the two measures of size.

As predicted in *Hypothesis 2-10*, size and both output control and control by socialisation and networks are positively related. For control by socialisation and networks this relationship acquires a high level of significance for both measures (p = 0.002 and p = 0.003, both 2-tailed), while for output control the relationship is marginally significant for the employees' measure only (p = 0.078, 2-tailed). These results also partially confirm *Hypothesis 2-11*, which predicted that the positive relationship between size and bureaucratic formalised control would be weaker than the relationship between size and the two indirect control mechanisms. Although this is true for control by socialisation and networks, the magnitudes of the correlation coefficients for bureaucratic formalised control and output control are comparable.

Concerning output control, no systematic differences are found between countries. For control by socialisation and networks, very small correlation coefficients and/or contradictory coefficients are found for Finland, Sweden, Switzerland and the USA. For the other five countries, however, correlation coefficients are very high, especially for the total sales measure (ranging from 0.642 to 0.954). Analysing the relationship for these five countries separately results in correlation coefficients of 0.477 (employees) and 0.540 (total sales), p = 0.000, 2-tailed for both measures.

The relationship between size and the various control mechanisms remains ambiguous. No clear results were found concerning either personal centralised control or output control. The well-documented positive relationship between size and bureaucratic formalised control could be confirmed for France, Switzerland and the UK only. The only control mechanism that is consistently positively related to size is control by socialisation and networks, especially for France, Germany, Japan, the Netherlands and the UK. Controlling for the other variables in this section (organisational model, size and level of multinationality) does not substantially change the relationships for three of the four control mechanisms. It does result, however, in a significant (p = 0.01, 2-tailed) positive relationship between both measures of size and output control, thus confirming both Hypotheses 2-10 and 2-11.

Level of multinationality
As discussed in Section 2 of Chapter 3, six different measures were used to represent the level of multinationality of the MNC as a whole: the percentage of foreign sales, the percentage of foreign employees, the years of foreign experience, the number of (manufacturing) subsidiaries and the number of countries in which the MNC operates. A scale reliability analysis in Section 3

of Chapter 4 indicated that the percentage of foreign sales had a negative item-total correlation. It was therefore excluded from the scale that now consisted of five items.

In conformity with *Hypothesis 2-12*, a negative relationship was found between the level of multinationality and personal centralised control. However, this negative relationship did not achieve statistical significance (Spearman's rho: -0.145, p = 0.207, 2-tailed). Contrary to *Hypothesis 2-13*, the relationship between multinationality and bureaucratic formalised control was found to be positive, though far from significant (Spearman's rho: 0.091, p = 0.436, 2-tailed). The relationship between the level of internationalisation and output control is indeed positive, as predicted in *Hypothesis 2-14*. However, this relationship does not achieve significance (Spearman's rho: 0.95, p = 0.416, 2-tailed).

As predicted in *Hypothesis 2-15*, there is a positive correlation between the level of multinationality and the extent of control by socialisation and networks that is nearly significant at 0.05 level. This positive correlation is mainly due to a strong and significant (p = 0.006, 2-tailed) correlation between multinationality and international management training. Controlling for the other variables in this section (organisational model, size and level of heterogeneity) reduces the level of significance of this relationship to 0.094 (2-tailed). The other relationships between multinationality and control mechanisms do not experience any major changes by including these control variables.

In sum, the level of multinationality of the MNC as a whole does not seem to have a major impact on the type of control mechanisms that are used in respect of subsidiaries. The positive correlation with international management training is not surprising, since highly internationalised MNCs would probably see more need for international management training.

Complexity/heterogeneity

Hypotheses 2-16 to *2-18* predicted a negative relationship between complexity/heterogeneity and both personal centralised control and bureaucratic formalised control and a positive relationship between complexity/heterogeneity and control by socialisation and networks. Unfortunately, no significant relationships were found between the number of 2- or 4-digit SIC codes and *any* of the control mechanisms included in the sample. Correlation coefficients are extremely low for most control mechanisms. Furthermore, the only correlation coefficients that surpass the (-)0.10 level are contrary to the expected direction. If we control for the other variables discussed in this section (organisational model, size and level of multinationality), all correlation coefficients are below (-)0.10 and all but one in eight below (-)0.05. In our sample of MNCs, the level of complexity/heterogeneity simply does not seem to have any significant influence on the type of control mechanisms used in respect of subsidiaries.

Conclusions

In this section, we discussed the various headquarters characteristics that were assumed to have an influence on the control portfolio used by headquarters in respect of their subsidiaries. Two of these characteristics, the level of multi-nationality and the level of heterogeneity/complexity, did not seem to have *any* major influence on the composition of the control portfolio. For a third characteristic, MNC size, the expected positive relationship with control by socialisation and networks was confirmed at a high level of significance. Controlling for the other variables, the same was true for output control. The expected positive relationship between size and bureaucratic formalised control could be confirmed for a subsample of countries only. Results for personal centralised control were very mixed across countries. However, using a 1-tailed significance level, which is acceptable since we predicted the direction of the difference in all cases, we can accept all of the hypotheses concerning size at 0.10 level of significance or better.

Concerning the fourth characteristic, organisational models, all predicted differences between multidomestic, global and transnational companies regarding the level of control and the composition of the control portfolio were in the expected direction. Differences between multidomestic companies, on the one hand, and global and transnational companies, on the other hand, were significant. At a conservative 2-tailed significance level, the differences in the type of control mechanisms used between global and transnational firms were not significant. Using a 1-tailed significance level, which is acceptable since we predicted the direction of the difference in all cases, the differences for control by socialisation and networks and bureaucratic formalised control are significant at the 0.10 level of significance, while the difference for personal centralised control narrowly misses this significance level.

In the next section, we will investigate whether specific subsidiary characteristics can explain the difference in control portfolios across subsidiaries.

Subsidiary characteristics

Subsidiary size

Although the relationship between the size of the subsidiary and the level of personal centralised control has received a lot of attention in previous studies, results were very mixed: negative, positive and insignificant relationships were found. In addition, theoretical motivations are equally contradictory. *Hypothesis 2-19* therefore predicted that no significant linear relationship would be found between the size of the subsidiary and the level of personal centralised control exercised over this subsidiary by headquarters. Correlation coefficients for both absolute and relative (subsidiary employees/headquarters employees) are very low and very insignificant. Visual inspection showed that the alternative suggested curvilinear relationship is not present either. A country-by-country analysis showed no significant relationship for any of the headquarters countries included in the sample. Finally, controlling for the other subsidiary characteristics included in this section did not change the relationships. Although subsidiary size might have an influence on the application of the other control mechanisms, there does not seem to be *any* major relationship between subsidiary size, whether absolute or relative, and the level of personal centralised control applied by headquarters to the subsidiary in question.

No hypotheses were offered for either bureaucratic formalised control or output control. Output control was deemed more likely, however, for larger subsidiaries. Our data show a weak and marginally significant positive relationship between absolute size and both bureaucratic formalised control and output control. Controlling for the other subsidiary characteristics included in this section makes these relationships insignificant, however. A country-by-country analysis showed no significant relationships between size and bureaucratic formalised control for any of the countries. Concerning output control, however, subsidiaries of MNCs headquartered in both Finland and France showed a significantly positive relationship between absolute and relative size and output control. A separate analysis for these two countries shows a highly significant ($p = 0.000$) and strong relationship between both absolute (Spearman's rho: 0.549) and relative (Spearman's rho: 0.485) size and output control.

As predicted in *Hypothesis 2-20*, there is a significant ($p = 0.000$) positive relationship between both absolute and relative subsidiary size, and the level of control by socialisation and networks applied by headquarters. This relationship remains equally strong when we control for the other subsidiary characteristics included in this section. Although a country-by-country analysis shows the relationship is positive for each country, it is particularly strong for France on both measures and for Germany, Japan, UK and the USA for absolute size.

In sum, personal centralised control and bureaucratic formalised control do not seem to be related to subsidiary size, whether absolute or relative. As predicted, the indirect control mechanisms are the ones that vary most with subsidiary size. In general, larger subsidiaries would be expected to experience higher control levels, since they are more important for headquarters. As direct control would probably be resisted by these subsidiaries, the resulting control gap should be filled by the more indirect control mechanisms. The relationship is particularly strong for control by socialisation and networks. Concerning output control, a significant positive relationship could be found for MNCs headquartered in Finland and France only.

Subsidiary age
In *Hypothesis 2-21*, subsidiary age is negatively related to the amount of personal centralised control exercised by headquarters over this subsidiary. Headquarters will supervise young subsidiaries more closely and centralise decision-making because the new investment brings specific uncertainties that have already been eliminated with older subsidiaries. This hypothesis is not confirmed by our data. Although the relationship is in the expected direction, it is far from being significant. Controlling for the other variables included in this section does not change this lack of significant relationship. A country-by-country analysis shows very low correlation coefficients (below 0.10) for most countries. Finland and France have higher - but still insignificant - negative correlation coefficients (0.30 and 0.25 respectively), while Germany has a marginally significant (0.327, $p = 0.078$, 2-tailed) *positive* correlation between age and personal centralised control.

As hypothesised in Chapter 1 and empirically confirmed in Chapter 4, the control mechanism that is most affected by the age of the subsidiary is the level of expatriation. Nevertheless, we also expected a positive relationship between subsidiary age and the two impersonal types of control: bureaucratic formalised control and output control (*Hypothesis 2-22*). However, our sample shows no significant relationships between subsidiary age and bureaucratic formalised control, output control or control by socialisation and networks, although the correlations are clearly stronger for the impersonal types of control. A significant negative relationship is found, however, between subsidiary age and direct expatriate control. This is not surprising, since older subsidiaries have a lower expatriate presence than younger subsidiaries. We might conclude that in this case expatriates take care of direct supervision and quasi-centralisation of decision-making. This expatriate role will be further explored in Section 2.

In sum, the age of the subsidiary does not seem to have a significant influence on the type of control mechanism that is exercised by headquarters in relation to this particular subsidiary. An exception to this is direct expatriate control, which is negatively related to the age of the subsidiary.

Interdependence
Increasing interdependence - measured as intra-company sales and purchases - between a particular subsidiary and either headquarters or other subsidiaries increases both the importance of this subsidiary for headquarters and the level of risk involved. Therefore, *Hypothesis 2-23* predicted a positive relationship

between the extent of interdependence of a subsidiary with the MNC as a whole, and the total amount of control that is exercised by headquarters in relation to this subsidiary. This hypothesis is indeed confirmed by our data (Spearman's rho: 0.141, p = 0.018, 2-tailed). As put forward in *Hypotheses 2-24* and *2-25* and following previous studies, this higher level of control is assumed to be mainly due to a higher level of personal centralised control and bureaucratic formalised control. Interdependence is indeed significantly positively related to both personal centralised control (Spearman's rho: 0.160, p = 0.007, 2-tailed) and bureaucratic formalised control (Spearman's rho: 0.163, p = 0.006, 2-tailed), while no significant relationships are found for the two indirect control mechanisms.

In Chapter 2, however, we also distinguished between *de*pendence and *inter*dependence. In our data set, *de*pendence is measured by the level of sales and purchases to and from headquarters, while *inter*dependence is represented by the level of sales and purchases to and from other subsidiaries. Headquarters-dependent subsidiaries were subsequently predicted to experience different dominant control mechanisms than subsidiary-dependent subsidiaries. More specifically, *Hypothesis 2-26* predicted subsidiary dependent subsidiaries to experience a higher level of control by socialisation and networks than headquarters-dependent subsidiaries. This hypothesis can indeed be accepted (Z: -2.190, p = 0.028, 2-tailed). Headquarters-dependent subsidiaries, on the other hand, show a significantly higher level of direct expatriate control (Z: -2.824, p = 0.005, 2-tailed). Apparently, a more direct form of personal control is preferred in headquarters-dependent subsidiaries, while a more indirect form is dominant in subsidiary-dependent subsidiaries.[135]

A final distinction that was made in Chapter 2 was the difference between input-dependent and output-dependent subsidiaries. In *Hypothesis 2-27* output-dependent subsidiaries were predicted to experience a higher level of control than input-dependent subsidiaries, since the former were expected to be more important nodes in the company network. This hypothesis could indeed be accepted at a significance level of 0.05 (Z: -1.989, p = 0.047, 2-tailed). This difference in the total level of control is mainly due to a higher level of personal centralised control and a higher level of bureaucratic formalised control for output-dependent subsidiaries.

In sum, the level of interdependence between a particular subsidiary and the rest of the MNC has a considerable influence on the level and type of control that is exerted by headquarters over this subsidiary. Highly interdependent subsidiaries, and in particular output-dependent subsidiaries experi-

---

[135] In Wolf's (1994) study a comparable difference was found. In headquarters-dependent subsidiaries, the level of shared values was lower than in headquarters-dependent subsidiaries and the managing director was more likely to be a parent-country national.

ence a higher level of control than other subsidiaries. The control mechanisms most affected in this respect are personal centralised control and bureaucratic formalised control. In addition, *de*pendent subsidiaries (HQ-dependent subsidiaries) are more likely to experience a high level of direct expatriate control, while *inter*dependent subsidiaries (subsidiary-dependent subsidiaries) are more likely to experience a high level of control by socialisation and networks.

Local responsiveness
The concept of local responsiveness is very important in the study of MNCs. Local responsiveness can be conceptualised at both headquarters and subsidiary level. At headquarters level local responsiveness is incorporated into the organisational models as discussed above. Multidomestic and transnational companies are assumed to be more locally responsive than global firms. Even within a certain organisational model, there might be differences at subsidiary level in the degree of local responsiveness. This responsiveness to the local market was measured with four questions that asked for the level of local production, R&D and local adaptation of marketing and products. Scale reliability showed a Cronbach's alpha of 0.73, which is considered acceptable.

As *Hypothesis 2-28* indicated, local responsiveness would be negatively related to total control levels. In order to be locally responsive, a subsidiary should not be strictly controlled by headquarters. This hypothesis can indeed be accepted (Spearman's rho: -0.125, p = 0.036, 2-tailed). However, as put forward in *Hypotheses 2-29* and *2-30*, we would expect a lower application of the two *direct* control mechanisms to be the cause of a lower total level of control for locally responsive subsidiaries. Our data do indeed reveal this picture. There is a significant negative relationship between local responsiveness and both personal centralised control (Spearman's rho: -0.158, p = 0.008, 2-tailed) and bureaucratic formalised control (Spearman's rho: -0.138, p = 0.021, 2-tailed), while no significant relationship is present for output control and control by socialisation and networks.

These relationships do not change when controlling for the other subsidiary characteristics included in this section. Interestingly, however, a country-by-country analysis shows that in contrast to all other countries, subsidiaries of Japanese MNCs show a significant (Spearman's rho: 0.478, p = 0.004, 2-tailed) positive relationship between local responsiveness and total control level. In fact, for subsidiaries of Japanese firms, all control mechanisms are positively correlated with local responsiveness. Apparently, Japanese MNCs consider local responsiveness as a factor that should induce a higher, rather than a lower, level of control. A tentative explanation for this might be that many Japanese MNCs have only recently started to localise their production and marketing (e.g. in response to the common European market), which might lead them to keep matters under rather strict control in this start-up period. Excluding Japan from our sample increases the size of the correlation coefficients for total control, personal centralised control and bureaucratic formalised control to -0.212, -0.199 and -0.191 respectively and increases the level of 2-tailed significance to 0.001, 0.002 and 0.003 (all 2-tailed).

Subsidiary roles

As indicated in Section 1 of Chapter 2, the specific role a subsidiary plays in the MNC as a whole might very well influence the level and type of control that is exercised in relation to this subsidiary. However, as also explained in that section, we realised the importance of this variable only after the empirical data were collected. Therefore, the only way in which we can characterise subsidiary roles is to look at their level of interdependence and local responsiveness as was also done by Martinez and Jarillo (1991). To this end, subsidiaries were divided into four groups. The first group represented the autonomous subsidiary and scores above the mean for local responsiveness and below the mean for interdependence. A second group has the reverse pattern and represents the receptive subsidiary. Active subsidiaries score above the mean for both local responsiveness and interdependence. Finally, although this type of subsidiary was not distinguished by Martinez and Jarillo, based on two input variables a fourth group was defined that has a combination of low local responsiveness and low interdependence. Following Taggart (1996c), we have called this type of subsidiary quiescent.

Table 5-2 indicates the number of subsidiaries in our sample that could be classified under these four roles and the total level of interdependence and local responsiveness for these four groups. Although for active subsidiaries the level of local responsiveness is somewhat lower than for autonomous subsidiaries, scoring for all of the other combinations is according to expectations. In addition, a Kruskal-Wallis analysis showed that the four groups differ significantly on each of the items used to measure interdependence and local responsiveness. As could be expected, active subsidiaries are least prevalent in the sample. As indicated by Martinez and Jarillo (1991), even transnational companies will have more autonomous or receptive subsidiaries than active subsidiaries. Also, in our sample, most subsidiaries have either a receptive or autonomous role.

When we compare the percentage of subsidiaries with different roles in MNCs headquartered in different countries, it becomes apparent that the largest differences are found with regard to the autonomous and receptive role. In Finnish, Dutch or British MNCs well over half of the subsidiaries have an autonomous role, while in German, Japanese and Swiss MNCs more than half of the subsidiaries have a receptive role. No dominant subsidiary roles are found in French, Swedish and American MNCs. These differences might be partly due to a difference in industry distribution. Around half of the subsidiaries in the (multidomestic) paper and food industries are characterised as autonomous, while receptive subsidiaries are dominant in the (global) electronics, computer, automobile and pharmaceutical industries. As we have seen before, many MNCs in the paper and food industries are Finnish or British and many MNCs in the electronics, computer and automobile industries Japanese or German. However, subsequent logistic regression showed that - in contrast to the organisational model applied by headquarters - with regard to subsidiary roles, the country of location of headquarters has a large and significant explanatory power, while this is not the case for the industry in which the MNC operates.

Table 5-2 Total level of interdependence and local responsiveness and number of cases for four groups of subsidiaries

Subsidiary role		Total level of interdependence	Total level of responsiveness
Autonomous	Mean	1.6556	4.0389
	N	90	90
Active	Mean	2.6319	3.5903
	N	36	36
Receptive	Mean	2.500	2.1187
	N	99	99
Quiescent	Mean	1.6944	2.0926
	N	54	54
Total	Mean	2.0887	2.9229
	N	279	279

Turning to the specific hypotheses that were formulated in 1 of Chapter 2, *Hypothesis 2-31* indicated that autonomous subsidiaries would be expected to experience a lower total level of control than both receptive and active subsidiaries. This difference is significant for both the comparison between autonomous and active subsidiaries (Z: -2.913, p = 0.004, 2-tailed) and the comparison between autonomous and receptive subsidiaries (Z: -3.014, p = 0.003, 2-tailed). Subsequently, *Hypothesis 2-32* predicted comparable levels of total control for active and receptive subsidiaries if active subsidiaries had a level of interdependence comparable to receptive subsidiaries and a level of local responsiveness comparable to autonomous subsidiaries. As can be seen in Table 5-2, active subsidiaries have a slightly higher level of interdependence than receptive subsidiaries and a somewhat lower level of local responsiveness than autonomous subsidiaries. The differences are not very large, however, and a comparison of the total control levels for both types of subsidiaries shows no significant differences (Z: -0.639, p = 0.523, 2-tailed).

In addition to hypotheses about the total level of control, two hypotheses were formulated about the dominant type of control applied in different types of subsidiaries. *Hypotheses 2-33* and *2-34* predicted receptive subsidiaries to experience a higher level of personal centralised control and a lower level of control by socialisation and networks than active subsidiaries. Although the difference was in the expected direction for both control mechanisms, it was not significant (Z: -1.281, p = 0.200, 2-tailed; Z: -0.872, p = 0.383, 2-tailed). Differences for the two other control mechanisms (bureaucratic formalised control and output control) are even much less significant, however. Active and receptive subsidiaries do differ significantly in the level of direct expatriate control (Z: -2.121, p = 0.034, 2-tailed). Active subsidiaries have a significantly higher level of direct expatriate control than receptive subsidiaries.

In addition to the level of interdependence and local responsiveness, we also typified subsidiaries with regard to their function (assembly, production, sales, service, country headquarters and R&D). In *Hypothesis 2-35* sales subsidiaries were predicted to have a relatively low level of total control, since their strategic importance to headquarters is limited. The dominant type of control in this type of subsidiary was hypothesised to be output control. The first part of this hypothesis could be accepted at a high level of significance (Z-value: -3.428, p = 0.001, 2-tailed). Furthermore, sales subsidiaries experience a lower than average level for each of the control mechanisms except for output control, which they experience to a higher than average extent. Output control can therefore clearly be seen as the dominant control mechanism for sales subsidiaries.

Hypothesis 2-36 related to R&D subsidiaries and predicted that these subsidiaries would experience a lower level of personal centralised control and bureaucratic formalised control and a higher level of control by socialisation and networks. Although the difference was in the expected direction, it was only (marginally) significant for bureaucratic formalised control (Z: -1.762, p = 0.078, 2-tailed) and control by socialisation and networks (Z: -1.785, p = 0.074, 2-tailed).

Uncertainty
Environmental uncertainty is a characteristic that has often been related to control mechanisms, both in a national and in an international context. In our survey environmental uncertainty was measured using five questions with regard to consumers, competition, (technological) change and the necessity for continuous adaptation. A scale reliability analysis showed that these questions had a Cronbach's alpha of 0.78, which is considered acceptable. In *Hypotheses 2-37* to *2-39* environmental uncertainty was predicted to be nega-

tively related to personal centralised control and bureaucratic formalised control and positively to control by socialisation and networks. These hypotheses could not be accepted. There is no systematic relationship between environmental uncertainty and personal centralised control, while the relationship between environmental uncertainty and bureaucratic formalised control is positive rather than negative, but not significant. Finally, although the relationship between environmental uncertainty and control by socialisation and networks is in the expected direction, it is not significant.

Since in Ghoshal and Nohria's (1989) study the correlation between environmental uncertainty and the various control mechanisms was strongest for the item "technological dynamism", we also calculated the correlation coefficients for this item only. This considerably "improves" the results. Control by socialisation and networks is now significantly (p = 0.001, 2-tailed) positively related to environmental uncertainty, while a weak negative relationship appears for personal centralised control. Controlling for the other subsidiary characteristics included in this section makes this relationship stronger and nearly significant at the 2-tailed 0.05 level. With regard to bureaucratic formalised control, the positive relationship nearly disappears when controlling for the other characteristics, and becomes highly insignificant. Apparently, there is no strong relationship between uncertainty and bureaucratic formalised control in either direction.

Again, however, a country-by-country analysis reveals different patterns across countries. The hypothesised relationship is very strong for American, British, Dutch and Finnish subsidiaries. Including only these subsidiaries in the analysis results in a significant negative correlation for personal centralised control (Spearman's rho: -0.195, p = 0.035, 2-tailed) and a significant positive correlation for control by socialisation and networks (Spearman's rho: 0.285, p = 0.002, 2-tailed). As above, correlations for the single item technological change are even stronger. Concerning bureaucratic formalised control, the positive correlation becomes stronger, but is still not significant. Of the other five countries, France and Sweden do not show any strong relationships, while for Japan, Germany and Switzerland a higher level of environmental uncertainty results in a *higher* instead of *lower* level of personal centralised control. Taking the results of Chapter 4 with regard to expatriation into account, Japanese, German and to a lesser extent Swiss MNCs seem more likely to respond with direct personal control in situations of high risk and/or uncertainty.

Cultural distance
Concerning the influence of cultural distance on control mechanisms, previous empirical research offered mostly insignificant findings, and theoretical contributions offered no clear motivations for their prescriptions. However, in

Chapter 2, we indicated that the international transfer of PCNs would probably be the most effective way to control subsidiaries in culturally distant countries. The empirical results in Section 3 of Chapter 4 have already showed that cultural distance was positively related to the number of expatriates in top-5 positions and to the likelihood of a PCN as managing director. In that chapter, we also showed that the main reason for this higher expatriate presence was transfer for organisational development, which included direct expatriate control. This positive relationship is also apparent when testing for direct expatriate control separate from the other two organisation development functions. This positive relationship between cultural distance and direct expatriate control is present for all headquarters countries included in the sample, although the relationship is stronger for some countries than for others. For Sweden, for instance, the relationship is very strong (Spearman's rho: 0.641, $p = 0.000$, 2-tailed).

Related to this preference for personal control through expatriates, *Hypothesis 2-40* predicted that impersonal control mechanisms would be used to a lesser extent in culturally distant countries. This relationship is indeed in the expected direction, but significant for output control only. However, controlling for the other subsidiary characteristics included in this section reveals a significant ($p = 0.008$, 2-tailed) negative relationship between cultural distance and both bureaucratic formalised control and output control.

Conclusions
The various subsidiary characteristics that were assumed to have an influence on the control portfolio in use in relation to them were discussed. One of these characteristics, subsidiary age, did not seem to have a major impact on the application of any of the control mechanisms except for direct expatriate control, to which subsidiary age is negatively related.

As expected, subsidiary size was positively related to the use of the more indirect control mechanisms: output control and control by socialisation and networks; interdependence was positively related to the use of direct control mechanisms: personal centralised control and bureaucratic formalised control; while local responsiveness was negatively related to the use of these direct control mechanisms. Concerning subsidiary roles, autonomous subsidiaries were found, as predicted, to experience less control than active and receptive subsidiaries. Furthermore, although they were not always significant, differences were also found between active and receptive subsidiaries and between subsidiaries with specific functions (sales, R&D) in the application of specific control mechanisms. For a subsample of countries, a higher level of environmental uncertainty was shown to lead to a lower level of personal centralised control and a higher level of control by socialisation and networks. As expected, cultural distance was negatively related to the two impersonal types of control: bureaucratic formalised control and output control, a relationship that became stronger when controlling for the other subsidiary characteristics.

Summary and regression models

In this section, we will first summarise the results with regard to the hypotheses that were tested in the two previous sections. Subsequently, regression analysis will be used to identify which of the characteristics discussed in both this section and the previous chapter have the highest explanatory power with regard to both total control and the four different control mechanisms: personal centralised control, bureaucratic formalised control, output control and control by socialisation and networks.

Summary

Table 5-3 summarises the results of the tests performed. The level of multinationality and heterogeneity do not seem to have a major impact on the type of control mechanisms applied. Of the seven hypotheses concerning these characteristics, only three were in the expected direction and only one was significant. On the other hand, there is no evidence of a relationship contrary to the hypotheses either, since none of these relationships was significant. It is likely that the different organisational models capture part of the variance in multinationality and heterogeneity. We will come back to this later when we will test the existence of configurations of MNCs.

Relationships between MNC size and the application of various control mechanisms were always in the predicted direction and, using a 1-tailed level of significance, at least marginally significant. The larger the MNC, the higher the level of output control and control by socialisation and networks and, to a lesser extent, bureaucratic formalised control. Concerning organisational models, the differences between multidomestic companies on the one hand and global and transnational companies on the other hand could be confirmed at high levels of significance. Subsidiaries from multidomestic companies clearly experience lower levels of total control and indirect control mechanisms are dominant. Concerning the difference between global and transnational companies, Table 5-3 shows that all differences were in the expected direction, but only marginally significant at a 1-tailed significance level. Following these data we can conclude that there is a slight tendency for subsidiaries of transnational companies to experience more control by socialisation and networks and less personal centralised control and bureaucratic formalised control, while there is no difference between the two organisational models in the level of output control.

Table 5-3 Summary results of the hypotheses concerning headquarters characteristics

No.	Headquarters characteristics: content of the hypothesis	Expected direction	Accepted 0.05 sign., 1-tailed	1-tailed sign.
1	MNCs use indirect control mechanism to a larger extent than direct ones.	Yes	-----	-----
2a	Subsidiaries from multidomestic firms less control than from global firms	Yes	Yes	**
2b	Subsidiaries from multidomestic firms less control than from transnational firms	Yes	Yes	*
3	Output control and CBSN dominant in multidomestic firms	Yes	-----	-----
4	Subsidiaries of transnational firms more CBSN than subsidiaries of global firms	Yes	**No**	†
5	Subsidiaries of global firms more PCC than subsidiaries of transnational firms	Yes	**No**	**n.s.**
6	Subsidiaries of global firms more BFC than subsidiaries of transnational firms	Yes	**No**	†
7	No difference in OC for subsidiaries from global or transnational firms	Yes	-----	-----
8*	No relationship between MNC size and PCC	Yes	-----	-----
9*	Positive relationship between MNC size and BFC	Yes	**No**	†
10a* **	Positive relationship between MNC size and OC	Yes	**No**/Yes	†/**
10b*	Positive relationship between MNC size and CBSN	Yes	Yes	**
11	Relationship between MNC size and BFC weaker than for output and CBSN**	Mix/Yes	-----	-----
12	Negative relationship between multinationality and PCC	Yes	**No**	**n.s.**
13	Negative relationship between multinationality and BFC	**No**	No	n.s.
14	Positive relationship between multinationality and OC	Yes	**No**	**n.s.**
15	Positive relationship between multinationality and CBSN	Yes	Yes	*
16	Negative relationship between heterogeneity and PCC	**No**	No	n.s.
17	Negative relationship between heterogeneity and BFC	**No**	No	n.s.
18	Positive relationship between heterogeneity and CBSN	**No**	No	n.s.

PCC = personal centralised control, BFC = bureaucratic formalised control, OC = output control, CBSN = control by socialisation and networks.

* These hypotheses were tested using two different measures of MNC size. If the direction of the difference was the same in both cases, the significance level was averaged over these two measures.

** Controlling for other variables results in a more significant relationship and/or acceptance of the hypothesis.

*** $p < 0.001$, ** $p < 0.01$, * $p < 0.05$, † $p < 0.10$, all 1-tailed.

----- = formal hypothesis testing not applicable.

As Table 5-4 shows, the results concerning subsidiary characteristics are more in conformity to the hypotheses. All but one of the differences were in the expected direction and only nine of the remaining 27 hypotheses could not be accepted at a (1-tailed) 0.05 level of significance. Of these nine, two could be accepted at the 0.10 level of significance, while three others were (very) significant for a subsample of countries or when controlling for other subsidiary characteristics.

In sum, Table 5-4 confirms a positive relationship between size and control by socialisation and networks, a positive relationships between interdependence and total control, personal centralised control and bureaucratic formalised control and a negative relationship between local responsiveness and the same control mechanisms. Environmental uncertainty is negatively related to personal centralised control and positively to control by socialisation and networks for a subsample of countries. An investigation of the relationship between cultural distance and control mechanisms showed that MNCs apparently prefer direct personal control in the form of expatriates to the more impersonal form of control (bureaucratic formalised control and output control) in culturally distant countries.

Concerning subsidiary type, output-dependent subsidiaries experience more control than input-dependent subsidiaries, and subsidiary-dependent subsidiaries experience more control by socialisation and networks than HQ-dependent subsidiaries. Autonomous subsidiaries clearly experience a lower level of control than both active and receptive subsidiaries. The same goes for sales subsidiaries, where the dominant control mechanism is output control. R&D subsidiaries can be differentiated from other subsidiaries in the sense that they experience less personal centralised control and bureaucratic formalised control and more control by socialisation and networks.

Multiple regression models
Using multiple regression analysis, we will try to ascertain which of the characteristics discussed in this section and Chapter 4 has the highest explanatory power with regard to the different control mechanisms. Headquarters and subsidiary characteristics have to be analysed separately, since most subsidiary characteristics cannot be logically aggregated at headquarters level and the transformation of headquarters characteristics to subsidiary level would inflate their importance. We will therefore present two different regression models: one that considers headquarters characteristics only (based on our sample of around 100 headquarters) and one that considers subsidiary characteristics only (based on our sample of nearly 300 subsidiaries). The application of multiple regression analysis requires that various assumptions are satisfied: linearity, equality of variance and normality. It is often difficult to comply with all assumptions. "Rarely are assumptions not violated in one way or another in regression analysis and other statistical procedures" (Norusis, Base System User's Guide Part 2, 1994: 249).

Table 5-4 Summary results of the hypotheses tested concerning subsidiary characteristics

No.	Subsidiary characteristics: content of the hypothesis	Expected direction	Accepted 0.05 sign., 1-tailed	1-tailed sign.
19	No relationship between subsidiary size and PCC	Yes	-----	-----
20	Positive relationship between subsidiary size and CBSN	Yes	Yes	***
21	Negative relationship between subsidiary age and PCC	Yes	**No**	**n.s**
22a	Positive relationship between subsidiary age and BFC	Yes	**No**	**n.s.**
22b	Positive relationship between subsidiary age and OC	Yes	**No**	†
23	Positive relationship between interdependence and total control	Yes	Yes	**
24	Positive relationship between interdependence and PCC	Yes	Yes	**
25	Positive relationship between interdependence and BFC	Yes	Yes	**
26	Subsidiary-dependent subsidiaries higher level of CBSN	Yes	Yes	*
27	Output-dependent subsidiaries higher level of total control	Yes	Yes	*
28	Negative relationship between local responsiveness and total control *	Yes	Yes	*/***
29	Negative relationship between local responsiveness and PCC *	Yes	Yes	**/***
30	Negative relationship between local responsiveness and BFC *	Yes	Yes	*/**
31a	Autonomous subsidiaries less total control than active subsidiaries	Yes	Yes	**
31b	Autonomous subsidiaries less total control than receptive subsidiaries	Yes	Yes	**
32	Active subsidiaries same level of control as receptive subsidiaries	Yes	-----	-----
33	Receptive subsidiaries more PCC than active subsidiaries	Yes	**No**	**n.s.**
34	Active subsidiaries more CBSN than receptive subsidiaries	Yes	**No**	**n.s.**
35a	Sales subsidiaries lower level of total control than other subsidiaries	Yes	Yes	***
35b	Output control dominant control mechanism in sales subsidiaries	Yes	-----	-----
36a	R&D subsidiaries less PCC than other subsidiaries	Yes	**No**	†
36b	R&D subsidiaries less BFC than other subsidiaries	Yes	Yes	*
36c	R&D subsidiaries more CBSN than other subsidiaries	Yes	Yes	*
37	Negative relationship between environmental uncertainty and PCC *	Yes	**No**/Yes	**n.s.**/*
38	Negative relationship between environmental uncertainty and BFC *	**No**	No	n.s./†
39	Positive relationship between environmental uncertainty and CBSN *	Yes	**No**/Yes	**n.s.**/***
40a	Negative relationship between cultural distance and BFC **	Yes	**No**/Yes	†/**
40b	Negative relationship between cultural distance and OC **	Yes	Yes	*/**

PCC = personal centralised control, BFC = bureaucratic formalised control, CBSN = control by socialisation and networks.

* These relationships become stronger and more significant when certain countries are excluded from the sample.

** These relationships become stronger and more significant when controlling for the other subsidiary characteristics.

*** p < 0.001, ** p < 0.01, * p < 0.05, † p < 0.10, all 1-tailed.

----- = formal hypothesis testing not applicable.

In our case linearity is not a problem. In the bivariate analyses, we systematically checked relationships for non-linearity, but did not find any indications for this. Plotting standardised residuals against standardised predicted values for each of the regression analyses confirmed this observation completely. The same plots also indicated that there was no reason to suspect violation of the equality of variance assumption, as had already been shown before for some of the variables. As also indicated before, however, many variables do not seem to be normally distributed. Since histograms of standardised residuals and cumulative normal probability plots showed that the deviation from normality was not very strong for most variables and the K-S Lilliefors normality tests did not generate very high statistics, we judged that multiple regression analysis would be appropriate in our case.

Table 5-5 and Table 5-6 show the regression models of the influence of various headquarters and subsidiary characteristics on the application of different control mechanisms. Since we wanted to create parsimonious models, stepwise selection (a combination of forward selection and backward elimination) was used to identify the subset of variables that were good predictors of the dependent variable. In order to allow marginally significant variables (2-tailed p-value between 0.05 and 0.10) to be included in the model, the entry requirement was modified to "probability of F-to-enter is less than or equal to 0.10". The variable enters the regression analysis if the probability associated with the F-test is less than or equal to 0.10.

Seventeen dummy variables were created, one for each of the headquarters countries and industries. To this end, values for each headquarters country or industry were recoded into 0 and 1, where 1 signified that the case was located in the country in question or was operating in the industry in question and 0 meant that it was not. Since there were no specific theoretical reasons to choose a particular order of variables, all independent variables were entered in one block. Above we have regularly referred to direct (personal centralised control and bureaucratic formalised control) and indirect (output control and control by socialisation and networks) control mechanisms. Therefore, we have also included separate regression analyses for these types of control mechanisms.

Table 5-5 Linear regression models of the influence of various headquarters characteristics on the application of different control mechanisms; percentage of explained variance (adjusted R-square) between brackets

Independent variables	PCC	BFC	OC	CBSN	Direct control	Indirect control	Total control
HQ Country							
Germany				-.424*** (7.5%)		-.222* (2.6%)	
Japan		-.286* (4.2%)		-.378*** (11.5%)		-.335*** (7.4%)	
UK	.265* (4.4%)				.214* (4.0%)		
Sweden				.187* (2.5%)		.233* (5.7%)	
Switzerland	-.176† (2.0%)					-.216* (2.7%)	
Industry							
Chemical	.359*** (7.0%)				.384*** (8.2%)		.235* (4.3%)
Electronics	.252* (3.9%)						
Food and Beverages		-.198† (2.4%)					
Paper		-.270* (3.9%)		-.350*** (13.1%)		-.223* (3.8%)	
Pharmaceutical	-187† (5.0%)						
HQ characteristics							
Multidom. model	-.363*** (12.2%)	-.268* (13.4%)		-.185* (2.4%)	-.405*** (19.1%)		-.308** (18.4%)
Log HQ employees			.366** (12.1%)		.211* (3.3%)		
Log total sales				.436*** (15.2%)		.558*** (20.1%)	.316** (5.9%)
Model statistics[136]							
R	.635	.533	.366	.752	.648	.665	.564
R-square	.403	.284	.134	.566	.420	.442	.318
Adjusted R-square	.345	.239	.121	.522	.373	.396	.286
F-value model	6.870	6.248	10.236	13.035	8.845	9.658	9.927
Sig. of model	.000	.000	.002	.000	.000	.000	.000

PCC = personal centralised control, BFC = bureaucratic formalised control, OC = output control, CBSN = control by socialisation and networks.
*** p < 0.001, ** p < 0.01, * p < 0.05, † p < 0.10, all 2-tailed.
Values for the independent variables are standardised beta coefficients.

---

[136] The statistics reported for regression models differ considerably between publications. Some publications do not mention adjusted R-square, which is the most conservative measure and most suitable for comparing models between different data sets, since it also takes sample size and the number of predictor variables into account (Hair et al, 1995). Further, regression models with small sample sizes and a relatively large number of predictor variables (see e.g. Garnier, 1982 and Wolf, 1994 who use sample sizes of 29-39 cases) can easily result in an 'over-fitting' of the variate to the sample. Through over-fitting, small sample sizes often result in high R and R-square values, which might be misleading if authors do not report adjusted R-squares.

All the regression models for headquarters characteristics are highly significant. There are considerable differences, however, between the models in terms of explained variance (adjusted R-square), which runs from a low of 12% for output control to a high of 52% for control by socialisation and networks.[137] The low R-square for output control is not surprising since the bivariate analysis has already shown that the level of output control was often nearly constant across different independent variables.

In conformity with what we found in the bivariate analysis, Table 5-5 shows that the level of both multinationality and heterogeneity do not exercise a major influence on the type of control mechanisms that are used in respect to subsidiaries. The type of organisational model, however, has a major impact on all control mechanisms except for output control and, related, indirect control. Subsidiaries of multidomestic companies experience a lower level of total control. As already apparent in the bivariate analysis, this is mainly due to a lower level of the two direct control mechanisms: personal centralised control and bureaucratic formalised control. The results for MNC size also confirm what was found in the bivariate analyses: the larger the MNC, the higher the level of both output control and control by socialisation and networks.

In addition to the variables discussed in this chapter, we also included headquarters country and industry in the models. The results with regard to headquarters country are broadly comparable to what we found in the analysis in Chapter 4 (see Table 4-8). Direct control mechanisms (personal centralised control and bureaucratic formalised control) are used to a larger extent in subsidiaries of British MNCs, while their application is rather low in subsidiaries of Swiss MNCs. Indirect control mechanisms (output control and especially control by socialisation and networks) are most prominent in subsidiaries of Swedish MNCs and least prominent in subsidiaries of both German and Japanese MNCs.

Somewhat surprisingly, however, there were also rather strong industry effects. Although an Anova analysis (see Section 1 of Chapter 4) did not show any significant differences in the application of control mechanisms across industries, considering the other variables reveals a different picture. Subsidiaries in the chemical industry are strongly controlled, especially with direct control mechanisms. To a much lesser extent, the same is true for subsidiaries in the electronics industry. The other end of the spectrum is occupied by subsidiaries in the paper industry that experience rather low levels of both bu-

---

[137] Although the percentage of explained variance is rather low in some cases, especially for subsidiary variables, this is by no means abnormal in the social sciences where models with adjusted R-squares around 0.10 or even lower are published in respected academic journals (see e.g. Banai, 1992; Black, 1992; Chang, 1996; Gencturk and Aulakh, 1995; Hannon et al, 1995; Parker, Zeira and Hatem, 1996; Waddock and Graves, 1997).

reaucratic formalised control and control by socialisation and networks. Finally, at a marginal level of significance, personal centralised control is applied to a lesser extent in the pharmaceutical industry and bureaucratic formalised control is less prominent in the food and beverages industry.

Looking at the total level of control, we see that the type of organisational model and the size of the MNC have the highest explanatory power. Exactly the same result was found in Wolf's (1994) study.[138] Since Wolf did not include industry as an independent variable and only differentiated between the USA and Europe, we cannot compare the findings concerning country and industry.

In sum, the results of the multiple regression analysis largely confirm our earlier analyses. In addition, however, strong industry effects were found that had not become apparent before. Broadly speaking, subsidiaries in multi-domestic industries experience lower levels of control than subsidiaries in global industries.

As Table 5-6 shows, the regression models for subsidiary characteristics are also highly significant for each of the control mechanisms. As above, differences are apparent in the level of the variance explained, and again output control has the lowest (2.6%) and control by socialisation and networks the highest (10.3%) level of explained variance. Overall, (adjusted) R-squares are much lower than for the headquarters characteristics, however.

The influence of the individual characteristics is again comparable to what we have found in the bivariate analysis, although not all differences detected there achieve statistical significance in a multivariate analysis. Subsidiary size has the largest influence on control by socialisation and networks, and is significantly positively related to the total level of control exercised by headquarters. This contradicts the findings by Wolf (1994), who discovered a (marginally) significant negative relationship. As explained in the theoretical part of this book, however, we would expect larger subsidiaries to experience a higher level of control because of their importance to headquarters. Although no significant relationships between subsidiary age and the various control mechanisms were found in the bivariate analysis, the multivariate analysis showed a negative relationship between subsidiary age and control by socialisation and networks. The older the subsidiary, the lower the level of control by socialisation and networks that is exercised by headquarters in respect of this subsidiary. We have not been able to find a clear rationale for

---

[138] Our results can be adequately compared to this study only, since most of the other studies discussed in the theoretical part of this book did not include multivariate analyses. Those that did included only one control mechanism and/or independent variables that were not completely comparable to ours.

this. Although a negative relationship would be expected between total control and subsidiary age, since younger subsidiaries are more likely to be closely controlled, it is not clear why it should be control by socialisation and networks that is applied to a lesser extent.

The independent variables interdependence and local responsiveness do not seem to have a large influence on the type of control mechanisms applied. It is likely that much of the variance for these factors is included in the different subsidiary roles and functions. Only the subsidiary-dependent subsidiary variable entered the regression analysis. As hypothesised and confirmed in the bivariate analysis, control by socialisation and networks is applied to a larger extent in these subsidiaries. The multivariate analysis shows that this is also the case for bureaucratic formalised control. In general, however, indirect control is more important for these subsidiaries.

Table 5-6 Linear regression models of the influence of various subsidiary characteristics on the application of different control mechanisms; percentage of explained variance (adjusted R-square) between brackets

Independent variables	PCC	BFC	OC	CBSN	Direct control	Indirect control	Total control
Subsidiary characteristics							
Log subsidiary employees		.145* (1.2%)		.284*** (6.7%)		.289*** (6.7%)	.156* (1.9%)
Subsidiary age				-.133* (1.3%)			
Subsidiary-dependent sub.		.132* (1.8%)		.146* (1.4%)		.104† (0.7%)	
Autonomous subsidiary	-.225*** (3.5%)	-.253*** (4.2%)			-.259*** (6.6%)	-.126* (0.7%)	-.257*** (4.5%)
Active subsidiary	-.117† (0.9%)						
Sales subsidiary	-.236*** (4.7%)				-.205*** (3.4%)		-.217*** (5.7%)
R & D subsidiary		-.106† (0.6%)					
Environ. characteristics							
Environmental uncertainty				.115† (0.9%)			
Cultural distance		-.126* (1.0%)	-.172** (2.6%)		-.131* (1.3%)		
Model statistics							
R	.318	.326	.172	.342	.352	.303	.363
R-square	.101	.106	.030	.117	.124	.092	.132
Adjusted R-square	.091	.088	.026	.103	.113	.081	.121
F-value model	9.668	6.045	7.877	8.457	12.042	8.652	12.878
Sig. of model	.000	.000	.005	.000	.000	.000	.000

PCC = personal centralised control, BFC = bureaucratic formalised control, OC = output control, CBSN = control by socialisation and networks.
*** $p < 0.001$, ** $p < 0.01$, * $p < 0.05$, † $p < 0.10$, all 2-tailed.
Values for the independent variables are standardised beta coefficients.

Subsidiary roles (a combination of interdependence and local responsiveness) have a considerable influence on many of the control mechanisms included in our survey. As also shown in the bivariate analysis, autonomous subsidiaries experience a significantly lower level of control than subsidiaries with either active or receptive roles. As Table 5-6 shows, this result is mainly due to a lower level for the two direct control mechanisms: personal centralised control and bureaucratic formalised control. In addition, active subsidiaries also experience a lower level of personal centralised control, a result that did not acquire significance in the bivariate analysis.

In the bivariate analysis, we found that the subsidiary function (sales or R&D) had a considerable influence on the level and type of control that was exercised by headquarters towards these subsidiaries. Concerning sales subsidiaries, the bivariate results are confirmed at very high levels of significance. For R&D subsidiaries, only the predicted lower level of bureaucratic formalised control is (marginally) significant.

Turning to the environmental variables, the hypothesised positive relationship between environmental uncertainty and control by socialisation and networks could be confirmed for a subsample of countries only in the bivariate analysis. As Table 5-6 shows, the multivariate analysis produces a (marginally) significant result for this relationship. However, no significant relationship was found for personal centralised control. Concerning cultural distance, a partial correlation analysis showed a significant negative relationship between cultural distance and the two impersonal types of control (bureaucratic formalised control and output control). As can be seen in Table 5-6, this result is confirmed in the multivariate analysis. Apparently, cultural distance leads MNCs to prefer a close personal control (in particular by means of expatriates) over more impersonal control mechanisms.

In sum, the results of the multiple regression analysis largely confirm our earlier analyses, although not all differences found in the bivariate analysis were statistically significant in the multivariate analysis.

Conclusions

In this section, we combined the first two building blocks of this thesis: control mechanisms and multinational firms. We investigated the influence of both headquarters and subsidiary characteristics on the level and type of control that is exercised by headquarters over its subsidiaries. A majority of the specific hypotheses that were put forward in Chapter 2 in this respect could be accepted at high levels of significance. A multiple regression analysis confirmed most of the findings of the bivariate analyses. At headquarters level, MNC size and the organisational model applied were the most influential characteristics. In addition, variables discussed in the previous chapter, headquarters country and industry, also had a high explanatory power. At subsidiary level, size, the subsidiary role and function and the extent of cultural distance between headquarters and subsidiary were shown to have a high explanatory power with regard to the level and type of control exercised by headquarters over a particular subsidiary. In the next section, Section 2, we will add our third building block to the analysis and look at international transfers as a control mechanism in MNCs.

2. INTERNATIONAL TRANSFERS AS A CONTROL MECHANISM IN MNCS

Introduction

In Section 1, we discussed the influence of various headquarters and subsidiary characteristics on the level and type of control exercised over subsidiaries. In this section, we will focus on the role of international transfers as a control mechanism. We will first investigate whether international transfers can indeed function as a way to achieve control by socialisation and networks and, more particularly, shared values and informal communication networks. The hypotheses put forward in Section 2 of Chapter 2 in this respect will be tested, and we will explore the situations in which the role of international transfers in achieving this informal type of control is strongest. Subsequently, we will discuss the alternatives to international transfers to achieve a high level of shared values and informal communication: formal networks and international management training. A fourth and final subsection then discusses the role of international transfers as a direct means of control.

In Chapter 4, we discussed the descriptive statistics concerning the nationality of the managing director. The majority of managing directors were shown to have the nationality of the host country, while nearly a third were parent-country nationals (see Table 4-16). Table 5-7 reports the descriptive statistics for the two other measures of expatriate presence: the number of expatriates in top-5 positions and the total number of expatriates working in the subsidiary. Since the latter measure is highly dependent on subsidiary size, we also calculated the percentage of expatriates in the total workforce. As can be seen in Table 5-7, expatriate presence differs considerably between subsidiaries.

Table 5-7 Expatriate presence in subsidiaries

	N	Minimum	Maximum	Mean	Std. Devia-tion
% expatriates in workforce	287	0	67	3.10	7.70
Number of expats in subsidiary	287	0	242	9.14	23.06
Number of expats in top 5 positions	287	0	5	1.33	1.35

International transfers as an indirect control mechanism

A review of the relevant literature in Section 2 of Chapter 2 showed that it is generally accepted that international transfers can be used to facilitate both shared values between headquarters and subsidiaries and the construction of informal information networks. However, as indicated in the same chapter, this relationship has so far not undergone any major empirical tests. If we can show that subsidiaries with a larger proportion of internationally transferred managers score higher on the shared values and informal communication aspects of control by socialisation and networks, this would certainly increase confidence in the existence of this relationship. *Hypotheses 2-41* and *2-42* predict that subsidiary scores on the "shared values" and "informal communication" elements of control by socialisation and networks will be positively related to the proportion of expatriate managers in the upper-level workforce.

The level of both shared values and informal communication is significantly positively related to the number of expatriates in top 5 positions (Spearman's rho shared values: 0.161, p = 0.007, 2-tailed; Spearman's rho informal communication: 0.182, p = 0.002, 2-tailed) and the number of expatriates in the total workforce (Spearman's rho shared values: 0.197, p = 0.001, 2-tailed; Spearman's rho informal communication: 0.163, p = 0.006, 2-tailed).[139] In addition, the level of both shared values and informal communication is significantly higher in subsidiaries that are headed by a PCN (Z: -3.360, p = 0.001, 2-tailed; Z: -2.462, p = 0.014, 2-tailed). The fact that the relationship between the *percentage* of expatriates in the total workforce and the level of shared values and informal communication is much weaker (Spearman's rho shared values: 0.093, p = 0.117, 2-tailed; Spearman's rho informal communication: 0.104, p = 0.087, 2-tailed), is due to the fact that this measure partly controls for subsidiary size. As we have seen before, the

---

[139] Controlling for international management training and task forces turns the relationship insignificant for the total number of expatriates. The strength of the relationship for top-5 managers hardly changes, however. In the next section, we will further investigate the relationship between international transfers and its alternatives.

relationship between subsidiary size and the level of shared values and informal communication is positive. Controlling for size makes the relationship weaker for the other measures of expatriate presence as well. We therefore conducted a multiple regression analysis to explore the relative importance of expatriate presence as a determinant of the level of shared values and informal communication.

Table 5-8 summarises the results of this regression analysis.[140] The first column for each dependent variable shows the regression model without including the measures of expatriate presence, while the second column does include these measures in the analysis. Starting with shared values, we see that the model without expatriate presence is highly significant and has an adjusted R-square of 0.106. Both the model statistics and the subsidiary characteristics that entered the model closely resemble the model that was specified for control by socialisation and networks in Table 5-6. This is of course not surprising, since shared values is one of the items of control by socialisation and networks. As for control by socialisation and networks, subsidiary size explains the largest percentage of the variance. Including the measures of expatriate presence results in a model that is even slightly more significant, and that has an adjusted R-square that is more than 50% higher than the model without them. The nationality of the managing director is the most influential of the various measures of expatriate presence. This measure entered the regression model in the first step with an adjusted R-square of 0.059. Although the beta coefficients and the percentage of variance explained for the other subsidiary characteristics change slightly, their level of significance remains very similar. From this analysis, we can therefore safely conclude that expatriate presence has indeed a significant influence on the level of shared values between headquarters and subsidiaries.[141]

Concerning informal communication, the model without inclusion of the measures of expatriate presence is very weak. Although the model is significant, its adjusted R-square is very low and its only predictor variable, subsidiary size, is not very strong. Including the measures of expatriate presence results in a better model, in which the nationality of the managing director

---

[140] As in the previous section, data were checked for violation of linear regression assumptions. No major violations were found, however.

[141] We might wonder, however, whether the positive relationship between expatriate presence and shared values/informal communication is not simply due to a response effect. Local managing directors might underestimate the level of shared values and informal communication, while 'PCN managing directors' do the reverse, thus creating a positive relationship between a PCN managing director and these variables. If we limit our analysis to a subsample of subsidiaries with a local managing director, the level of shared values and informal communication is significantly positively related to another measure of expatriate presence: the percentage of expatriates in the total workforce. The chance that the relationship is due to a response effect only is therefore very small.

was the first predictor variable to enter the model with an adjusted R-square of 0.037. We can therefore conclude that expatriate presence also has a significant influence on the level of informal communication.

Table 5-8 Linear regression models of the influence of various subsidiary characteristics on the level of shared values and informal communication; percentage of explained variance (adjusted R-square) between brackets

Independent variables	Shared values 1	Shared values 2	Informal commu- nication 1	Informal commu- nication 2	Output control 1	Output control 2
Subsidiary characteristics						
Log sub. employees	.281*** (3.9%)	231*** (3.2%)	.122* (1.1%)			
Subsidiary age	-.158* (1.9%)	-.133* (1.2%)				
Subsidiary-dependent subsidiary	.186** (2.4%)	.240*** (3.6%)				
Autonomous subsidiary	-.188** (2.4%)	-.213*** (2.7%)				
R&D subsidiary				.139* (1.2%)		
Sales subsidiary				-.116† (0.9%)		
Cultural distance					-.172** (2.6%)	-.188** (3.0%)
Expatriate presence						
Managing director PCN		.225*** (5.9%)		.194** (3.7%)		
% expats in workforce						-.203** (4.9%)
Model statistics						
R	.347	.430	.122	.266	.172	.296
R-square	.120	.185	.015	.071	.030	.088
Adjusted R-square	.106	.166	.011	.058	.026	.079
F-value model	8.637	9.611	3.884	5.494	7.877	10.500
Sig. of model	.000	.000	.005	.001	.005	.000

*** $p < 0.001$, ** $p < 0.01$, * $p < 0.05$, † $p < 0.10$, all 2-tailed.
Values for the independent variables are standardised beta coefficients.

Regression analyses were also run for each of the other control mechanisms (personal centralised control, bureaucratic formalised control and output control) and for the two other elements of control by socialisation and networks (task forces and management training). Except for output control, none of the other control mechanisms was significantly influenced by any of the measures of expatriate presence. Including expatriate presence considerably improved the regression model for output control, however. The explanatory power of cultural distance remained fairly similar, but the percentage of expatriates in the total workforce entered the regression analysis in the first step with an adjusted R-square of 0.049. The larger the cultural distance between headquarters and subsidiary, and the higher the expatriate presence in the subsidiary, the lower the level of output control exercised over this subsidiary. Apparently, expatriate presence and output control are seen as alternative ways to control subsidiaries.

Although we can conclude that expatriate presence influences the level of shared values and informal communication in subsidiaries significantly, this relationship is not equally strong in all situations. An exploratory analysis showed that this relationship is much stronger in acquisitions than in greenfields, in subsidiary-dependent subsidiaries than in headquarters-dependent subsidiaries, in autonomous subsidiaries and in subsidiaries with a higher than average local responsiveness (the last two measures overlap partially). What these situations have in common is that they all represent a higher level of independence in respect of headquarters. Apparently, expatriate presence is most effective in facilitating informal control in subsidiaries that are otherwise relatively independent from headquarters. Since absolute expatriate presence is generally rather low in these circumstances, we might also conclude that the "marginal effectiveness" of expatriates in facilitating informal control decreases if expatriate presence increases. In other words: if there are no or only a few expatriates employed in a particular subsidiary, "adding" additional expatriates has a strong positive effect[142] on shared values and informal communication, while the effect of adding another expatriate is much weaker in a situation where there is already a high expatriate presence.

Table 5-9 Strength of the relationship between expatriate presence and informal control in various headquarters countries, subsidiary regions and industries

	Relation for shared values stronger in:	Relation for shared values weaker in:	Relation for informal communication stronger in:	Relation for informal communication weaker in:
HQ country	Japan, Netherlands	Sweden, USA	Netherlands, UK	Finland, USA
Subsidiary region	Latin American, Anglo-Saxon	Far Eastern, Germanic	Nordic, Anglo-Saxon	Latin American, Germanic
Industry	Computer, Paper	Pharmaceutical, Food & Beverages	Food & Beverages, Paper	Automobile, Pharmaceutical

In addition, we can distinguish certain headquarters countries, subsidiary regions and industries in which the investigated relationship is either much stronger or much weaker than in others. Unfortunately, we have not been able

---

[142] For the moment, we accept a causal relationship, which of course cannot be formally concluded from our cross-sectional survey.

to find a clear rationale for these differences, summarised in Table 5-9. However, the conclusion that might be drawn from this table is that the role of expatriate presence in establishing informal control is limited in American MNCs, in subsidiaries in the Germanic countries and in the pharmaceutical industry. On the other hand, expatriate presence is a very important facilitator of informal control in Dutch MNCs, in subsidiaries in the Anglo-Saxon countries and in the paper industry. Nevertheless, much more research is still needed to get a clearer picture of the role of international transfers as an indirect control mechanism.

Hypothesis 2-43 refers to another way to assess the importance of international transfers in achieving informal control. As already described in Section 3 of Chapter 4, subsidiary and headquarters managers were asked to indicate the importance of various functions of expatriation. Two of these functions, "ensuring a homogeneous corporate culture throughout the company" and "improving information and communication channels" are closely related to the control mechanisms shared values and informal communication. *Hypothesis 2-43* predicted these functions to be as important as the other functions of expatriation. As can be seen in Table 4-17 in Chapter 4, at subsidiary level[143] the improvement of communication channels is seen as the second most important function of expatriation, while the transfer of corporate culture shares a third/fourth place with "training for future positions at headquarters". The mean for both functions lies around 3 (= important). They therefore certainly have a more than marginal importance.

Table 5-10 Average importance of the three main functions of expatriation on a scale of 1-5

	N	Minimum	Maximum	Mean	Std Deviation
Management development	212	1	5	2.634	1.072
Organisation development	212	1	5	2.875	0.979
Position filling	212	1	5	2.804	0.908

Table 5-10 compares the three main functions of expatriation: organisational development, position filling and management development. As can be seen, there are no major differences between the various functions. If anything,

---

[143] At headquarters level (responses from 25 HR-managers) both transfer for corporate culture and transfer to improve information and communication channels were seen as (much) less important than transfer for management development or position filling As discussed in Chapter 4, expatriate managers might not be specifically sent out for these reasons (corporate HR-managers' responses), while in actual practice (subsidiary managers' responses) this function might turn out to be very important.

however, organisational development is more important than the other functions, thereby again confirming the role of expatriation in facilitating informal control.

Alternatives to international transfers

In Section 2 of Chapter 2, we discussed various alternatives to international transfers to facilitate shared values and informal communication. Of these alternatives, formal networks and international management training were judged most important. For internationally transferred managers themselves, we hypothesised that international transfers would probably be most effective in achieving a high level of shared values and informal communication. For the other subsidiary managers, however, the direct effect of participation in formal networks and international management training programmes on shared values and informal communication might very well be stronger than the indirect effect of expatriate presence.

Hypotheses 2-44 and *2-45* therefore predicted that the relationship between both management training and formal networks and the subsidiary scores on the shared values and informal communication elements of control by socialisation and networks would be stronger than the relationship between expatriate presence and these scores. These hypotheses are confirmed, although the difference in correlation coefficients is larger for international management training than for formal networks.

Hypotheses 2-46 and *2-47* predicted that the influence of international management training would be largest on the level of shared values, while formal networks would have the highest effect on the level of informal communication. These hypotheses can be partially confirmed. Participation in international management training is indeed more strongly related to shared values than participation in formal networks. However, although the influence of formal networks is stronger on informal communication than on shared values, the influence of international management training on informal communication is even slightly more important. The difference between the effect of international management training and task forces is smaller in the case of informal communication, though.

To further explore the relative importance of international management training, task forces and expatriate presence on both the level of shared values and informal communication, we performed a regression analysis including the subsidiary characteristics as discussed above, various measures of expatriate presence *and* participation of subsidiary managers in international management training and formal networks. Except for the variable subsidiary-dependent subsidiary, none of the subsidiary characteristics entered the regression analysis.

Table 5-11 Linear regression models of the influence of various subsidiary characteristics on the level of shared values and informal communication; percentage of explained variance (adjusted R-square) between brackets

Independent variables	Shared values	Informal communication
Subsidiary characteristics		
Participation subsidiary managers in international management training	.400*** (21%)	.199** (2.9%)
Participation subsidiary managers in formal (international) networks	.122* (0.9%)	.229*** (8.9%)
Subsidiary-dependent subsidiary	.149** (1.9%)	
Expatriate presence		
Managing director PCN	.276*** (5.9%)	.205*** (3.9%)
Model statistics		
R	.556	.410
R-square	.309	.168
Adjusted R-square	.297	.157
F-value model	25.867	15.622
Sig. of model	.000	.000

*** $p < 0.001$, ** $p < 0.01$, all 2-tailed.
Values for the independent variables are standardised beta coefficients.

Participation of subsidiary managers in international training had the largest explanatory power for the level of shared values. In contrast to the result for Hypothesis 2-44, however, expatriate presence had a larger explanatory power than participation of subsidiary managers in formal networks. The same result is found for informal communication, although in this case it is participation of subsidiary managers in formal (international) networks that explains the largest percentage of the variance (therewith confirming Hypothesis 2-47 that had to be rejected in the bivariate analysis). In conclusion, we can say that alternatives to international transfers certainly play an important role in explaining differences in the level of shared values and informal communication in subsidiaries. Even including these alternatives, expatriate presence continues to play a major role in achieving this informal type of control.

International transfers as a direct control mechanism

As indicated in Section 2 of Chapter 1, expatriates can also be seen as a direct way to control subsidiaries. In this sense, they will be used to effectuate personal centralised control. In Chapter 4 (Table 4-1) we saw that although direct expatriate control should be seen as a separate control mechanism, it is most strongly related to direct supervision and centralisation of decision-making at headquarters. In this section, we will give an overview of the circumstances in which direct expatriate control is most prominent.

Table 5-12 Mean level of direct expatriate control in MNCs headquartered in different countries, in different subsidiary regions and in different industries

	Direct expatriate control much higher in:	Direct expatriate control much lower in:
Headquarters country	Japan, Germany, Netherlands	USA, France, UK
Subsidiary region	Far East, Latin American	Nordic, Anglo-Saxon
Industry	Automobile, Electronics	Food and Beverages, Paper

Looking at the mean level of direct expatriate control, we see that the results in Table 5-12 closely conform to what we found in Section 3 of Chapter 4 concerning expatriate presence. This is only logical, since direct expatriate control is strongly related to the presence of expatriates (correlation coefficients of 0.46 and 0.56 for the percentage of expatriates in the subsidiary and the number of expatriates in top-5 positions respectively and a Z-value of -8.212 for the nationality of the managing director). There is no one-to-one relationship, however, since subsidiaries can have a high expatriate presence, but still feel that this presence is mainly aimed at facilitating informal control or that the transfer was mainly administered for management development reasons or for the transfer of technical know-how.

Although there is some indication that the strength of the *relationship* between expatriate presence and direct expatriate control is not equally strong in all situations, the differences are not as clear as in the case of informal control and will therefore not be discussed in detail. Again, however, there is some evidence that there might be a declining "marginal effectiveness" of expatriates in achieving direct expatriate control.

Conclusions

We explored the role of international transfers and their alternatives as control mechanisms. Table 5-13 summarises the hypotheses tested in this section.[144] Although formal testing was not always possible, given the structure of the hypothesis, the portent of the hypothesis could be accepted in most cases.

---

[144] Only the nationality of the managing director and the number of expatriates in top-5 positions were used to test Hypotheses 2-36 and 2-37, since the proportion of expatriate managers in the upper-level workforce was judged to be the most important determinant of shared values and informal communication.

Table 5-13 Summary of the hypotheses tested in this section

NO.	International transfers as informal control mechanisms: content of the hypotheses	Expected direction	Accepted 0.05 sign., 1-tailed	1-tailed sign.
41	Positive relationship expatriate presence and shared values *	Yes	Yes	**
42	Positive relationship expatriate presence and informal communication *	Yes	Yes	**
43	Organisation development as important as other functions	Yes	-----	-----
44a	Relationship between international management training and shared values stronger than relationship between expatriate presence and shared values	Yes	-----	-----
44b	Relationship between formal networks and shared values stronger than relationship between expatriate presence and shared values	Yes/No+	-----	-----
45a	Relationship between international management training and informal communication stronger than relationship between expatriate presence and informal communication	Yes/No+	-----	-----
45b	Relationship between formal networks and informal communication stronger than relationship between expatriate presence and informal communication	Yes	-----	-----
46	Relationship between international management training and shared values stronger than relationship between formal networks and shared values	Yes	-----	-----
47	Relationship between formal networks and informal communication stronger than relationship between international management training and informal communication	No/Yes+	-----	-----

* These hypotheses were tested using two different measures of expatriate presence (nationality managing director and number of expatriates in top 5 positions). If the direction of the difference was the same in both cases, the significance level was averaged over these two measures.
+ Multivariate analysis resulted in the rejection/acceptance of this hypothesis.
----- = formal hypothesis testing not applicable.
*** $p < 0.001$, ** $p < 0.01$, * $p < 0.05$, † $p < 0.10$, all 1-tailed

International transfers were shown to play an important role in facilitating both indirect and direct control. As expected, however, participation of subsidiary managers in international management training and task forces was even more strongly related to the level of shared values and informal communication. Nevertheless, multivariate analysis showed that - contrary to Hypotheses 2-40 and 2-41 - expatriate presence was a (close) second most important explanatory factor of variance in the level of shared values and informal communication. For shared values, international management training was the most important explanatory factor, while for informal communication it was formal networks.

Given our findings, we can conclude that expatriate presence is significantly related to the level of shared values and informal communication in subsidiaries. However, it was also shown that this relationship was not equally strong in all situations, and that there might be a declining "marginal effectiveness" of expatriate presence. As could be expected, the relationship between expatriate presence and direct expatriate control was even stronger. Again, the strength of this relationship differed across countries and industries and there was some evidence of a declining "marginal effectiveness". Therefore, much more research is needed to get a clearer picture of the role of international transfers as an indirect control mechanism, and to disentangle the direct and indirect control effects of expatriation.

3. CONFIGURATIONS AND PERFORMANCE IMPLICATIONS

Introduction

In the two previous sections, we discussed the empirical results with regard to the integration of our theoretical building blocks. Section 1 combined control mechanisms and MNCs, while Section 2 added international transfers to the picture. As indicated before, many of the variables discussed above might be interrelated. We therefore decided to construct configurations of multinational companies that integrate many of the variables discussed before. A description and justification for these configurations can be found in Section 3 of Chapter 2. In the next section, we will investigate whether these configurations can be distinguished in our empirical data.

A second main element of Section 3 is performance analysis. Previous research, as discussed in Chapter 2, discovered that, next to the country of origin, both "economic" and "organisational" factors are significant determinants of firm performance. In this book, the focus is on organisational factors: the type of organisational model and control mechanisms applied and the fit between the two of them. However, in order to appreciate the relative importance of organisational factors in determining performance differences, it is important to look at some of the other factors as well.

Configurations tested

In this section, we will empirically test the configurations that have been theoretically derived in Chapter 2. In order to do so, we have reproduced the theoretical predictions in Table 5-14. In addition, the table includes the mean levels of the different variables for each of the three main organisational models. For variables where the mean did not represent a "logical" value, standardised scores were used. This occurred when variables that were measured on a 6- or 7-point (Likert) scale, instead of asking the respondent for an exact value. Column 5 of Table 5-14 first indicates whether the differences between the three organisational models were in the expected direction. The chi-square value resulting from a Kruskal-Wallis-Anova analysis subsequently reveals whether there is an overall difference between the three models. Finally, the sixth column summarises which of the pairs are different at a 0.05 significance level (Mann-Whitney tests). Concerning the headquarters characteristics, the level of measurement is obviously the headquarters level. The level and type of control were consolidated to headquarters level. All of the other characteristics were tested at subsidiary level, since they cannot be logically consolidated to headquarters level.

Table 5-14 Test of configurations of multinational companies; deviations from theoretical configurations printed in bold

Organisational model	Multido-mestic	Global	Transnational	Exp. Diff.?/ chi-square	Pairs diff. at 0.05 (1-tailed)
HQ characteristics					
Size of the company	small 49046 empl.	large 120313 empl.	large/**medium** 62892 empl.	**Partly** 10.545, .005	G>M&T
Extent of multinationality (standardised scores)	medium .07	medium -.08	high .16	Yes 1.436, .488	**None**
Level of diversity, number of 2/4-digit SIC codes	medium 3.17/6.20	low/**high** 3.87/6.33	high/**low** 2.73/5.32	**No** 5.569, .062/ 1.99, .368	G>T
Subsidiary characteristics					
Average size of subsidiaries (employees)	small 468 empl.	large 1023 empl.	large 885 empl.	Yes 5.933, .051	G&T>M
Average age of subsidiaries	old 51 years	young 39 years	med./**young** 34 years	**Partly** 6.892, .032	M>T
Total level of interdependence (standardised score)	low -.55	high .26	High .07	Yes 27.923, .000	G&T>M
Level of HQ dependence (standardised score)	low -.47	high .30	medium -.07	Yes 26.073, .000	G>T>M
Level of subsidiary dependence (standardised score)	low -.23	medium .02	high .16	Yes 5.625, .060	T>M
Local responsiveness (standardised score)	high .29	low -.32	high .24	Yes 18.967, .000	M&T>G
% autonomous subsidiaries	high 52%	low 18%	medium 41%	Yes 24.417, .000	M&T>G
% receptive subsidiaries	low 30%	high 43%	medium/**low** 23%	**Partly** 7.897, .019	G>M&T
% active subsidiaries	low 2%	low/**high** 15%	high 19%	**Partly** 9.981, .007	G&T>M
% production subsidiaries	high 66%	low 55%	high 70%	Yes 4.772, .092	T>G
% R&D subsidiaries	low 22%	low 28%	high 40%	Yes 5.602, .061	T>M&G

% acquired subsidiaries	high 41%	low 27%	medium 30%	Yes 3.635, .162	M>G
Level and type of control (all standardised scores)					
Total level of control	low -.40	high .24	high .11	Yes 10.211, .006	G&T>M
Level of personal centralised control	low -.44	high .32	medium -.02	Yes 11.527, .003	G&T>M
Level of bureaucratic formalised control	low -.41	high .27	medium -.07	Yes 10.049, .007	G&T>M
Level of output control	medium .007	medium .0009	medium -.01	Yes .141, .932	none
Level of control by socialisation and networks	medium/**low** -.26	medium .07	high .22	**Partly** 3.951, .139	T>M
Level and type of expatriation					
Expatriate presence	low	high	high		
Number of expatriates	3.5	11.8	12.3	Yes 15.527, .000	G&T>M
% PCN as MD	27%	42%	44%	Yes 4.320, .115	G&T>M
Number expatriates in top 5 positions	.91	1.63	1.37	Yes 11.210, .004	G&T>M
Type of expatriate control	--	more direct	more indirect		
Correlations + effect MD for direct control	weaker than average	stronger than average	weaker than average	Yes	---
Correlations + effect MD for indirect control	stronger than average	weaker than average	stronger than average	Yes	---

Starting with the *headquarters characteristics*, we see that, as predicted, multidomestic companies are relatively small in *size*. Contrary to our expectations, however, transnational companies are also significantly smaller than global companies. This difference remains present if we measure size in terms of total assets or total sales. Apparently, it is the focus on economies of scale, dominant in global companies, that increases company size. The combined emphasis on efficiency, differentiation and world-wide learning, as found in transnational companies, does not seem to lead to larger companies, although transnational companies are slightly larger than multidomestic companies.

With regard to the extent of *multinationality*, transnational companies are indeed found to be more internationalised than their multidomestic and especially their global counterparts. However, these differences are generally small and insignificant. Although transnational companies are slightly more and global companies slightly less internationalised than average, the level of multinationality is not a major differentiator between different types of companies.

Differences concerning the level of *diversity* are the complete opposite of what was expected. Global companies have the highest and transnational companies the lowest level of diversity. Retrospectively, however, we doubt whether the number of SIC codes in which a company operates adequately captures the level of diversity in the way interpreted in the theoretical framework. Another line of reasoning might be that global companies can more easily operate in a larger number of different areas, simply because they focus on standardised products. This means that for global companies the level of diversity *within* each activity is rather low, but that they could take up a larger number of different, even seemingly unrelated, activities. If this is true, we would expect global companies to show a larger extent of unrelated diversification. Using Varadarajan and Ramanujam's (1987) categories as described in Section 2 of Chapter 3, we can distinguish related (high mean narrow-spectrum diversity, low broad-spectrum diversity) and unrelated diversification (high broad-spectrum diversity, low mean narrow-spectrum diversity). Broad-spectrum diversity is operationalised by the number of 2-digit SIC codes in which a firms operates, while mean narrow-spectrum diversity is calculated by the dividing the number of 4-digit SIC codes in which a firm operates by the number of 2-digit SIC codes in which it operates (Varadarajan and Ramanujam, 1987:383). If we compare global and transnational firms on these categories, we see that although the difference is not significant, transnational companies have a higher level of related diversification (Z: -1.112, p = 0.266, 2-tailed) than global companies. Global companies, on the other hand, indeed have a significantly higher (Z: 1.979, p = 0.048, 2-tailed) level of unrelated diversification than transnational companies. This would seem to support our assumption that global companies operate a larger number of different activities that in themselves might be rather standardised. Unfortunately, our available empirical data do not allow us to measure differences in diversity in the way it was originally intended in the theoretical framework.

Regarding *subsidiary characteristics*, the difference in average *size* between subsidiaries of different types of multinational companies conforms to our expectations. Subsidiaries of both global and transnational companies are larger than subsidiaries of multidomestic companies. The difference in *age* conforms only partly to our predictions. Although subsidiaries of multidomestic companies are indeed older than subsidiaries of both transnational and - marginally significantly - global companies, transnational companies and not global companies seem to have the youngest subsidiaries. This is partly due to the fact that transnational are on average younger than both global and multidomestic companies. Apparently, not all transnational companies grow out of multidomestic and global companies.

As expected, subsidiaries of both global and transnational companies show a higher total level of *interdependence* than subsidiaries of multidomestic companies. Further, as predicted, the level of *de*pendence, that is dependence on headquarters, is highest for subsidiaries of global companies and lowest for subsidiaries of multidomestic companies. Differences in the level of *inter*-dependence, that is, dependence on other subsidiaries, are also in the expected direction, that is the level is highest for transnational companies and lowest for multidomestic companies. In general, however, differences for subsidiary dependence are more modest than for headquarters dependence. Concerning *local responsiveness*, differences conform perfectly to our predictions. Local responsiveness is high for subsidiaries of both multidomestic and transnational firms and low for subsidiaries of global firms.

Looking at subsidiary roles, the highest percentage of *autonomous* subsidiaries can be found, as expected, in multidomestic companies. More than half of the subsidiaries in multidomestic companies play an autonomous role, while for global companies this goes for only one in five subsidiaries. As predicted, the dominant subsidiary role in global companies is a *receptive* one, which is taken by more than 40% of subsidiaries in global companies. Partly contradicting our expectations, the percentage of receptive subsidiaries is lowest in transnational companies and not in multidomestic companies. As already described in Section 3 of Chapter 2, we expected the average percentage of active subsidiaries to be rather small, since even in transnational companies only a limited of subsidiaries will fulfil this strategically important role. As can be seen in Table 5-14, the percentage of active subsidiaries is indeed lowest for each type of company. As foreseen, most active subsidiaries are found in transnational companies, but contrary to our expectations, nearly as high a percentage of active subsidiaries is found in global companies. An active role is very unlikely for subsidiaries in a multidomestic company.

Concerning subsidiary types, global companies were expected to have the lowest percentage of *production* subsidiaries, since they would be more likely than both multidomestic and transnational companies to concentrate production in a limited number of locations. This tendency is indeed apparent in our empirical data, although the difference is significant only between transnational and global companies. Subsidiaries with an *R&D* function were expected to occur more frequently in transnational companies, since in this type of company subsidiaries are more likely to have a strategic role. As Table 5-14 shows, there is indeed a significant difference in the percentage of subsidiaries with an R&D function between transnational companies on the one hand and both global and multidomestic companies on the other hand. Finally, as anticipated, the percentage of acquired subsidiaries is highest in multidomestic companies and lowest in global companies.

Most of the differences between different types of companies concerning *control mechanisms* were already tested in Section 1. The summary in Table 5-14 shows that the predicted differences were largely present in the empirical data. However, the anticipated differences between global and transnational companies concerning personal centralised control, bureaucratic formalised control and control by socialisation and networks were not significant. Further, contrary to our predictions, the level of control by socialisation and networks in subsidiaries of multidomestic companies is lower than in global companies. The data do reconfirm, however, that output control and control by socialisation and networks are the dominant control mechanisms in multidomestic firms.

A final issue on which the three types of firms were assumed to differ was the *level and type of expatriation*. Expatriate presence was expected to be rather high in subsidiaries of both global and transnational firms, and low in subsidiaries of multidomestic firms. As can be seen in Table 5-14, this prediction could be confirmed for all three measures of expatriation. As anticipated, however, the main function of expatriation differs between global and transnational firms. In global companies, the emphasis is on direct expatriate control, while in transnational companies expatriates seem to be used to achieve informal control through the fostering of socialisation and the strengthening of informal communication channels. Multidomestic firms resemble transnational firms in this respect. Although subsidiaries of multidomestic firms have a low expatriate presence, where expatriates are present they mainly serve to achieve an informal type of control.

In sum, we can conclude that the theoretically derived configurations of multinational companies fit the empirical data well. Of the 25 comparisons that were made, only one, the level of diversity, was contrary to expectations. As explained above, this might also be due to an inadequate operationalisation of this construct. Five other comparisons conformed only partly to our expectations. Transnational companies were shown to be medium-sized rather than large, while subsidiaries of transnational companies were young rather than average-aged. In addition, receptive subsidiaries are less prominent in transnational companies than expected, while active subsidiaries are more prominent in global companies than expected. Finally, the level of control by socialisation and networks in multidomestic companies is lower than expected.

In Table 5-14, we have included the results that were partly contradictory to our expectations in bold. Again, a visual inspection shows that the empirical results conform quite closely to the theoretical assumptions. It therefore certainly seems possible to define different ideal types of multinational companies that vary systematically on many of the characteristics discussed in this thesis. A further question would then be whether firms that conform more closely to an ideal type, in particular concerning their fit between organisa-tional model and control mechanisms, outperform other firms. This question will be answered shortly. First, however, the next section will be devoted to empirically testing the performance consequences of a number of other fac-tors as discussed in Section 3 of Chapter 2.

Performance implications: county-of-origin and "economic" factors

In the next section, we will discuss the performance implications concerning organisational factors. However, since previous literature has shown that both country-of-origin and several "economic" factors, i.e. factors mainly re-searched in the economic tradition, might be as important as organisational factors in explaining differences in performance between companies, we will pay some attention to a number of these factors in this section. In the first subsection, we will test a number of bivariate hypotheses concerning five factors: country of origin, size, diversification, extent of multinationality and industry. A second subsection summarises these findings and uses multiple regression analysis to assess which of the factors discussed is most important in explaining differences in performance between companies.

Bivariate analyses

Country of origin Previous research revealed considerable and consistent differences in performance between MNCs headquartered in different coun-tries. Since many of the organisational factors discussed below might be dis-tributed differently between countries, it is very important to identify the country-of-origin effect on performance. As already indicated in Chapter 2, not doing so might lead to an erroneous attribution of performance differ-ences to factors that - for reasons that might be totally unrelated to perform-ance - differ across countries. All studies identified in Section 3 of Chapter 2 focused - explicitly or implicitly - on multinationals and used either ROS, ROE or ROA or a combination of these ratios to measure performance and can therefore easily be compared to our own results.

Hypothesis 2-48 predicted that MNCs from different countries would dif-fer significantly in performance, and that American MNCs would outperform both their Japanese and their European counterparts. There are indeed vast differences in performance between MNCs headquartered in different coun-tries. For all but one performance indicator, differences are significant at the 0.000 level of significance. In general, differences are larger for the single-year comparisons than for the five-year-average comparisons. This is to be expected since idiosyncratic results in one particular year are averaged out when taking a five-year average.

Table 5-15 Mean performance (measured as ROA, ROE and ROS) for different countries

HQ Country		ROA 94	ROA 90-94	ROE 94	ROE 90-94	ROS 94	ROS 90-94
Finland	Mean	7.7	1.1	12.7	-1.1	4.2	0.5
	N	3	4	5	6	5	6
France	Mean	3.2	3.4	8.2	8.8	4.1	4.7
	N	10	11	10	11	10	11
Germany	Mean	1.9	2.4	6.7	7.5	1.9	2.2
	N	7	8	7	8	8	9
Japan	Mean	0.7	1.6	1.5	4.6	0.8	1.7
	N	16	18	16	18	16	18
Netherlands	Mean	5.5	3.5	14.3	7.9	5.3	3.4
	N	4	4	4	4	4	4
Sweden	Mean	7.8	4.7	20.1	10.2	9.5	5.5
	N	7	8	7	8	7	8
Switzerland	Mean	4.7	4.1	13.5	10.6	7.4	5.9
	N	5	5	5	5	5	5
UK	Mean	10.0	8.7	22.2	23.6	8.2	7.8
	N	9	9	9	9	9	9
USA	Mean	7.1	6.1	20.1	14.4	7.1	5.3
	N	30	30	30	30	30	30
Total	Mean	5.3	4.3	13.8	10.6	5.3	4.2
	N	91	97	93	99	94	100

American MNCs are found to outperform Japanese MNCs with considerable margins on all of the six performance indicators. The difference in performance between American and European MNCs is smaller, although at a 1-tailed significance level the difference on all indicators is at least marginally significant in favour of American MNCs. Again, however, there are large differences between the different European countries. Table 5-15 summarises the mean performance levels on all six indicators for the nine countries included in our sample. Although the results should be interpreted with care, since the number of observations for some countries is quite small, interesting differences become apparent.

As already identified above, the American MNCs outperform Japanese MNCs on all indicators. For most indicators Japanese MNCs score lowest of the total sample only Finnish companies performed worse during the 1990-1993 period.[145] Even higher in performance than American MNCs, however, are British MNCs. On all six indicators, their performance is roughly twice as high as average. If we exclude British MNCs from the sample of European companies, the difference in performance between American and European

---

[145] The low performance of Finnish companies in this period reflects the very severe recession in the Finnish economy in the early nineties, due to declining trade levels with some of their main trading partners (Russia, Estonia, Latvia and Lithuania) in the unrest following the opening up of Eastern Europe.

companies becomes nearly as significant as the difference between American and Japanese companies. German companies resemble Japanese companies closest, having the lowest overall performance of all European companies (except for Finnish companies in 1990-93). Sweden, and to a lesser extent Finland, seem to have made a remarkable recovery during the last year included in our survey. In general, except for Germany and Japan and to a lesser extent France,[146] all countries seem to have recovered from the early nineties recession that struck most of countries included in our survey. The less than sparkling performance of the Japanese economy in the nineties, and the fact that the difficulties of the German economy since the reunification are far from being solved yet, is reflected in both the short- and the long-term performance of companies headquartered in these countries.

Comparing our actual figures with the studies discussed in Chapter 2 reveals that both the level of performance and the differences between countries remain quite stable.[147] The similarity for many of the countries is striking. In general, however, European firms seem to do slightly better between 1990 and 1994 than in the period covered by the earlier studies, although this might partly be a result of the inclusion of different countries. German and Japanese firms, on the other hand, fare much worse in the nineties than before (see Blaine, 1994, who covered the 1984-1990 period). In sum, we can conclude that nationality is an important determinant of differences in performance. Below, using multiple regression analysis, we will investigate whether this conclusion holds if we take the other variables into account.

Hypothesis 2-49 predicted that performance differences between countries would (partly) be due to differences in corporate tax rates. Unfortunately, we have not been able to find a reliable comparison of tax rates for all of the countries included in our survey. Also, tax systems differ considerably between countries. We therefore decided not to recalculate our data taking tax differences into account, since this would lead to a cumulation of inaccuracies. In general, we can say, however, that for most countries corporate tax rates fall in the 25-35% bracket. However, tax rates in both Japan and Germany lie around 50%. Although these tax differences could partly explain the lower performance of Japanese and German MNCs, performance differences are so large that it is unlikely that they would be nullified by taking different tax rates into account.

---

[146] Part of the lower performance of France can be explained by the rather high proportion of state-owned companies in this country in general and in our sample in particular. Earlier studies (see e.g. Haar, 1989) have found state ownership to have an important negative effect on the performance indicators used in this survey.

[147] Although not all studies cover all the countries discussed, combining the older studies with our study allows us to cover a 25-year period (1970-1994).

Size As discussed in Chapter 2, size is interpreted as a source of organisational costs or as a source of inefficiencies and was therefore expected to be
negatively related to performance *(Hypothesis 2-50)*. To facilitate comparison
with previous studies, which all used total sales and total assets as a measure
of size, Spearman correlation coefficients were calculated for both measures.
There is indeed a strong (correlation coefficients varying from -0.179 and -
0.519) and significant negative relationship between size and all six performance indicators. Especially in the last year included in our survey (1994)
larger companies performed far worse than smaller companies. Again, however, there are some differences between countries. The negative relationship
is particularly strong for American companies, but much weaker for Japanese
companies and some of the European companies. Industry-wise the relationship holds for most industries, although in the paper industry larger firms
seem to do better.

Diversification A number of previous studies found that firms that diversify
based on one particular strength (related diversification) are more profitable
than firms that employ unrelated diversification. This finding has even become popular management wisdom since the publications of Peters and Wa-
terman. However, as for some other studies regarding diversification and performance, our sample did not show any support for this contention, which was
summarised in *Hypothesis 2-51*. Although companies employing related diversification perform slightly better than firms that rely on unrelated diversification, the difference is far from significant. No major differences were found
in this relationship when investigating it for different countries and industries.

Extent of multinationality The more internationalised companies are, the better they will be able to profit from world-wide opportunities and hence the
higher their performance *(Hypothesis 2-52)*. Using a combined scale of the
various measures of multinationality as discussed in Section 2 of Chapter 3,
the level of multinationality is indeed shown to be positively related to all six
performance indicators.[148] The relationship is particularly strong for the 1990-
94 averages of ROS (Spearman's rho: 0.378, p = 0.001, 2-tailed) and ROE
(Spearman's rho: 0.363, p = 0.001, 2-tailed). Although this positive relation-

---

[148] We did find some support for Geringer et al's (1989) contention that a threshold of internationalisation might exist. Classifying our firms into five equal categories based on their level of
multinationality resulted in a continuously rising profitability from category 1 to 4 and a decline
in profitability from category 4 to 5. This result is remarkable since our measure of multinationality excluded the single-item measure used by Geringer et al. (% foreign sales) Nevertheless, as
Sullivan (1994a) indicated in a replication, extension and reinterpretation of this study, the
original study might be criticised as suffering from some conceptual, methodological and analytical anomalies. Pursuing the idea of a threshold of internationalisation further, however,
would lead us too far from the focus of our story.

ship was stronger for some countries than for others, it was present for all of them. Interestingly, the pharmaceutical industry shows a negative relationship between multinationality and performance, both for the five-year average and for 1994. This is very likely to be a small sample idiosyncrasy, however. Due to missing data, there are only six cases in this subsample.

Industry The industry in which a company operates might be an important determinant of performance. Unfortunately, most of the previous research either did not pay any attention to industry differences or if it did, did not indicate which industries were high or low performers. We therefore put forward a general hypothesis, *Hypothesis 2-53*, which predicted that there would be significant differences in performance between firms operating in different industries. This is indeed the case in our sample, performance differences between industries are large and very significant. Remarkably, differences are smaller for the last year than for the five-year average. Since overall performance was higher in 1994, a tentative explanation might be that industries differ in their vulnerability concerning economic downturns.

As could be expected, the highest performers are found in the pharmaceutical industry, an industry well known for its large (sometimes called excessive) profit margins. The overall performance of this industry is significantly higher than for each of the other industries on all six performance measures. Even if we exclude the pharmaceutical industry, however, the remaining seven industries still differ significantly in performance. Other high-performing industries are the food and beverages industry and the petroleum industry, while the five remaining industries are rather close together in performance levels.

Summary and multiple regression analysis: country-of-origin and "economic" factors

Table 5-16 summarises the results of the hypotheses tested in this section. Most hypotheses could be accepted at high levels of significance. MNCs headquartered in different countries and operating in different industries differed significantly in performance. Smaller and more internationalised firms outperformed their larger less internationalised colleagues. Only the type of diversification did not have a major impact on performance in our sample.

Since the independent variables tested in this section might be interrelated, we also performed a multiple regression analysis to assess the relative importance of each of the variables. The results of this regression analysis are shown in Table 5-17.[149] The type of diversification was not entered in this

---

[149] As in the previous sections, data were checked for violation of linear regression assumptions. No major deviations were found.

regression analysis, since it would drastically reduce the number of cases. Its omission was not considered problematic, since in the bivariate analysis this variable did not appear to have any impact on performance. As can be deduced from the model statistics, all models are highly significant and have a large explanatory power.

Table 5-16 Summary of the results of the hypotheses tested in this section with regard to country-of-origin/"economic" factors and performance; results contrary to hypotheses in bold

No.*	Performance implications: content of the hypotheses	Expected direction	Accepted 0.05 sign., 1-tailed	1-tailed sign.
48a	MNCs from different countries differ significantly in performance	Yes	Yes	***
48b	American MNCs outperform Japanese MNCs	Yes	Yes	***
48c	American MNCs outperform European MNCs**	Yes	**No**/Yes	†/**
49	Performance differences disappear when adjusted for tax differences	No test	No test	No test
50	Negative relationship between MNC size and performance ***	Yes	Yes	*
51	Related diversification more profitable than unrelated diversification	Yes	**No**	n.s.
52	Multinationality positively related to performance	Yes	Yes	**
53	MNCs from different industries differ significantly in performance	Yes	Yes	***

* All hypotheses were tested using the three average (1990-94) measures of performance. If the direction of the difference was the same for all measures, the significance level was averaged over these three measures.
** Excluding UK from the European sample leads to the acceptance of this hypothesis.
*** Two different measures for size were used. If the direction of the difference was the same for both measures, the significance level was averaged over both measures.
*** $p < 0.001$, ** $p < 0.01$, * $p < 0.05$, † $p < 0.10$, all 1-tailed

Much of the variability in the extent of multinationality between companies might be captured in the country of origin (or even the industry) variable, since this variable did not enter any of the eight regression analyses. As signalled in the bivariate analysis, the size of the company has a negative impact mainly for the 1994 performance indicators. The industry in which a firm operates and its country of origin are by far the most important explanatory factors for differences in performance, however. Confirming the bivariate analysis, operating in the pharmaceutical industry was found to have a *very* strong positive influence on profitability, while for the five-year-average performance, the food and beverages industry also had a higher than average performance. Japanese firms are consistent underperformers, while the same goes for German (and partly French) firms concerning 1994 figures. A consistently higher than average performance is found for British and to a lesser extent American firms.

Table 5-17 Linear regression models of the influence of country-of-origin and "economic" factors on performance; percentage of explained variance (adjusted R-square) between brackets

Independent variables	ROA 94	ROE 94	ROS 94	Total 1994[150]	ROA 90-94	ROE 90-94	ROS 90-94	Total 90-94
HQ country								
Finland		-.153† (1.7%)				-.250** (6.7%)	-.155* (1.4%)	
France	-.153* (2.2%)	-.315*** (7.4%)		-.222 **				
Germany	-.213** (1.9%)	-.374*** (8.1%)	-.231*** (4.8%)	-.275*** (8.2%)			-.131† (1.2%)	
Japan	-.328*** (8.9%)	-.603*** (25.6%)	-.303*** (6.6%)	-.489*** (16.5%)	-.139† (3.2%)	-161† (4.6%)	-.207** (3.6%)	-.155† (3.2%)
UK	.183* (3.6%)			.113† (0.8%)	.240** (4.4%)	.237** (2.9%)		.236** (4.2%)
USA					.172* (1.6%)	.167† (1.7%)		.151† (1.4%)
Industry								
Chemical	.151* (1.7%)							
Food and Beverages					.186* (7.4%)	.303*** (12.6%)	.130† (1.8%)	.249** (9.9%)
Paper			-.137* (1.3%)	-.159* (1.7%)				
Pharmaceutical	.487*** (36.0%)	.286*** (14.5%)	.679*** (60.2%)	.429*** (37.3%)	.633*** (49.3%)	.441*** (24.0%)	.764*** (64.1%)	.633*** (44.7%)
HQ characteristics								
Size (sales)	-.247*** (12.2%)		-.186** (1.8%)	-.249*** (3.5%)	-.158* (2.1%)			
Size (assets)								
Multinationality								
Model statistics								
R	.837	.778	.875	.870	.842	.753	.856	.813
R-square	.701	.605	.766	.758	.709	.567	.732	.662
Adjusted R-square	.665	.573	.747	.728	.680	.525	.711	.634
F-value model	19.404	18.971	41.223	25.900	24.325	13.543	35.019	23.861
Sig. of model	.000	.000	.000	.000	.000	.000	.000	.000

*** $p < 0.001$, ** $p < 0.01$, * $p < 0.05$, † $p < 0.10$, all 2-tailed.
Values for the independent variables are standardised beta coefficients.

Part of the high performance of American and British companies and part of the low performance of German and Japanese companies can be explained by

---

[150] Total performance 1994 and 1990-94 is calculated as the average of the three different indicators.

different industry distribution. American and British MNCs are much more prominent in the high-performing pharmaceutical and food industries than German and Japanese MNCs. As the regression model shows, however, even when taking the industry variable into account, country of origin explains a significant proportion of variance in performance.

Because of the very strong effect of the pharmaceutical industry, industry effects explained a larger percentage of variance than country-of-origin effects. Since the pharmaceutical industry had such a dominant influence, regression analyses were rerun excluding this industry dummy. Although the adjusted R-squares were considerably reduced by this omission, all models remained highly significant. There were no major differences concerning the inclusion of variables, except with regard to company size and the level of multinationality. When the pharmaceutical dummy is excluded, size has a significant (negative) impact for each of the five-year-average performance indicators and the total five-year-average performance indicator. In addition, the level of multinationality has a significant positive impact on both the five-year-average ROE and the total five-year-average performance indicator.

The multivariate analysis largely confirms the findings of the bivariate analyses. Industry and country-of-origin factors have the largest explanatory power concerning performance differences, but in some cases company size and the level of multinationality are important as well. In the next section, we will focus on the impact of organisational factors on performance.

Performance implications: organisational factors

In this section, we will discuss the performance implications concerning organisational factors. In the first subsection, we will test a number of bivariate hypotheses with regard to two organisational factors that were identified in Chapter 2 as possible explanatory factors of differences in the level of shared values and the application of a transnational organisational model. A second subsection investigates whether various types of external and internal fit are positively related to performance. Subsequently, the relative importance of each of the organisational factors will be tested using multiple regression analysis. A final subsection then combines organisational factors with the country-of-origin and "economic" factors discussed before.

Performance effects of shared values and transnational model
As discussed in Chapter 2, both national and international studies found a strong relationship between the strength of corporate culture and company performance. We therefore put forward the hypothesis (*Hypothesis 2-54*) that the level of shared values between headquarters and subsidiaries would be positively related to the performance of the MNC as a whole. The level of

shared values is positively related to all performance measures included in this survey. In none of the cases, however, does this relationship achieve statistical significance, although at a 1-tailed level of significance the relationship with the five-year ROS and ROA averages is marginally significant. The lack of a very strong relationship with objective performance indicators is not really surprising, since the influence of shared values on MNC financial performance will work through intermediate, so-called "soft" performance indicators such as personnel turnover, employee involvement, absenteeism and social climate.

We do find, however, a significantly positive relationship between control by socialisation and networks as a whole and almost all financial performance indicators. This positive relationship is far weaker and insignificant for bureaucratic formalised control and output control. Personal centralised control even has a negative relationship with performance. All elements of control by socialisation and networks are positively related to performance, although the relationship is especially strong for international management training. This of course begs the recurrent question about the direction of the causal relationship between training (and HRM in general) and performance (see e.g. d'Arcimoles, 1995; Hendry, Pettigrew and Sparrow, 1989; Kalleberg and Moody, 1994, Russell et al., 1985). Do companies with higher levels of training or more sophisticated HRM practices have higher performance levels or can successful companies afford to spend more on training and sophisticated HRM?

Many publications in the field of international management, either implicitly or explicitly, assume that transnational companies are best equipped for today's competitive environment. So far, the performance implications of the various organisational models have hardly been investigated. Two studies referred to in the theoretical framework (Brinkgreve, 1993 and Roth and Morrison, 1990) found transnational companies, or their equivalents, to outperform global or multidomestic companies, but in neither of the studies were results statistically significant. Using the three organisational models as a classification system (companies are *either* transnational *or* global *or* multidomestic), the same results are found for our data. Although transnational companies consistently outperform their global and multidomestic counterparts on each of the six performance indicators, significance is obtained only for 1994 ROE and (in the comparison with global companies) for 1994 ROA. In general, transnational companies have the highest and global companies the lowest performance, while multidomestic companies fall in between.

However, treating the different models as categories implies that marginal transnational companies (those that conform only partly to transnational characteristics) are assumed to be as effective as full-blown transnational companies, which is unlikely. Using the original factor scores for each company on each of the three organisational models resolves this problem, since it takes a higher or lower application of a certain model into account. In this way we measure whether the *extent* to which a company applies a transnational model (even if its dominant strategy is identified as global or multidomestic) is positively related to performance. A positive relationship is present and, for some performance indicators, this relationship is significant. As could be expected from our earlier categorical analysis, the extent of application of a global model is negatively, and for some indicators significantly so, related to performance, while the extent of application of a multidomestic model does not seem to have a major impact on performance. Overall, we can therefore say that our *Hypothesis 2-55*, which predicted transnational companies to outperform global and multidomestic companies receives some empirical support.

Hypothesis 2-56 predicted that the difference in performance between headquarters countries would be smaller for transnational and global companies then for multidomestic companies since the latter would be less subject to the homogenising effect of globalisation. Unfortunately, the division of a limited number of cases for each headquarters country over three strategies, combined with a number of missing performance indicators resulted in a large number of cell sizes between 1 and 5. Formal hypothesis testing was therefore considered inappropriate.

Performance effects of external and internal fits

Industry/model fit In Section 2 of Chapter 1, we identified ideal-type models for the different industries included in our sample. Companies in the electronics, computer, automobile and petroleum industries would preferably use a global organisational model, while a multidomestic model would be best suited for companies in the paper industry. Companies in the food and beverages industry would preferably use either a multidomestic or a transnational model, while for companies in the pharmaceutical industry a choice between a global and a transnational model would be ideal. We will now investigate whether companies that employ an organisational model that "fits" the industry outperform companies that have a misfit.

In order to quantity (mis)fit the mean factor score for the preferred model was calculated for each industry. This mean score was subtracted from the actual score for each company. Companies with positive values had a fit between industry and organisational model, while companies with negative values had a misfit. Since the extent of (mis)fit might be more important than an (arbitrary) classification as fit or misfit, the resulting original values - showing the extent of (mis)fit - were correlated with performance. These correlations are generally positive and for the five-year-average performance indicators also (marginally) significant. We can thus conclude that the extent to which a company applies an organisational model that fits its industry explains part of the variance in performance across companies.

Organisational model/control mechanisms fit When we discussed the organisational configurations, we noticed that the empirical profiles concerning control mechanisms conform reasonably well to the ideal profiles. In that section, however, we used the broad concepts: low, medium and high, to indicate the intensity of a certain control mechanism. In this section, we will try to quantify these broad concepts. As indicated by Gresov (1989) ideal profiles can be derived either theoretically or empirically. A purely theoretical profile would be to use the end-points of the scale (1 and 7) as representing low and high values and the mean of the scale (4) as medium. However, in most surveys, scores on the variables will often take other values than end-points. Also, an empirically derived profile can be considered appropriate where the theory is stated in ordinal terms (high/low). We are, for instance, not interested to know whether global companies have a high level of personal centralised control in an absolute sense, but rather whether they have a high level of personal centralised control *compared* to multidomestic and transnational companies.

Gresov (1989) and Roth, Schweiger and Morrison (1991) and Venkatraman and Prescott (1990) derive ideal profiles by computing the mean scores for high-performing firms. High performers would subsequently have to be excluded from further analysis to avoid an upward bias created by using the same set of observations to derive and test the profile. In our view, taking only the top five performers, as done by Roth, Schweiger and Morrison (1991), would result in a small sample bias. Taking more than five observations to derive the ideal profile, however, would mean that a large proportion of our sample would have to be removed from further analysis, especially if we also follow the recommendation of Gresov (1989) to remove the middle quintile and the recommendations of Venkatraman and Prescott (1990) to exclude an equal number of low performers to prevent a bias resulting from the shift in mean performance. Since the remaining sample size would be too small for reliable statistical analysis, we chose to follow another approach, inspired by Wolf (1996a), which quantifies the high/low values by using respectively the 75th and 25th quartile values and the medium value using the mean value of the sample.

A comparison of quantified ideal profiles and actual profiles for the various organisational models can be found in Figure 5-1 to Figure 5-3. The quantitative analysis confirms our findings in testing the configurations: actual profiles conform to ideal profiles rather well. Only in three out of twelve comparisons are the actual profiles significantly different from the ideal profiles: the lower than expect value of bureaucratic formalised control (t-value

2.855, p = 0.007, 2-tailed) for global companies, the lower than expected value for control by socialisation and networks for transnational companies (t-value 3.736, p = 0.012, 2-tailed) and the higher than expected value of personal centralised control for multidomestic companies (t-value 3.725, p = 0.001, 2-tailed).

Figure 5-1 Application of control mechanisms in global companies, ideal vs actual

Figure 5-2 Application of control mechanisms in transnational companies, ideal vs actual

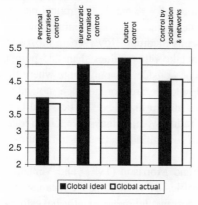

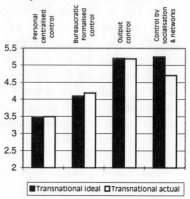

Figure 5-3 Application of control mechanisms in multidomestic companies, ideal vs actual

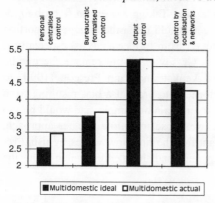

Subsequently, in order to test *Hypothesis 2-58*, which predicted that the closer the fit between the organisational model applied at headquarters and the control mechanisms applied towards subsidiaries, the higher the performance of the MNC as a whole, this fit was calculated for each combination of organisational model and control mechanism and then summarised over the four control mechanisms. For an ideal-type high intensity there is a penalty of being below the 75th quartile and a bonus for being above. For an ideal-type low intensity, there will be a penalty of being above the 25th quartile and a bonus for being below. For a medium intensity, there will be a penalty of deviating from the mean to either side. The actual (mis)fit calculations were as follows:

- Ideal profile high: Actual level of control mechanism - 75th quartile value.
- Ideal profile low: 25th quartile value - actual level of control mechanism.
- Ideal profile medium: -| Mean - actual level of control mechanism |.

In this way, a negative value denotes a deviation from the ideal profile, while a positive denotes conformity to the ideal profile. The higher the negative (positive) value, the higher the deviation (conformity).

The results of a correlation analysis between these summarised fit measures and the various performance indicators show a positive correlation for all performance measures, but never achieve significance. A separate analysis correlating the fit for each individual control mechanism with performance showed that the fit score for personal centralised control had a strong negative relationship with performance, while the fit scores for all of the other control mechanisms had a positive relationship with performance. If we subsequently exclude personal centralised control, the relationship between fit and performance is significant for all but one of the six performance indicators. The negative relationship between personal centralised control fit and performance is especially strong for transnational and global companies that "require" a medium or high level of personal centralised control. This then confirms our observation above that a high level of personal centralised control is negatively related to performance. Ideal profiles for personal centralised control in a performance context would have to be adjusted downwards.

As already indicated in the theoretical framework, another way to interpret the ideal profiles is to see them as minimum profiles. Conceptually, this would mean that for each type of organisational model there is a minimum level of control for each of the four control mechanisms. In general, the level of necessary control would thus be lower for multidomestic companies than for global and transnational companies, but an intensity lower than the threshold level would result in a penalty with regard to performance. The idea of fit as a minimum profile gets some support since all correlation coefficients are positive and higher than for the "regular" fit analysis. In addition, correlations only become significant when excluding personal centralised control from the analysis.

In sum, we can conclude that, although there is considerable support for the applicability of ideal control profiles for different organisational models, adherence to these ideal profiles does not seem to have major performance effects. In particular, a high use of personal centralised control seems to have a negative impact on performance, so that ideal profiles, whether as "regular" or as minimum fit, would perhaps have to be adjusted downwards for this particular control mechanism.

Subsidiary strategy/control mechanisms fit Just as at headquarters level, at subsidiary level a positive performance effect would be expected of a fit between subsidiary strategy or role (active, receptive or autonomous) and the type of control mechanisms that headquarters exerts over this subsidiary. Since overall MNC performance would be an aggregation of the performance of the different subsidiary-units, a fit at subsidiary level should have a positive impact on the performance of the MNC as a whole (*Hypothesis 2-59*). As indicated in Section 3 of Chapter 2, the ideal control profile concerning organisational models is hypothesised to apply for the "most characteristic" subsidiary role of a given organisational model as well. This means that active subsidiaries would have the same ideal profile as transnational companies, receptive subsidiaries would resemble global companies and autonomous subsidiaries would be most like multidomestic companies.

The calculation of the fit between subsidiary role and control mechanisms was performed in the same way as above. Means and quartile values were calculated for the sample, deviation/conformity levels were calculated for each subsidiary role/control mechanism combination using the same formulas as above, and were subsequently summarised over the four control mechanisms. Since performance is measured at headquarters level, in cases where more than one subsidiary of a given headquarters was included in the sample, the fit scores were then consolidated to this level. As could be expected given the results above and the fact that subsidiary fit would have a more indirect effect on MNC performance than headquarters fit, the resulting correlation coefficients are generally very low and insignificant. Excluding personal centralised control as above, does not improve this lack of results.

Again, however, the profiles might be interpreted as minimum profiles, which would mean that receptive and active subsidiaries would require a higher minimum level of control to be effective than autonomous subsidiaries. There is some support for this interpretation, especially when personal centralised control is excluded. Having a control intensity below the threshold level for a given subsidiary would thus negatively impact performance.

The shared values alternative A final hypothesis we would like to test combines the aspect of fit (at subsidiary level) with the importance of shared values as discussed in the previous section. Following Nohria and Ghoshal (1994), we predicted that companies that combine a high level of shared values with a high level of fit at subsidiary level would outperform other companies (*Hypothesis 2-60*). In order to test this hypothesis companies were divided into four different groups based on the dichotomies of high/low fit and high/low shared values. The cut-off point for the categories was the mean value of fit and shared values respectively. This of course introduces the problems discussed in Chapter 2 relating to categorisation (arbitrary cut-off points, marginal members as important as "full" members), but it allows us to test Nohria and Ghoshal's results with a different sample and a slightly different operationalisation of variables.

Table 5-18 The relationship between subsidiary level fit/shared values and performance

		ROA 90-94	ROE 90-94	ROS 90-94	Overall 90-94	ROA 94	ROE 94	ROS 94	Overall 94
High SV, high fit	Mean	5.22	11.58	5.27	22.06	6.73	16.65	7.42	30.80
	N	28	8	28	28	25	25	5	25
High SV, low fit	Mean	4.57	12.04	4.73	21.34	4.65	13.40	5.46	23.52
	N	24	24	24	24	24	24	24	24
Low SV, High fit	Mean	3.82	10.57	3.42	18.87	4.32	13.35	4.00	22.16
	N	23	24	25	23	21	22	23	21
Low SV, low fit	Mean	3.59	7.85	3.28	14.70	5.56	11.86	4.36	12.93
	N	21	22	22	21	20	21	21	20
Total	Mean	4.36	10.61	4.23	19.51	5.35	13.92	5.38	24.87
	N	96	98	99	96	90	92	93	90

As Table 5-18 shows, the results largely confirm our hypothesis (equal to Nohria and Ghoshal's simultaneity hypothesis). Applying a high level of both shared values and fit has a positive relation on performance. In all but one of the eight comparisons, performance is highest in the high shared values, high-fit category. The exception (ROE 90-94) shows the highest performance for the high shared values, low-fit group and a marginally lower performance for the high shared values, low-fit group. In all but two (ROA 94 and ROS 94) of the eight cases performance is lowest in the low/low category. Since the high shared values, low-fit category performs consistently higher than the low shared values, high-fit category, we cannot confirm Nohria and Ghoshal's equifinality hypothesis. As will be confirmed below in the multiple regression analysis, the level of shared values has a larger explanatory power than the level of fit.

Unfortunately, although the differences in performance are largely in the expected direction, none of the pair-wise comparisons achieves a 0.05 level of significance. However, for the only performance indicator that is used in both our and Nohria and Ghoshal's study (ROA), their results are very weak as well. In fact, the relative difference in performance in their study is even smaller than in our study. The two performance indicators that *do* provide significant results in Nohria and Ghoshal's study are both growth indicators (ROA growth and sales growth). For reasons extensively explained in Section 3 of Chapter 2, we did not use growth indicators in our study.

Summary and linear regression analysis: Organisational factors

Table 5-19 summarises the results of the hypotheses tested in this section concerning the influence of organisational factors on performance. Although all differences or correlations predicted in the various hypotheses were in the expected direction, only few achieved significance. There is a modest indication that the level of shared values, and more generally the level of control by socialisation and networks, is positively related to performance.

Table 5-19 Summary of the results of the hypotheses tested in this section with regard to organisational factors and performance; results contrary to hypotheses in bold

No.*	Performance implications: organisational factors: content of the hypotheses	Expected direction	Accepted 0.05 sign., 1-tailed	1-tailed sign.
54	The level of shared values is positively related to performance	Yes	**No**	†
55a	Transnational companies will outperform multi-domestic companies	Yes	**No**	n.s.
55b	Transnational companies will outperform global companies	Yes	**No**/Yes**	n.s./*
56	Performance differences between countries smaller for transnational and global firms than for multidomestic firms	No test	No test	No test
57	MNCs that employ organisational models that fit the industry orientation outperform MNCs with a misfit in this respect	Yes	Yes	*
58	Positive relationship between extent of organisational model/control mechanisms fit and performance	Yes	**No**	n.s.
59	Positive relationship between extent of subsidiary strategy/control mechanisms fit and performance	Yes	**No**	n.s.
60	Positive relationship between a combination of high shared values and subsidiary level fit and performance.	Yes	**No**	n.s.

* All hypotheses were tested using only the three average (90-94) measures of performance. If the direction of the difference was the same for all measures, the significance level was averaged over these three measures.

** When interpreted as the extent to which a transnational/global model is used.

*** $p < 0.001$, ** $p < 0.01$, * $p < 0.05$, † $p < 0.10$, all 1-tailed

The differences in performance between transnational companies on the one hand and multidomestic and global companies on the other hand were not significant when organisational models were defined in a categorical way. If we interpret the hypothesis as the *extent* to which companies apply a certain organisational model, there is a marginally significant (p = 0.0523, 1-tailed) positive correlation between long-term performance (five-year averages) and the application of a transnational model and a marginally significant (p = 0.0515, 1-tailed) negative correlation for the global model. Of the hypotheses concerning fit, only the one concerning external fit could be accepted. Although in all other cases results were in the expected direction, correlations were too weak to be significant.

Table 5-20 Linear regression models of the influence of organisational factors on performance; percentage of explained variance (adjusted R-square) between brackets

Independent variables	ROA 94	ROE 94	ROS 94	Total 1994	ROA 90-94	ROE 90-94	ROS 90-94	Total 90-94
Control mechanisms								
Shared values					.329*** (4.4%)	.272** (5.9%)	.282** (3.2%)	.306** (3.8%)
Organisation models								
Global	-.214† (3.3%)				-.395*** (6.2%)	-.333*** (4.2%)	-.334*** (3.0%)	-.371*** (3.9%)
Multidomestic								
Transnational		.290** (7.3%)		.252* (5.2%)				
Fit measures								
Industry/model fit					.284** (5.9%)	.357*** (4.7%)	.282** (5.6%)	.342*** (9.0%)
Model/control fit								
Subsidiary strategy/-control fit								
Model statistics								
R	.214	.290	--	.252	.441	.422	.385	.444
R-square	.046	.084	--	.064	.195	.178	.148	.197
Adjusted R-square	.033	.073	--	.052	.165	.148	.118	.167
F-value model	3.730	7.267	--	5.303	6.602	5.997	4.865	6.696
Sig. of model	.057	.009	n.s.	.024	.000	.001	.004	.000

*** p < 0.001, ** p < 0.01, * p < 0.05, † p < 0.10, all 2-tailed.
Values for the independent variables are standardised beta coefficients.

A multiple regression analysis confirmed the results of the bivariate analyses. Only the variables shared values, organisational model and the industry/-model fit entered the regression analysis. Table 5-20 summarises the results of these regression models. Although the percentage of explained variance is modest in most cases, both the models and the beta coefficients of the included variables for the five-year-average performance indicators are highly significant.

Country-of-origin, "economic" and "organisational" factors combined
We have discussed the influence of country-of-origin and "economic" factors on performance, while in this section we focused on organisational factors. We will now combine all factors to see whether they have an independent impact on performance. Table 5-21 reports the results of the multiple analyses including country-of-origin, "economic" and "organisational" factors.

As becomes immediately apparent, these regression models resemble very closely the "economic" models presented earlier. Neither shared values, nor any of three fit measures enters the regression analysis. Only one of the organisational factors, the organisational model applied, seems to have additional explanatory power when non-organisational factors are included. Much of the variability in, for instance, the level of shared values is related to industry (higher in the pharmaceutical industry) or country (higher in American MNCs). In order to truly disentangle organisational effects from country/industry effects, we should run separate regression analyses for each different country/industry. Unfortunately, this is not feasible since the resulting sample sizes are too small for regression analysis.

Since the pharmaceutical industry has such a dominant influence, we reran regression analyses excluding this industry dummy. Although the adjusted R-squares were considerably reduced by this omission, all models remained highly significant. The result of this exclusion is that some of the other factors become (more) significant. The negative influence of the application of a global organisational model becomes stronger and more significant in most of the regression models, while the level of shared values becomes significant in two out of three five-year-average models (ROA 90-94 and ROS 90-94). Furthermore, the negative influence of size now becomes significant in six of the eight models. There is no effect, however, on the importance of any of the fit measures.

Table 5-21 Linear regression models of the influence of both country-of-origin/"economic" and "organisational" factors on performance, percentage of explained variance (adjusted R-square) between brackets

Independent variables	ROA 94	ROE 94	ROS 94	Total 94	ROA 90-94	ROE 90-94	ROS 90-94	Total 90-94
HQ country								
Finland	.176* (2.4%)							
France		-.262** (5.9%)	-.138† (1.3%)	-.195* (2.7%)				
Germany		-.401*** (14.6%)	-.162* (2.8%)	-.300*** (10.4%)				
Japan		-.598*** (26.8%)	-.297*** (8.2%)	-.456*** (16.7%)			-.183* (2.8%)	
Sweden	.237** (2.7%)		.131† (1.4%)			.211* (3.3%)		.213* (3.7%)
UK	.373*** (9.8%)			.130† (1.1%)	.323*** (9.1%)	.360*** (6.1%)		.331*** (5.3%)
USA	.408*** (7.8%)				.267** (5.0%)	.277** (4.0%)		.235** (2.6%)
Industry								
Chemical	.304*** (6.8%)		.188* (1.7%)	.176* (1.8%)				
Food and Beverages						.304** (13.7%)		.252** (9.6%)
Pharmaceutical	.377*** (17.5%)	.267** (8.6%)	.547*** (36.9%)	.472*** (35.1%)	.548*** (42.3%)	.401*** (18.8%)	.750*** (63%)	.590*** (39.8%)
HQ characteristics								
Size (assets)					-.209** (3.7%)			
Extent of multinationality								
Control mechanisms	--	--	--	--	--	--	--	--
Organisation models								
Global	-.194* (1.7%)		-.159* (1.3%)	-.208** (2.7%)	-.239** (6.6%)		-.194* (3.0%)	
Multidomestic								
Transnational								
Fit measures	--	--	--	--	--	--	--	--
Model statistics								
R	.728	.768	.758	.861	.834	.713	.840	.803
R-square	.530	.591	.574	.742	.696	.508	.705	.645
Adjusted R-square	.487	.559	.536	.705	.667	.459	.688	.610
F-value model	12.395	18.750	14.852	20.102	23.387	10.521	42.254	18.525
Sig. of model	.000	.000	.000	.000	.000	.000	.000	.000

*** $p < 0.001$, ** $p < 0.01$, * $p < 0.05$, † $p < 0.10$, all 2-tailed.

Values for the independent variables are standardised beta coefficients.

The dominant influence of country of origin and industry on performance is rather disappointing, since this still leaves open the question of why companies headquartered in certain countries and operating in certain industries are more profitable than others. Concerning the country of origin several explanatory factors can be suggested. First, difference in corporate *tax rates* between countries can have a direct and indirect effect on the performance measures included in this study. Although we have not been able to find reliable figures comparing corporate tax rates between all of the countries included in our survey, in general we can say that corporate tax rates in Japan and Germany are higher than in all of the other countries. The direct effect of higher tax rates will be that the numerator of the ratios used to calculate financial performance in most studies, profit after tax, will be lower in both Japan and Germany, thus leading to lower return (net profit) on sales, assets and equity. The indirect effect of higher tax rates is that companies will want to minimise their actual *profits* and make extensive use of reserve funds.

These reserve funds bring us to a second explanatory factor: differences in *accounting practices*. Unlike the United States and the UK, there is a widespread use of both general and special reserve funds in both Germany and Japan (Blaine, 1994). In addition to legal reserves equalling 10% (Germany) to 25% (Japan) of company's capital stock, firms in these countries are allowed to create reserves for issues as diverse as R&D development, dividend equalisation, overseas market development or reserves to cover for requirements of certain social or economic legislation (Blaine, 1994). The result is that, although there might be returns, they will partly take the form of reserves rather than profits. In addition to differences in the use of reserves, Blaine (1994) gives an overview of 16 other differences in accounting practices, of which the net effect on profitability is negative for both Japanese and German firms and positive for American firms.

In addition to differences in tax rates and accounting practices, difference in *capital structure* and the *importance of stock markets* may also contribute to the explanation of differences in performance between countries. British and American companies raise their funds mainly by selling stock (are equity-based), while German and Japanese companies are mainly credit-based (Prowse, 1994). In 1985, stock market capitalisation as a percentage of GNP amounted to 81% in Britain compared with a mere 14% in Germany, while the USA and Japan fell in between with 48% and 37% respectively (Prowse, 1994:30, table 6). Since interest payments on debts are deducted before - and dividend payments after - net income has been calculated, companies that have a high debt/equity ratio will show lower levels of net income and hence lower ROS, ROA and ROE.

More importantly, however, these different capital structures are also reflected in *different philosophies* about the management of companies. While

Anglo-Saxon companies are mainly managed in the interest of shareholders and focus on the maximisation of short-term profits, German and Japanese companies are more concerned about long-term viability and stability. In German and Japanese companies and also in many other European companies, the interest of stakeholders other than shareholders (e.g. employees, unions, community, government) is given serious consideration and companies are seen more as social institutions than as profit-generating machines. This phenomenon is reinforced by the fact that in the Anglo-Saxon countries, around 80% or more of the shares are held for trading purposes, while in Germany and Japan the overwhelming majority of shares are held for control purposes (Prowse, 1994:24, table 3). Obviously, investors holding shares for trading purposes are more likely to focus on short-term returns than on long-term stability. As Lane (1995:50) indicates, in British companies "every major financial decision has to be taken with an eye on the movement of the stock market". The result is that in the USA and the UK a quick return on investments is an absolute necessity to keep the confidence of shareholders. Although this might lead in an underinvestment in training, R&D and other activities leading to long-term benefits only, the overall effect on the traditional performance measures is positive.

Tax differences, differences in accounting practices, differences in the importance of the stock market and in the reasons for which shares are held thus all lead to a higher measured *financial* performance for American and British companies and a lower performance for German and Japanese companies, without necessarily reflecting a higher/lower *business* performance. Further, although it is difficult to separate this from the previous issues, we would say that, in general, the national culture in the UK and especially in the USA is more oriented towards financial achievements than in many other countries, including Japan and Germany.

The reasons for differences in performance between industries fall somewhat outside the scope of this book, and the author's area of knowledge. However, issues such as a (protected) monopoly positions and the high use of knowledge-intensive labour might lead to less competition in general and less competition from low-wage countries in particular for the pharmaceutical industry. Hence prices can be (far) above production costs and profits will therefore be higher. With regard to the other high-performing industry, the food industry, production is also unlikely to take place far away from the major markets, because of the non-durability of some of the products, and the fact that transportation costs would weigh rather heavily on these products, which are relatively inexpensive per unit. Again, competition from low-wage countries is therefore not as likely as in the computer, automobile and electronics industries. In addition, for many branded packaged goods their value is more in their image than in the actual product, thus leading to the possibility of demanding premium prices. Although of course premium prices are also customary for some segments in the automobile (e.g. Rolls Royce, Jaguar), computer (IBM) and electronics (B&O) industries, in the mass markets for these products the focus is much more on price competition.

In addition to the unique effects of country of origin and industry, there might be an interaction effect between these two independent variables. In his book *The Competitive Advantage of Nations*, Porter (1990) offers an intricate analysis of why countries have a competitive advantage in certain industries and not in others.[151] Brown, Soybel and Stickney (1994) show that for the eleven industries they investigated, American firms outperformed Japanese firms in five industries (automobile, chemical, food processing, metals, and pharmaceuticals), while the reverse was true for three industries (electronics, instruments and machinery). Multiple-industry samples might therefore be biased in the sense that industries in which one particular country has a competitive advantage (and hence a higher performance) are over-represented.

These large differences in performance between countries and industries lead to considerable problems in explaining performance by certain characteristics when country and industry are not explicitly included in the statistical analysis. An extreme example was already reported in Chapter 2 (Peterson et al., 1996), where certain "best-practice" IHRM practices were statistically "proven" to be strongly negatively related to performance, without the proviso that this would most probably be a country-of-origin effect (Japanese and European companies score lower on the traditional financial performance indicators and have a higher application of best practices in expatriate management such as language training). In addition, comparisons on performance implications between studies with different industry/country distributions should be made with extreme care only.

Conclusion

This last section of Chapter 5 further explored the interaction between variables included in our survey. To do so, the empirical validity of the three organisational configurations that were derived theoretically in Chapter 2 was tested. Overall, we could conclude that the theoretically derived MNC configurations performed quite well. Of the 25 comparisons that were made, only one was contrary to the hypothesised differences, while four other comparisons conformed only partly to our expectations. Subsequently, the implica-

---

[151] Our sample is too small to perform separate industry analyses in order to investigate whether particular countries outperform others in certain industries. Overall, however, Manova analysis shows the interaction effect between country of origin and industry to be significant at the 0.05 level for the five-year-average ROA and at the 0.01 level for the five-year-average ROS.

tions of country-of-origin, "economic" and "organisational" factors on performance were explored. The country of origin, the industry, and the size and level of multinationality of the company were shown to explain a large proportion of variation in performance between companies. Although the influence of the organisational factors: shared values, type of organisational model and external and internal fit was in the expected direction, their explanatory power was much lower than for the other factors. A combined regression analysis showed that of the organisational factors only the type of organisational model was significantly related to performance.

Chapter 5 is the last of the two empirical chapters. In the next and final chapter, we will summarise and discuss our findings relating to the three main research questions, signal the limitations of our research and suggest possibilities for further research. We will also include a brief note on the managerial implications of our study.

6. Conclusion, discussion, limitations and implications

In this final chapter, we will first summarise our study's main findings concerning the three major research questions. A subsequent discussion will place these results in a broader context. Further, the study's limitations will be identified and we will offer some suggestions for further research. Finally, we will briefly indicate the study's managerial implications.

1. SUMMARY OF THE MAIN FINDINGS

Headquarters/subsidiary characteristics and the control portfolio

Research question 1: Which characteristics of both headquarters and subsidiaries of MNCs can explain differences in the composition of the portfolio of control mechanisms that is used by headquarters in respect of its subsidiaries?

At *headquarters* level, six characteristics were discussed: the country of origin of headquarters, the industry in which the MNC operates, the organisational model applied, the size of the MNC and its level of multinationality and heterogeneity. Country of origin has a high explanatory power concerning the type of control mechanisms used. Direct personal control mechanisms (personal centralised control) are used to a larger extent in respect of subsidiaries of British and German MNCs, while their application is rather low for subsidiaries of Swiss and Swedish MNCs. Indirect personal control mechanisms (control by socialisation and networks) are most prominent in respect of subsidiaries of Swiss and Swedish MNCs and least prominent for subsidiaries of both French and Japanese MNCs. Both direct and indirect impersonal control mechanisms (bureaucratic formalised control and output control) are used to a high extent in respect of subsidiaries of Anglo-Saxon and German MNCs and to a relatively low extent for subsidiaries of Japanese and Finnish MNCs. Concerning industry, the most remarkable finding was that subsidiaries in the chemical industry are very strongly controlled, especially with the use of direct control mechanisms.

Contrary to our expectations, the level of both multinationality and hetero-geneity does not seem to have a significant relationship with the type of control mechanisms used in respect of subsidiaries. The type of organisational model applied, however, has a large explanatory power for all control mechanisms except for output control and, related, indirect control. Subsidiaries of multidomestic companies experience a lower level of total control. This is mainly due to a lower level of the two direct control mechanisms: personal centralised control and bureaucratic formalised control. Concerning MNC size, we found that, as anticipated, the larger the MNC, the higher the level of both output control and control by socialisation and networks.

At *subsidiary* level, we investigated seven different characteristics: subsidiary size, subsidiary age, the level and type of interdependence, the level of local responsiveness, the subsidiary's role and function, the uncertainty of the subsidiary's environment and the extent of cultural distance between head-quarters and subsidiary. Bivariate analyses showed that the influence of virtually all characteristics was in the expected direction. A multivariate analysis, used to ascertain which of the characteristics had the highest explanatory power, showed first of all that the specific role and/or function of subsidiaries explains a large amount of the variance in the type and level of control used in respect of them. Autonomous subsidiaries experience a significantly lower level of control than subsidiaries with either active or receptive roles. This result is mainly due to a lower level of intensity for the two direct control mechanisms: personal centralised control and bureaucratic formalised control. The subsidiary function also seems to have a considerable influence on the level and type of control that is exercised by headquarters over these subsidiaries. Sales subsidiaries experience lower total levels of control, mainly because the level of personal centralised control is much less pronounced for these subsidiaries. R&D subsidiaries experience a significantly lower level of bureaucratic formalised control.

Subsidiary age and the level of interdependence and local responsiveness did not have a high explanatory power once other characteristics were included in the analysis. Subsidiary-dependent subsidiaries, however, experienced a significantly higher level of indirect control than headquarters-dependent subsidiaries. As with the size of the MNC as a whole, the size of the subsidiary had a considerable (positive) impact on the total level of control exercised in respect of this subsidiary. Conforming to the results at head-quarters level, the level of indirect control, in particular, is strongly positively related to the size of the subsidiary.

Turning to the environmental variables, the multivariate analysis produced a (marginally) significant result for the expected positive relationship between environmental uncertainty and control by socialisation and networks. With regard to cultural distance, a significant negative relationship was found with the two impersonal types of control (bureaucratic formalised control and output control). Apparently, cultural distance leads MNCs to prefer a personal control mechanism (in particular by means of expatriates, as shown below) over the more impersonal control mechanisms.

The role of international transfers as a control mechanism

Research question 2: What role do international transfers play in controlling MNC subsidiaries? Are there alternative ways to achieve a high level of informal control in MNC subsidiaries?

Our second research question brought the aspect of international transfers into the picture, and investigated the role of expatriates in controlling subsidiaries. We have seen that expatriates can form both a direct and an indirect means of control. In exercising the direct type of control, expatriates directly supervise decisions taken at headquarters. This role is particularly strong in Far Eastern or Latin American subsidiaries of Japanese and German MNCs operating in the automobile or electronics industries. It is much less important in subsidiaries of American, French and British MNCs located in Scandinavian or Anglo-Saxon countries and operating in the food or paper industry.[152]

Previous studies on expatriate management have often claimed that expatriates also play a role in realising an informal type of control. So far, however, none has provided an adequate empirical test of this relationship. Our study has provided such a test, and shown that there is indeed a positive relationship between the level of expatriate presence and the level of both shared values between headquarters and subsidiary managers, and informal communication between them. Including expatriate presence significantly improved the regression models that were constructed to explain the variance in the level of shared values and informal communication across subsidiaries. In addition, the level of output control exercised in respect of a particular subsidiary could also be partly explained by the level of expatriate presence. The higher the percentage of expatriates in the workforce of a subsidiary, the lower the levels of output control used in respect of this subsidiary. Output control and expatriate control appear to be seen as alternative ways to control subsidiaries.

Two alternatives to international transfers were identified, however, that were also able to facilitate an informal type of control: international management training and formal networks. Participation of subsidiary managers in international management training and formal networks was positively related

---

[152] All these factors have an independent effect on the type of expatriate control. Therefore the strongest effect is found when all three factors (country of location of subsidiary, country of origin of headquarters and industry) work in the same direction.

to the level of both shared values between headquarters and subsidiaries, and informal communication between them. Linear regression analysis showed that the strongest explanatory factor of a high level of shared values between headquarters and subsidiaries was participation of subsidiary managers in international management training, while the level of expatriate presence and the participation of subsidiary managers in formal networks ranked second and third. All three, however, were significantly positively related to the level of shared values, so that companies using all three mechanisms to a large extent had the highest level of shared values. Concerning informal communication, the order was exactly reversed participation in formal networks had the highest explanatory power, while participation in management training had the lowest. The level of expatriate presence again took second place. Once more, all three mechanisms had an independent and significant impact on the level of informal communication, so that this was highest in companies using all three mechanisms to a large extent.

In addition, our study also provided information on the various factors that influenced the level of expatriate presence in subsidiaries. Expatriate presence was shown to vary considerably across countries and industries in a way that partly confirmed, but also supplemented, results from earlier studies. Further, expatriate presence was shown to be positively related to the level of cultural distance between headquarters and subsidiary, and subsidiary size. A negative relationship was found between both subsidiary age and expatriate presence, and between performance and expatriate presence. In addition, expatriate presence was lower in acquisitions than in greenfields, and lower in sales/service subsidiaries than in subsidiaries with a strategic function. These results considerably extend our knowledge about the factors influencing MNC staffing policies.

Configurations and performance implications

Research question 3a: Can we distinguish (both theoretically and empirically) MNC configurations that summarise the various MNC characteristics included in our study?

In answer to this research question, three configurations of MNCs were theoretically derived in Section 3 of Chapter 2. These configurations were partly based on previous research and partly on our own deductions, and comprised most of the variables included our study. An empirical test of these configurations showed that, although some of the specific differences in characteristics could not be fully confirmed, overall the firms in our sample could be described as approaching one of the following three ideal types of configurations:

Global companies operate in industries with fairly standardised consumer needs, making the realisation of economies of scale very important. They are therefore usually rather large in terms of their number of employees. Although they operate in a relatively large number of different areas, *within* each of their activities the level of diversity is quite low. Many industries have turned global during the last decades, but the consumer electronics, computer and automobile industries remain prime examples. Since price competition is very important, the dominant strategic requirement is efficiency, and these companies therefore integrate and rationalise their production to produce standardised products in a very cost-efficient manner. The result is that their subsidiaries are relatively large. Subsidiaries in global companies are usually very dependent on headquarters for their sales and purchases, and are not supposed to respond actively to the local market demands in terms of, for instance, product adaptation. Their role is receptive rather than active or autonomous, and they are typically greenfields rather than acquisitions. The total level of control exercised by headquarters over these subsidiaries is quite high. This is mainly caused by a high level of the two direct control mechanisms: personal centralised control and bureaucratic formalised control. The indirect control mechanisms, output control and control by socialisation and networks, are not used to a higher than average extent. Expatriate presence in subsidiaries of this type of companies is high, and the main role of these expatriates is to exercise direct control through the supervision of decisions taken at headquarters. The global configuration is most typical of German and Japanese MNCs.

Multidomestic companies are the complete opposite of global companies. Products or services are differentiated to meet differing local demands, and policies are differentiated to conform to differing governmental and market demands. Local demand is strongly influenced by cultural, social and political differences between countries. The food and beverages industry is a classical example of a multidomestic type of industry. Since economies of scale are unimportant in these types of companies, both the company as a whole and the different subsidiaries are rather small in terms of employees. Subsidiaries operate relatively independently from headquarters, in the sense that they buy/sell a very low proportion of their input/output from headquarters. They are responsive to the local market, and adapt both products and marketing to local circumstances. This is made easier by the fact that products are often produced locally. The role of subsidiaries can therefore be characterised as autonomous. A relatively large number of these subsidiaries are acquisitions, and partly because of that, subsidiaries in multidomestic companies are usually older than in other companies. Not surprisingly, the total level of control exercised by headquarters in respect of these subsidiaries is rather low. In particular, the two direct control mechanisms, personal centralised control and bureaucratic formalised control, are used to a very low extent, while the use of output control and control by socialisation and networks lies around average. Expatriate presence is also rather low. If expatriates are present, they are more likely to exercise an indirect than a direct type of control. The multidomestic configuration is most typical of French and British and to a lesser extent Finnish and Swedish MNCs.

In a sense, a *transnational* company combines characteristics of both global and multidomestic companies, in that it tries to respond simultaneously to the sometimes conflicting strategic needs of global efficiency and national responsiveness. In addition, the transfer of knowledge is very important for these companies. Expertise is spread throughout the organisation, and subsidiaries can serve as a strategic centre for a particular product-market combination. Although we cannot yet identify "typical" transnational industries, the pharmaceutical industry comes close, and many MNCs in the food industry are moving towards a more transnational type of company. In terms of size, transnational firms and their subsidiaries can also be located between global and multidomestic companies. Subsidiaries in this type of company are more dependent on *other* subsidiaries for their inputs and outputs than on headquarters, which confirms the network type of organisational structure that is said to be typical for transnational companies. Subsidiaries are usually also very responsive to the local market, and many of them play an autonomous role. The level of active subsidiaries, that is subsidiaries that are both highly integrated and responsive to the local market, is highest in these types of firms. Although the level of control exercised in respect of subsidiaries in transnational companies is nearly as high as for global companies, this is mainly due to a high level of control by socialisation and networks. Relatedly, although expatriate presence in subsidiaries is also rather high, the main role of expatriates in this type of companies is to facilitate an informal and indirect, rather than a direct, type of control. The transnational configuration is most typical of American, Dutch and Swiss MNCs.[153]

Research question 3b: Which of the MNC characteristics included in this study can be used to explain differences in performance between MNCs?

This last research question investigated the importance of various MNC characteristics in explaining performance differences between MNCs. Contrary to our predictions, no significant relationship was found between diversification strategy and performance. As expected, smaller and highly internationalised companies outperformed their larger and less internationalised colleagues.

---

[153] See Harzing (1998b) for a more detailed analysis of these configurations and Harzing (1998d) for a more detailed analysis of the difference between acquisitions and greenfields.

The highest explanatory power, however, could be attributed to the country of origin of headquarters and the industry in which the MNC operated. American and British companies consistently outperformed Japanese and German companies, while the performance of companies in the pharmaceutical industry was unmatched by that of companies in any of the other industries. We suggested, however, that differences in *financial* performance between countries could be mainly due to differences in tax rates, accounting practices, capital structure and the importance of the stock markets, without necessarily reflecting differences in actual *business* performance.

The influence of the organisational factors: shared values, type of organisational model, external and internal fit was in the expected direction. The higher the level of shared values, and the higher the level of external and internal fit, the higher the performance. Further, transnational companies were shown to outperform global companies. The explanatory power of these factors, however, was much lower than for the country of origin, the industry and MNC size. When all factors where combined in a single regression analysis, only one of the organisational factors - the type of organisational model - was significantly related to performance. Companies with a global organisational model performed worse than both multidomestic and transnational companies.

2. DISCUSSION AND SUGGESTIONS FOR FURTHER RESEARCH

The visual model in Figure 6-1 gives a simplified overview of the relationships tested in this book, and will serve as the basis for our discussion, which will place a number of remarkable findings in a somewhat broader context. Issues related to headquarters and subsidiary characteristics will be discussed first. Concerning headquarters characteristics, we will highlight the importance of the country-of-origin effect, and discuss our contribution towards testing empirically the Bartlett and Ghoshal typology of multinational companies. A number of headquarters and subsidiary characteristics in our survey were clearly linked to "traditional" organisation theory. The implications of our findings in this respect, for both organisation theory and international management, will be discussed. In relation to subsidiary characteristics, we will indicate the importance of subsidiary roles in explaining differences in the control portfolio. Subsequently, we will focus on the role of expatriation, and discuss why a strategic view of this field is necessary. The usefulness of configuration analysis in international management and the uselessness of a comparison of financial performance across countries will be discussed next. Finally, the myth of a European monolith will be repudiated.

Figure 6-1 Simplified overview of the relationships described and tested in this thesis

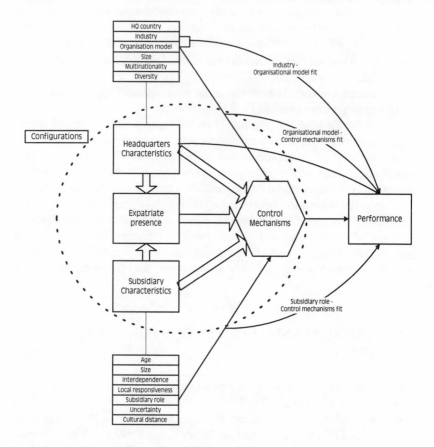

HQ characteristics: the country-of-origin effect

For most issues discussed in this book, the country of origin was shown to be very important. Even when considering other variables, as was done with the help of linear and logistic regression analysis, the country of origin had a high explanatory power. If we look at the main subject of this thesis: control port-folios, we find strong differences between MNCs headquartered in different countries in the application of the various control mechanisms. In addition, some of the relationships between headquarters and/or subsidiary charac-teristics and control mechanisms differ between countries. The direction of the relationship between MNC size and both personal centralised control and bureaucratic formalised control, for instance, differs between countries.

We did not really anticipate this dominant country-of-origin effect. Multinational companies would be expected to be the first to be influenced by the globalisation and organisational effects as identified by Mueller (1994). The world-wide diffusion of technologies, knowledge and information, and the convergence between national monetary and fiscal policies - issues usually subsumed under the globalisation effect - would be expected to lead to a declining importance of national differences. In addition, the organisational effect, in the form of the diffusion of best practices and corporate culture, would lead to a mitigation of the country-of-origin effect. As our study shows, the country-of-origin effect has anything but lost its significance. On second thoughts, this is perhaps less surprising if we consider the subject of this thesis. Referring to Child (1981), as we did in Chapter 3, the effect of culture/society will be particularly strong in micro-level organisation processes, relating to authority, style, conduct, participation and attitudes. Control mechanisms would be a good example of a micro-level organisation process.

The overall conclusion we can draw from these observations is that in studies about control mechanisms (and many other micro-level subjects) in MNCs, the country of origin of the MNC should be given due emphasis in the research design. It does not seem very useful to select a large enough number of countries to randomise the variance on non-matched cultural/societal variables, as suggested by Brislin et al. (1973). Rather, researchers should be recommended to focus on a comparison across a well-motivated selection of a *limited* number of countries, to make sure that sample sizes per country are large enough to separate the country-of-origin effect from the other effects under investigation. Since there is some indication that contingency relationships are societally/culturally determined as well, it also does not seem very useful to investigate contingency relationships across a large number of different countries without anticipating the possibility of a country-by-country analysis in advance. In selecting the countries to be included into the research design, we would welcome an increased focus on individual European countries, since differences between them are larger than most American researchers seem to realise.

HQ characteristics: Bartlett and Ghoshal's typology

In our description of different organisational models in the theoretical chapters, we relied heavily on the typology constructed by Bartlett and Ghoshal. As identified in Chapter 1, this typology is very well accepted in the field of international management. Bartlett and Ghoshal's typology was based on in-depth clinical, action-oriented/case study research. The typology would therefore be expected to lie close to the organisational reality as experienced by multinational companies. Using the distinction described in Chapter 2, the classification could be seen as taxonomical (derived from actual data) rather than typological (the result of theoretical deduction).

In Chapter 1, we also indicated, however, that there is no overwhelming empirical support that can justify the use of this taxonomy, based on nine MNCs, as a typology for MNCs in general. Exploratory factor analysis of our data for 97 headquarters resulted in three factors that could be clearly interpreted as the three major organisational models identified by Bartlett and Ghoshal.[154] These results therefore show considerable support for the use of their classification as a general typology of MNCs. Based on theoretical justifications, these organisational models were subsequently supplemented with a number of other headquarters and subsidiary characteristics to form configurations of MNCs. The fact that these configurations performed very well in the empirical analysis increases our confidence in the basic Bartlett and Ghoshal classification.

However, two additional remarks should be made in this respect. First, Chapter 4 showed that the typology did not seem to be very meaningful for the petroleum industry. No dominant organisation model could be identified for this industry, since respondents in this industry provided us with relatively low scores for all items measuring the various organisational models. We can therefore conclude that we cannot necessarily generalise the typology to other industries than the ones included in Bartlett and Ghoshal's sample (consumer electronics, telecommunications and branded packaged goods). On the other hand, the specific items we used to operationalise the various organisational models might simply be inapplicable to the petroleum industry. Another model may be necessary to describe the petroleum industry and possibly other capital-intensive process industries. Further, still different models may have to be constructed to portray the specificities of various service sectors. This would plead for including a limited number of industries in future samples, so that operationalisations can be more specifically tailored to these industries.

Second, inherent in Bartlett and Ghoshal's theory is the idea that many multidomestic and global companies will eventually evolve to be transnational companies. Based on this assumption, we expected the age of both subsidiaries and headquarters of transnational companies to lie in between their global and multidomestic counterparts. Our empirical analysis, however, showed that both headquarters and subsidiaries of transnational companies were younger than their global and multidomestic counterparts. We can therefore conclude that apparently not all transnational companies grew out of global and multidomestic companies. On closer examination, we found the younger age of transnational headquarters to be caused by two factors. First, a

---

[154] As indicated in Chapter 1, the international model was not included in our survey, since it is the least clearly defined and is not present in many other typologies.

number of recently established computer companies apparently started out as transnational companies. Second, four of our 22 transnational companies are recent mergers and indicated the year of their merger as the year of their foundation. In a sense, these companies can be considered to be operating as transnational companies from the merger onwards. Overall, however, we would hesitate to draw any far-reaching conclusions in this respect, since the sample of transnational companies was rather small, and may have been influenced by extreme values with regard to the age of both headquarters and subsidiaries.

HQ and subsidiary characteristics: organisation theory and international management research

In the introduction to this book, we already indicated that many authors called for a more systematic inclusion of existing results from the field of organisation theory in research designs investigating multinational organisations. We therefore included four variables that in "traditional" organisation theory are usually considered to have a large influence on the applicability of the different control mechanisms: size, interdependence (the level of dependence of different parts of the organisation on each other for e.g. inputs), uncertainty and heterogeneity/diversity. Overall, the results from our study show that it seems to have been a wise choice to include these variables in the analysis. The results for MNCs largely confirm, but also extend, results for domestic organisations.

The variable *size* explained a considerable proportion of the variance in the application of control mechanisms, both at headquarters and at subsidiary level. At headquarters level, size was the largest explanatory factor of the variance for the indirect control mechanisms (output control and control by socialisation and networks), both separately and combined. At subsidiary level, the same was true for control by socialisation and networks and the two indirect control mechanisms combined. These results thus confirm previous studies in the field of organisation theory, in the sense that size is an important explanatory factor for differences in control mechanisms. In contrast to these studies, however, a dominant effect was found only for the *indirect* control mechanisms. As was indicated in Chapter 2, very few previous studies were available that investigated the effect of size on the two indirect control mechanisms. Most previous studies focused on the *direct* control mechanisms (personal centralised control and bureaucratic formalised control) only. Our study thus reconfirms the importance of the variable size, but concludes that it is mainly associated with higher levels of indirect control. This again pleads for the inclusion of a complete portfolio of control mechanisms in future studies, both for domestic and for multinational companies.

In our bivariate analyses, *interdependence* was also found to be an important variable, although in the multivariate analysis its effect was more limited. In general, as in most "traditional" organisation studies, interdependence was found to be positively associated with the direct control mechanisms (personal centralised control and bureaucratic formalised control). More importantly, however, we found that the *type* of interdependence (dependence on either headquarters or other subsidiaries) was a crucial factor in explaining differences in control mechanisms, and would therefore like to plead for a more differentiated view of interdependence. A variant of Thompson's (1967) classification scheme, adapted to MNCs, could be very useful in this respect.

Our results concerning *uncertainty* also confirmed previous studies in the field of organisation theory. In the multivariate analysis, there was a positive relationship between the level of uncertainty and the level of control by socialisation and networks. Uncertain environments would be expected to be associated with more indirect and informal control mechanisms. This relationship was rather weak, however. Two other important conclusions could be drawn concerning this variable, though. *First*, correlations were much stronger when only the item regarding technological dynamism (the extent to which the technology in the industry is subject to change) was included in the analysis. The actual type of technology used, however, is one of the important variables identified in organisation studies that was *not* included in our study. The fact that control mechanisms also varied between industries can also be reinterpreted with the factor technology in mind, since the type of technology used is an important differentiator between industries. The high level of direct control in the chemical industry might for instance be due to its continuous process production technology. It would therefore seem wise to include technology as an independent variable in future studies. *Second*, contrasting findings appeared for MNCs headquartered in different countries. The relationship between uncertainty and personal centralised control, for instance, was positive for Japanese, German and Swiss MNCs and negative for American, British, Dutch and Finnish MNCs.

The level of *complexity/heterogeneity* was one of the very few variables in our study that did not give the expected results. Retrospectively, however, we doubt whether the number of 2- or 4-digit SIC codes in which a company operates adequately captures the level of complexity/heterogeneity in the way in which it was interpreted in our theoretical framework. Although the number of different SIC codes is a very commonly used operationalisation, we might wonder whether operating in different SIC-areas necessarily means that the organisation's markets and customers have different characteristics and needs, as was put forward in the original definition. Consumer needs might very well differ as much within industries as between industries. In addition, it might have been better to differentiate between complexity and heterogeneity after all. Companies may operate in heterogeneous environments that in themselves are very simple, while companies operating in one single environment may experience a high level of complexity. Future studies should therefore pay closer attention to the operationalisation of this concept. Combined with our observations regarding the uncertainty concept, it would be a good idea to include technological complexity as an independent variable. The diversity variable might more adequately be captured as the different market demands an MNC has to comply with. In this interpretation, it also includes the complexity concept. Unfortunately, this operationalisation would be almost tautological with elements of the organisational model variable.

In sum, we can conclude that many concepts important in "traditional" organisation theory have proven their usefulness in the study of multinational companies. Researchers in the field of international management should therefore pay closer attention to a more systematic grounding of their research in organisation theory. At the same time, studies of MNCs might lead to a considerable enrichment of organisation theory.

Subsidiary characteristics: differentiating the control portfolio to take different subsidiary roles into account

In Chapter 2, we discussed a number of subsidiary characteristics that might lead headquarters managers to differentiate the control portfolio for different subsidiaries. Chapter 5 showed that next to the variable subsidiary size, a traditional organisation characteristic discussed above, many subsidiary characteristics related to the role or function of subsidiaries had a relatively large explanatory power. Control mechanisms in headquarters-dependent subsidiaries could be clearly delineated from control mechanism in subsidiary-dependent subsidiaries. The latter experienced more informal and indirect control (especially control by socialisation and networks), while the former experienced more direct control (direct expatriate control). These findings are especially interesting, since a previous study by Wolf (1994) found the same result in a different sample using different operationalisations. Subsidiary-dependent subsidiaries are typical of a network type of firm, in which various nodes of the network are equally important. Our study thus clearly confirms the often-claimed use of more indirect control mechanisms in this type of firm. We might wonder, however, whether a decreasing level of (direct) control by headquarters would not be compensated by an increasing level of (direct) control by *other* subsidiaries. Since our measurement of control was focused on headquarters-subsidiary interactions only (see also Section 3 below), we cannot answer this question, but it would be an interesting subject for future research.

As already indicated in Chapter 2, our measurement of subsidiary roles was not very sophisticated, since the importance of this characteristic became apparent only after the empirical part of this study had been concluded. However, subsidiary roles based on a simple combination of interdependence and local responsiveness were shown to have a relatively large explanatory power concerning the variance in control mechanisms applied. In addition, two of the subsidiary functions (sales and R&D) were significantly related to the higher or lower use of particular control mechanisms. Since all of the characteristics discussed in this section are related to the role a subsidiary occupies in the corporate network, we would strongly recommend future researchers to pay closer attention to this characteristic. It would seem useful to construct configurations of subsidiaries roles based on more than a simple two-way classification scheme, and to relate these configurations to the application of various control mechanisms. Of course, it would be very suitable to combine research in this area with an increased emphasis on relationships *between* subsidiaries.

Expatriation: towards a more strategic view

As repeated several times in this book, research in the field of expatriation has focused too much on practical issues alone. This is not surprising, since the interest in the strategic aspects of human resources is very recent in domestic personnel management as well. Our study showed that international transfers could play an important role in the transfer of organisational culture, and in the improvement of informal communication channels between headquarters and subsidiaries. Thus, expatriates do not only transfer technical or managerial knowledge, but also culture and information. Once this is realised, it becomes apparent that the operational functions such as selection, training and repatriation should also be adapted to the specific goal that is pursued with expatriation.

If the only goal of expatriation is a transfer of technical knowledge or the filling of a position for which no locals are available, selection may be based on technical skills alone and extensive cross-cultural training might not be necessary.[155] When the expatriate is expected to transfer mostly "soft issues", such as culture and informal information, soft skills such as interpersonal skills and cultural empathy might be more important, and might have to be taught if not present. The problem is that few companies identify culture and information transfer in advance as important reasons for expatriation. Our

---

[155] Of course one could argue that some degree of cross-cultural training is always necessary, since transferring skills to locals might be very difficult if the expatriate does not respect cultural differences.

study showed that the transfer of corporate culture and the improvement of communication channels were seen as more important by subsidiary managers than by HR-managers at headquarters, thus indicating that the actual importance of these functions in practice may be larger than corporate HR-managers realise. This can therefore also explain the lack of cross-cultural training, and the emphasis on technical skills in some companies. Finally, if transfer is mainly motivated by managing development reasons, repatriation is of course of crucial importance. If companies do not use the knowledge that expatriates have gathered abroad, which unfortunately seems to be common practice (Smeets, 1997; Kneebone, 1997), much of the management development objective is lost.

In sum, expatriates are powerful links between the various units of an MNC. In Mueller's (1994) terms, they are crucial in the realisation of the organisational effect. Transfer of best practices and learning from each other can be greatly facilitated by these cross-pollinating bumble-bees. It is therefore time that this strategic function is given due attention, both in theory and in practice.

The usefulness of configurations in international management research

In Section 3 of Chapter 2, we identified various configurations of MNCs based on theoretical justifications. The empirical results conform fairly closely to our theoretical assumptions. It therefore certainly seems possible to condense a number of headquarters and subsidiary characteristics into a limited number of clearly delineated "ideal types". Although in this book we have not been able to show that adherence to these ideal types has significant performance implications, we do feel that research along these lines would be more useful than a continued focus on bivariate contingency relationships. More focused studies could try to elaborate the idea of fit in MNCs, profiting from the recent attention to configuration analysis in strategic management literature. A recent (Ketchen et al., 1997) meta-analysis of 40 tests of the configuration-performance relationship showed that: "organisations' configurations contributed more to performance explanation to the extent that studies used (1) broad definitions of configurations, (2) single-industry samples, and (3) longitudinal designs" (Ketchen et al., 1997:223). Although these observations are aimed at researchers in the field of strategic management, they will presumably be valid for researchers in the field of international management as well. We also support Ketchen et al's call for more programmatic configurational research and the reduction of competing theories and models by identifying commonalties among configurations. Our study gave a start to this in the field of international management.

A focus on configuration analysis would also seem to be quite compatible with the societal effect approach. Both the configurational and the societal effect approach emphasise that there is no one best way to achieve certain goals. Certain constellations of organisational or societal factors, however, do form logical patterns. Changing or copying one of these elements in isolation will not lead to the desired results. In comparing organisations across countries, configuration analysis could even be incorporated into the societal effect analysis, in the sense that societal patterns in different countries lead to a "preference" for one configuration over another. Comparing the link between configurations and performance in a multi-country sample leads to additional problems, however. These problems will be discussed in the next subsection.

The uselessness of comparing financial performance across countries

In considering performance differences between companies, the highest explanatory power could be attributed to the country of origin of headquarters and the industry in which the MNC operates. In discussing our results concerning differences in performance between countries in Chapter 5, we identified the considerable difficulties in this respect. Differences in *financial* performance between countries could very well be mainly due to differences in tax rates, accounting practices, capital structure and the importance of the stock markets, without necessarily reflecting differences in actual *business* performance. Furthermore, financial measures that are not based on ratios run the risk of identifying performance differences that are simply caused by fluctuations in exchange rates.

There is a vast amount of literature that compares traditional performance indicators such as ROS, ROA and ROE across countries. Companies in different countries, however, do not necessarily attach equal importance to these performance indicators. In comparing several countries on the same performance indicator(s), which might be important (and thus high) in a subset of these countries only, the researcher runs a considerable risk of explaining performance differences by any characteristic that is "accidentally" high in the country(ies) for which the performance indicator used in the study is important. This means that any study that compares performance or the relationship between an (organisational) characteristic and performance across countries with different "performance orientations" would be of limited scientific and practical value. It would seem much more useful to investigate which performance indicators are considered important in various countries and to relate this to the country's societal/legal/cultural background.

The myth of the European monolith

In addition to the conclusions above, which are all in one way or another related to our specific research questions, we would like to draw attention to one remarkable general finding of our study: the fact that there are large differences in virtually every field investigated *between* European countries. In many cases, companies from the USA and Japan can be found at opposite extremes, while European companies as a whole fall in between. Within this group of European companies, however, some can be found close to the US pattern, while others resemble the Japanese pattern.

More specifically, we find in the field of control mechanisms that Swiss and Swedish companies resemble each other closely. German and British companies, however, show a pattern that, for most control mechanisms, resembles American companies, while Finnish companies come very close to Japanese companies with respect to the impersonal forms of control (bureaucratic formalised control and output control). Looking at the various organisational models, we find that Finnish, French and British companies share a preference for the multidomestic model. German companies, however, join their Japanese counterparts in having the global model as the dominant one, while Dutch and Swiss multinationals resemble American companies with their preference for the transnational model. With regard to expatriation, we find Japan and Germany at the one extreme with a high level of expatriate presence in subsidiaries and a high application of direct expatriate control, while the USA and the UK are at the opposite extreme. The same distinction can be made concerning financial performance, where Japanese and German companies are found at the low end, and the American and the British companies at the high end. Even concerning response rates, there are tremendous differences between European countries, with the Danish response being more than three times as high as the French response rate.

Overall, we can find a broad pattern in which German companies resemble Japanese companies most closely, while British companies are very similar to their American counterparts. The other five European countries usually fall in between these two extreme patterns, with no consistent country pairs across the various fields of interest. It would therefore seem very inappropriate to either generalise findings from one or two European countries to a European pattern, or to consider European companies as a homogeneous whole, both of which are common practice in previous (American) research in the various fields. We would therefore like to recommend future researchers to consider their choice of countries in cross-national comparisons very carefully.

In sum

Briefly summarising our discussion above, we would like to plead for research with a holistic approach, paying attention to constellations of factors related to each other (configurations) rather than to traditional bivariate contingency analyses. Configurations can be defined at both headquarters and subsidiary level and, in their construction, researchers would do well to pay due attention to existing organisation theory. Both the country of origin and the industry should be carefully considered in the choice of population. Ideally, studies should focus on a limited number of countries and industries, so that subsample analysis is feasible. Since Europe appears to host a large variety of patterns within a small geographical area, for almost every aspect studied in this book, more attention to a comparison between different European countries seems justified. In these studies, special attention should be paid to the comparability of performance indicators across countries. This summary expresses our overall view as to the direction of future research in this area. In addition to a discussion of the limitations of our study, the next section will offer some specific recommendations and issues that could be taken into account by future researchers in this field.

3. LIMITATIONS OF THE STUDY AND RECOMMENDATIONS FOR FUTURE RESEARCHERS

This section will discuss the limitations of our study and, where applicable, offer some recommendations for further research. We would first like to indicate, however, which of the limitations apparent in many other studies have been remedied in our own study. As already occasionally referred to in some of the previous chapters, our study does *not* suffer from many of the "conventional" limitations in this field of research in the sense that it:

- focused on more than one or two control mechanisms;
- included a whole range of predictor variables instead of only one or two;
- included non-American MNCs in the sample;
- investigated subsidiaries in more than one or two countries;
- explicitly dealt with the strategic aspects of international HRM;
- provided an integrated perspective on control mechanisms, including the often-referred-to but never systematically investigated role of expatriate managers;
- provided a solid theoretical foundation by reviewing contributions in the field of organisation studies and expatriate management, in addition to

international management literature;
- included studies overlooked by the mainstream (Anglo-Saxon) research community in its literature review;
- questioned subsidiary managers instead of headquarters managers, in order to increase the accuracy and diminish the social desirability of the answers;
- paid due attention to the process aspects of doing international research and included a solid literature review on the execution of (international) mail surveys;
- used well-motivated and innovative incentives to increase response rates;
- resulted in a response rate that was higher than for many other studies, so that the sample size was relatively large;
- paid attention to the cross-cultural equivalence of the various measures used in the study.

In spite of the fact that many limitations of previous studies have been remedied, our study does have its own limitations. These will be discussed in more detail below. Where applicable, we will include recommendations for further research.

First, since we used a key-informant approach, our results are based on the opinions of a single respondent in each organisation, a limitation this study shares with virtually all large-scale international studies. As discussed in detail in Chapter 3, the prevalent response rates in international mail surveys make another approach practically infeasible. A solution to this problem might be to try to gain cooperation of key people within the various organisations and have them distribute questionnaires and persuade their colleagues to cooperate. This approach, however, is very time-intensive and does not remove the risk of low response rates.

Second, although every care was taken to formulate questions as unambiguously as possible, our study used perceptual measures to operationalise some of the constructs. This was done first because of the not immediately quantifiable nature of, for instance, strategy and control mechanisms. Although for some of these constructs quantification would have been possible, it would have made the questionnaire longer and more complicated, thus reducing the likelihood of a high response rate. The result is, however, that the answers to our questions might contain an element of perception. Combined with the reliance on single or two- to four-item constructs, this might reduce the validity of our findings. On the other hand, as discussed extensively in Chapter 4, the results of our study display a high level of conformity with the results of many other studies that focused on a more limited number of relationships using multiple and/or more quantitative measures.

Third, since our study is cross-sectional rather than longitudinal, statistical correlations cannot unambiguously be interpreted as causal relationships. We tried to alleviate this problem by including an extensive literature review to justify the hypothesised causal relationships tested in our study. However, a true test of the causality of the relationships tested in this book can only be offered by qualitative and/or longitudinal research.

Fourth, although many of the specific hypotheses tested in this study could be accepted, in some cases the magnitude of the predicted differences or correlations was rather small, although usually significant. In Abelson's terms (1995), we conclude that the magnitude of our results might have suffered from our striving for generalisability.[156] The same striving for generalisability resulted in the need for a large sample and hence a relatively high response rate. Previous research (see Chapter 3) showed that the length of the questionnaire is one of the most, if not *the* most important influencing factor on response rates. The longer the questionnaire, the lower the response rate. This size limit led us to decide to keep our questions on a rather general level, instead of differentiating them towards different functional areas, and in most cases to use scales of only two to four items. Based on the results of our study, future researchers might try to enhance magnitude, without compromising too much on generality, by strategically choosing the countries, industries, control mechanisms and predictor variables to be included in their study.

Fifth, because of our emphasis on generalisability and the method of data collection - questionnaires with closed-ended question - our results mainly focus on outcomes. The actual process underlying much of the relationships has remained a black box. Of course, other research methods are more suitable in adding flesh to the bones dug up and the skeleton constructed in this study. For instance, now that the role of international transfers in achieving an informal type of control has been empirically confirmed on a large scale, more detailed analysis, by means of, for instance, case studies, should give better insight into the way in which this process actually works (see Marschan, 1995, Marschan et al., 1996a/b; and Nurmi, 1995 for examples of this

---

[156] Abelson (1995) proposes a five fold set of criteria to judge the quality of scientific research, together forming the acronym MAGIC (Magnitude, Articulation, Generality, Interestingness and Credibility). Magnitude refers to the quantitative magnitude of support for a qualitative claim. Articulation refers to the level of detail in which conclusions are described. A conclusion such as the level of control by socialisation and networks in Swedish and Swiss MNCs is higher than in French and Japanese MNCs has a higher level of articulation than the conclusion that there are systematic differences between countries in this respect. Generality refers to the breadth of the applicability of the conclusions, and can be enhanced by including a wide range of contextual variations in a comprehensive research plan. A study's interestingness is a function of its capacity to change beliefs and its importance, while its credibility is enhanced by methodological and theoretical soundness. Although we would like to leave the verdict on the last two issues to our readers, we feel we may comfortably claim a high level of articulation and generality, combined with - in some cases - a lower level of magnitude.

type of analysis). An important, but potentially very difficult, issue would be to distinguish between direct and indirect expatriate control.

Sixth, in spite of the fact that our study has a much larger geographical spread than previous studies, some areas have been neglected. Although Japanese MNCs were included in the survey, our study did not include any other Asian MNCs (e.g. from Hong Kong, Singapore, South Korea, Taiwan, Thailand, Malaysia). Ulgado et al. (1994) report that MNCs from Asian developing countries show patterns that resemble Japanese firms concerning expatriation, control and structure. However, since developments in this region are becoming increasingly important for the Western world, it would be worthwhile to include MNCs from this region in future studies. Unfortunately, in view of the large cultural differences between "East" and "West", this would aggravate the problems associated with cross-cultural research and would make multi-cultural research teams indispensable. At subsidiary level, Eastern European, Middle Eastern and African subsidiaries were not included in our survey. In view of recent political developments, especially the first of these would be a highly intriguing research domain. Additional problems associated with cross-cultural research should not be taken lightly, although at subsidiary level many of the respondents will be (Western) expatriates.

Seventh, our study included only wholly owned subsidiaries. The level of control and the portfolio of control mechanisms that is used might very well be different for e.g. joint ventures and minority participations. Staffing policies could be especially crucial in these types of subsidiaries. A current research project undertaken by the author investigates the influence of ownership on the nationality of the managing director and other top-level functions in subsidiaries. Related to this, non-equity forms of cooperation, such as the contractual alliances that have become very important in high-tech industries (Hagedoorn and Narula, 1996), were outside the scope of this survey. Controlling these "virtual organisations" might be even more complex. Unfortunately, investigating this type of contractual agreements might be equally complex, because of their often temporary and volatile nature.

Eighth, our study - as most of the other studies in this field - only included the application of control mechanisms by headquarters in respect of their subsidiaries. As Forsgren and Pahlberg (1992:41) rightly indicate: "if we adopt the view of the international firm as a multi-centre structure, it is relevant to broaden the question of control beyond the issue of conflict between the subsidiary's local adaptation and the top management's overall integration". The behaviour of subsidiaries can have an effect not only at the local level but also for the whole or part of the MNC to which it belongs. Therefore, control issues within an MNC should not only consider the design of various control systems by headquarters, but also pay attention to the control exercised by powerful subsidiaries. This question also relates to the importance of distinguishing various subsidiary roles, and the effect these roles may have on the level and type of control exercised in respect of and by these subsidiaries. The fact that the multi-centre - or in our terms transnational - firm is a rather recent discovery led most researchers to focus on "top-down" control. Future research could try to remedy this limitation and include "bottom-up" or "lateral" types of control. This is particularly important in investigating the role of expatriates, since transfers from subsidiaries to headquarters and from subsidiaries to other subsidiaries are slowly becoming more important.

Ninth, and related to the previous point, our interpretation of shared values has been rather headquarters-oriented. Respondents were asked to indicate the extent to which subsidiary executives shared the company's main values. We could ask ourselves whether, especially in a more transnationally oriented company, the aim would indeed be to socialise every employee into one uniform parent-company culture. Viewing corporate culture in this way does have a somewhat totalitarian touch (see Welch and Welch, 1997 for a particularly fierce argument against the fashionable idea of using culture as a control mechanism). Perhaps the aim of a truly geocentric or transnational company should be to create a kind of "super-organisational culture", using the best of all different cultures (see also Adler and Ghadar, 1990). This super-organisational culture would then explicitly be based on diversity, not on conformity. Investigating the dynamics of this type of corporate culture and its interactions with national culture is a fascinating, but very large and so far virtually unexplored, research task.

A *final* limitation of this study is related to performance measurement. Following virtually all other research in this field, we measured performance as return on sales, return on assets and return on equity. Retrospectively, we feel that these measures are too narrow to capture firm performance adequately. Further, they are considerably influenced by differences in tax rates and especially differences in accounting practices across countries. In addition, these accounting-based financial measures are past-, rather than future-oriented. A broader, less distorted and more future-oriented picture of performance could be found in operational measures such as market share, manufacturing value added, growth, investments in research and development and training, product/service quality, productivity or even various measures of employee morale. Future studies could therefore try to include these operational performance measures and, as indicated above, explore their relative importance across countries. Unfortunately, for most of these measures studies would run into the same problems that induced us to use the more conventional measures in the first place: the necessity to rely on cooperation of respondents to provide sensitive or even confidential data and/or the very time-consuming task of providing reliable growth figures that are not too much influenced by exchange rate differences.

4. IMPLICATIONS FOR MANAGEMENT

Although research in the field of (international) management may seem more practice-oriented than research in many other areas, it rarely contributes directly to practice and it is often difficult to find clear-cut applications of research results. Knowledge building in any field is gradual and cumulative, so that the results of one single study can hardly be used to offer firm recommendations. This is even more true since the functioning of organisations is influenced by a multitude of factors, so that any isolated advice may be of limited use. In spite of these reservations, we will try to give some idea of the possible managerial implications of our research.[157]

First, our data show clearly that MNCs from different countries often have different dominant control mechanisms and organisational models (see Tables 4-8 and 4-14 for a summary of these differences). This could partly be due to different industry distributions, but it is also at least partly related to cultural-/societal differences between countries. It would be wise to consider these differences when searching for a partner in cross-national mergers and acquisitions. Failure to do so could hinder the successful operation of a merger that seemed to be perfect from a financial and competitive point of view. Although the difficulties in merging with Japanese companies might be apparent for most Westerns MNCs, there are also other "country combinations" that might be less successful. The recent merger between the Swedish Asea and the Swiss Brown Boveri would seem to have been a wise choice in terms of the compatibility of dominant control mechanisms and organisational models in these respective countries. The control portfolios of Swedish and Swiss MNCs are extremely comparable. Although their dominant organisational

---

[157] Although we have not been able to offer clear-cut guidelines, the fact that over 90% of the respondents indicated that they would like to receive a summary report indicates that companies are indeed interested in the results of a study like this. On the other hand, it is of course very easy and non-committing to request a free report, if the only thing you have to do is indicate this on the questionnaire. However, four respondents at subsidiary level requested an additional report to be sent to headquarters. In addition, one respondent - who we hope was impressed by the professional design of the report - forgot that the study had been conducted by a university and requested more information about the products and services of our company. With the summary report, we included an order form with which respondents could order additional reports for a price varying from $100 to $250. All reports counted between 12 and 24 pages. Three thematic reports were offered that focused on specific issues: environment/strategy/structure, control mechanisms and expatriation. In addition, nine country and eight industry reports could be ordered, which provided detailed data on how the particular headquarters country or industry differed from the total sample on each of the issues included in the survey. We received orders from three different companies (two subsidiaries and one headquarters). One company ordered all thematic reports, while the second was only interested in the expatriation report. The third company ordered two thematic reports, four country reports and one industry report.

models are slightly less comparable, they are not as different from each other as, for instance, the dominant models of German and French firms.

In addition, the relationship between some of the explanatory variables and specific control mechanisms proved to be different for MNCs from different countries. A higher level of uncertainty in the environment, for instance, led German, Japanese and Swiss MNCs to centralise decisions and exert a closer surveillance on subsidiaries' operations, while the reverse was true for American, British, Dutch and Finnish companies. MNCs from the latter companies responded with a higher level of control by socialisation and networks. These differential results might be caused by the generally higher level of uncertainty avoidance present in the national cultures of Japan, Germany and Switzerland. This might lead MNCs in these countries to prefer a close personal control in situations of high risk/uncertainty. The common prescription in organisational theory for situations of high uncertainty is to decentralise operations, release strict personal control and rely on more informal control mechanisms. Our results show, however, that this might be an example of the many American (or Anglo-Saxon) management prescriptions that cannot simply be transferred to other countries/cultures. MNCs that originate from countries with a cultural/societal profile that is markedly different from the USA (in our sample Japan, Germany, Switzerland and France, and to a lesser extent Finland, Sweden and the Netherlands) would therefore be wise not to accept the prescriptions of American management theorists and gurus without questioning. There is simply no "best way of management" that is universally applicable across countries.

Most MNCs also differentiated their application of control mechanisms for different types of subsidiaries. Larger subsidiaries were more strongly controlled than smaller subsidiaries, especially through control by socialisation and networks. Subsidiaries that were highly integrated within the company network were also more strongly controlled, especially through the two direct control mechanisms, personal centralised control and bureaucratic formalised control, than their less integrated counterparts. The reverse was true for subsidiaries that scored high on local responsiveness. Overall, autonomous subsidiaries with strong links with the local environment experienced less control than receptive subsidiaries that had a predominance of internal rather than external links. In addition, MNCs preferred personal control mechanisms (personal centralised control, direct expatriate control and control by socialisation and networks) over impersonal (bureaucratic formalised control and output control) control mechanisms for subsidiaries located in culturally distant countries. These findings were consistent with our theoretical expectations. It would therefore not seem wise to take an undifferentiated approach to control, but rather to consider differences in subsidiary characteristics when deciding on the level and type of control exercised. A high level of control, especially of the direct type, might be very dysfunctional for relatively autonomous subsidiaries, whose main function is to be responsive to the local market. For highly integrated subsidiaries, however, that play a crucial role in the MNC's integrated international production system, a higher level of control might be needed and appropriate. Because of their importance, large subsidiaries might also need to be more strongly controlled, but because of their generally higher level of local resources and competences, a direct type of control is likely to be resisted. The less obtrusive control by socialisation and networks might indeed be a better solution in this case. Finally, personal control mechanisms appear to be preferable to impersonal control mechanisms for bridging cultural distance.

Some interesting results can be reported concerning international transfers. Expatriate presence in (top positions in) subsidiaries differs considerably across countries and industries. The largest number of expatriates can be found in Asian and Latin American subsidiaries of Japanese or German MNCs in the automobile industry. The lowest expatriate presence can be found in Scandinavian subsidiaries of American or British MNCs in the food industry. In addition, subsidiary characteristics such as size, age, entry mode and function were shown to have an impact on the level of expatriate presence in subsidiaries. More expatriates are found in large, young and underperforming subsidiaries. In addition, expatriate presence was lower in acquisitions than in greenfields, and lower in sales/service subsidiaries than in subsidiaries with a strategic function. Finally, expatriates often seem to be used to bridge cultural distance they are more numerous in subsidiaries that are culturally distant from headquarters. We have not been able to relate these particular choices to performance, and cannot therefore offer any firm conclusions concerning their effectiveness. In spite of this, our results could be helpful for newly internationalising companies that would like to learn from their more experienced colleagues concerning subsidiary staffing policies.

What can also be concluded from our research is that international transfers can play a strategic role. In addition to being a means of knowledge transfer and position filling when no qualified locals are available, international transfers play a role in both management and organisation development. International transfers can be a very effective way to internationalise managers, and to prepare them for important positions at either headquarters or other subsidiaries. In addition, expatriates were shown not only to exercise direct control, but also to facilitate indirect control over subsidiaries. The higher the expatriate presence in a subsidiary, the higher the level of both shared values and informal communication with headquarters. However, participation of subsidiary managers in international management training and formal networks was found to be an important alternative to international transfers to achieve a high level of informal control. Companies striving to achieve a high level of informal control would therefore do well to use all three alternatives.

The questioning of HR-managers at headquarters resulted in some interesting results concerning expatriate management. HR-managers in MNCs from countries with a high relative use of expatriates reported larger problems in attracting and retaining local managers. The higher presence of expatriates in these subsidiaries might block career opportunities for local managers and hence result in motivational problems. HR-managers in MNCs from countries that showed a preference for local managers reported higher problems concerning dual-career couples and expatriate re-entry. MNCs from these countries might have been forced to rely more on local managers because of their increasing problems in managing expatriates. In general, corporate HR-managers feel that there are no serious problems concerning the number of parent-country nationals who are prepared to work abroad. Three quarters of the HR-managers, however, feel that there is a lack of PCNs with sufficient international management skills. Companies that send out expatriates for management development reasons report fewer problems with a lack of international management skills. This suggests that companies that take training and development seriously have a more internationally competent workforce. Repatriation is seen as a problem by slightly more than half of the companies. Expatriate re-entry problems are less prominent in companies that maintain a centralised roster of managerial employees and attach a high importance to management development as a reason for expatriation. Again, paying more attention to personnel development issues seems to be rewarded by fewer problems in expatriate management.

The configurational analysis performed in Chapter 5 and summarised above will be of interest to a managerial audience. Three clearly delineated MNC configurations were found: global, multidomestic and transnational. Each of these configurations showed a distinct pattern of coherent internal characteristics. The fit between some of these internal characteristics was assumed to lead to higher performance. Unfortunately, we have not been able to show very strong performance effects of a fit between the organisational model applied at headquarters and control mechanisms, or between subsidiary role and control mechanisms. However, overall the effect of fit was positive. Also, the three theoretically derived organisational configurations were to a large extent confirmed in practice, thus giving at least some indication that adherence to these configurations is seen as wise management practice. Again, especially for newly internationalising companies, the configurations could be a helpful yardstick to evaluate their own internal fit.

In addition to internal fit as described above, a number of other company characteristics were investigated for their effect on financial performance. Smaller and highly internationalised companies were found to outperform their larger and less internationalised colleagues. As expected, companies with transnational characteristics showed higher levels of performance than more global-type companies. A high level of shared values between headquarters and subsidiaries was also shown to be positively related to performance, as was a fit between the characteristics of the industry in which the company operated and its organisational model (i.e. a global model for global industries, etc.). None of these characteristics, however, had a very strong impact on performance. Most of the difference in performance between the MNCs in our sample could be explained by the industry in which they operated and the country in which they were headquartered. American and British MNCs consistently outperformed Japanese and German companies, while the performance of companies in the pharmaceutical industry was unmatched by that of companies in any of the other industries. Differences in *financial* performance between countries, however, could be mainly due to differences in tax rates, accounting practices, capital structure and the importance of the stock markets, without necessarily reflecting differences in actual *business* performance. We would therefore strongly recommend MNCs in different countries to focus on performance indicators that are relevant for *their* major stakeholders and not blindly to emphasise (short-term) financial performance, although with the globalisation of financial markets, stock market performance may gain prominence for many companies.

References

Abelson, R.P. (1995): *Statistics as Principled Argument*, Hillsdale, NJ: Lawrence Erlbaum Associates Publishers.

Ackermann, K.-F., Pohl, G. (1989): Entlohnung, internationale, in Macharzina, K., Welge, M.K.: *Handwörterbuch Export und internationale Unternehmung*, pp. 379-391, Stuttgart: Poeschel.

Acuff, F. (1984): *International and Domestic Human Resources Functions: Innovations in International Compensation*, New York: Organization Resources Counselers.

Adler, N.J (1983a): A Typology of Management Studies Involving Culture, *Journal of International Business Studies*, vol. 14 (Fall), pp. 29-47.

Adler, N.J (1983b): Cross-Cultural Management Research: The Ostrich and the Trend, *Academy of Management Review*, vol. 8 no. 2, pp. 226-232.

Adler, N.J (1983c): Cross-Cultural Management: Issues to be faced, *International Studies of Management and Organization*, vol. XIII no. 1-2, pp. 7-45.

Adler, N.J. (1984a): Understanding the ways of understanding: Cross-Cultural management methodology reviewed, in Farmer, R.N.: *Advances in international comparative management*, vol. 1, pp. 31-67, Greenwich, CT: JAI Press.

Adler, N.J (1984b): Women Do Not Want International Careers: And Other Myths About International Management, *Organizational Dynamics*, vol. 13 no. 2, pp. 66-79.

Adler, N.J. (1987): Pacific Basin Managers: A Gaijin, Not A Woman, *Human Resource Management*, vol. 26 no. 2, pp. 169-191.

Adler, N.J., Doktor, R., Redding, S.G. (1989): From the Atlantic to the Pacific Century: Cross-Cultural Management Reviewed, in Osigweh, C.A.B.: *Organizational Science Abroad, Constraints and Perspectives*, pp. 27-54, New York: Plenum Press.

Adler, N.J., Ghadar, F. (1990): Strategic Human Resource Management: A Global Perspective, in Pieper, R.: *Human Resource Management: An International Comparison*, pp. 235-260, Berlin: Walter de Gruyter.

Adler, N.J. (1992): Globally Competitive: Women Managing Worldwide, *Applied Psychology: An International Review*.

Adler, N.J., Bartholomew, S. (1992a): Academic and Professional Communities of Discourse: Generating Knowledge on Transnational Human Resource Management, *Journal of International Business Studies*, vol. 23 no. 3, pp. 551-569.

Adler, N.J., Bartholomew, S. (1992b): Managing Globally Competent People, *Academy of Management Executive*, vol. 6 no. 3, pp. 52-65.

Agarwal, S. (1993): Influence of Formalization, Role Stress, Organization Commitment and Work Alienation of Salespersons, *Journal of International Business Studies*, vol. 24 no. 4, pp. 715-739.

Agathe, K.E. (1990): Managing the mixed marriage, *Business Horizons* (Jan/Feb), pp. 37-43.

Albaum, G., et al. (1987): Likert Scale and Semantic Differential Issues Relevant to Cross-Cultural Research, paper presented at the Second Symposium on Cross-Cultural Consumer and Business (Dec.), Honolulu, Hawaii.

Albaum, G., Strandskov, J. (1989): Participation in a Mail Survey of International Marketers: Effects of Pre-Contact and Detailed Project Explanation, *Journal of Global Marketing*, vol. 2 no. 4, pp. 7-23.

Albaum, G., Strandskov, J., Erickson, R. (1989): Translation in Questionnaire Design for International and Cross-Cultural Research, *Working Paper 2/1989*, Copenhagen: Copenhagen School of Economics and Business Administration.

Andersson, U., Forsgren, M. (1995a): Subsidiary Embeddedness and its Implications for Integration in the MNC, in Schiattarella, R.: *Proceedings of the 21st annual conference*, vol. 2 (10-12 December), pp. 235-256, Urbino: EIBA.

Andersson, U., Forsgren, M. (1995b): Using Networks to Determine Multinational Parental Control of Subsidiaries, in Paliwoda, S.J., Ryans, Jr., J.K.: *International Marketing Reader*, pp. 72-87.

Angur, M.G., Nataraajan, R. (1995): Do Source of Mailing and Monetary Incentives Matter in International Industrial Mail Surveys?, *Industrial Marketing Management*, vol. 24, pp. 351-357.

Armstrong, J.S., Yokum, J.T. (1994): Effectiveness of Monetary Incentives. Mail Surveys to Members of Multinational Professional Groups, *Industrial Marketing Management*, vol. 23, pp. 133-136.

Arvey, R.D., Bhagat, R.S., Salas, E. (1991): Cross-cultural and cross-national issues in personnel and human resources management, in Rowland, K.M.; Ferris, G.R.: *Research in Personnel Management and Human Resource Management*, vol. 9, pp. 367-407, Greenwich: JAI Press Inc.

Aulakh, P.S., Kotabe, M. (1993): An assessment of theoretical and methodological developments in international marketing: 1980-1990, *Journal of International Marketing*, vol. 1 no. 2, pp. 5-28.

Ayal, I., Hornik, J. (1986): Foreign source effects on response behavior in cross-national mail surveys, *International Journal of Research in Marketing*, vol. 3, pp. 157-167.

Baker, J.C., Ivancevich, J.M. (1971): The Assignment of American Executives Abroad: Systematic, Haphazard, or Chaotic?, *California Management Review*, vol. XIII no. 3, pp. 39-44.

Baliga, B.R., Jaeger, A.M. (1984): Multinational Corporations: Control Systems and Delegation Issues, *Journal of International Business Studies*, vol. 15 (Fall), pp. 25-40.

Banai, M (1992): The Ethnocentric Staffing Policy in Multinational Corporations: A Self-Fulfilling Prophecy, *The International Journal of Human Resource Management*, vol. 3 no. 3 (December), pp. 451-472.

Banai, M., Reisel, W.D. (1993): Expatriate Managers' Loyalty to the MNC: Myth or Reality? An Exploratory Study, *Journal of International Business Studies* (Second Quarter), pp. 233-248.

Barham, K. (1995): Developing Intenational Management Competencies, paper presented at the 2nd European Conference on International Staffing and Expatriate Management (26-27 June), Braga, Portugal.

Barnett, S.T., Toyne, B. (1991): The Socialization, Acculturation, and Career Progression of Headquartered Foreign Nationals, in Prasad, S.B., Peterson, R.B.: *Advances in International Comparative Management*, vol. 6, pp. 3-34, London: JAI Press.

Bartlett, C.A. (1986): Building and Managing the Transnational: The New Organizational Challenge, in Porter, M.E.: *Competition in Global Industries*, pp. 367-401, Boston, MA: Harvard Business School Press.

Bartlett, C.A., Goshal, S. (1987a): Managing Across Borders: New Strategic Requirements, *Sloan Management Review*, vol. 28 (Summer), pp. 7-17.

Bartlett, C.A., Ghoshal, S. (1987b): Managing Across Borders: New Organizational Responses, *Sloan Management Review* (Fall), pp. 43-52.

Bartlett, C.A., Goshal, S. (1988): Organizing for Worlwide Effectiveness: The Transnational Solution, *California Management Review*, vol. 31 no. 1, pp. 54-74.

Bartlett, C.A., Ghoshal, S. (1989): *Managing Across Borders. The Transnational Solution*, Boston, MA.: Harvard Business School Press.

Bartlett, C.A., Ghoshal, S. (1991): Global Strategic Management: Impact on the New Frontiers of Strategy Research, *Strategic Management Journal*, vol. 12, pp. 5-16.

Bartlett, C.A., Ghoshal, S. (1992a): *Transnational Management: Text, Cases and Readings in Cross-Border Management*, Chicago: Irwin.

Bartlett, C.A., Ghoshal, S. (1995): Changing the role of top management: beyond systems to people, *Harvard Business Review*, vol. 73 no. 3, pp. 132-142.

Baty, G.B., Evan, W.M., Rothermel, T.W. (1971): Personnel flows as interorganizational relations, *Administrative Science Quarterly*, vol. 16, pp. 430-443.

Baumgarten, K.E.E. (1992a): Expatriate failure and success: a search for potential predictors, Unpublished master's thesis, Enschede: University of Twente.

Baumgarten, K.E.E. (1992b): A profile for international managers and its implications for selection and training, Unpublished master's thesis, Enschede: University of Twente.

Baumgarten, K.E.E. (1995): Training and development of international staff, in Harzing, A.W.K., Van Ruysseveldt, J.: *International Human Resource Management*, pp. 205-228, London: Sage.

Baumler, J.V. (1971): Defined Criteria of Performance in Organizational Control, *Administrative Science Quarterly* (September), pp. 340-350.

Beer, M., Spector, B., Lawrence, P.R., Quin Mills, D., Walton, R.E. (1984): *Managing Human Assets*, New York: Macmillan.

Biggadike, E.R. (1990): Research on managing the multinational company: a practitioner's experiences, in Bartlett, C.A.; Doz, Y., Hedlund, G.: *Managing the global firm*, pp. 303-325, London: Routledge.

Birdseye, M.G., Hill, J.S. (1995): Individual, Organizational/Work and Environmental Influences on Expatriate Turnover Tendencies: An Empirical Study, *Journal of International Business Studies*, vol. 26 no. 4, pp. 787-814.

Birkinshaw, J.M. (1994): Approaching Heterarchy. A Review of the Literature on Multinational Strategy and Structure, in Prasad, B., Peterson, R.B.: *Advances in International Comparative Management*, vol. 9, pp. 111-144, Greenwich, CT: JAI Press.

Birkinshaw, J., Morrison, A.J. (1995): Configurations of Strategy and Structure in Subsidiaries of Multinational Corporations, *Journal of International Business Studies*, vol. 26 no. 4, pp. 729-754.

Birkinshaw, J., Jonsson, S., Hood, N. (1995): The determinants of subsidiary mandates and subsdiary initiative: a three-country study, paper submitted to the Academy of Management annual confererence, Cincinnati OH, 1996, International Division.

Birkinshaw, J. (1997): Entrepreneurship in Multinational Companies: The Characteristics of Subsidiary Initiatives, *Strategic Management Journal*, vol. 18 no. 3, pp. 207-230.

Birnberg, J.G., Snodgrass, C. (1988): Culture and control: a field study, *Accounting, Organization and Society*, vol. 13 no. 5, pp. 447-464.

Black, J.S. (1988): Work Role Transitions: A Study of American Expatriate Managers in Japan, *Journal of International Business Studies* (Summer), pp. 277-294.

Black, J.S., Mendenhall, M. (1989): A Practical but Theory-based Framework for Selecting Cross-Cultural Training Methods, *Human Resource Management*, vol. 28 (Winter), pp. 511-539.

Black, J.S., Mendenhall, M. Oddou, G. (1991): Toward a Comprehensive Model of International Adjustment: An Integration of Multiple Theoretical Perspectives, *Academy of Management Review*, vol. 16 no. 2, pp. 291-317.

Black, J.S., Porter, L.W. (1991): Managerial behaviors and job performance: a successful manager in Los Angeles may not succeed in Hong Kong, *Journal of International Business Studies* vol. 22 no.1, pp. 99-113.

Black, J.S., Gregersen, H.B., Mendenhall, M.E. (1992): Toward a Theoretical Framework of Repatriation Adjustment, *Journal of International Business Studies*, vol. 23 no. 4, pp. 737-760.

Black, J.S., Gregersen, H.B., Mendenhall, M.E. (1992): *Global Assignments*, San Francisco: Jossey Bass.

Black, J.S., Gregersen, H.B. (1992): Serving Two Masters: Managing the Dual Allegiance of Expatriate Employees, *Sloan Management Review* (Summer), pp. 61-71.

Black, J.S. (1992): Socializing American Expatriate Managers Overseas: Tactics, Tenure and Role Innovation, *Group and Organization Management*, vol. 17 no. 2, pp. 171-192.

Blackwell, N., Bizet, J.P., Child, P., Hensley, D. (1991): Shaping a pan-European organization, *McKinsey Quarterly* no. 2, pp. 95-111.

Blaine, M. (1994): Comparing the Profitability of Firms in Germany, Japan, and the United States, *Management International Review*, vol. 34 no. 2, pp. 125-148.

Blau, P.M., Scott, W.R. (1963): *Formal Organizations*, London: Routledge and Kegan Paul.

Blau, P.M., Schoenherr, R.A. (1971): *The Structure of Organizations*, New York: Basic Books.

Bolwijn, P.T., Kumpe, T. (1990): Manufacturing in the 1990s - Productivity, Flexibility and Innovation, *Long Range Planning*, vol. 23 no. 4, pp. 44-57.

Borg, M. (1988): *International Transfers of Managers in Multinational Corporations*, Uppsala: Acta Universitatis Upsaliensis.

Borg, M., Harzing, A.W.K. (1995): Composing an international staff, in Harzing, A.W.K., Van Ruysseveldt, J.: *International Human Resource Management*, pp. 179-204, London: Sage.

Borg, M., Harzing, A.W.K. (1996): Karrierepfade und Effektivität internationaler Führungskräfte - Profile und Erfolgspotentiale, in Macharzina, K., Wolf, J. (eds.), *Handbuch Internationales Führungskräfte-Management*, Stuttgart: RAABE Verlag, pp. 267-278.

Böttcher, R., Welge, M.K. (1996): Global Strategies of European Firms, *The International Executive*, vol. 38 no. 2, pp. 185-216.

Bowman, C., Ambrosini, V. (1997): Using Single Respondents in Strategy Research, *British Journal of Management*, vol. 8, pp. 119-131.

Boyacigiller, N. (1990): The role of expatriates in the management of interdependence, complexity and risk in multinational corporations, *Journal of International Business Studies*, vol. 21 no. 3, pp. 357-381.

Boyacigiller, N. (1991): The International Assignment Reconsidered, in Mendenhall, M., Oddou, G.: *Readings and Cases in International Human Resouce Management*, pp. 148-155, Boston: PWS-Kent.

Boyacigiller, N., Adler, N.J. (1991): The parochial dinosaur: The organizational sciences in a global context, *Academy of Management Review*, vol. 16 no. 2, pp. 262-290.

Boyacigiller, N., Adler, N.J. (1993): Insiders and outsiders: Bridging the worlds of organizational behavior and international management, in Toyne, B.; Nigh, D.: *The State of International Business Inquiry*, Westport, Connecticut: Greenwood Publishing Company.

Boyacigiller, N., Kleinberg, J., Phillips, M., Sackmann, S. (1996): Conceptualizing Culture, in Punnett, B.J.; Shenkar, O.: *Handbook for International Management Research*, pp. 155-208, Cambridge, MA: Blackwell.

Brett, J.M., Stroh, L.K. (1995): Willingness to Relocate Internationally, *Human Resource Management*, vol. 34 no. 3, pp. 405-424.

Brewster, C. (1991): *The Management of Expatriates*, London: Kogan Page.

Brewster, C., Hegewisch, A.; Mayne, L., Tregaskis, O. (1994): Methodology of the Price Waterhouse Cranfield Project, in Brewster, C.; Hegewisch: *Policy and Practice in European Human Resource Management*, London: Routledge.

Brewster, C., et al. (1996): Comparative research in human resource management: a review and an example, *The International Journal of Human Resource Management*, vol. 7 no. 3, pp. 585-604.

Brinkgreve, O.E. (1993): *The development and performance of transnational organizations* (Dec.), Rotterdam: Erasmus University, Afstudeerscriptie.

Briscoe, D.R. (1995): *International Human Resource Management*, Englewood Cliffs, NJ: Prentice Hall.

Brislin, R.W., Lonner, W.J.,. Thorndike, R.M. (1973): *Cross-Cultural Research Methods*, New York: Wiley.

Brislin, R.W. (1986): The Wording and Translation of Research Instruments, in Lonner, W.J., Berry, J.W.: *Field methods in cross-cultural research*, pp. 137-164, Beverly Hills: Sage Publications.

Brossard, M., Maurice, M. (1976): Is there a Universal Model of Organization Structure?, *International Studies on Management and Organizations*, vol. 6, pp. 11-45.

Brown, P., Soybel, V., Stickney, C. (1994): Comparing US and Japanese corporate-level operating performance using financial statement data, *Strategic Management Journal*, vol. 15, pp. 75-83.

Buchanan, B. (1974): Building organizational commitment: Socialization of managers in work organizations, *Administrative Science Quarterly*, vol. 19, pp. 533-546.

Buckley, P., Dunning, J.H., Pearce, R.D. (1978): The Influence of Firm Size, Nationality, and Degree of Multinationality on the Growth and Profitability of the World's Largest Firms, 1962-1972, *Welwirtschaftliches Archiv*, vol. 114 no. 2, pp. 243-257.

Buckley, P.J., Brooke, M.Z. (1992): International Human Resource Management, in Buckley, P.J., Brooke, M.Z.: *International Business Studies*, pp. 523-539, Oxford: Blackwell.

Burns, T., Stalker, G.M. (1961): *The Management of Innovation*, London: Tavistock Publications.

Bush, J.B., Frohman, A.L. (1992): Communication in a "Network" Organization, *Organizational Dynamics*, pp. 23-36.

Buzzell, R., Quelch, J.A. (1988): *Multinational Marketing Management*, Reading: Addison-Wesley.

Caligiuri, P.M., Stroh, L.K. (1995): Multinational corporation management strategies and international human resources practices: bringing IHRM to the bottom line, *The International Journal of Human Resource Management*, vol. 6 no. 3 (Sept.), pp. 494-507.

Calori, R., Sarnin, P. (1991): Corporate Culture and Economic Performance, *Organization Studies*, vol. 12 no. 1, pp. 49-74.

Calori, R., Lubatkin, M., Very, Philippe (1994): Control Mechanisms in Cross-border Acquisitions: An International Comparison, *Organization Studies*, vol. 15 no. 3, pp. 361-379.

Cardel Gertsten, M. (1990): Intercultural Competence and Expatriates, *The International Journal of Human Resource Management*, vol. 1 no. 3, pp. 341-362.

Casson, M., Loveridge, R., Singh, F. (1996): The Ethical Significance of Corporate Culture in Large Multinational Enterprises, in Brady, F.N.: *Ethical Universals in International Business*, pp. 303-356, Berlin: Springer.

Cavusgil, S.T., Das, A. (1997): Methodological Issues in Empirical Cross-Cultural Research: A Survey of the Management Literature and a Framework, *Management International Review*, vol. 37 no. 1, pp. 71-96.

Chandler, A.D. (1962): Strategy and Structure: Chapters in the History of the Industrial Entreprise, Cambridge, MA: MIT Press.

Chang, S.J. (1996): An Evolutionary Perspective on Diversification and Corporate Restructuring: Entry, Exit, and Economic Performance during 1981-1989, *Strategic Management Journal*, vol. 17 no. 8 (October), pp. 587-612.

Child, J. (1972): Organizational Structure, Environment and Performance: The Role of Strategic Choice, *Sociology*, vol. 6, pp. 1-22.

Child, J. (1973): Strategies of Control and Organization Behavior, *Administrative Science Quarterly*, vol. 18 (March), pp. 1-17.

Child, J. (1981): Culture, Contingency and Capitalism in the Cross-National Study of Organizations, in Staw, B.M., Cummings, L.L.: *Research in Organizational Behavior*, vol. 3, pp. 303-356, Greenwich, CT: JAI Press.

Child, J., Tayeb, M. (1983): Theoretical Perspectives in Cross-National Organizational Research, *International Studies on Management and Organization*, pp. 23-70.

Child, J. (1984): *Organization: a Guide to Problems and Practice*, London: Harper and Row.

Chow, C.W., Shields, M.D., Chan, Y.K. (1991): The effects of management controls and national culture on manufacturing performance: an experimental investigation, *Accounting, Organization and Society*, vol. 16 no. 3, pp. 209-226.

Chow, C.W., Kato, Y., Shields, M.D. (1994): National Culture and the preference for management controls: an exploratory study of the firm-labor market interface, *Accounting, Organization and Society*, vol. 19 no. 4/5, pp. 381-400.

Church, A.H. (1993): Estimating the effect of incentives on mail survey response rates: a meta-analysis, *Public Opinion Quarterly*, vol. 57, pp. 62-79.

Clark, P.C., Mueller, F. (1996): Organizations and Nations: from Universalism to Institutionalism, *British Journal of Management*, vol. 7, pp. 125-139.

Coase, R.H. (1937): The nature of the firm, *Economica*, vol. 4, pp. 386-405.

Collis, D.J. (1991): A Resource-Based Analysis of Global Competition: The Case of the Bearings Industry, *Strategic Management Journal*, vol. 12, pp. 49-68.

Conant, J.S., Mowak, M.P., Varadarjan, P.R. (1990): Strategic types, distinctive competencies and organizational performance: A multiple measure-based study, *Strategic Management Journal*, vol. 11, pp. 365-383.

Cool, K., Schendel, D. (1987): Strategic Group Formation and Performance, *Management Science*, vol. 33, pp. 1102-1124.

Cooper, C.L., Cox, C.J. (1989): Applying American Organizational Sciences in Europe and the United Kingdom: The Problems, in Osigweh, C.A.B.: *Organizational Science Abroad, Constraints and Perspectives*, pp. 57-66, New York: Plenum Press.

Cortina, J.M. (1993): What is Coefficient Alpha? An Examination of Theory and Applications, *Journal of Applied Psychology*, vol. 78 no. 1, pp. 98-104.

Cray, D. (1984): Control and Coordination in Multinational Corporations, *Journal of International Business Studies*, vol. 15 (Fall), pp. 85-99.

Cullen, J.B., Johnson, J.L., Sakano, T. (1995): Japanese and Local Partner Commitment to IJVs: Psychological Consequences of Outcomes and Investments in the IJV Relationship, *Journal of International Business Studies*, vol. 26 no. 1, pp. 91-116.

D'Arcimoles, C.-H. (1995): *Human Resource Policies and Company Performance: An analysis of French firms using panel data* (Sept.), Rotterdam: Rotterdam Institute for Business Economic Studies.

Daft, R.L. (1992): *Organization Theory and Design*, New York: West Publishing Company.

Daley, L., et al. (1985): Attitudes toward financial control systems in the United States and Japan, *Journal of International Business Studies* no. Fall, pp. 91-110.

Daniel, S.J., Reitsperger, W.D. (1991): Management Control Systems for J.I.T.: An Empirical Comparison of Japan and the U.S., *Journal of International Business Studies*, vol. 22 no.4, pp. 603-617.

Daniels, J.D., Arpan, J. (1972): Comparative Home Country Influences on Management Practices Abroad, *Academy of Management Journal*, vol. 15 no. 3, pp. 305-315.

Daniels, J.D., Pitts, R.A., Tretter, M.J. (1984): Strategy and Structure of U.S. Multinationals: An Exploratory Study, *Academy of Management Journal*, vol. 27 no. 2, pp. 292-307.

Daniels, J.D., Pitts, R.A., Tretter, M.J. (1985): Organizing for Dual Strategies of Product Diversity and International Expansion, *Strategic Management Journal*, vol. 6 no. 3, pp. 223-237.

Daniels, J.D., Bracker, J. (1989): Profit performance: Do foreign operations make a difference?, *Management International Review*, vol. 29, pp. 46-56.

Daniels, J.D., Radebaugh, L.H. (1989): *International Business. Environment and Operations*, Reading, MA: Addison-Wesley.

Datta, D., Rajagopolan, N., Rajheed, A. (1991): Diversification and Performance: a Critical Review, *Journal of Management Studies*, vol. 25 no. 5, pp. 529-557.

Dawson, S., Dickinson, D. (1988): Conducting international mail surveys: The effect of incentivess on response rates within an industrial population, *Journal of International Business Studies*, vol. 19, pp. 491-496.

De Cieri, H., Dowling, P.J., Taylor, K.F. (1991): The psychological impact of expatriate relocation on partners, *The International Journal of Human Resource Management*, vol. 2 no. 3 (December), pp. 377-414.

De Meyer, A. (1991): Tech Talk: How Managers Are Stimulating Global R&D Communication, *Sloan Management Review* (Spring), pp. 49-58.

Delaney, E. (1996): Strategic Development of multinational subsidiaries in Ireland, Paper presented at the 22nd EIBA conference (15-17 Dec.), Stockholm.

Denison, D.R. (1990): *Corporate culture and organizational effectiveness*, New York: Wiley.

Denison, D.R., Mishra, A.K. (1995): Toward a Theory of Organizational Culture and Effectiveness, *Organization Science*, vol. 6 no. 2, pp. 204-223.

Denison, D.R. (1996): What IS the Difference Between Organizational Culture and Organizational Climate? A Native's Point of View on a Decade of Paradigm Wars, *Academy of Management Review*, vol. 21 no. 3, pp. 619-654.

Derr, C.D., Oddou, G. (1991): Are U.S. Multinationals adequately preparing future American leaders for global competition?, *The International Journal of Human Resource Management*, vol. 2 no. 2, pp. 227-244.

Derr, C.D., Oddou, G. (1993): Internationalizing Managers - Speeding Up the Process, *European Management Journal*, vol. 11 no. 4, pp. 435-442.

Desatnick, R.L., Bennett, M.L. (1978): *Human Resource Management in the Multinational Company*, New York: Nichols.

Dess, G., Davis, P. (1984): Porter's generic strategies as determinants of strategic group membership and organizational performance, *Academy of Management Journal*, vol. 27, pp. 467-488.

Diamantopoulos, A., Schlegelmilch, B.B., Webb, L. (1991): Factors Affecting Industrial Mail Response Rates, *Industrial Marketing Management*, vol. 20, pp. 327-339.

Dichter, S.F. (1991): The organization of the '90s, *McKinsey Quarterly*, no. 1, pp. 145-155.

Dillman, R. (1978): *The total design method*, New York: John Wiley and Sons.

Dobry, A. (1983): *Die Steuerung ausländischer Tochtergesellschaften - Eine theoretische und empirische Untersuchung ihrer Grundlagen und Instrumente*, Giessen.

Doty, D.H., Glick, W.H., Huber, G.P. (1993): Fit, Equifinality, and Organizational Effectiveness - A Test of Two Configurational Theories, *Academy of Management Journal*, vol. 36, pp. 1196-1250.

Doty, H.D., Glick, W. (1994): Typologies as a unique form of theory building, *Academy of Management Review*, vol. 19, pp. 230-251.

Douglas, S.P., Craig, C.S. (1983): *International Marketing Research*, Englewood Cliffs: Prentice Hall.

Douma, S., Schreuder, H. (1991): *Economic Approaches to Organizations*, New York: Prentice Hall.

Dowling, P.J. (1986): Human Resource Issues in International Business, *Syracuse Journal of International Law and Commerce*, vol. 13 no. 2, pp. 255-271.

Dowling, P.J., Welch, D.E. (1988): International Human Resource Management: An Australian Perspective, *Asia Pacific Journal of Management*, vol. 6 no. 1, pp. 3965.

Dowling, P.J., Schuler, R.S. (1990): *International Dimensions of Human Resource Management*, Boston: PWS-Kent.

Doyle, P., Saunders, J., Wong, V. (1992): Competition in global markets: A case study of American and Japanese competition in the British market, *Journal of International Business Studies*, vol. 23 no. 3, pp. 419-442.

Doz, Y.L. (1976): *National policies and multinational management*, Unpublished doctoral dissertation: Harvard Business School,.

Doz, Y.L. (1980): Strategic Management in Multinational Companies, *Sloan Management Review*, vol. 21 (Winter), pp. 27-46.

Doz, Y.L., Prahalad, C.K. (1984): Patterns of Strategic Control Within Multinational Firms, *Journal of International Business Studies*, vol. 15 no. 2, pp. 55-72.

Doz, Y.L., Prahalad, C.K. (1986): Controlled Variety: A Challenge for Human Resource Management in the MNC, *Human Resource Management*, vol. 25 (Spring), pp. 55-71.

Doz, Y.L. (1986): *Strategic Management in Multinational Companies*, New York.

Doz, Y.L., Prahalad, C.K. (1991): Managing DMNCs: A Search for a New Paradigm, *Strategic Management Journal*, vol. 12, pp. 145-164.

Drasgow, F., Kanfer, R. (1985): Equivalence of psychological measurement in heterogeneous populations, *Journal of Applied Psychology*, vol. 70, pp. 662-680.

Drazin, R., Van de Ven, A.H. (1985): Alternate forms of fit in contingency theory, *Administrative Science Quarterly*, vol. 30, pp. 514-539.

Early, P.C. (1987): Intercultural Training for Managers: A Comparison of Documentary and Interpersonal Methods, *Academy of Management Journal*, vol. 30 no. 4, pp. 685-698.

Edström, A., Galbraith, J.R. (1977a): Alternative Policies for International Transfers of Managers, *Management International Review*, vol. 17 no. 2, pp. 11-22.

Edström, A., Galbraith, J.R. (1977b): Transfer of Managers as a Coordination and Control Strategy in Multinational Organizations, *Administrative Science Quarterly*, vol. 22 (June), pp. 248-263.

Edström, A., Galbraith, J.R. (1978): The Impact of Managerial Transfers on Headquarters-Subsidiary Relationships in a Multinational Company, in Ghertman, M., Leontiades, J.: *European Research in International Business*, pp. 331-349, Amsterdam.

Edström, A., Lorange, P. (1984): Matching Strategy and Human Resources in Multinational Corporations, *Journal of International Business Studies*, vol. 15 (Fall), pp. 125-137.

Edwards, P., Ferner, A., Sisson, K. (1996): The conditions for international human resource management: two case studies, *The International Journal of Human Resource Management*, vol. 7 no. 1 (Feb.), pp. 20-40.

Egelhoff, W.G (1984): Patterns of Control in US, UK, and European Multinational Corporations, *Journal of International Business Studies*, vol. 15 (Fall), pp. 73-83.

Egelhoff, W.G (1988a): *Organizing the Multinational Enterprise*, Cambridge: Ballinger.

Egelhoff, W.G. (1988b): Strategy and Structure in Multinational Corporations: A Revision of the Stopford and Wells Model, *Strategic Management Journal*, vol. 9, pp. 1-14.

Egelhoff, W.G. (1993): Information-processing Theory and the Multinational Corporation, in Ghoshal, S., Westney, D.E.: *Organization Theory and the Multinational Corporation*, pp. 182-210, New York: St. Martin's Press.

Ellison, L.M., Nicholas. D.A. (1986): Employee Benefits and Special Policies, in Famularo, J.J.: *Handbook of Human Resources Administration*, New York: McGraw-Hill.

Enz, C.A. (1986): New Directions for cross-cultural studies: Linking organizational and societal cultures, in Farmer, R.N.: *Advances in international comparative management* (vol. 2), pp. 173-189, Greenwich, CT: JAI Press.

Eramilli, M.K. (1996): Nationality and Subsidiary Ownership Patterns in Multinational Corporations, *Journal of International Business Studies*, vol. 27 no. 2, pp. 225-248.

Evans, P.A.L. (1986): The Strategic Outcomes of Human Resource Management, *Human Resource Management*, vol. 25 (Spring), pp. 149-167.

Evans, P.A.J , Lorange, P. (1989): The Two Logics Behind Human Resource Management, in Evans, P.A.L., Doz, Y., Lorange, P.: *Human Resource Management in International Firms: Change, Globalization, Innovation*, pp. 144-161, London: Macmillan.

Evans, P.A.L. (1989): Organizational development in the transnational enterprise, in Woodman, R., Pasmore, W.: *Research in Organizational Change and Development*, vol. 3, New York: JAI Press.

Evans, P.A.L., Lank, E., Farquhar, A. (1989): Managing Human Resources in the International Firm: Lessons From Practice, in Evans, P.A.L., Doz, Y., Lorange, P.: *Human Resource Management in International Firms: Change, Globalization, Innovation*, pp. 113-143, London: Macmillan.

Evans, P.A.L. (1991): *Management Development as Glue Technology*, Fontainebleau: INSEAD, Working Paper, no. 91/59/0B.

Farmer, R.N., Richman, B.M. (1965): *Comparative Management and Economic Progress*, Homewood, IL: Irwin.

Fatehi, K. (1996): *International Management*, Englewood Cliffs, New Jersey: Prentice Hall.

Feldman, D.C., Thompson, H.B. (1993): Expatriation, Repatriation and Domestic Geographical Relocation: An Empirical Investigation of Adjustment to New Job Assignments, *Journal of International Business Studies* vol. 24 no. 3, pp. 507-529.

Fenwick, M., Welch, D., De Cieri, H. (1993): Organizational Control through Staff Transfers: A Concept Revisited, Lisbon, paper presented at the 19th EIBA Annual Conference.

Fenwick, M.S., DeCieri, H. (1995): An Integrative Approach to International Compensation: Meeting Emerging Challenges, paper presented at the 21st annual Conference of the European International Business Academy (10-12 December), Urbino, Italy.

Ferner, A. (1994): Multinational Companies and Human Resource Management: An Overview of Research Issues, *Human Resource Management Journal*, vol. 4 no. 3, pp. 79-102.

Ferner, A. (1997): Country of origin effects and human resource management in multinational companies, *Human Resource Management Journal*, vol. 7 no. 1, pp. 19-37.

Ferner, A., Edwards, P., Sisson, K. (1995): Coming Unstuck? In Search of the "Corporate Glue" in an International Professional Service Firm, *Human Resource Management*, vol. 34 no. 3 (Fall), pp. 343-361.

Festing, A. (1996a): *Strategisches Internationales Personalmanagement*, München und Mering: Rainer Hamp Verlag.

Festing, A. (1996b): Strategic International Human Resource Managment in German Multinational Enterprises, *Innovation and International Business, Proceedings of the 22nd EIBA conference*, vol. 1, pp. 251-276, Stockholm: Stockholm School of Economics, IIB.

Fiegenbaum, A., Thomas, H. (1990): Strategic Groups and Performance: The U.S. Insurance Industry, 1970-1984, *Strategic Management Journal*, vol. 11 no. 3, pp. 197-215.

Finkelstein, S. (1992): Power in Top Management Teams: Dimensions, Measurement and Validation, *Academy of Management Journal*, vol. 35 no. 3, pp. 505-538.

Flamholtz, E.G., Das, T.K., Tsui, A.S. (1985): Toward an integrative framework of organizational control, *Accounting, Organization and Society*, vol. 10 no. 1, pp. 35-50.

Fombrun, C., Tichy, N.M, Devanna, M.A. (1984): *Strategic Human Resource Management*, New York: John Wiley.

Forsgren, M. (1990): Managing the International Multi-Centre Firm, *European Management Journal*, vol. 8 no. 2 (June), pp. 261-267.

Forsgren, M., Pahlberg, C. (1992): Subsidiary Influence and Autonomy in International Firms, *Scandinavian International Business Review*, vol. 1 no. 3, pp. 41-51.

Forsgren, M., Holm, U. (1995): Internationalization of management: dominance and distance, in Buckley, P.J., Ghauri, P.N.: *The internationalization of the firm*, pp. 337-349, London: The Dryden Press.

Forsgren, M., Holm, U., Johanson, J. (1995): Division Headquarters go Abroad - A Step in the Internationalization of the Multinational Corporation, *Journal of Management Studies*, vol. 32 no. 4 (July), pp. 475-492.

Forster, N. (1992): International managers and mobile families: the professional and personal dynamics of transnational career pathing and job mobility in the 1990s, *The International Journal of Human Resource Management*, vol. 3 no. 3 (December), pp. 605-623.

Forster, N. (1994): The forgotten employees? The experience of expatriate staff returning to the UK, *The International Journal of Human Resource Management*, vol. 5 no. 2 (May), pp. 405-425.

Forster, N., Johnsen, M. (1996): Expatriate management policies in UK companies new to the international scene, *The International Journal of Human Resource Management*, vol. 7 no. 1 (Feb.), pp. 179-205.

Fox, R.J., Crask, M.R., Kim, J. (1988): Mail survey response rate: a meta analysis of selected techniques for inducing response, *Public Opinion Quarterly*, vol. 52, pp. 467-491.

Franko, L.G. (1973): Who Manages Multinational Enterprises?, *Columbia Journal of World Business*, vol. 8 (Summer), pp. 30-42.

Franko, L.G. (1976): *The European Multinationals*, London: Harper and Row.

Galbraith, J.R. (1973): *Designing complex organizations*, Reading, MA: Addison-Wesley.

Galbraith, J.R., Edström, A. (1976): International Transfer of Managers: Some Important Policy Considerations, *Columbia Journal of World Business*, vol. 11 (Summer), pp. 100-112.

Galbraith, J.R., Kazanjian, R.K. (1986): Organizing to Implement Strategies of Diversity and Globalization: The Role of Matrix Designs, *Human Resource Management*, vol. 25 (Spring), pp. 37-54.

Garnier, G. (1982): Context and decision making autonomy in the foreign affiliates of U.S. multinational corporations, *Academy of Management Journal* (December), pp. 893-908.

Garnier, G. (1984): The Autonomy of Foreign Subsidiaries - Environmental and National Influences, *Journal of General Management*, vol. 10 no. 1, pp. 57-82.

Gates, S.R., Egelhoff, W.G. (1986): Centralization in Headquarters-Subsidiary Relationships, *Journal of International Business Studies*, vol. 17 (Summer), pp. 71-92.

Gaugler, E. (1989): Repatriierung von Stammhausdelegierte(n), in Macharzina, K., Welge, M.K.: *Handwörterbuch Export und internationale Unternehmung*, pp. 1937-1951, Stuttgart: Poeschel.

Gencturk, E.F., Aulakh, P.S. (1995): The Use of Process and Output Controls in Foreign Markets, *Journal of International Business Studies*, vol. 26 no. 4, pp. 755-786.

Geringer, J.M., Beamish, P.W., daCosta, R. (1989): Diversification Strategy and Internationalization: Implications for MNE Performance, *Strategic Management Journal*, vol. 10, pp. 109-119.

Gerpott, T.J. (1990): Strategieadäquates Personalmanagement bei der Integration von internationalen Akquisitionen, *Betriebswirtschaftliche Forschung und Praxis*, vol. 5, pp. 439-462.

Gerrichhauzen, J.T.G. (1991): Groupthink en organisatiecultuur, *M&O*, no. 3, pp. 169-183.

Ghauri, P. (1995): New structures in MNCs based in small countries: a network approach, in Ghauri, P.N., Prasad, S.B.: *International Management: A reader*, pp. 51-63, London: The Dryden Press.

Ghoshal, S., Bartlett, C.A. (1988): Creation, adoption and diffusion of innovations by subsidiaries of multinational corporations, *Journal of International Business Studies* (Fall), pp. 365-388.

Ghoshal, S., Nohria, N. (1989): Internal Differentiation within Multinational Corporations, *Strategic Management Journal*, vol. 10, pp. 323-337.

Ghoshal, S., Bartlett, C.A. (1990): The multinational corporation as an interorganizational network, *Academy of Management Review*, vol. 15, pp. 603-625.

Ghoshal, S., Westney, D.E. (1993): Introduction and Overview, in Ghoshal, S., Westney, D.E.: *Organization Theory and the Multinational Corporation*, pp. 1-23, New York: St Martin's Press.

Ghoshal, S., Nohria, N. (1993): Horses for Courses: Organizational Forms for Multinational Corporations, *Sloan Management Review* (Winter), pp. 23-35.

Ghoshal, S., Korine, H., Szulanski, G. (1994): Interunit communication within MNCs, *Management Science*, vol. 40 no. 1, pp. 96-110.

Godkin, L., Braye, C.E., Caunch, C.L. (1989): U.S. based cross-cultural management research in the eighties, *Journal of Business and Economic Perspectives*, vol. 15 no. 2, pp. 37-45.

Goehle, D.G. (1980): *Decision making in Multinational Corporations*, Ann Arbor: UMI Research Press.

Gonzalez, R.F., Negandhi, A.R. (1967): *The United States Executive: His Orientation and Career Patterns*, Michigan: East Lansing: MI.

Gordon, G.G., DiTomasso, N. (1992): Predicting corporate performance from organizational culture, *Journal of Management Studies*, vol. 29 no. 6, pp. 783-798.

Gosling, D.H. (1988): Measuring the performance of divisional cost centres, *CMA Magazine* (July-August), pp. 30-33.

Govindarajan, V., Gupta, A.K. (1985): Linking control systems to business unit strategy: impact on performance, *Accounting, Organization and Society*, vol. 10 no. 1, pp. 51-66.

Goyder, J. (1994): An experiment with cash incentives on a personal interview study, *Journal of the Market Research Society*, vol. 36 no. 4, pp. 360-366.

Grant, R.M. (1987): Multinationality and performance among British manufacturing companies, *Journal of International Business Studies*, vol. 18 no. 3, pp. 79-89.

Green, R.T., White, P.D. (1976): Methodological considerations in cross-national consumer research, *Journal of International Business Studies*, vol. 7 no. 3, pp. 81-87.

Greer, T.V., Lohtia, R. (1994): Effects of Source and Paper Color on Response Rates in Mail Surveys, *Industrial Marketing Management*, vol. 23, pp. 47-54.

Gregersen, H.B., Black, J.S. (1990): A Multifaceted Approach to Expatriate Retention in International Assignments, *Group and Organization Studies*, vol. 15 no. 4 (December), pp. 461-485.

Gresov, C. (1989): Exploring fit and misfit with multiple contingencies, *Administrative Science Quarterly*, vol. 34, pp. 431-453.

Groenewald, H., Sapozhnikov, A. (1990): Auslandentsendungen von Führungskräften. Vorgehenweisen internationaler Fluggesellschaften, *Die Unternehmung*, vol. 44 no. 1, pp. 28-42.

Gronhaug, K., Nordhaug, O. (1992): International human resource management: an environmental perspective, *The International Journal of Human Resource Management*, vol. 3 no. 1 (May), pp. 1-14.

Grunow, D. (1995): The Research Design in Organization Studies: Problems and Prospects, *Organization Science*, vol. 6 no. 1, pp. 93-103.

Gullahorn, J.E., Gullahorn, J.T. (1963): An investigation of the effects of three factors on response to mail questionnaires, *Public Opinion Quarterly*, vol. 27, pp. 294-296.

Gupta, A.K., Govindarajan, V. (1984): Business unit strategy, managerial characteristics, and business unit effectiveness at strategy implementation, *Academy of Management Journal*, vol. 27, pp. 25-41.

Gupta, A.K., Govindarajan, V. (1991): Knowledge Flows and the Structure of Control within Multinational Corporations, *Academy of Management Review*, vol. 16 no. 4, pp. 768-792.

Gupta, A.K., Govindarajan, V. (1994): Organizing for Knowledge Flows within MNCs, *International Business Review*, vol. 3 no. 4, pp. 443-457.

Haar, J. (1989): A Comparative Analysis of the Profitability Performance of the Largest U.S., European and Japanese Multinational Enterprises, *Management International Review*, vol. 29 no. 3, pp. 5-19.

Hage, J., Aiken, M., Marrett, C.B. (1971): Organization Structure and Communications, *American Sociological Review* (October), pp. 860-871.

Hagedoorn, J., Narula, R. (1994): Choosing Models of Governance for Strategic Technology Partnering: International and Sectoral Differences, in Obłój, K.: *Proceedings of the 20th annual conference*, vol. 1 (11-13 December), pp. 103-130, Warsaw: EIBA.

Hair, J., Anderson, R.E., Tatham, R.L., Black, W.C. (1995): *Multivariate Data Analysis with Readings*, Englewood Cliffs, NJ: Prentice Hall.

Hall, D., Saias, M. (1980): Strategy Follows Structure, *Strategic Management Journal*, vol. 1 no. 2, pp. 149-163.

Hall, W.K. (1980): Survival strategies in hostile environments, *Harvard Business Review* (September/October), pp. 75-85.

Halsberghe, E., Van den Bulcke, D. (1982): *Beleidsautonomie van buitenlandse dochterondernemingen in België*, Brussel: Instituut van de Onderneming.

Hambrick, D. (1983): High profit strategies in mature capital goods industries: A contingency approach, *Academy of Management Journal*, vol. 26, pp. 687-707.

Hamill, J. (1989): Expatriate Policies in British Multinationals, *Journal of General Management*, vol. 14 no. 4, pp. 18-33.

Hamilton III, R.D., Taylor, V.A.: Kashlak, R.J. (1996): Designing a control system for a multinational subsidiary, *Long Range Planning*, vol. 29 no. 6, pp. 857-868.

Hannon, J.M., Huang, I.-C., Jaw, B.-S. (1995): International Human Resource Strategy and Its Determinants: The Case of Subsidiaries in Taiwan, *Journal of International Business Studies*, vol. 26 no. 3, pp. 531-554.

Hansen, G.S., Wernerfelt, B. (1989): Determinants of Firm Performance: The Relative Importance of Economic and Organizational Factors, *Strategic Management Journal*, vol. 10, pp. 399-411.

Harbison, F., Myers, C.A. (1959): *Management in the Industrial World*, New York: McGraw-Hill.

Harpaz, I. (1996): International Management Survey Research, in Punnett, B.J., Shenkar, O.: *Handbook for International Management Research*, pp. 37-62, Cambridge, MA: Blackwell.

Harris, P.R., Moran, R.T. (1979): *Managing cultural differences*, Houston: Gulf Publishing Company.

Harris, H. (1995): Women's role in (international) management, in Harzing, A.W.K., Van Ruysseveldt, J.: *International Human Resource Management*, pp. 229-251, London: Sage.

Harrison, G.L., et al. (1994): The Influence of Culture on Organization Design and Planning and Control in Australia and the United States Compared with Singapore and Hong Kong, *Journal of International Financial Management and Accounting* (Oct.), pp. 242-261.

Harvey, M.G. (1982): The Other Side of Foreign Assignments: Dealing with the Repatriation Dilemma, *Columbia Journal of World Business*, vol. 17 no. 1, pp. 52-59.

Harvey, M.G. (1983): The Multinational Corporations Expatriate Problem: An Application of Murphy's Law, *Business Horizons*, vol. 26 no. 1, pp. 71-78.

Harvey, M.G. (1985): The Executive Family: An Overlooked Variable in International Assignments, *Columbia Journal of World Business*, vol. 20 (Spring), pp. 84-93.

Harvey, L. (1987): Factors affecting response rates to mailed questionnares: a comprehensive literature review, *Journal of the Market Research Society*, vol. 29, pp. 341-353.

Harvey, M.G. (1989): Repatriation of Corporate Executives - An Empirical Study, *Journal of International Business Studies*, vol. 20 no. 1, pp. 131-144.

Harvey, M. (1993a): Designing a Global Compensation System: The Logic and a Model, *Columbia Journal of World Business* Winter, pp. 57-72.

Harvey, M. (1993b): Empirical Evidence of Recurring International Compensation Problems, *Journal of International Business Studies* vol.24 no. 4, pp. 785-799.

Harzing, A.W.K. (1991): *National culture and organizational change: fit or failure*, Maastricht: University of Limburg, unpublished master's thesis.

Harzing, A.W.K. (1994): Organizational Bumblebees: International Transfers as a control mechanism in multinational companies, paper presented at the doctoral tutorial of the 20th annual meeting of the European International Business Academy (December), Warsaw.

Harzing, A.W.K., Van Ruysseveldt, J. (1995): *International Human Resource Management*, London: Sage.

Harzing, A.W.K. (1995a): Strategic planning in multinational firms, in Harzing, A.W.K., Van Ruysseveldt, J.: *International Human Resource Management*, pp. 25-50, London: Sage.

Harzing, A.W.K. (1995b): The Persistent Myth of High Expatriate Failure Rates, *The International Journal of Human Resource Management*, vol. 6 no. 2, pp. 457-475.

Harzing, A.W.K. (1995c): MNC staffing policies: in search of explanations for variety, paper presented at the 21th annual meeting of the European International Business Academy (December), Urbino.

Harzing, A.W.K., Hofstede, G. (1996): Planned change in organizations: the influence of national culture, in Bacharach, S.B., Bamberger, P.A., Erez, M.: *Research in the Sociology of Organizations: Cross-cultural analysis of organizations*, vol. 14, pp. 297-340, Greenwich: JAI Press.

Harzing, A.W.K. (1996a): Environment, Strategy, Structure, Control Mechanisms, and Human Resource Management, *Company report of doctoral research project*, Maastricht: University of Limburg.

Harzing, A.W.K. (1996b): How to survive international mail surveys: an inside story, *Innovation and International Business, Proceedings of the 22nd EIBA conference*, vol. 1, pp. 313-339, Stockholm: Stockholm School of Economics, IIB.

Harzing, A.W.K. (1997a): Research note: about the paucity of empirical research in IHRM: A test of Downes framework of staffing foreign subsidiaries, *Journal of International Management*, vol. 3 no. 2, pp. 153-167.

Harzing, A.W.K. (1997b): Response rates in international mail surveys: Results of a 22 country study, *International Business Review*, vol. 6 no. 6, pp. 641-665.

Harzing, A.W.K. (1998a): MNC staffing policies for the CEO position in foreign subsidiaries: the results of an innovative research method, in: Brewster, C., Harris, H.: *International HRM: Contemporary issues in Europe*, London: Routledge.

Harzing, A.W.K. (1998b): Configuration analysis in international management: the way forward?, under review at *Journal of International Business Studies*.

Harzing, A.W.K. (1998c): The effect of nationality on response rates in international mail surveys, under review at *Industrial Marketing Management*.

Harzing, A.W.K. (1998d): Acquisitions versus greenfields: both sides of the picture, paper presented at the 1998 Meeting of the Academy of International Business, Vienna, 7-10 October.

Harzing, A.W.K. (1998e): Who's in Charge? : an empirical study of executive staffing practices in foreign subsidiaries, under review at *Journal of Management Studies*.

Hays, R.D. (1974): Expatriate Selection: Insuring Success and Avoiding Failure, *Journal of International Business Studies*, vol. 5 no. 1, pp. 25-37.

Hedlund, G. (1981): Autonomy of subsidiaries and formalization of headquarters-subsidiary relationships in Swedish MNCs, in Otterbeck, L.: *The management of headquarter-subsidiary relationships in multinational corporations*, pp. 25-78, New York: St Martin's Press.

Hedlund, G. (1986): The Hypermodern MNC - A Heterarchy?, *Human Resource Management*, vol. 25 (Spring), pp. 9-35.

Hedlund, G., Rolander, D. (1990): Action in heterarchies: new approaches to managing the MNC, in Bartlett, C.A., Doz, Y., Hedlund, G.: *Managing the global firm*, pp. 15-46, London: Routledge.

Hedlund, G., Ridderstrale, J. (1992): *Toward the N-form Corporation: Exploration and Creation in the MNC*, Stockholm: Institute of International Business, Stockholm School of Economics, Working Paper.

Hedlund, G. (1993): Assumptions of Hierarchy and Heterarchy, with Applications to the Management of the Multinational Corporation, in Ghoshal, S., Westney, D.E.: *Organization Theory and the Multinational Corporation*, pp. 211-236, New York: St Martin's Press.

Hedlund, G. (1994): A model of knowledge management and the N-form corporation, *Strategic Management Journal*, vol. 15, pp. 73-90.

Heenan, D.A., Perlmutter, H.V. (1979): *Multinational Organization Development*, pp. 1-85, Reading, MA: Addison-Wesley Publishing Company.

Helgeson, J.G. (1994): Receiving and responding to a mail survey: a phenomenological examination, *Journal of the Market Research Society*, vol. 36 no. 4, pp. 339-347.

Helms, M. (1991): International Executive Compensation Practices, in Mendenhall, M., Oddou, G.: *Readings and Cases in International Human Resouce Management*, pp. 375-384, Boston: PWS-Kent.

Hendry, C.A., Pettigrew, A., Sparrow, P. (1989): Linking strategic change, competitive performance and human resource management: results of a UK empirical study, in Mansfield, R.: *Frontiers of Management*, pp. 195-220, London: Routledge.

Hendry, C.A. (1994): *Human Resource Strategies for International Growth*, London: Routledge.

Hendry, C. (1996): Continuities in Human Resource Processes in Internationalization and Domestic Business Management, *Journal of Management Studies*, vol. 33 no. 4 (July), pp. 475-494.

Hennart, J.-F. (1991): Control in Multinational Firms: The Role of Price and Hierarchy, *Management International Review*, vol. 31 Special Issue, pp. 71-96.

Henry, E.R. (1965): What business can learn form Peace Corps selection and training, *Personnel*, vol. 42 no. 4, pp. 17-25.

Hickson, D.J., et al. (1974): The Culture-Free Context of Organization Structure: A Tri-National Comparison, *Sociology*, vol. 8, pp. 59-80.

Hilb, M. (1992): The challenge of management development in Western Europe in the 1990s, *The International Journal of Human Resource Management*, vol. 3 no. 3 (December), pp. 575-584.

Hillman, F., Rudolph, H. (1996): Jenseits des brain drain, *WZB Discussion Paper* no. FS I 96-103.

Hines, A.M. (1993): Linking Qualitative and Quantitative Methods in Cross-Cultural Survey Research: Techniques from Cognitive Science, *Amercian Journal of Community Psychology*, vol. 21 no. 6, pp. 729-746.

Hodgetts, R.M., Luthans, F. (1994): *International Management*, New York: McGraw-Hill.

Hoeksema, L.H. (1995): *Learning Strategy as a Guide to Career Success in Organizations*, Leiden: DSWO Press.

Hoffman, R.C. (1988): The General Management of Foreign Subsidiaries in the U.S.A. - An Exploratory Study, *Management International Review*, vol. 28 no. 2, pp. 41-55.

Hofstede, G. (1980a): Culture's Consequences. International Differences in Work-Related Values, London: Sage Publications.

Hofstede, G. (1980b): Motivation, Leadership and Organizations: Do American Theories Apply Abroad?, *Organizational Dynamics* (Summer), pp. 42-63.

Hofstede, G., Spangenberg, J.F.A. (1986): Methodology of International Comparative Research, Maastricht: Faculty of Economics, Limburg University, Research Memoran-dum, 86-013.

Hofstede, G. (1991): *Cultures and Organizations: Software of the Mind*, London: McGraw-Hill.

Hoopes, D. (1994): Worldwide Branch Locations of Multinational Companies, Detroit: Gale Research Inc.

Hoppe, M.H. (1993): The Effects of National Culture on the Theory and Practice of Managing R&D Professionals Abroad, *R&D Management*, vol. 23 no. 4, pp. 313-325.

Horng, C. (1993): Cultural Differences, Trust and their Relationships to Business Strategy and Control, in Prasad, S.B., Peterson, R.B.: *Advances in International Comparative Management*, vol. 8, pp. 175-197, Greenwich: JAI Press.

Horvath, D., et al. (1981): The cultural context of organizational control. An international comparison, in Hickson, D., McMillan, C.: *Organization and the Nation: The Aston Programme IV*, London: Gower.

Hossain, S., Davis, H.J. (1989): Some Thoughts on International Personnel Management as an Emerging Field, *Research in Personnel and Human Resources Management, Suppl. 1*, pp. 121-136, Greenwich: JAI Press Inc..

Hout, T., Porter, M.E., Rudden, E. (1982): How Global Companies Win Out, reprinted in Bartlett, C., Ghoshal, S. (1992): *Transnational Management, Text Cases and Readings*, pp. 371-381, Homewood, Boston: Irwin.

Houten, G. van (1989): The Implications of Globalism: New Management Realities at Philips, in Evans, P., Doz, Y., Laurent, A.: *Human Resource Management in International Firms: Change, Globalization, Innovation*, pp. 101-112, London: Macmillan.

Hulbert, J.M, Brandt, W.K. (1980): *Managing the Multinational Subsidiary*, New York: Holt, Rinehart and Winston.

Imai, K., Itami, H. (1984): Interpenetration of Organization and Market. Japan's Firm and Market in Comparison with the U.S., *International Journal of Industrial Organization* no. 2, pp. 285-310.

Ishida, H. (1986): Transferability of Japanese Human Resource Management Abroad, *Human Resource Management*, vol. 25 (Spring), pp. 103-120.

Jaeger, A.M. (1982): Contrasting Control Modes in the Multinational Corporation: Theory, Practice, and Implications, *International Studies of Management and Organization*, vol. XII no. 1, pp. 59-82.

Jaeger, A.M. (1983): The Transfer of Organizational Culture Overseas: An Approach to Control in the Multinational Corporation, *Journal of International Business Studies*, vol. 15 (Fall), pp. 91-114.

Jaeger, A.M., Baliga, B. (1985): Control Systems and Strategic Adaptation: Lessons from the Japanese Experience, *Strategic Management Journal*, vol. 6, pp. 115-134.

Jain, S.C., Tucker, L.R. (1995): The Influence of Culture on Strategic Constructs in the Process of Globalization: an Empirical Study of North American and Japanese MNCs, *International Business Review*, vol. 4 no. 1, pp. 19-37.

Janis, I.L. (1972): Groupthink, reprinted in Hackman, J.R. et al (1983): *Perspectives on Behavior in Organizations*, pp. 378-384, New York: McGraw-Hill.

Jarillo, J.C., Martinez, J.I. (1990): Different Roles for Subsidiaries: The Case of Multinational Corporations in Spain, *Strategic Management Journal*, vol. 11, pp. 501-512.

Jeelof, G. (1989): Global Strategies of Philips, *European Management Journal*, vol. 7 no. 1, pp. 84-91.

Jobber, D., Sanderson, S. (1983): The effects of a prior letter and coloured questionnaire paper on mail survey response rates, *Journal of the Market research society*, vol. 25 (Oct.), pp. 339-349.

Jobber, D., Sanderson, S. (1985): The Effect of Two Variables on Industrial Mail Survey Returns, *Industrial Marketing Management*, vol. 14, pp. 119-121.

Jobber, D. (1986): Improving Response Rates in Industrial Mail Surveys, *Industrial Marketing Management*, vol. 15, pp. 183-195.

Jobber, D., Saunders, J. (1986): The specificiation and estimation of a robust mail survey response model, *Proceedings of the XVth Annual Conference of the European Marketing Academy* (June), pp. 865-880, Helsinki.

Jobber, D., Saunders, J. (1988): An experimental investigation into cross-national mail survey response rates, *Journal of International Business Studies*, vol. 19, pp. 483-489.

Jobber, D., Mirza, H., Wee, K.H. (1991): Incentives and response rates to cross-national business surveys: a logit model analysis, *Journal of International Business Studies*, vol. 22 no. 4, pp. 711-721.

Jobber, D., Saunders, J. (1993): A Note on the Applicability of the Bruvold-Comer Model of Mail Survey Response to Commercial Populations, *Journal of Business Research*, vol. 26, pp. 223-236.

Johnson Jr, J.H. (1995): An Empirical Analysis of the Integration-Responsiveness Framework: U.S. Construction Equipment Industry Firms in Global Competition, *Journal of International Business Studies*, vol. 26 no. 3 (Third Quarter), pp. 621-636.

Jong, H.W. de (1996): Rijnlandse ondernemingen presteren beter, *Economisch Statistische Berichten* 13 March, pp. 228-232.

Kalafatis, S.P., Tsogas, M.H. (1994): Impact of the Inclusion of an Article as an Incentive in Industrial Mail Surveys, *Industrial Marketing Management*, vol. 23, pp. 137-143.

Kalleberg, A.L., Moody, J.W. (1994): Human Resource Management and Organizational Performance, *American Behavioral Scientist*, vol. 37 no. 7, pp. 948-962.

Kamoche, K. (1996): The integration-differentiation puzzle: a resource-capability perspective in international human resource management, *The International Journal of Human Resource Management*, vol. 7 no. 1 (Feb.), pp. 230-244.

Keegan, W.J. (1974): Multinational Scanning: A Study on the Information Sources Utilized by Headquarters Executives in Multinational Companies, *Administrative Science Quarterly* (September), pp. 411-421.

Kelley, L., Worthley, R. (1981): The Role of Culture in Comparative Management: A Cross-Cultural Perspective, *Academy of Management Journal*, vol. 24 no. 1, pp. 164-173.

Kelley, L., Whatley, A., Worthley, R. (1987): Assessing the Effects of Culture on Managerial Attitudes: A Three-Culture Test, *Journal of International Business Studies*, vol. 23, pp. 17-31.

Kenter, M.E. (1985): *Die Steuerung ausländischer Tochtergesellschaften. Instrumente und Effizienz*, Frankfurt am Main/Berlin/New York: P. Lang.

Kenter, M.E. (1989): Stammhausdelegierte(n), Entsendung von, in Macharzina, K., Welge, M.K.: *Handwörterbuch Export und internationale Unternehmung*, pp. 1925-1937, Stuttgart: Poeschel.

Keown, C.F. (1985): Foreign Mail Surveys: Response Rates Using Monetary Incentives, *Journal of International Business Studies* (Fall), pp. 151-153.

Kepos, P. (1995): *International Directory of Company Histories*, vols I-VIII, Chicago: St James Press.

Kerin, R.A., et al. (1981): Offer of Results and Mail Survey Response From a Commercial Population, paper presented at the 13th meeting of the American Institute for Decision Sciences (Nov.), Boston.

Kerr, J.L., Jackofsky, E.F. (1989): Aligning Managers with Strategies: Management Development versus Selection, *Strategic Management Journal*, vol. 10, pp. 157-170.

Ketchen, Jr, D.J., Thomas, B., Snow, C.C. (1993): Organizational Configurations and Performance, *Academy of Management Journal*, vol. 36, pp. 1278-1313.

Ketchen, Jr, D.J., Shook, C.L. (1996): The Application of Cluster Analysis in Strategic Management Research: An Analysis and Critique, *Strategic Management Journal*, vol. 17 no. 6, pp. 441-458.

Ketchen, Jr, D.J., et al. (1997): Organizational Configurations and Performance: A Meta-Analysis, *Academy of Management Journal*, vol. 40 no. 1, pp. 222-240.

Khandwalla, P.N. (1974): Mass output orientation of operations technology and organizational structure, *Administrative Science Quarterly*, vol. 19, pp. 74-79.

Khandwalla, P.M. (1977): *The Design of Organizations*, New York: Harcourt Brace Jovanovic.

Kiesler, S., Sproull, L.S. (1986): Response Effects in the Electronic Survey, *Public Opinion Quarterly*, vol. 50, pp. 402-413.

Kilgore, J.E. (1991): International Relocation: The future of spouse relocation assistance, *Journal of Career Development*, vol. 17 no. 4, pp. 271-284.

Klein, K.J., Dansereau, F., Hall, R.J. (1994): Levels issues in theory development, data collection, and analysis, *Journal of Applied Psychology*, vol. 19, 195-229.

Kneebone, T. (1997): Lecture about repatriation based on the results of a survey by Bennett Associates, Seminar: Legal Aliens: Expatriates in today's world (22 April), Maastricht.

Kobrin, S.J. (1988): Expatriate Reduction and Strategic Control in American Multinational Corporations, *Human Resource Management*, vol. 27 (Spring), pp. 63-75.

Kobrin, S.J. (1991): An Empirical Analysis of the Determinants of Global Integration, *Strategic Management Journal*, vol. 12, pp. 17-31.

Kobrin, S.J. (1994): Is there a Relationship between a Geocentric Mind-Set and Multinational Strategy?, *Journal of International Business Studies* vol. 25 no. 3, pp. 493-511.

Koene, B.A.S. (1996): *Organizational Culture, Leadership and Performance in Context. Trust and Rationality in Organizations*, Maastricht: Datawyse.

Kogut, B., Singh, H. (1988): The Effect of National Culture on the Choice of Entry Mode, *Journal of International Business Studies* (Fall), pp. 411-432.

Kopp, R. (1994): International Human Resource Policies and Practices in Japanese, European and United States Multinationals, *Human Resource Management*, vol. 33 no. 4 (Winter), pp. 581-599.

Kotabe, M., Duhan, D.F., Smith, D.K., Wilson, R.D. (1991): The perceived veracity of PIMS strategy principles in Japan: An empirical inquiry, *Journal of Marketing*, vol. 55 no. 1, pp. 26-41.

Kriger, M.P., Solomon, E.E. (1992): Strategic Mindset and Decision-making Autonomy in U.S. and Japanese MNCs, *Management International Review*, vol. 32 no. 4, pp. 327-343.

Kuhn, T.S. (1970): *The Structure of Scientific Revolutions*, Chicago: University of Chicago Press, 2nd enlarged edn..

Kuin, P. (1972): The Magic of Multinational Management, *Harvard Business Review*, vol. 72 (Nov.-Dec.), pp. 89-97.

Kumar, M. (1984): Comparative Analysis of UK Domestic and International Firms, *Journal of Economic Studies*, vol. 4 no. 3, pp. 26-42.

Kumar, B.N., Steinmann, H. (1986): Japanische Fuhrungskrafte zwischen ensandten und lokalen Fuhrungskraften in Deutschland, *Zeitschrift fur Betriebswirtschaftliche Forschung*, vol. 38 no. 6, pp. 493-516.

Kumar, B.N., Karlshaus, M. (1992): Auslandseinsatz und Personalentwicklung. Ergebnisse einer empirischen Studie über den Beitrag der Auslandsentsendung., *Zeitschrift für Personalforschung*, vol. 6 no. 1, pp. 59-74.

Kumar, B.N. (1993): Globale Wettbewerbstrategien für den Europäischen Binnenmarkt, in Haller, M. et al: *Globalisierung der Wirtschaft - Einwirkungen auf die Betriebswirtschaftlehre*, pp. 49-76, Bern, Stuttgart, Wien: Verlag Paul Haupt.

Kusters, E.J.N. (1994): *Shell we go abroad?*, Tilburg University, Unpublished Master's Thesis.

Kustin, R.A., Jones, R.A. (1996): An Investigation of Japanese/American Managers' Leadership Styles in US Corporations, *Journal of International Management*, vol. 2 no. 2, pp. 111-126.

Kwok, C.C.Y., Apran, J.S. (1994): A Comparison of International Business Education at U.S. and European Business Schools in the 1990s, *Management International Review*, vol. 34 no. 4, pp. 357-379.

LaGarce, R., Kuhn, L.D. (1995): The Effect of Visual Stimuli on Mail Survey Response Rates, *Industrial Marketing Management*, vol. 24, pp. 11-18.

Lane, C. (1995): *Industry and society in Europe: Stability and Change in Britain, Germany and France*, Aldershot: Edward Elgar.

Lanier, A.R. (1979): Selecting and preparing personnel for overseas transfers, *Personnel Journal*, vol. 58 no. 3, pp. 160-163.

Laurent, A. (1983): The Cultural Diversity of Western Concepts of Management, *International Studies of Management and Organization*, vol. XIII no. 1-2, pp. 75-96.

Laurent, A. (1986): The Cross-Cultural Puzzle of International Human Resource Management, *Human Resource Management*, vol. 25 (Spring), pp. 91-102.

Lawler, E.E. (1981): *Pay and organization development*, Reading: Addison-Wesley.

Lawrence, J.W., Lorsch, P.R. (1967): *Organization and Environment*, Harvard University Press.

Lebas, M., Weigenstein, J. (1986): Management Control: The Roles of Rules, Markets and Culture, *Journal of Management Studies*, vol. 23 no. 3, pp. 259-271.

Lee, J., Blevins, D. (1990): Profitability and Sales Growth in Industrialized Versus Newly Industrializing Countries, *Management International Review*, vol. 30 no. 1, pp. 87-100.

Lee, C., Green, R.T. (1991): Cross-cultural examination of the Fishbein behavioral intentions model, *Journal of International Business Studies*, vol. 22 no. 2, pp. 289-305.

Lei, D., Slocum, J.W., Slater, R.W. (1990): Global Strategy and Reward Systems: The Key Roles of Management Development and Corporate Culture, *Organizational Dynamics*, vol. 19, pp. 27-41.

Leksell, L. (1981): *Headquarter-Subsidiary Relationships in Multinational Companies*, Stockholm: Stockholm School of Economics.

Leong, S.M., Tan, C.T. (1993): Managing across borders: an empirical test of the Bartlett and Ghoshal [1989] organizational typology, *Journal of International Business Studies*, vol. 24 no. 3, pp. 449-464.

Levitt, T. (1983): The globalization of markets, *Harvard Business Review* (May-June), pp. 92-102.

Levolger, E. (1995): *Internationale uitzending*, Tilburg: Tilburg University, Unpublished Master's Thesis.

Likert, R. (1967): The Principle of Supportive Relationships, in Pugh, D.S.: (1987) *Organization Theory: selected Readings*, pp. 293-316, Harmondsworth: Penguin Books.

Lincoln, J.R., Kalleberg, A.L. (1985): Work organization and workforce commitment: A study of plants and employees in the U.S. and Japan, *American Sociological Review*, vol. 50 (December), pp. 738-760.

Lincoln, J., Hanada, M., McBride, K. (1986): Organizational Structures in Japanese and U.S. Manufacturing, *Administrative Science Quarterly*, pp. 289-312.

Lindblom, C.E. (1987): The Science of Muddling Through, in Pugh, D.S.: *Organization Theory: selected Readings*, pp. 238-255, Harmondsworth: Penguin Books.

Logger, E., Vinke, R. (1995): Compensation and appraisal of international staff, in Harzing, A.W.K., Van Ruysseveldt, J.: *International Human Resource Management*, pp. 252-270, London: Sage.

London, S.J., Dommeyer, C.J. (1990): Increasing Response to Industrial Mail Surveys, *Industrial Marketing Management*, vol. 19, pp. 235-241.

Lorenz, C. (1989): The Birth of a Transnational: Striving to Exploit an Elusive Balance, *Financial Times* (19 June).

Lorenz, C. (1990): IBM joins the ranks of "transnationals", *Financial Times* (10 December).

Lorenz, C. (1991): Sharing Power around the World, *Financial Times* (29 November).

Lowe, S. (1996b): Hermes Revisited: A Replication of Hofstede's Study in Hong Kong and the UK, *Asia Pacific Business Review*, vol. 2 no. 3 (Spring), pp. 101-119.

Lytle, A.L., et al. (1995): A Paradigm for Confirmatory Cross-Cultural Research in Organizational Behavior, in Staw, B.M., Cummings, L.L.: *Research in Organizational Behavior*, vol. 17, pp. 167-214, Greenwich: JAI Press.

Maanen, J. van, Schein, E.H. (1979): Toward a theory of organizational socialization, in Cummings, L.L., Staw, B.M.: *Research in Organizational Behavior*, vol. 1, pp. 209-264, Greenwich: JAI Press.

Maanen, J. van (1985): People Processing: Strategies of Organizational Socialization, in Sathe, V.: *Culture and related corporate realities*, pp. 223-244, Homewood, IL: Irwin.

Macharzina, K., Engelhard, J. (1991): Paradigm Shift in International Business Research: From Partist and Eclectic Approaches to the GAINS Paradigm, *Management International Review*, vol. 31 no. Special Issue, pp. 23-43.

Macharzina, K. (1992): Internationaler Transfer von Führungskraften, *Zeitschrift fur Personalforschung*, vol. 6 no. 3, pp. 366-384.

Macharzina, K. (1993): Steuerung von Auslandsgesellschaften bei Internationalisierungsstrategien, in Haller, M. et al: *Globalisierung der Wirtschaft - Einwirkungen auf die Betriebswirtschaftslehre*, pp. 77-109, Bern-Stuttgart-Wien: Verlag Paul Haupt.

Macharzina, K. (1995): Interkulturelle Perspektiven einer management- und führungsorientierten Betriebswirtschaftslehre, in Wunderer, R.: *Betriebswirtschaftslehre als Management- und Führungslehre*, pp. 266-283, Stuttgart: Schaffer-Poeschel Verlag.

Macharzina, K., Wolf, J. (1996): Internationales Führungskräfte-Management-Zukunftsherausforderung erfolgsorientierter Unternehmensführung, in Macharzina, K., Wolf, J.: *Handbuch Internationales Führungskräfte-Management*, pp. 3-14, Stuttgart: RAABE Verlag.

Maljers, F.A. (1992): Inside Unilever: The Evolving Transnational Company, *Harvard Business Review* (September-October), pp. 46-51.

Malnight, T.W. (1996): The Transition from Decentralized to Network-Based MNC Structures: An Evolutionary Perspective, *Journal of International Business Studies*, vol. 27 no. 1, pp. 43-66.

March, J.G., Simon, H.A. (1958): *Organizations*, New York: John Wiley and Sons, Inc..

Marschan, R. (1995): Building bridges for horizontal communication: a case study, *Paper presented at the 21st annual Conference of the European International Business Academy* (10-12 December), Urbino, Italy.

Marschan, R., Welch, D., Welch, L. (1996a): Control in Less-Hierarchical Multinationals: The Role of Personal Networks and Informal Communication, *International Business Review*, vol. 5 no. 2.

Marschan, R., Welch, D., Welch, L. (1996b): Language, Power and Structure: Communication and Control in the Multinational, *Innovation and International Business, Proceedings of the 22nd EIBA conference*, vol. 2, pp. 459-482, Stockholm: Stockholm School of Economics, IIB.

Martinez, J.I., Jarillo, J.C. (1989): The evolution of research on coordination mechanisms in multinational corporations, *Journal of International Business Studies*, vol. 20 no. 3, pp. 489-514.

Martinez, Z.L., Ricks, D.A. (1989): Multinational Parent Companies' Influence over Human Resource Decisions of Affiliates: US Firms in Mexico, *Journal of International Business Studies*, vol. 20 (Fall), pp. 465-487.

Martinez, J.I., Jarillo, J.C. (1991): Coordination demands of international strategies, *Journal of International Business Studies* vol. 22, no. 3, pp. 429-444.

Martinez, J.I., Quelch, J.A. (1996): Country managers: the next generation, *International Marketing Review*, vol. 13 no. 3, pp. 43-55.

Mascarenhas, B. (1984): The Coordination of Manufacturing Interdependence in Multinational Companies, *Journal of International Business Studies* vol. 15 no. 4, pp. 91-106.

Matteson, M.T. (1974): Type of Transmittal Letter and Questionnaire Color as Two Variables Influencing Response Rates in a Mail Survey, *Journal of Applied Psychology*, vol. 59, pp. 535-536.

McDonald, P., Gandz, J. (1992): Getting value from shared values, *Organizational Dynamics* (Winter), pp. 64-77.

Meffert, H. (1989): Globalisierungsstrategien und ihre Umsetzung im internationalen Wettbewerb, *Die Betriebswirtschaft*, vol. 49 no. 4, pp. 445-463.

Meffert, H. (1991): Wettbewerbstrategien auf globalen Märkten, *Betriebswirtschaftliche Forschung und Praxis*, vol. 43 no. 5, pp. 399-415.

Melin, L. (1992): Internationalization as a Strategy Process, *Strategic Management Journal*, vol. 13, pp. 99-118.

Mendenhall, M.E., Oddou, G. (1985): The Dimensions of Expatriate Acculturation: A Review, *Academy of Management Review*, vol. 10 no. 1, pp. 39-47.

Mendenhall, M.E., Dunbar, E., Oddou, G.R. (1987): Expatriate Selection, Training and Career-Pathing: A Review and Critique, *Human Resource Management*, vol. 26 (Fall), pp. 331-345.

Mendenhall, M.E., Oddou, G. (1988): The Overseas Assignment: A Practical Look, *Business Horizons* (Sept./Oct.), pp. 78-84.

Merchant, K.A. (1985): *Control in Business Organizations*, Cambridge, MA:Balinger Publishing Company.

Merchant, K.A., Chow, C.W., Wu, A. (1995): Measurement, evaluation and reward of profit center managers: a cross-cultural field study, *Accounting, Organization and Society*, vol. 20 no. 7/8, pp. 619-638.

Merchant, K.A. (1996): *Management Control Systems: Text and Cases*, Englewood Cliffs, NJ: Prentice Hall.

Meyer, A.D., Tsui, A.S., Hinings, C.R. (1993): Configurational Approaches to Organizational Analysis, *Academy of Management Journal*, vol. 36, pp. 1175-1195.

Miles, R.E., Snow, C.C. (1978): *Organization strategy, structure and process*, New York: McGraw-Hill.

Miles, R.E., Snow, C.C. (1984): Fit, Failure and the Hall of Fame, *California Management Review*, vol. 26 no. 3, pp. 10-28.

Miles, R.E., Snow, C. (1992): Causes of failure in network organizations, *California Management Review*, vol. 27 no. 3, pp. 62-73.

Miller, E.L. (1972): The selection decision for an international assignment: a study of the decision maker's behavior, *Journal of International Business Studies*, vol. 3, pp. 49-65.

Miller, D., Friesen, P.H. (1977): Strategy making in context: ten empirical archetypes, *Journal of Management Studies*, vol. 14, pp. 259-280.

Miller, D., Friesen, P.H. (1978): Archetypes of strategy formulation, *Management Science*, vol. 24, pp. 921-933.

Miller, D. (1981): Toward a new contingency approach: The search for organizational gestalts, *Journal of Management Studies*, vol. 18 no. 1, pp. 1-26.

Miller, D. (1982): Evolution and Revolution: A Quantum View of Structural Change in Organizations, *Journal of Management Studies*, vol. 19 no. 2, pp. 131-151.

Miller, D. (1983): The correlates of entrepreneurship in three types of firms, *Management Science*, vol. 29, pp. 770-191.

Miller, D., Dröge, C. (1986): Psychological and Traditional Determinants of Structure, *Administrative Science Quarterly*, vol. 31 (December), pp. 539-560.

Miller, D. (1986): Configurations of Strategy and Structure: Towards a Synthesis, *Strategic Management Journal*, vol. 7 no. 3, pp. 233-249.

Miller, D., Friesen, P. (1986): Porter's generic strategies and performance: An Empirical Examination with American Data. Part II: Performance Implications, *Organization Studies*, vol. 7, pp. 255-263.

Miller, D. (1987a): Strategy Making and Structure: Analysis and Implications for Performance, *Academy of Management Journal*, vol. 30 no. 1, pp. 7-32.

Miller, D. (1987b): The Structural and Environmental Correlates of Business Strategy, *Strategic Management Journal*, vol. 8, pp. 55-76.

Miller, D., Friesen, P.H. (1987): Porter's (1980) Generic Strategies and Performance: An Empirical Examination with American Data, Part 1: Testing Porter, *Organization Studies*, vol. 7 no. 1, pp. 37-55.

Miller, D. (1996): Configurations Revisited, *Strategic Managment Journal*, vol. 17 no. 7, pp. 505-512.

Milliken, F.J., Martins, L.L. (1996): Searching For Common Threads: Understanding the Multiple Effects of Diversity in Organizational Groups, *Academy of Management Review*, vol. 21 no. 2 (April), pp. 402-433.

Milliman, J., Von Glinow, M.A., Nathan, M. (1991): Organizationnal Life Cycles and Strategic International Human Resource Management in Multinational Companies: Implications for Congruence Theory, *Academy of Management Review*, vol. 16 no. 2, pp. 318-339.

Mintu, A.T., Calantone, R.J., Gassenheimer, J.B. (1993): International Mail Surveys: Some Guidelines for Marketing Researchers, *Journal of International Consumer Marketing*, vol. 5 no. 1, pp. 69-83.

Mintzberg, H. (1973): *The Nature of Managerial Work*, Englewood Cliffs, NJ: Prentice-Hall.

Mintzberg, H. (1979): *The structuring of organizations*, Englewood Cliffs, NJ: Prentice Hall.

Mintzberg, H. (1983): *Structure in Fives. Designing Effective Organizations*, Englewood Cliffs, NJ: Prentice-Hall.

Mintzberg, H. (1988a): Strategy-Making in Three Modes, in Quinn, J.B., Mintzberg, H., James, R.M.: *The Strategy Process*, pp. 82-88, Englewood Cliffs, NJ: Prentice-Hall.

Mintzberg, H. (1988b): Opening up the Definition of Strategy, in Quinn, J.B., Mintzberg, H., James, R.M.: *The Strategy Process*, pp. 13-20, Englewood Cliffs, NJ: Prentice-Hall.

Mintzberg, H. (1989): *Mintzberg on Management*, Glencoe, NY: The Free Press.

Misa, K.F., Fabricatore, J.M. (1979): Return on investment of overseas personnel, *Financial Executive*, vol. 47 no. 4, pp. 42-46.

Mitchell, T.R. (1985): An evaluation of the validity in correlational research conducted in organizations, *Academy of Management Review*, vol. 10, pp. 192-205.

Moenaert, R.K., Caeldries, F., Commandeur, H.R., Peelen, E. (1994): Managing Technology in the International Firm: an Exploratory Survey on Organizational Strategies, paper presented at the 20th Annual Conference of the EIBA (11-13 December), Warsaw.

Morgan, G. (1993): *Imaginization, the art of creative management*, London: Sage.

Morris, M.H., Davis, D.L., Allen, J.W. (1994): Fostering Corporate Entrepreneurship: Cross-Cultural Comparisons of the Importance of Individualism Versus Collectivism, *Journal of International Business Studies*, vol. 25 no. 1, pp. 65-90.

Morrison, D. (1974): Discriminant Analysis, in Ferber, R.: *Handbook of Marketing Research*, pp. 2442-2457, New York: Wiley.

Mueller, F. (1994): Societal Effect, Organizational Effect and Globalization, *Organization Studies*, vol. 15 no. 3, pp. 407-428.

Mullen, M.R. (1995): Diagnosing Measurement Equivalence in Cross-National Research, *Journal of International Business Studies*, vol. 26 no. 3, pp. 573-596.

Murphy, P.R., Dalenberg, D.R., Daley, J.M. (1990): Improving Survey Responses with Postcards, *Industrial Marketing Management*, vol. 19, pp. 349-355.

Murray, F., Murray, A. (1986): Global managers for global businesses, *Sloan Management Review*, vol. 27 no. 2 (Winter), pp. 75-80.

Murray, J.Y., Wildt, A., Kotabe, M. (1995): Global Sourcing Strategies of U.S. Subsidiaries of Foreign Multinationals, *Management International Review*, vol. 35 no. 4, pp. 307-324.

Napier, N.K., Peterson, R.B (1991): Expatriate Re-Entry - What Do Repatriates Have to Say, *Human Resource Planning*, vol. 14 no. 1, pp. 19-28.

Nasif, E.G., et al. (1991): Methodological Problems in Cross-Cultural Research. An Updated Review, *Management International Review*, vol. 31 no. 1, pp. 79-91.

Naumann, E. (1992): A conceptual model of expatriate turnover, *Journal of International Business Studies*, vol. 23, pp. 499-531.

Negandhi, A.R. (1975): Comparative Management and Organization Theory: A Marriage Needed, *Academy of Management Journal*, vol. 18 no. 2, pp. 334-344.

Negandhi, A.R., Baliga, B.R. (1981): Internal Functioning of American, German and Japanese Multinational Corporations, in Otterbeck, L.: *The Management of Headquarters Subsidiary Relationships in Multinational Corporations*, pp. 107-120, Aldershot: Gower.

Negandhi, A.R., Welge, M. (1984): Beyond Theory Z: Global Rationalization Strategies of American, German and Japanese Multinational Companies, *Advances in International Comparative Management*, Greenwich, CA: JAI Press.

Negandhi, A.R. (1987): *International Management*, Newton, Massachusetts: Allyn and Bacon.

NFTC (1995): *Global Relocations Trends. 1995 Survey Report*, New York: Windham International and the National Foreign Trade Council.

NN (1996): *Directory of Corporate Affiliations*, New Providence, NJ: Reed Elsevier.

Nobel, R., Birkinshaw, J. (1998): Innovation in Multinational Corporations: Control and Communication Patterns in International R&D Operations, *Strategic Management Journal*, vol. 19 no.5, pp. 479-496.

Nohria, N., Ghoshal, S. (1994): Differentiated Fit and Shared Values: Alternatives for Managing Headquarters-Subsidiary Relations, *Strategic Management Journal*, vol. 15, pp. 491-502.

Norburn, D., et al. (1990): A four-nation study of the relationship between marketing effectiveness, corporate culture, corporate values, and market orientation, *Journal of International Business Studies*, vol. 21 no. 3, pp. 451-468.

Norusis, M.J. (1994): *Manuals for SPSS 6.1*, Chicago, IL: SPSS, Inc.

Nurmi, T. (1995): Expatriate's role in influencing the communication within multi-nationals: an ignored resource?, paper presented at the 21st annual Conference of the European International Business Academy (10-12 December), Urbino, Italy.

O'Connor, N.G. (1995): The influence of organizational culture on the usefulness of budget participation by Singaporean-Chinese managers, *Accounting, Organization and Society*, vol. 20 no. 5, pp. 383-405.

O'Neill, T.W., et al. (1995): Survey response rates: national and regional differences in a European multicentre study of vertebral osteoporosis, *Journal of Epidemology and Community Health*, vol. 49, pp. 87-93.

Oberg, W. (1963): Cross-Cultural Perspectives on Management Principles, *Academy of Management*, vol. 6 (June), pp. 129-143.

Oddou, G., Mendenhall, M. (1991): Expatriate Performance Appraisal: Problems and Solutions, in Mendenhall, M., Oddou, G.: *Readings and Cases in International Human Resouce Management*, pp. 364-374, Boston: PWS-Kent.

Oddou, G., Gregersen, H.B., Brooklyn Derr, C., Black, J.S. (1995): Building Global Leaders: Strategy Differences Among European, U.S. and Japanese Multinationals, paper presented at the AIB Annual Conference, (November), Seoul, Korea.

Ondrack, D.A. (1985a): International Transfers of Managers in North American and European MNE's, *Journal of International Business Studies*, vol. 16 no. 3, pp. 1-20.

Ondrack, D.A. (1985b): International Human-Resources Management in European and North-American Firms, *International Studies of Management and Organisation*, vol. XV no. 1, pp. 6-32.

Ondrack, D.A., Saks, A. (1990): Research Activities in International Human Resource Management, in Rugman, A.M.: *Research in Global Strategic Management*, vol. 1, pp. 213-221, Greenwich: JAI Press.

Osigweh, C.A.B. (1989): The Myth of Universality in Transitional Organizational Science, in Osigweh, C.A.B.: *Organizational Science Abroad, Constraints and Perspectives*, pp. 3-26, New York: Plenum Press.

Otterbeck, L. (1981): Concluding Remarks - And a Review of Subsidiary Autonomy, in Otterbeck, L.: *The Management of Headquarters Subsidiary Relationships in Multinational Corporations*, pp. 337-343, Aldershot, Hampshire: Gower.

Ouchi, W.G. (1977): The Relationship Between Organizational Structure and Organizational Control, *Administrative Science Quarterly*, vol. 22 (March), pp. 95-112.

Ouchi, W.G., Jaeger, A.M. (1978): Type Z Organisation: Stability in the Midst of Mobility, *Academy of Management Review*, vol. 3 no. 2, pp. 305-314.

Ouchi, W.G. (1979): A Conceptual Framework for the Design of Organizational Control Mechanisms, *Management Science*, vol. 25 no. 9, pp. 833-848.

Ouchi, W.G (1980): Markets, Bureaucracies and Clans, *Administrative Science Quarterly*, vol. 25 (March), pp. 129-141.

Ouchi, W.G., Price, R.L. (1993): Hierarchies, Clans and Theory Z: A New Perspective on Organization Development, *Organization Dynamics*, condensed reprint from 1978.

Paauwe, J., Dewe, P. (1995): Organizational structure of multinational firms: theories and models, in Harzing, A.W.K., Van Ruysseveldt, J.: *International Human Resource Management*, pp. 75-98, London: Sage.

Paauwe, J. (1996): HRM and peformance: the linkage between resources and institutional context, ESRC Seminar Series: the contribution of HRM to Business Performance (Oct.).

Parker, L. (1992): Collecting Data the E-Mail Way, *Training and Development* (July), pp. 52-54.

Parker, B., Zeira, Y., Hatem, T. (1996): International Joint Venture Managers: Factors Affecting Personal Success and Organizational Performance, *Journal of International Management*, vol. 2 no. 1, pp. 1-30.

Pausenberger, E., Noelle, G.F. (1977): Entsendung von Führungskraften in ausländische Niederlassungen, *Zeitschrift für betriebswirtschaftliche Forschung*, vol. 29 no. 6, pp. 346-366.

Pausenberger, E., Glaum, M. (1993): Informations- und Kommunikationsprobleme in internationalen Konzernen, *Betriebswirtschaftliche Forschung und Praxis* no. 6, pp. 602-627.

Pazy, A., Zeira, Y. (1983): Training Parent-country Professionals in Host-country Organizations, *Academy of Management Review*, vol. 8 no. 2, pp. 262-272.

Peccei, R., Warner, M. (1976): Decision-making in a multinational firm, *Journal of General Management*, vol. 2 no. 2, pp. 66-71.

Peng, T.K., Peterson, M.F., Shyi, Y.P. (1991): Quantitative methods in cross-national management research: Trends and equivalence issues, *Journal of Organizational Behavior*, vol. 12 no. 2, pp. 87-108.

Perlmutter, H.V. (1969): The Tortuous Evolution of the Multinational Company, *Columbia Journal of World Business* (Jan./Febr.), pp. 9-18.

Peterson, K.D. (1984): Mechanisms of Administrative Control over Managers in Educational Organizations, *Administrative Science Quarterly*, vol. 29, pp. 573-597.

Peterson, R.B., Sargent, J., Napier, N.K., Shim, W.S. (1996): Corporate Expatriate HRM Policies, Internationalization, and Performance in the World's Largest MNCs, *Management International Review*, vol. 36 no. 3, pp. 215-230.

Pfeffer, J., Leblebici, H. (1973): Executive recruitment and the development of interfirm organizations, *Administrative Science Quarterly*, vol. 18, pp. 449-461.

Phatak, A.V. (1989): *International Dimensions of Management*, Boston.

Philips, L.W. (1981): Assessing measurement error in key informant reports: A methodological note on organizational analysis in marketing, *Journal of Marketing Research*, vol. 18, pp. 395-415.

Picard, J. (1979): Factors of variance in multinational marketing control, in Mattson, L.G., Widersheim-Paul: *Recent Research on the Internationalization of Business*, Uppsala: Almqvist and Wiksel.

Picard, J. (1980): Organizational Structures and Integrative Devices in European Multinational Corporations, *Columbia Journal of World Business* (Spring), pp. 30-35.

Podsakoff, P.M., Organ, D.W. (1986): Self-Reports in Organizational Research: Problems and Prospects, *Journal of Management*, vol. 12 no. 4, pp. 531-544.

Porter, M.E. (1980): *Competitive Strategy: Techniques for Analyzing Industries and Competitors*, New York: The Free Press.

Porter, M.E. (1985): *Competitive Advantage: Creating and Sustaining Superior Performance*, New York: The Free Press.

Porter, M.E. (1986a): Changing Patterns of International Competition, *California Management Review*, vol. 27 (Winter), pp. 9-40.

Porter, M.E. (1986b): Competition in Global Industries: A Conceptual Framework, in Porter, M.E.: *Competition in Global Industries*, pp. 15-56, Boston MA: Harvard Business School Press.

Porter, M.E. (1990): *The Competitive Advantage of Nations*, London: MacMillan Press.

Posner, B.Z., Kouzes, J.M., Schmidt, W.H. (1985): Shared values make a difference: an empirical test of corporate culture, *Human Resource Management*, vol. 24 no. 3, pp. 293-309.

Prahalad, C.K. (1975): *The strategic process in a multinational corporation*, : School of Business Adminstration, Harvard University, unpublished doctoral dissertation.

Prahalad, C.K., Doz, Y.L. (1987): *The Multinational Mission*, New York: The Free Press.

Pressley, M.M., Tullar, W.L. (1977): A factor interactive investigation of mail survey response rates from a commercial population, *Journal of Marketing Research*, vol. 14, pp. 108-111.

Prowse, S. (1994): Corporate Governance in an international perspective: a survey of corporate control mechanisms in the United States, the United Kingdom, Japan and Germany, no. 41 (July), Basle: Bank for International Settlements, BIS Economic Papers.

Pucel, D.J., Nelson, H.F., Wheeler, D.N. (1971): Questionnaire follow-up returns as a function of incentives and responder characteristics, *Vocation Guidance Quarterly*, vol. 19, pp. 188-193.

Pucik, V. (1984): The International Management of Human Resources, in Fombrun, C.J., Tichy, N.M., Devana, M.A.: *Strategic HRM*, pp. 403-419, New York: Wiley.

Pucik, V., Katz, J.H. (1986): Information, Control, and Human Resource Management in Multinational Firms, *Human Resource Management*, vol. 25 (Spring), pp. 121-132.

Pucik, V. (1991): *Revolution or Evolution: The Tranformation of Japanese Personnel Practices*, : Center for Advanced Human Resource Studies, School of Industrial and Labor Relations, Cornell University, Working Paper 91-04.

Pugh, D.S., Hickson, D.J., Hinings, C.R., Turner, C. (1968): Dimensions of Organization Structure, *Administrative Science Quarterly*, vol. 13, pp. 65-105.

Pugh, D.S., Hickson, D.J., Hinings, C.R., Turner, C. (1969): Dimensions of Organization Structure, *Administrative Science Quarterly*, vol. 14, pp. 91-114.

Punnett, B.J., Withane, S. (1990): Hofstede's Value Survey Module: To Embrace or Abandon?, in Prasad, B., Peterson, R.B.: *Advances in International Comparative Management*, vol. 5, pp. 69-89, Greenwich: JAI Press.

Punnett, B.J., Crocker, O., Stevens, M.A. (1992): The challenge for women expatriates and spouses: some empirical evidence, *The International Journal of Human Resource Management*, vol. 3 no. 3 (December), pp. 585-592.

Punnett, B.J., Shenkar, O. (1994): International Management Research: Toward a Contingency Approach, in Prasad, B., Peterson, R.B.: *Advances in International Comparative Management*, vol. 9, pp. 39-55, Greenwich: JAI Press.

Punnett, B.J., Shenkar, O. (1996): *Handbook for international management research*, Cambridge, MA: Blackwell.

Quester, P.G., Conduit, J. (1996): Standardisation, Centralisation and Marketing in Multinational Companies, *International Business Review*, vol. 5 no. 4, pp. 395-421.

Quinn, J.B. (1988): Strategic Change: "Logical Incrementalism", in Quinn, J.B., Mintzberg, H., James, R.M.: *The Strategy Process*, pp. 94-103, Englewood Cliffs, NJ: Prentice Hall.

Rall, W. (1989): Organisation für den Weltmarkt, *Zeitschrift für Betriebswirtschaft*, vol. 59 no. 10, pp. 1074-1089.

Ramaswamy, K. (1992): Multinationality and performance: A synthesis and redirection, *Advances in International Comparative Management*, vol. 10, pp. 435-454.

Ramaswamy, K., Kroeck, K.G., Renforth, W. (1996): Measuring the Degree of Internationalization of a Firm: A Comment, *Journal of International Business Studies*, vol. 27 no. 1, pp. 167-178.

Reynolds, C. (1986): Compensation of overseas personnel, in Famularo, J.J.: *Handbook of Human Resources Administration*, New York: McGraw-Hill.

Reynolds, C., Bennett, R. (1991): The Career Couple Challenge, *Personnel Journal*, vol. 70 no. 3, pp. 46-48.

Rhoen, A. (1995): Japan: HRM op de helling?, *In, door, uitstroom van personeel*, no. 4/5, pp. 31-44, : Samson.

Riordan, C.M., Vandenberg, R.J. (1994): A Central Question in Cross-Cultural Research: Do Employees of Different Cultures Interpret Work-related Measures in an Equivalent Manner, *Journal of Management*, vol. 20 no. 3, pp. 643-671.

Robbins, S.P. (1993): *Organizational Behavior*, Englewood Cliffs, NJ: Prentice Hall.

Roberts, K.H. (1970): On Looking at an Elephant: An Evaluation of Cross-Cultural Research Related to Organizations, *Psychological Bulletin*, vol. 74 no. 3, pp. 327-350.

Robinson, R.D. (1978): *International Business Management. A Guide to Decision Making*, Hinsdale, IL: The Dryden Press.

Robock, S.H., Simmonds, K. (1983): *International Business and Multinational Entreprises*, Homewood, Illinois: Irwin.

Roessel, R. von (1988): *Führungskräfte-Transfer in internationalen Unternehmungen*, Köln: Wirtschaftsverlag Bachem in Köln.

Ronen, S., Shenkar, O. (1985): Clustering Countries on Attitudinal Dimensions: A Review and Synthesis, *Academy of Management Review*, vol. 10 no. 3, pp. 435-454.

Ronen, S. (1986): *Comparative and Multinational Magement*, New York.

Root, F.R. (1986): Staffing the overseas unit, in Famularo, J.J.: *Handbook of Human Resources Administration*, New York: McGraw-Hill.

Rosenzweig, P.M., Singh, J.V. (1991): Organizational Environments and the Multinational Enterprise, *Academy of Management Review*, vol. 16 no. 2, pp. 340-361.

Rosenzweig, P.M. (1994): When Can Management Science Research Be Generalized Internationally?, *Management Science*, vol. 40 no. 1, pp. 28-39.

Rosenzweig, P.M., Nohria, N. (1994): Influences on Human Resource Management Practices in Multinational Corporations, *Journal of International Business Studies*, vol. 25 no. 2, pp. 229-251.

Roth, K., Morrison, A.J. (1990): An empirical analysis of the integration-responsiveness framework in global industries, *Journal of International Business Studies*, vol. 21 no. 3, pp. 541-561.

Roth, K., Schweiger, D.M., Morrison, A.J. (1991): Global Strategy Implementation at the Business Unit Level - Operational Capabilities and Administrative Mechanisms, *Journal of International Business Studies*, vol. 22 no. 3, pp. 369-402.

Roth, K., Nigh, D. (1992): The Effectiveness of Headquarter Subsidiary Relationships: The Role of Coordination, Control, and Conflict, *Journal of Business Research*, vol. 25 no. 4, pp. 277-301.

Rugman, A.M. (1983): The Comparative Performance of U.S. and European Multinational Enterprises, 1970-1979, reprinted in *Management International Review*, vol. 34 no. 1, pp. 51-61, 1994.

Rumelt, R.P. (1974): *Strategy, Structure and Economic Performance*, Harvard Business School, Division of Research.

Rumelt, R.P. (1982): Diversification strategy and profitability, *Strategic Management Journal*, vol. 3, pp. 359-369.

Russell, J.S., Terborg, J.R., Powers, M.L. (1985): Organizationl Performance and Organizational Level Training and Support, *Personnel Psychology*, vol. 38, pp. 849-863.

Samuelson, P.A., Nordhaus, W.D. (1985): *Economics*, 12th edn, New York: McGraw-Hill.

Sano, Y. (1996): Management education in Japan, in Warner, M.: *International Encyclopedia of Business and Management*, pp. 1161-1171, London: Routledge.

Schaffer, R.A., Rhee, J.H. (1996): Should an expatriate or a host-national manager be utilized to establish a foreign, wholly-owned subsidiary: an integration of economic theory and organizational theory concepts, paper presented at the Academy of Management Conference, Cincinnati.

Schlegelmilch, B.B., Robertson, D.C. (1995): The Influence of Country and Industry on Ethical Perceptions of Senior Executives in the U.S. and Europe, *Journal of International Business Studies*, vol. 26 no. 4, pp. 859-881.

Schmalensee, R. (1985): Do markets differ much?, *American Economic Review*, vol. 75, pp. 341-351.

Schneider, S.C. (1988): National vs Corporate Culture: Implications for Human Resource Management, *Human Resource Management*, vol. 27 (Summer), pp. 231-246.

Schollhammer, H. (1971): Organization Structures of Multinational Corporations, *Academy of Management Journal*, vol. 14 no. 3 (Sept.), pp. 345-365.

Schoonhoven, G.B. (1981): Problems with contingency theory testing assumptions hidden within the language of contingency theory, *Administrative Science Quarterly*, vol. 26, pp. 349-377.

Schreuder, H., Spangenberg, J., Kunst, P., Romme, A.G.L. (1988): *The Structure of Organizations: An empiral assessment of Mintzberg's typology*, Maastricht: University of Limburg, Working Paper.

Schreuder, H. (1990): *Coase, Hayek, and Hierarchy*), Maastricht: University of Limburg, Working paper.

Schreyögg, G. (1993): Unternehmungskultur zwischen Globalisierung und Regionalisierung, in Haller, M. et al: *Globalisierung der Wirtschaft - Einwirkungen auf die Betriebswirtschaftlehre*, pp. 149-170, Bern, Stuttgart, Wien.

Schuldt, B.A., Totten, J.W. (1994): Electronic mail versus mail survey response rates, *Marketing research*, vol. 6 no. 1, pp. 36-39.

Schuler, R.S., Jackson, S.E. (1987): Linking Competitive Strategies with Human Resource Management Practices, *The Academy of Management EXECUTIVE*, vol. 1 no. 3, pp. 207-219.

Schuler, R.S., Dowling, P.J., DeCieri, H. (1993): An Integrative Framework of Strategic international Human Resource Management, *The International Journal of Human Resource Management*, vol. 4, pp. 717-764.

Schuler, R., Florkowski, G. (1996): International Human Resource Management, in Punnett, B.J., Shenkar, O.: *Handbook for International Management Research*, pp. 351-402, Cambridge, MA: Blackwell.

Schütte, H. (1996): Between Headquarters and Subsidiaries: The RHQ Solution, paper presented at the 22nd EIBA Conference (Dec.), Stockholm.

Scullion, H. (1991): Why Companies Prefer to Use Expatriates, *Personnel Management*, vol. 23 no. 11, pp. 32-35.

Scullion, H. (1992): Attracting Management Globetrotters, *Personnel Management*, vol. 24 no. 1, pp. 28-32.

Sekaran, U. (1983): Methodological and analytical considerations in cross-national research, *Journal of International Business Studies*, vol. 14 no. 2, pp. 61-74.

Seror, A.C. (1989): An empirical analysis of strategies for managerial control: The United States and Japan, in Prasad, S.B. (ed.): *Advances in International Comparative Management*, vol. 4, pp. 19-44, Greenwich: JAI Press.

Shipchandler, Z.E., Terpstra, V., Shaheen, D. (1994): A Study of Marketing Strategies of European and Japanese Firms Manufacturing in the US, *International Business Review*, vol. 3 no. 3, pp. 181-199.

Simon, H.A. (1965): *Administrative Behavior*, New York: The Free Press.

Singh, J. (1995): Measurement Issues in Cross-National Research, *Journal of International Business Studies*, vol. 26 no. 3, pp. 597-620.

Smeets, B. (1997): *Repatriation, the situation in Dutch international organisations*, unpublished Master's thesis, Maastricht: Maastricht University.

Smith, A. (1776): An Inquiry into the Nature and Causes of the Wealth of Nations, London: Dent and Sons.

Snodgrass, C.R., Grant, J.H. (1986): Cultural Influences on Strategic Planning and Control Systems, in Shirvastava, P., Huff, A., Dutton, J.: *Advances in Strategic Management*, vol. 4, pp. 205-228, Greenwich: JAI Press.

Snow, C.C., Hambrick, D.C. (1980): Measuring organizational strategies: Some theoretical and methodological problems, *Academy of Management Review*, vol. 5, pp. 527-538.

Soenen, L.A., Van den Bulcke, D. (1988): Belgium's Largest Industrial Companies: A Comparison of Size and Financial Performance between Foreign and Belgian Owned Firms, *Management International Review*, vol. 28 no. 1, pp. 51-63.

Solomon, C.M. (1995): Repatriation: Up, Down or Out?, *Personnel Journal*, vol. 74 (Jan.), pp. 28-37.

Sondergaard, M. (1994): Research Note: Hofstede's Consequences: A Study of Reviews, Citations and Replications, *Organization Studies*, vol. 15 no. 3, pp. 447-456.

Sorge, A. (1977): The Cultural Context of Organization Structure: Administrative Rationality, Constraints and Choice, in Warner, M.: *Organizational Choice of Constraints*, pp. 57-78, Farnborough, UK: Saxon House.

Sorge, A. (1983): Cultured Organization, *International Studies of Management and Organization*, vol. XII, pp. 106-138.

Sorge, A. (1995): Cross-national differences in personnel and organization: describing and explaining variables, in Harzing, A.W.K., Van Ruysseveldt, J.: *International Human Resource Management*, pp. 99-123, London: Sage.

Sproull, L.S. (1986): Using Electronic Mail for Data Collection in Organizational Research, *Academy of Management Journal*, vol. 29, pp. 159-169.

Steers, R.M. (1989): Organizational Science in a Global Environment: Future Directions, in Osigweh, C.A.B.: *Organizational Science Abroad, Constraints and Perspectives*, pp. 293-304, New York: Plenum Press.

Stening, B.W., Hammer, M.R. (1992): Cultural Baggage and the Adaptation of Expatriate American and Japanese Managers, *Management International Review*, vol. 32 no. 1, pp. 77-89.

Stone, R.J. (1991): Expatriate Selection and Failure, *Human Resource Planning*, vol. 14 no. 1, pp. 9-18.

Stopford, J.M., Wells, L.T. (1972): *Managing the Multinational Entreprise. Organization of the Firm and Ownership of the Subsidiaries*, New York: Basic Books.

Stopford, J. (1992): *Directory of multinationals*, 4th edn, New York: Stockton Press.

Sullivan, D., Bauersmidt, A. (1991): The "Basic Concepts" of International Business Strategy: A Review and Reconsideration, *Management International Review*, vol. 31 (Special Issue), pp. 111-124.

Sullivan, D. (1994a): The threshold of internationalization: Replication, extension, and reinterpretation, *Management International Review*, vol. 34 no. 2, pp. 165-186.

Sullivan, D. (1994b): Measuring the Degree of Internationalization of a Firm, *Journal of International Business Studies*, vol. 25 no. 2, pp. 325-342.

Sullivan, D. (1996): Measuring the Degree of Internationalization of a Firm: A Reply, *Journal of International Business Studies*, vol. 27 no. 1, pp. 179-192.

Summer, C., et al. (1990): Doctoral Education in the field of business policy and strategy, *Journal of Management*, vol. 16, pp. 361-398.

Sundaram, A.K., Black, J.S. (1992): The Environment and Internal Organization of Multinational Enterprises, *Academy of Management Review*, vol. 17 no. 4, pp. 729-757.

Taggart, J.H. (1996a): *An Empirical Evaluation of the Coordination-Configuration Paradigm*, Glasgow: Strathclyde International Business Unit, Working Paper Series 1996/5.

Taggart, J.H. (1996b): Multinational Manufacturing Subsidiaries in Scotland: Strategic Role and Economic Impact, *International Business Review*, vol. 5 no. 5, pp. 447-468.

Taggart, J.H. (1996c): *Subsidiary Strategy: Augmenting Jarillo Martinez*, Glasgow: Strathclyde International Business Unit, Working Paper Series 1996/5.

Talaga, J., Buch, J. (1992): Credit Practices of European Subsidiaries of US Multinational Companies, *Management International Review*, vol. 32 no. 2, pp. 149-162.

Tannenbaum, R. (1968): *Control in Organizations*, New York: McGraw-Hill.

Tayeb, M.H. (1988): *Organizations and National Culture*, London: Sage Publications.

Taylor, W. (1991): The Logic of Global Business: An Interview with ABB's Percy Barnevik, *Harvard Business Review* March-April, pp. 91-105.

Taylor, S., Beechler, S., Napier, N. (1996): Toward an integrative model of Strategic International Human Resource Management, *Academy of Management Review*, vol. 21 no. 4 (Oct.), pp. 959-985.

Teagarden, M.B., et al. (1995): Toward a Theory of Comparative Management Research: An Idiographic Case Study of the Best International Resources Management Project, *Academy of Management Journal*, vol. 38 no. 5 (Oct.), pp. 1261-1288.

Thavanainen, M., Welch, D.E. (1995): Expatriate Job Performance Management: a Review and Critique, in Schiattarella, R.: *Proceedings of the 21th annual conference*, vol. 1 (10-12 December), pp. 191-212, Urbino: EIBA.

Theuerkauf, I. (1991): Reshaping the global organization, *McKinsey Quarterly*, no. 3, pp. 102-119.

Thomas, D.C., Ravlin, E.C., Wallace, A.W. (1996): Effect of cultural diversity in work groups, in Bacharach, S.B., Bamberger, P.A., Erez, M.: *Research in the Sociology of Organizations: Cross-cultural analysis of organizations*, vol. 14, pp. 1-34, Greenwich: JAI Press.

Thompson, J.D. (1967): *Organizations in Action*, New York: McGraw-Hill.

Torbiörn, I. (1982): *Living Abroad: Personal Adjustment and Personnel Policy in the Overseas Setting*, New York: Wiley.

Torbiörn, I. (1994): Operative and Strategic Use of Expatriates in New Organizations and Market Structures, *International Studies of Management and Organization*, vol. 24 no. 3, pp. 5-17.

Toyne, B., Kuhne, R.J. (1983): The Management of the International Executive Compensation and Benefits Process, *Journal of International Business Studies*, vol. 14 (Winter), pp. 37-50.

Triandis, H.C. (1983): Dimensions of Cultural Variation as Parameters of Organizational Theories, *International Studies of Management and Organization*, vol. XIII no. 1-2, pp. 139-169.

Trompenaars, F. (1993): *Riding the waves of culture*, London: Nicholas Brealey Publishing.

Tse, A., et al. (1994): A comparison of the effectiveness of mail and facsimile as survey media on response rate, speed and quality, *Journal of the Market Research Society*, vol. 36 no. 4, pp. 349-355.

Tuggle, F.D., Saunders, C.B. (1979): Control and its Organizational Manifestations: A Propositional Inventory, *Review of Business and Economic Research* (Spring).

Tung, R.L. (1981): Selection and Training of Personnel for Overseas Assignments, *Columbia Journal of World Business*, vol. 15 (Spring), pp. 68-78.

Tung, R.L. (1982): Selection and Training Procedures of U.S., European, and Japanese Multinationals, *California Management Review*, vol. 25 no. 1 (Fall), pp. 57-71.

Tung, R.L. (1984): Strategic Management of Resources in the Multinational Entreprise, *Human Resource Management*, vol. 23 no. 2, pp. 129-144.

Tung, R.L. (1987): Expatriate Assignments: Enhancing Success and Minimizing Failure, *Academy of Management Executive*, vol. 1 no. 2, pp. 117-125.

Tung, R.L. (1988): The New Expatriates: Managing Human Resources Abroad, Cambridge, MA.: Ballinger.

Tung, R.L., Punnett, B.J. (1993): Research in International Human Resource Management, in Wong-Rieger, D., Rieger, F.: *International Management Research: Looking to the Future*, pp. 35-53, Berlin: De Gruyter.

Turner, I., Henry, I. (1994): Managing International Organisations. Lessons from the Field, *European Management Journal*, vol. 12 no. 4 (December), pp. 417-431.

Tzeng, R. (1995): International Labor Migration through Multinational Enterprises, *International Migration Review*, vol. 29 no. 1, pp. 139-145.

Ueno, S., Sekaran, U. (1992): The Influence of Culture on Budget Control Practices in the USA and Japan: An Empirical Study, *Journal of International Business Studies*, vol. 23 no. 4, pp. 659-674.

Ulgado, F.M., Yu, C.-M. J., Negandhi, A.R. (1994): Multinational Enterprises from Asian Developing Countries: Management and Organizational Characteristics, *International Business Review*, vol. 3 no. 2, pp. 123-133.

United Nations (1993), *World Investment Report: Transnational Corporations and Integrated International Production*, New York: United Nations.

Van de Ven, A.H., Delbecq, A.L., Koenig, R. (1976): Determinants of Coordination Modes Within Organizations, *American Sociological Review* (April), pp. 332-338.

Van de Ven, A.H., Drazin, R. (1985): The concept of fit in contingency theory, in Cummings, L.L., Staw, B.M: *Research in organizational behavior*, vol. 7, pp. 333-365, Greenwich, CT: JAI Press.

Van den Bulcke, D., Halsberghe, E. (1984): Employment Decision-Making in Multinational Enterprises - Survey Results from Belgium, *ILO Working Paper* no. 32, Gent.

Van den Bulcke, D. (1984): Autonomy of decision making by subsidiaries of multinational enterprises, in Vandamme, J.: *Employee Consultation and Information in Multination Corporations*, pp. 219-251, London: Croom Helm.

Varadarajan, P., Ramanujam, V. (1987): Diversification and Performance - A Reexamination Using a New Two-Dimensional Conceptualization of Diversity in Firms, *Academy of Management Journal*, vol. 30 no. 2, pp. 380-393.

Veliyath, R., Srinivasan, T.C. (1995): Gestalt Approaches to Assessing Strategic Coalignment - A Conceptual Integration, *British Journal of Management*, vol. 6, pp. 205-219.

Venkatraman, N., Ramanujam, V. (1986): Measurement of business performance in strategy research: A comparison of approaches, *Academy of Management Review*, vol. 11 no. 4, pp. 801-814.

Venkatraman, N., Prescott, J.E. (1990): Environment-strategy Coalignment: An Empirical Test of its Performance Implications, *Strategic Management Journal*, vol. 11, pp. 1-23.

Vernon, R.G. (1966): International investment and international trade in the product cycle, *Quarterly Journal of Economics* (May), pp. 190-207.

Vernon, R. (1971): *Sovereignty at bay: The multinational spread of U.S. enterprises*, New York: Basic Books.

Waddock, S.A., Graves, S.B. (1997): The Corporate Social Performance - Financial Performance Link, *Strategic Management Journal*, vol. 18 no. 4, pp. 303-320.

Walker, B.J., Kirchmann, W., Conant, J.S. (1987): A Method to Improve Response to Industrial Mail Surveys, *Industrial Marketing Management*, vol. 16, pp. 305-314.

Wanous, (1980): 1. What is Organizational Entry?, 2. Organizational Recruitment, 3. Realistic Recruitment, 6. Socialization of Newcomers, *Organizational Entry*, Reading: Addison-Wesley.

Watson, W.E., Kumar, K., Michaelson, L.K. (1993): Cultural Diversity's Impact on Interaction Process and Performance: Comparing Homogeneous and Diverse Task Groups, *Academy of Management Journal*, vol. 36, pp. 590-602.

Webber, R.A. (1969): *Culture and Management: Text and Readings in Comparative Management*, Homewood IL: Irwin.

Weber, M. (1947): *The theory of social and economic organization*, New York: Oxford University Press.

Weick, K.E. (1979): *The Social Psychology of Organizing*, Reading: Addison-Wesley.

Welch, D.E., Welch, L.S. (1993): Using Personnel to Develop Networks: An Approach to Subsidiary Management, *International Business Review*, vol. 2 no. 2, pp. 157-168.

Welch, D.E., Welch, L. (1994): Linking operation mode diversity and IHRM, *The International Journal of Human Resource Management*, vol. 5 no. 4 (December), pp. 911-926.

Welch, D.E., Fenwick, M., De Cieri, H. (1994): Staff Transfers as a control strategy: an exploratory study of two Australian organizations, *The International Journal of Human Resource Management*, vol. 5 no. 2 (May), pp. 173-189.

Welch, D.E. (1994a): Determinants of International Human Resource Management Approaches and Activities: A Suggested Framework, *Journal of Management Studies*, vol. 31 no. 2, pp. 139-64.

Welch, D.E. (1994b): HRM Implications of Globalization, *Journal of General Management*, vol. 19 no. 4 (Summer), pp. 52-68.

Welch, D.E., Welch, L. (1997): Being Flexible and Accommodating Diversity: The Challenge for Multinational Management, *European Management Journal*, vol. 15 no. (December).

Welge, M.K. (1996): Strukturen für weltweit tätige Unternehmungen, in Corsten, H., Reiss, M.: *Handbuch Unternehmungsführung. Konzepte-Instrumente-Schnittstellen*, pp. 661-671, Wiesbaden:Gabler.

Welge, M.K. (1980): *Management in deutschen multinationalen Unternehmungen. Ergebnisse einer empirischen Untersuchung*, Stuttgart: Poeschel Verlag.

Welge, M.K. (1981): The Effective Design of Headquarter-Subsidiary Relationships in German MNCs, in Otterbeck, L.: *The management of headquarter-subsidiary relationships in multinational corporations*, pp. 79-106, New York: St Martin's Press.

Welge, M.K. (1982): Entscheidungsprozesse in komplexe, international tätige Unternehmungen, *Zeitschrift für Betriebswirtschaft*, vol. 52, pp. 810-833.

Welge, M.K. (1987a): Multinationale Unternehmen, Führung in, in Kieser, A., Reber, G., Wunderer, R.: *Handwörterbuch der Führung*, pp. 1532-1542, Stuttgart: Poeschel.

Welge, M.K. (1987b): Subsidiary Autonomy in Multinational Corporations, in Van Den Bulcke, D.: *International Business Issues*, Antwerpen, Proceedings of the 13th annual meeting of EIBA.

Welge, M.K. (1989): Koordinations- und Steuerungs-instrumente, in Macharzina, K., Welge, M.K.: *Handwörterbuch Export und internationale Unternehmung*, pp. 1182-1191, Stuttgart: Poeschel.

Westwood, R.I., Leung, S.M. (1994): The Female Expatriate Manager Experience. Coping with Gender and Culture, *International Studies of Management and Organization*, vol. 24 no. 3, pp. 64-85.

White, R.E., Poynter, T.A. (1990): Organizing for world-wide advantage, in Bartlett, C.A., Doz, Y., Hedlund, G.: *Managing the global firm*, pp. 95-113, London: Routledge.

Whitt, S.Y., Whitt, J.D. (1988): What professional service firms can learn from manufacturing, *Management Accounting* (Nov.), pp. 39-42.

Wiechmann, U. (1974): Integrating Multinational Marketing Activities, *Columbia Journal of World Business*, vol. 9 no. 4, pp. 7-16.

Williamson, O.E. (1975): *Markets and Hierarchies, Analyis and Antitrust Implications*, New York: The Free Press.

Williamson, O.E. (1981): The economics of organization: The transaction cost approach, *American Journal of Sociology*, vol. 87, pp. 548-577.

Williamson, O.E., Ouchi, W.G. (1981): The markets and hierarchies program of research: Origins, implications, prospects, in Ven, A. van de, Joyce, W.F.: *Perspectives on organization design and behaviour*, pp. 347-370, New York: Wiley.

Wills, S., Barham, K. (1994): Being an International Manager, *European Management Journal*, vol. 12 no. 1 (March), pp. 49-58.

Winch, G., Millar, C., Clifton, N. (1997): Culture and Organization: The Case of Transmache-Link, *British Journal of Management*, vol. 8, pp. 237-249.

Wolf, J. (1994): Internationales Personalmanagement. Kontext - Koordination - Erfolg, Wiesbaden: Gabler, MIR Edition.

Wolf, J. (1996a): "Sein" und "Sollen" im internationalen Personalmanagement - Grenzüberschreitende Koordinationsprozesse im Spanungsfeld von Zufallssteuerung und strategische Ausrichting, in Engelhard, J. (Hrsg.): *Strategische Führung internationaler Unternehmen*, pp. 119-147, Wiesbaden: Gabler.

Wolf, J. (1996b): Gestalts, Networks, and Heterarchies: Innovative Management Concepts and (the Study of) Human Resource Management Coordination in Multinational Corporations, paper presented at the 22nd EIBA Conference (Dec.).

Wong, G.Y.Y., Birnbaum-More, P.H. (1994): Culture, Context and Structure: A Test on Hong Kong Banks, *Organization Studies*, vol. 15 no. 1, pp. 99-123.

Woodward, J. (1958): Management and Technology, in Pugh, D.S. (1987): *Organization Theory: Selected Readings*, pp. 52-66, Harmondsworth: Penguin Books.

Wright, L.L., Lane, H.W., Beamish, P.W. (1988): International Management Research: Lessons from the Field, *International Studies of Management and Organisation*, vol. 18 no. 3, pp. 55-71.

Wrigley, L. (1970): *Divisional autonomy and diversification*, Harvard Business School, Doctoral thesis.

Yeung, H.W. (1995): Qualitative Personal Interviews in International Business Research: Some Lessons from a Study of Hong Kong Transnational Corporations, *International Business Review*, vol. 4 no. 3, pp. 313-339.

Youssef, S.M. (1973): The Integration of Local Nationals into the Managerial Hierarchy of American Overseas Subsidiaries: An Exploratory Study, *Academy of Management Journal*, vol. 16 no. 1, pp. 24-34.

Youssef, S.M. (1975): Contextual Factors Influencing Control Strategy of Multinational Corporations, *Academy of Management Journal* (March), pp. 136-145.

Yu, J., Cooper, H. (1983): A Quantative Review of Research Design Effects on Response Rates to Questionnaires, *Journal of Marketing Research*, vol. XX (Feb.), pp. 36-44.

Yuen, E., Hui Tak Kee (1993): Headquarters, host-culture and organizational influences on HRM policies and practices, *Management International Review*, vol. 33 no. 4, pp. 361-383.

Yunker, P.J. (1983): A Survey Study of Subsidiary Autonomy Performance Evaluation and Transfer Pricing in Multinational Corporations, *Columbia Journal of World Business*, vol. 17 no. 3, pp. 51-64.

Zaheer, S. (1995): Circadian Rhythms: The Effects of Global Market Integration in the Currency Trading Industry, *Journal of International Business Studies*, vol. 26 no. 4, pp. 699-728.

Zajac, E.J., Shortell, S.M. (1989): Changing generic strategies: Likelihood, direction, and performance implications, *Strategic Management Journal*, vol. 10, pp. 413-430.

Zeira, Y., Harari, E. (1977): Genuine Multinational Staffing Policy: Expectations and Realities, *Academy of Management Journal*, vol. 20 no. 2, pp. 327-333.

Zeira, Y., Banai, M. (1984): Present and Desired Methods of Selecting Expatriate Managers for International Assignments, *Personnel Review*, vol. 13 no. 3, pp. 29-35.

Zeira, Y., Banai, M. (1985): Selection of Expatriate Managers in MNCs: The Host-Environment Point of View, *International Studies of Management and Organisation*, vol. XV no. 1, pp. 33-51.

Index

Abelson, R.P. 368
accounting practices 344, 345
Ackerman, K.-F. 75
Acuff, F. 69
adhocracy 49
Adler, N.J. 5, 24, 25, 36, 71, 72, 73, 76, 77, 161, 163, 164, 167, 170, 171, 172, 173, 174, 176, 265, 370
Agarwal, S. 25
Agathe, K.E. 44
Aiken, M. 83
Albaum, G. 174, 175
Allen, J.W. 211
Andersson, U. 99
Angur, M.G. 198
appraisal schemes 75, 123–4
Armstrong, J.S. 204
Arpan, J. 27, 211
Arvey, R.D. 69, 76, 77
Asea Brown Boveri (ABB) 44, 371
atmosphere 15–16
Aulakh, P.S. 89, 91, 177
Australia, control mechanisms 28
automobile industry
control mechanisms 295
international managers 60, 268
performance differences 155
strategies and structures 52, 53, 252
Ayal, I. 198, 202

B&O 346
Baker, J.C. 70, 74
Baliga, B.R. 8, 20, 26, 28, 100, 101, 109, 110, 111, 122, 127
Banai, M. 56, 71, 72, 211
Barham, K. 74
Barnevik, Percy 44
Bartholomew, S. 36, 77
Bartlett, C.A. 1, 4, 27, 28, 32, 36, 37, 38, 41, 43, 44, 47, 50–51, 52, 70, 77, 85, 88, 104, 105, 107, 108, 116, 117,

118, 125, 138–9, 156, 158, 178, 189, 357–9
Baty, G.B. 118
Bauersmidt, A. 44–5
Baumgarten, K.E.E. 70, 74, 75, 76
Baumler, J.V. 82
Beamish, P.W. 148, 151, 171
Becton Dickinson 44
Beechler, S. 77
Beer, M. 69
Belgium, performance differences 151
Bennett, M.L. 75
Bennett, R. 73
biases 227–8, 247–8
Biggadike, E.R. 44
Birdseye, M.G. 211
Birkinshaw, J. 104, 140, 235
Birnbaum-More, P.H. 25, 28, 61
Birnberg, J.G. 28
Black, J.S. 42, 69, 71, 74, 75, 119, 210
Blackwell, N. 45, 104, 178
Blaine, M. 148, 150, 152, 157, 158, 327, 344
Blau, P.M. 82
Blevins, D. 148, 151
Bolwijn, P.T. 46–7
Borg, M. 55, 64, 65, 71, 119, 120, 126
Böttcher, R. 36
bounded rationality 12
Boyacigiller, N. 5, 59, 60, 61, 77, 166
Bracker, J. 154
Brandt, W.K. 28, 29, 58, 90
Braye, C.E. 25, 164
Brewster, C. 69, 70, 75, 171, 175, 211
Brinkgreve, O.E. 52, 157, 333
Briscoe, D.R. 56
Brislin, R.W. 172, 174, 357
Brooke, M.Z. 55, 71, 75
Brossard, M. 163
Brown, P. 151, 346
Buch, J. 211